A History of the
9th (Highlanders) Royal Scots
The Dandy Ninth

Neill Gilhooley

Pen & Sword
MILITARY

First published in Great Britain in 2019 by
PEN & SWORD MILITARY
an imprint of
Pen and Sword Books Ltd
47 Church Street
Barnsley
South Yorkshire S70 2AS

ISBN 978 1 52673 527 0

Printed and bound in England by
TJ International Ltd, Padstow, Cornwall

Typeset in Times New Roman
by CHIC GRAPHICS

Pen & Sword Books Ltd incorporates the imprints of
Pen & Sword Archaeology, Atlas, Aviation, Battleground, Discovery, Family
History, History, Maritime, Military, Naval, Politics, Railways, Select, Social
History, Transport, True Crime, Claymore Press, Frontline Books, Leo Cooper,
Praetorian Press, Remember When, Seaforth Publishing and Wharncliffe.

For a complete list of Pen and Sword titles please contact
Pen and Sword Books Limited
47 Church Street, Barnsley, South Yorkshire, S70 2AS, England
E-mail: enquiries@pen-and-sword.co.uk
Website: www.pen-and-sword.co.uk

The author's proceeds have been remitted to charity.

Contents

LIST OF MAPS...vii
FOREWORD...ix
PREFACE xv
QUOTES xix

CHAPTER ONE   Volunteers and Territorials, 1900-1913 1
Establishment • Boer War • Territorial Force

CHAPTER TWO   Defence of the Realm, 1914...34
Mobilisation • Imperial Service

CHAPTER THREE France and Flanders, 1915 52
Second Ypres • Armentières • Somme Valley

CHAPTER FOUR Highland Division, 1916 122
Labyrinth • High Wood • Beaumont Hamel • Courcelette

CHAPTER FIVE   The Home Front, 1914-1918...............................159
Recruitment • Second- and Third-Line Battalions

CHAPTER SIX   Offensive Spirit, 1917 187
Arras • Third Ypres • Cambrai

CHAPTER SEVEN Defeat and Victory, 1918......................................234
Saint Quentin • Lys • Soissons • Hundred Days

POSTSCRIPT   1919 to date 284
Repatriation • Defence Force • Amalgamation
Second World War • Army Reserve

APPENDICES 301
NOTES..316
FURTHER READING 323
ABBREVIATIONS...324
BIBLIOGRAPHY...325
IMAGES 333
THE FALLEN...337
INDEX 350

List of Maps

Any page numbers in italics denote maps that appear in the colour plate section found between pages 108/109

I	The Lost Battalion – Cemeteries and Memorials	xvii
II	South Africa	11
III	Scotland	19
IV	Lothian	28
V	Edinburgh	43
VI	Section 3	45
VII	Ypres	63
VIII	The Western Front	*1*
IX	The Ypres Salient	*2*
X	St Jean – Second Ypres	*3*
XI	The Somme Valley	*3*
XII	High Wood	*4*
XIII	Beaumont Hamel	*4*
XIV	Arras	*5*
XV	Thélus – Vimy Ridge	*6*
XVI	Rœux	*6*
XVII	Poelcappelle – Third Ypres – Plan of Attack	*7*
XVIII	Poelcappelle – 20 September 1917	*7*
XIX	Cambrai	*8*
XX	Mœuvres	*8*
XXI	Operation Michael – St Quentin to Amiens	*9*
XXII	Omignon	*9*
XXIII	Somme Crossing	*10*
XXIV	Marcelcave	*10*
XXV	Operation Georgette – Lys River	*11*
XXVI	Villemontoire	*12*
XXVII	Vendin-le-Vieil	*12*
XXVIII	Walcheren 1944	294

Foreword

WHEN I started to get seriously interested in the First World War, I suppose when I started to earn some reasonable money in the latter part of the 70s, it was just a few years after British formation and unit histories (I am particularly concerned here with the infantry) and memoirs of the conflict began to rise substantially in cost on the second hand market as a result of increasing interest. This was a time before technical developments in printing, along with other innovations, meant that short run reprints of titles were not an economic possibility except in very exceptional cases. By the mid 1980s, however, things had changed and continued to do so at a rapid pace; the arrival of new specialist military publishers, the costs involved, electronic technology and the impact of the internet as a means of sales have meant that the great majority of these histories (particularly) and memoirs are now available at a reasonable price and have remained in print.

Formation and unit histories – for want of a better term, regimental histories – of the Great War appeared, unsurprisingly, in large numbers in the years immediately after the Armistice. Some military historians and literary military figures, such as Everard Wyrall (who had ten or so published) and C.T. Atkinson (a half dozen or so), made a living out of writing these on commission from the subject of their work.

With the notable exception of the Dominions and India, no British formation above a division produced a history – for the rather obvious reason that the former had composite divisions that remained, more or less, within a 'national' Corps. Nearly all the British infantry regiments produced a history of the part that each played, although some of these had numerous battalions and several were restricted to, for example, the regular battalions.

The quality of these histories, naturally, was rather uneven. To some extent this was dictated by the amount of money that was available for the exercise. Some of the divisions were able to make use of funds allocated by the trustees of the money that the division had 'earned' from the running of divisional canteens or similar, for example. A divisional history also had the advantage of a large potential market of former members or of their relatives – in most cases, this was <u>the</u> market for them.

Regimental committees, especially of the larger regiments, also had access to at least some funds; in the end, almost every regiment ended up with a history of some sort, even if it was concentrated or exclusively concerned with the regular battalions. However, it was the nature of the structure of British wartime infantry regiments that had the greatest influence on the battalion histories that appeared post war.

The richer regiments obtained the services of established historians or authors – one thinks of the Irish Guards who had Rudyard Kipling to write their history, largely as a result of the close affinity he had with the regiment as his only son was killed whilst fighting in it. Others made use of a regimental committee to oversee the work and some had multiple authors.

The histories of the Territorial battalions tend to be of a different type and often reflect their nature: ie that these were battalions comprising part time volunteers that, for the most part, had a pre-war existence (even if one allows for the emergence of the second and third line battalions). Generally, these were quite well served, often very well served, by single battalion histories. This often reflected the fact that such battalions had members in civilian life who were well off and who could afford to support such a venture in the days when publishing was an expensive business. Territorial battalions also had a longer history – their origins went back several years before the outbreak of war, when the TF was first formed in 1907, and were often continuations or adaptations from previous Volunteer Force battalions. In nearly all cases they had an existence after the war – and therefore a ready, potential future market for their history.

This situation also largely applied to the 'Kitchener' battalions that were raised in the war, the Service battalions; however, these were wartime only battalions and they were formed and disbanded within the duration of the conflict. Those who had recruited from a relatively well-off pool of men were far more likely to produce a history than those who did not have that advantage. In the case of these latter types of battalion histories, therefore, it was a matter of money that determined whether or not a history was published.

Although the historical value of such works – especially as regards a critical review of operations – has often been denigrated by professional military historians, they do have certain advantages over the more recent histories. Above all, they were written when there were a large number of survivors of the war, who could contribute their recollections, who had actually been there and who could offer criticism of the various drafts. On the other hand, they were usually directed at a particular group of people, of those who had served or of relatives of those who had served. There would be a natural tendency to gloss over any failures, whilst the sources available were restricted and they were often published to a schedule and certainly to a budget. So the various factors at play: restricted access to the official records, possibly only their own War Diary; limited finances; the nature of the market at which they were aimed; the proximity to the war – meant that many of them have the feel of a superior school magazine. The better ones have rolls of honour, lists of the original members of the battalion and their fate, lists of honours and decorations, combining to provide an invaluable resource to historians in the pre internet years.

And this was how the situation remained for decades; by the end of the 1920s almost any history that was going to be written of a regiment's or battalion's war record had been written and published. A number of things combined to change this and was to produce a whole new wave of publications. Over the last thirty years a new history of a Great War unit has not been a particularly unusual event. Much of this can be ascribed to the accessibility of publishing books with a very limited sales market, as described above. Above all, the public interest in the Great War has mushroomed over the same period so that the number of people interested in, say, the 1/5th Leicestershire Regiment, is vastly bigger than it was in the 1970s.

These technological advances and the growth in the potential market for such books came at a time when information on formations, units and individuals of that war became much more easily available to the researcher, academic or amateur. There was a massive increase in those who research their family history. Visits to the battlefields of France and Flanders in particular, but also of important campaign areas such as Gallipoli, became far less adventurous undertakings; whilst new tour companies came on the scene and school trips to the battlefields became common.

All of these factors, reinforced by the extensive media attention on the centenary, have led to the publication of numerous studies of aspects of the war, such that possibly there have been more new titles on that conflict published in the last thirty years or so than there were in the immediate post war deluge of memoirs, battle narratives and formation and unit histories. It is not, therefore, just 'regimental' histories that have benefitted. Nearly all aspects of the war have received scholarly attention and the results of that work have been able to be printed rather than languishing as typed copies on university or regimental museum shelves. One area that has received particular attention has been single battalion histories of infantry regiments of the British army, almost invariably centred on their experience during the First World War.

Of these, a high proportion have been of Service battalions, that is those battalions of regiments that were created during the Great War under particular conditions of service and which ceased to exist at its end or very shortly thereafter. In turn, a good number of these were what was popularly known at the time as 'Pals' battalions, recruited from the same locality (e.g. Barnsley, Sheffield, Leeds Pals etc), often from the same industry (e.g. Newcastle and Hull Commercials, Glasgow Tramdrivers), or from friends who shared the same sorts of background or interests (e.g. Public School and Sportsmen's battalions). These histories have usually benefitted from concentrating on the origins of the battalion and thus delve into the social and economic conditions from which the initial recruits came. When the rush to the colours was at its peak after the Retreat from Mons and extending into the early months of 1915, these aspects were, of course, taken for granted when they were being published in the 1920s. Some of these histories have been very heavily weighted to the first years of a particular battalion's existence – its formation, its training, its arrival (usually, but far from always) on the Western Front, early encounters with the enemy, life at the Front and then the events of its participation in its first major offensive, almost invariably the Battle of the Somme 1916 and quite often on the fateful 1st July.

It is not uncommon for the books to become less detailed as the life of the battalion goes on through the remaining two years or so of the war. The reason for this is understandable, as the nature of the battalion often changed. The exigencies of the service meant that recruits were increasingly made up of men who had enlisted as a result of some form of conscription and quite often from different parts of the country, so that replacements in, say, a Yorkshire battalion might come, for example, from London, Scotland or Liverpool. The books tend to end on a 'what happened afterwards' section, disbandment (which for a good number happened with the reorganisation of the BEF in February and March 1918), the gatherings of Old Comrades and then the threat of being forgotten entirely, rather as their colours gradually disintegrate in the churches or cathedrals where they were hung after their disbandment.

There have been, of course, new books on regular battalions; either for those who never had a battalion history written about them (or were merely a part of a bigger regimental history that covered all the battalions that served in the Great War) or for a modern history to go in conjunction with one that was written in the immediate post war years. Of the more recent histories of Territorial battalions, most have followed along the lines of the service battalion histories. One or two have focussed on a more sociological basis: one thinks of Bill Mitchison's outstanding work on the London Rifle Brigade during the war, *Gentlemen and Officers* (1995). All of them have benefitted, especially the more recent ones, from the wealth of readily accessible resources and technology that were not available to those who wrote those early histories, from critical books on generals to detailed analysis of offensives, battles and even small-scale actions. There are far more books on the German and French armies in English.

A significant proportion of the War Diaries are now available online; as are medal rolls, silver badge rolls, Soldiers Died, disability pension awards, some service records, *The London Gazette*, a good range of trench mapping – and the list continues to grow. There are numerous associations that have brought together enthusiasts, such as the Western Front Association and the Gallipoli Association, producing professional publications. Online resources include the Commonwealth War Graves Commission's web site and Chris Baker's excellent Long Long Trail; whilst various forums (for example, the Great War Forum) bring the researcher into contact with a community of fellow enthusiasts and experts on a huge range of Great War specialist topics – which brings us to this book.

An account of a Territorial battalion of the Royal Scots, it falls neatly into the category of several types of battalion history of the Great War, but manages to do this by using the merits of each type without falling into some of the pitfalls. What we have here is an outstanding history in the sense of the narrative of the battalion during the war – and its second and third line battalions – which is given in full and is well illustrated by mapping. Crucially, it is preceded by the context of the battalion – that is its early existence and evolution from Volunteer Force unit into a territorial battalion and its existence in its Edinburgh home; and it takes it through the various vicissitudes of the post war period through to the present day, where it still has a place in the British Army's order of battle as a company in the Army Reserve, in the 6th Battalion the Royal Regiment of Scotland.

This book will be one of those that will find a place on the shelf of a military historian of the generations to come. Neill Gilhooley has taken advantage of every avenue that has been open to him: all those now available official records; personal accounts from a wide variety of sources; a clear understanding of the ethos and the morale of the battalion and its members, as well as of the time in which they lived; a most impressive range of illustrations; clear and annotated aerial photography; a formidable bibliography and useful appendices. All of this material has been combined into a clear, readable and accessible text.

In the whole it provides not only an eloquent tribute to the members of the Dandy Ninth but also a book that will have a lasting value to those who come afterwards and wish to study the phenomenon that was the British Army of 1914-1918.

Nigel Cave
Ratcliffe College

Preface

The train arrived at CASSEL at 10 a.m. Detraining was completed by 11 a.m. A hot meal was prepared for the men & the battalion moved off at 12.30 p.m. & marched to L'ABEELE station (12 miles) arriving there at 5 p.m. The two platoons of A Coy under Capt. P.A. Blair rejoined the battalion there. The battalion was billeted in farm buildings in the neighbourhood of L'ABEELE station.[1]

The Battalion War Diary, 28 February 1915

ON the last day of February 1915, a week from home, the battalion formed up on the road in companies to complete their journey. Along routes known to Caesar's *IX Legion* of Hispania and Napoleon's *Incomparable 9th* of Carcassonne, now passed Colonel Ferguson's *Dandy Ninth* of East Claremont Street, Edinburgh. 'Didn't the cobbled roads of Flanders feel hard,'[2] recalled Lance Corporal Jimmy Elliot, 'simply beastly for marching,'[3] agreed Private Russell 'Cherry' Thin. The morrow was March, since antiquity the first day of the campaign season, named even for the god of war. The 1/9th Battalion (Highlanders) Royal Scots joined 81 Brigade, 27th Division of the British Expeditionary Force on the French-Belgian border at the start of nigh on four years of fighting. They were the latest generation of Royal Scots, but by no means the last to 'trail their pikes in the low countries'.[4]

"Going In."
Flanders
March · 1915

Nº 1827.

The Royal Scots (1633-2006), oldest regiment of the British Army, had been established by royal warrant permitting Colonel John Hepburn of Athelstaneford (*Elsonf'd*) to recruit a corps in Scotland to serve the French King Louis XIII, counterparts to Dumas's Musketeers. Over the centuries they served around the world and fought in France and Flanders many times. By nineteenth century reforms the Royal Scots had been established as two battalions of full-time regulars, one to serve overseas whilst the other was at home to recruit and train, and been given Lothian and Edinburgh as their recruiting district. The regulars were augmented by the Volunteer Battalions, part-time soldiers later termed the Territorial Army.

This is a history of one of those battalions, the 9th Royal Scots, and expands somewhat on the previous history (1925) that ran to twelve pages. Formed in 1900 as a Volunteer Battalion, they served in the Territorial Force and Territorial Army until amalgamated in 1921. As the Highland Battalion, they were intended to be made up of Highlanders or those of Highland descent, living in Edinburgh. As such they were the only battalion in the regiment to wear the kilt, and not just ceremonially but on the march, in the trench and going 'over the bags'. They were affectionately known as the *Dandy Ninth* and fought on the Western Front from 1915 through to the Armistice.

A century hence we may follow them on the map, where the adjutant's stub of pencil has carefully recorded the place names in capitals. We may follow them on foot, where the *pavé*, though 'restored to man' as Kipling enumerated in his *Song of French Roads*, has yet to yield to busy roads. Yet more than a thousand men of the Ninth remain on the Western Front, a number equal to the original strength of the battalion: defending still the Salient or the wooded slopes of the Somme, advancing over the shoulder of Vimy Ridge, simply going about their day in fetching rations or water. Some have marked graves and others do not. Some went missing and were presumed dead only when hope had run to its last drop.

Pilgrims can pick out the front line east of the cemeteries and memorials that remain, and that frequently form milestones for battles, casualty clearing stations and hospitals. From the Channel it runs along ridges and reverse slopes, or all too often rather less favourably in an overlooked valley, tentatively crosses the marshes of the Scarpe and Somme and then on south to the largely French-held part of the line. Here, far further south than the familiar British battlefields of Ypres, Arras and Amiens, are the dead of the battalion's blackest day, the fateful First of August 1918. Around Raperie, a hundred odd miles from Poelcappelle in the north, lie a hundred *Dandy Ninths*, almost a company.

To lionise a subject is the prerogative of a history, to repeat some of the praise and perpetuate a fraction of their *esprit de corps*, but is not intended invidiously to promote them over all others. In the Great War the Royal Scots consisted of thirty-five battalions, and the Ninth had some 6,000 men pass through their ranks, one-hundredth of those recruited from Scotland and one-thousandth of the total the British Army raised from the empire. Whilst war diaries deem fighting withdrawals necessary because the units on their flanks have been routed – more so if they are from other divisions, almost without exception if they are French – there is a limit to how much

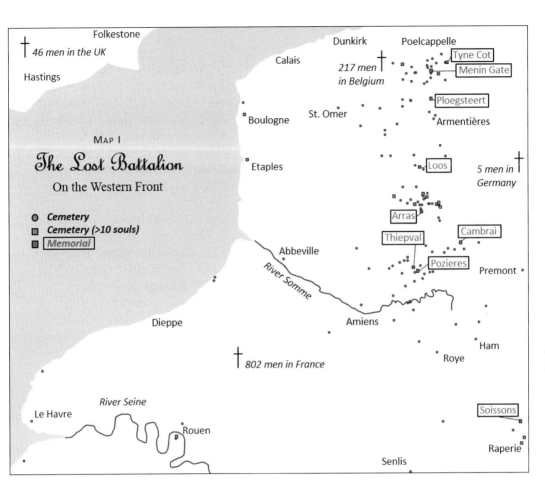

Folkestone
† 46 men in the UK

Hastings

MAP I

The Lost Battalion

On the Western Front

○ Cemetery
▢ Cemetery (>10 souls)
▢ Memorial

Dunkirk   Poelcappelle

Calais   Tyne Cot
              217 men †   Menin Gate
              in Belgium

Boulogne   St. Omer   Ploegsteert

                                        Armentières

Etaples   Loos   5 men in †
                                         Germany

                          Arras
                                    Cambrai
                        Thiepval
Abbeville   Pozieres
River Somme   Premont ·

Dieppe   Amiens

                                        Ham
† 802 men in France   Roye

River Seine   Soissons
Le Havre
         Rouen
                                        Raperie

                        Senlis

context may be offered. A battalion history advances on a narrow front. Moreover, for all that the axe of the armed forces may have a long oak haft and a heavy head, it still needs a keen cutting edge. The 9th Royal Scots can rightly claim to have stood on that infinitesimal edge and demonstrated character, determination, discipline and *élan* in days bright and dark, though the battalion has long since moved on into the mists.

This history follows a broadly chronological, rather pedestrian path. The reader will readily discern that it is not a soaring narrative; instead it treads heavily on a *pavé* of source material, at times well set and corroborated, at others contradictory, singular or incomplete. I am acutely conscious that some have picked up this book to follow in the footsteps of a relative and seek a good deal of detail, but that such a long trail may not suit everyone.

Where this book cannot follow so closely is in adopting the often light-hearted expectations of serving personnel, such as Private Wull Grossart: 'It will be good fun even if it does not alter the record of world history.'[5] Instead the words of Sir Ian Hamilton, speaking at the first anniversary dinner of the battalion, rightly humble any history:

'They fell as thick as the leaves of autumn fell in Sanctuary Wood. They lay in double rank at Ypres. In High Wood, at Beaumont Hamel, on the Vimy Ridge, at Armentières, Soissons and Loos their comrades are lying… the 9th Royal Scots have left behind them a trail of glory, a cloud of witnesses to their deathless fame. No living man could speak so eloquently of the 9th Royal Scots' achievements as that huge percentage of them whose self-sacrifice had spoken, still speak, and ever would speak for the brave battalion to which they once belonged.'[6]

Perhaps the greatest service that this book can do is to add another stone to the memorial cairn of the fallen.

Neill Gilhooley
12 October 2018

Notes on the text

The battalion is generally referred to here as the Ninth, as it frequently is in contemporary references. It has the advantages of brevity over 9th Battalion (Highlanders) The Royal Scots (The Lothian Regiment) (Territorial Force) and of clarity over merely the 9th.

Biographical information is, on the whole, available online in *An Index of the 9th Royal Scots*.

Generally, both Imperial and metric units are used, the exception being yards as these tended to be approximations. For reference 100 yards = 91 metres; half a mile = 880 yards = 2,640 feet = 805m.

The basic pay of a private was a shilling a day, though with proficiency pay this could be expected to be 1s 3d or 1s 6d. In the £sd system £1 = 20 shillings, and in turn 1s = 12 pence. In France, a decimalised currency gave 1 Franc = 100 centimes. A British penny was worth a little over ten French centimes during the First World War. Therefore a ha'penny, known to Scots as a *bawbee*, was roughly equivalent to a French *sous*, or five centimes.

Quotes

In an attempt, successful or not, to keep the text uncluttered, quotes are linked to the following sources by superscript numbers:

1 War Diaries
2 Jim Elliot
3 Russell 'Cherry' G. Thin
4 John 'Jock' Brown
5 Wull Grossart
6 *The Scotsman*
7 James Ferguson
8 *Edinburgh Evening News*
9 J.H.A. Macdonald
10 *The Leather Sporran*
11 J. Stirling
12 J.M. Grierson
13 Diary of Services...
14 L. Creswicke
15 The Watsonian
16 Thomas Wilfrid Bennet Clark (Letters)
17 *Aberdeen Journal*
18 *Glasgow Herald*
19 Bobby Johnston
20 Charles Carrington
21 J.R.S. Bell
22 A.A. Gordon
23 Jimmy Quinn
24 Bernard Holmer
25 P. Simkins
26 *Edinburgh Evening Dispatch*
27 *The Sketch*
28 Arthur Anderson
29 William Murray
30 L. Sellers (translated)
31 S. Manz
32 W.N. Nicholson
33 J. Ewing
34 *Dublin Daily Express*
35 William P. Young includes J/A Shannon
36 David Rorie

37 Clarence Gibb
38 Wattie Scott
39 James Lawson Cairns
40 *The Feilding Star* (N.Z.)
41 *Daily Record*
42 James Beatson
43 J.E. Edmonds et al
44 Arthur Lawson, courtesy Alistair Murdoch
45 I.V. Hogg
46 L. Macdonald
47 *The Times*
48 I.F.W. Beckett
49 E.H.D. Sewell
50 John Young
51 F.W. Bewsher
52 N.C. Down
53 William Ross
54 F.P. Crozier
55 A.H. Hussey
56 Bill Hay
57 C. Campbell
58 Ernst Jünger
59 F.C.B. Cadell
60 P. Hindenburg
61 Alexander F. MacPherson
62 R.B. Ross
63 C. Duffy
64 *The Independent*
65 Andrew G. Lees (PoW)
66 J.R.P. Sclater
67 T. Newark
68 F. Thackeray
69 T.A. Mackenzie
70 G. Blake
71 J. Stewart
72 John P. Fidler
73 *Manchester Evening News*
74 B. Seton

75 John W. Clapperton
76 *Dundee People's Journal*
77 *Southern Reporter*
78 *Kerry Evening Post*
79 J. Nicholls
80 P. Gibbs
81 A. Weekes
82 William Dea
83 Histories of the Two Hundred...
84 C.E. Crutchley
85 Douglas Wimberley
86 Fred Farrell
87 Andrew R. Bain
88 B. Hammond
89 A.S.G. Lee (pilot)
90 61st Division, dissertation
91 Arthur Conan Doyle
92 Colin Rice
93 Gustav Goes (translated by Robert Dunlop)
94 G.K. Rose
95 P. Münstermann (translated)
96 William Rennoldson
97 Memorials of Rugbeians
98 F.J. Reynolds
99 Pamphlet 9th Battalion (Highlanders)
100 Silver Parrish
101 John Alastair Shannon
102 T.E. Lawrence
103 David Murdoch, grandson
104 John McGurk
105 Robert G. Love
106 Robert H. Paterson
107 Hansard
108 J.C. Swann

See bibliography for full listing.

Chapter 1

Volunteers and Territorials
1900–1913

Establishment 1900
'TERRIBLE REVERSE OF BRITISH TROOPS', 'HIGHLAND BRIGADE DECIMATED' ran the newspaper headlines in December 1899. These, the consequence of 'Black Week' in the Second Boer War, were the result of defeats at Stormberg, Magersfontein and Colenso in South Africa. The Highland Brigade was part of the British advance to relieve Kimberley and a night march, intended to surprise the Boers, instead brought them unexpectedly onto Boer trenches at Magersfontein whilst still in column. There they suffered losses throughout the day as they lay in the open under the blistering sun. It was belatedly realised that the British Army was faltering in South Africa.

The Highland Brigade at Magersfontein.

1

The reserves were empty and a recruitment drive was soon underway that, notwithstanding the disasters in South Africa and indeed because of them, met with considerable enthusiasm from the peoples of Britain, Ireland, Canada, Australia and New Zealand. In this upsurge of patriotism, an Edinburgh solicitor by the name of Andrew Gordon felt that many young men in Edinburgh from, or descended from north of the Forth and Clyde, would join a Volunteer Battalion modelled on the Highland regiments, complete with kilt.

Numerous new volunteer companies, the forerunner of the Territorial Army, were being formed, but a whole new battalion was a rather more ambitious undertaking. In the spring of 1900 Gordon placed adverts in the press and began to take the names of interested parties.

With over 800 applications received in a few weeks, Andrew Gordon approached Colonel William Gordon of Threave, of Black Douglas renown, commanding the First Regimental District, to request the formation of a kilted battalion. This military district encompassed Lothian – then Peebleshire, Haddingtonshire, Linlithgowshire, Edinburghshire – and formed the recruiting area of the Royal Scots consisting of two Regular army battalions, a militia battalion and eight battalions of the Volunteer Force.

'The dark days of Magersfontein'[7]

KILTED CORPS FOR EDINBURGH.

PARTIES wishing to JOIN the above CORPS are requested to communicate with the Subscriber.

AND. GORDON,

3 Thistle Court,
Edinburgh, 20th March 1900.

In the ensuing silence the newspapers gave voice to the speculations circulating in the city. First, the correspondents wrote, far from being an anomaly to have a Highland battalion in Edinburgh, it was an omission that Aberdeen, Dundee, Glasgow and even London (and soon Liverpool) had Scottish volunteers in 'national garb', but the capital did not. It was suggested that each company in the battalion should be associated with a clan, such as Campbell, Macdonald and Cameron. The Macleod Society gathered eighty-three names for a Macleod Company, but for historical reasons they held hopes the new battalion would be attached to the Black Watch across the Forth.

Possible commanding officers were put forward including Colonel William Ivison Macadam, former commander of the 5th Volunteer Battalion Royal Scots (and incidentally shot dead in the Royal College of Surgeons in 1902); and Major James Ferguson, an officer of the 3rd Volunteer Battalion Gordon Highlanders.

The next requirement was that the new battalion would have to fit into the existing Volunteer Force of the Royal Scots. The 4th (Edinburgh) and 5th (Leith) Volunteer Battalions had no objection, but Colonel Horatio Macrae insisted it form part of his command consisting of the 1st, 2nd, and 3rd Volunteer Battalions, formed together as the Queen's Rifle Volunteer Brigade (QRVB), The Royal Scots.

The QRVB were opposed to the competition there might be on recruiting, though it was pointed out that they were at full strength. In May it was reported that the organisers of the 'kilties' preferred to be independent, but 'rather than have their project slaughtered' they consented to Macrae. There was then 'a great deal of balderdash' from QRVB officers as to seniority until it was agreed that seniority in the kilted corps would advance separately to the rest of the brigade. Macrae finally withdrew his objection and forwarded the proposal to the War Office for an unnumbered Highland Battalion, so as not to upset the Volunteer Force numbering:

Andrew Gordon.

'Sir, I have the honour to report that there is a strong desire for the formation of a Highland Volunteer Battalion in Edinburgh, to be clothed in the kilt, but otherwise to wear the uniform of the Territorial regiment, The Royal Scots.

Over 800 men not enrolled in existing Volunteer corps have put down their names as willing to join a Kilted Battalion, and I have to ask that authority may be given for the formation of a fourth battalion in connection with the Queen's Brigade, but to wear the kilt and be clothed in scarlet'.[7]

Horatio Macrae, Commandant Colonel QRVB, RS

The War Office had various 'points to settle' and the letter for authority was not issued until 12 July, although as the name of the commanding officer was still not announced, enrolment could not begin. The first officer, Lieutenant Colonel James Ferguson, was gazetted on 24 July 1900 as commanding officer, The Highland Battalion, Queen's Rifle Volunteer Brigade, The Royal Scots (Lothian Regiment). Two days later Andrew Gordon wrote to the men on his list asking them to enrol urgently. When the brigade returned from the Firth of Forth Infantry Brigade summer camp at Lochcote, West Lothian, Sergeant James Mitchell opened an orderly room for the Highland Battalion at the brigade's drill hall on Forrest Road, Edinburgh. However, in the intervening period enthusiasm had cooled, men had joined other units, and attempting to recruit in early August was not well timed so that in the first three weeks:

'A beggardly two hundred recruits are forward. The movement threatens to end in a fiasco… The prime blunder appears to have been attaching the new corps to the Queen's Brigade… the Highland Battalion is still at the stage of uncertainty whether it will have a history at all… Begging and praying for Highland recruits in the capital of Scotland simply makes Scotland ridiculous.'[8]

The friction had started immediately. Another correspondent to the newspapers asked why they were not an independent corps as originally intended, why not the 9th Royal Scots with their own drill hall, instead 'Master Queen's says "No, you come here" and then the fun commences.'[8] There was even a return to the question of seniority of officers before the first march out in August. Nevertheless, the first course of squad drills took place on Monday 13 August at the Forrest Road drill hall, near Greyfriars Bobby and alongside the old Flodden wall of the city.

The other battalions of the Queen's Rifle Volunteer Brigade (QRVB) were all dressed in dark rifle grey, as 'black Brunswickers'[9] known as 'Blackies', and stood in stark contrast to the scarlet tunics and Hunting Stewart kilts of the Highlanders, who soon earned the nickname *The Dandy Ninth*.

James Ferguson the younger of Kinmundy, Aberdeenshire, was an experienced volunteer officer of twenty-five years with the Gordon Highlanders, and spent part of the year at the courts in Parliament House in Edinburgh. An advocate at the early age of 22 in 1879, with considerable work for the Great North of Scotland Railway Company, he became Sheriff of Argyll in 1898 and took silk to become King's Counsel in 1902.

With a 'somewhat stiff and frigid exterior,' he possessed 'some of the foibles supposed to be characteristic of the Aberdeenshire laird. But those who were fortunate enough to know him intimately were well aware that behind the veil of an unprepossessing manner there lay concealed abundance of talent and commonsense, as well as a singularly kind heart.'[6]

Ferguson went to some lengths to stress that he had been asked to command the battalion and set his own preconditions to guarantee the independence of his command. In reality it seems likely that he was the driving force behind the battalion from the start, he had even drafted the letter of application to the War Office.

Archibald Alexander Gordon was the second officer appointed to the battalion and given command of A Company. His account of the battalion's origins is the more straightforward – that himself, James Ferguson and Gordon raised the battalion. Archibald

James Ferguson.

Gordon, an accountant, was a well-travelled and well-connected man, having been around the world and met Gordon of Khartoum, General Sherman, three French Presidents and a Jamaican who had been his grandfather's slave.

Ferguson was determined from the outset to set his battalion above the rest and to establish a strong sense of '*esprit de corps*... "Smartness" in appearance...was inculcated, and it was noticed that in coming to and from parade the men generally carried themselves as soldiers, with their rifles at the slope instead of lounging along with arms at the trail or carried like a bag of golf clubs.'[7]

On his instructions each man on enrolment had to demonstrate his commitment by making a deposit of ten shillings, nominally toward their uniform, to be returned after five years of satisfactory service, which was seen as 'rather stiff on apprentice lads and others... when the other corps are free'.[8] They were expected to contribute 2s 6d annually to battalion funds. Men normally signed on for three years but, given the extra costs of a Highland battalion, principally uniform, Ferguson extended this to five years. He also introduced a requirement for each recruit to be nominated by two members of the battalion. The first government grant to the battalion was for £800. To finance the initial costs, £3,000 was borrowed from the bank, guaranteed by the senior officers and repaid in 1905. The men's uniform came to £3 6s 4d, of which the kilt was the largest single expense at £1 3s. Four hundred uniforms were promptly ordered with a payment on account of £1,000.

The unit had an authorised strength of 600-904 yet, with a view to the end of the volunteering year on 31 October, they were only 200 strong. In addition, Ferguson was sanctioned to raise the full eight companies, rather than the six he had been working on and he would now have to find more officers and non commissioned officers (NCOs). It was decided to recruit six companies initially and to group together men of similar backgrounds, as follows:

Table 1. Company Composition in 1901

Lieutenant Colonel James Ferguson		
A Company	Captain Archibald A. Gordon	Men employed in offices
B Company	Captain James Clark	Men employed in law offices, or whose arrangements were affected by the sittings of the Court
C Company	Captain Thomas G. Clark	Men residing in the north of the town or employed in printing works
D Company	Captain Alexander S. Blair	General
E Company	Captain Alastair M. Campbell	Argyll and West
F Company	Captain Norman D. Macdonald	Inverness and North
Captain and Adjutant Henry S. Wedderburn, 1st Gordon Highlanders Honorary Lieutenant and Quartermaster Mr Andrew Gordon		

The last company commander appointed was Alexander Blair, on 12 December 1900, completing the full complement of six captains. Second Lieutenant Donald Rose had previously served for ten years in the Dutch Militia in Java. Adjutants, colour sergeant instructors and other permanent staff usually came from the regular battalions of the Gordon Highlanders, with whom the Ninth enjoyed a long association. Captain Henry Wedderburn, 1st Gordon Highlanders, and recently invalided back from South Africa, became adjutant.

Near the very end of the volunteer year, at first inspection, battalion strength was 399. Colonel Gordon was 'glad to see a good many grown men in the ranks'[7] and this number earned them a capitation of £1,690 11s for the following year.

Independence 1901

> *Highlanders, attention; advance in column of route from the right. A Company leading.*
>
> Colonel Ferguson's 'invariable word of command'.[10]

IN the winter of 1900-01 discontent grew between Ferguson and his superior, Macrae. The battalions were not, in Ferguson's view, the distinct units they should be but instead autonomy was eroded, the transfer of companies between battalions was threatened and the finances between the battalion and brigade were mixed up. Ferguson went as far as to say that the brigade 'resembled a French, German or Russian regiment than any British military unit'.[7] It was also reported in the press that the brigade might be broken up into battalions as their financial situation was unsatisfactory. This all came to a head when Macrae refused to cash the battalion cheques and Ferguson applied to become an independent corps. Once more there was a lengthy wait and, although not officially announced, it became known that the connection between the brigade and the Highland Battalion had been virtually cut, with official communications to be addressed to the 9th Battalion Royal Scots. The War Office replied in July 1901 with His Majesty's approval that the unit be separated and designated the 9th Volunteer Battalion (Highlanders) The Royal Scots (Lothian Regiment).

The battalion relocated to 7 Wemyss Place (telephone no. 3628), Edinburgh, an upstairs hall that had been in use as St Stephen's Free Church. A limited company was formed with Ferguson as chairman and Blair as secretary, which bought the property for £3,612 1s 6d. They leased the two houses underneath, the hall to the Ninth for £125 p.a. and the upper premises, No.10, to Ferguson himself. The chain of command closely matched social status, passing down from the headquarters and Ferguson's residence on Wemyss Place. On a par lived the captains, around the corner in elegant India Street lived Captain Blair. Moving further downhill we pass the homes of the junior officers in such addresses as Royal Circus and St Vincent Street. The sergeants lived further north again in respectable Stockbridge houses on Comely Bank and the like. Finally, the privates were scattered further afield, in residences out as far as Granton, Leith and Portobello.

The pews were cleared from the hall, a flag and flagstaff were furnished by the corporals and the sergeants contributed the clock. Finally, a Morris Tube Range was established that adapted service rifles to fire small calibre rounds so that the battalion could practise on an indoor range in the winter months. Given this is one of the most exclusive addresses in Edinburgh, overlooking the New Town's Queen Street Gardens, it comes as some surprise that rifle shooting was taking place here. For the rest of the year six targets, at up to 1,100 yards, were erected at the Hunter's Bog rifle range, Arthur's Seat. It was not the safest location with the occasional sheep shot, and at least once a bullet went through the window of a house, but 'none the worse for being a little difficult',[7] thought Ferguson who took a keen interest in the shooting results and the pride and competitive spirit they instilled. Though they were later placed well in the league tables, it is unsurprising the battalion had a poor start. Only sixty men were present for the musketry returns and in a brigade competition in April 1901 they trailed the leaders by 650 points. The best shot in the battalion was Sergeant George Strachan, a law student born in Kimberley, South Africa. He was commissioned in 1908 and was part of the Scotland team at Bisley.

The Minto Cup was an annual competition between Scottish units, pitching the Ninth against regulars as well as other volunteers. Like the regulars' Kitchener Tests it involved each team of sixteen setting out at twenty-minute intervals on a 10-mile march, with points deducted for exceeding two-and-a-half hours, followed by rifle firing at targets scattered at unknown distances. Although usually beaten by regulars, the Ninth could console themselves with good performances in their rivalry with the QRVB, except in 1912 when the team was disqualified having lost their way on the march.

Training was carried out at headquarters, Waverley Market and later at Inverleith Park, King's Park (Arthur's Seat) and Woodhouselee. This included section and company drills and battalion exercises, route marches, gymnastic classes and bayonet exercise, or 'tooth pick handling'[2] to the irreverent. An example night exercise, carried out in October 1901, was on the Almond River from Cammo to Cramond; in another, 'A march through the City on a winter evening was given the objective of the occupation as quickly as possible of a position on the Calton Hill.'[7] In March 1902 the tactical exercise comprised:

'A Northern Force has landed a small body of troops at Granton, further disembarkation being delayed. The Officer Commanding half battalion receives the following orders near Fettes College: It is essential to secure and hold the railway junction at Craigleith and ascertain strength and position of enemy. Advance at once, and secure position protecting Craigleith Junction. You will then push forward two companies to feel for enemy, and destroy the bridges over the Water of Leith from Coltbridge to Saughton Hall (inclusive).'[7]

Other exercises were carried out on the Braid and Craiglockhart Hills, near Colinton and Blackford Hill and a cancelled parade was signalled by a triangular flag flown from the Nelson Monument on Calton Hill. Ferguson despaired that open spaces about the city were unregulated and were becoming monopolised by golf and football. Drills had been:

> 'conducted in the midst of a mob of undisciplined children, who keep up a continuous shrieking in shrill voices, run in between the companies, and pick up and mimic the words of command. Three of four people golfing on a putting green consider themselves aggrieved in waiting for a little for the convenience of a battalion of some hundreds... playing second fiddle to a few individuals indulging in an inferior form of golf.'[7]

A general meeting of the battalion was held on 22 August to consider the rules of the corps. The scale of fines included 10s for pointing a rifle, loaded or unloaded, at any person without orders. Wearing corps clothing at unauthorised times cost 5s; curiously the same was levied for discharging a rifle accidentally. The Reverend Archibald Fleming was appointed chaplain and the first church parade was held in late May 1901, assembling in Charlotte Square with the service in the Tron Kirk. In August 1901 Major General Sir Ian Hamilton was appointed as honorary colonel.

The first general parade as an independent unit took place on 12 October 1901 in the Meadows, the Burgh loch drained, well known to some of the Ninth who were also members of the Royal Company of Archers, the King's Bodyguard in Scotland. At the end of the volunteer year, on 31 October 1901 the Ninth had a much-improved strength of 602. However, the target was moving, as from September 1901 the establishment was to be raised from 800 of all ranks to 800 rank and file and 932 all ranks. Ferguson still had 330 men to find as well as replacing annual losses.

Boer War

> 'Now when old Kruger heard the news, That the Lothians were sending
> Crack companies of Volunteers, A most judicious blending
> It's said he told a company, Of confidential frien's,
> "The Royal Scots are awfu' chaps, But Lord save us frae the Queen's."'[9]

THE Ninth had been raised in 1900 in response to the South African War, then seemingly in crisis, but without any real prospect of serving overseas as a complete corps. However, forty-five men of the Ninth did serve in South Africa (Appendix A). Half a dozen of them were with the Volunteer Service Companies of the Royal Scots; the rest enrolled in other units, mainly the Imperial Yeomanry and Baden-Powell's South African Constabulary. In addition, seven men joined the regulars.

The war is conventionally divided into three phases: the Boer invasion of British Natal and Cape Colony, beginning in October 1899; the British offensive, securing Pretoria in June 1900; and the drawn-out guerrilla war from March 1900 to war's end in May 1902. Like all wars, the causes were complex but included imperial expansion and the ambitious *gold bugs* making vast profits from the rand gold fields in Boer territory.

Imperial Volunteers

FROM the outset the Boer War, even before the final phase against the commandos, was a war of movement. The Boers, farmers on the wide-open pastures of the veldt, had ridden all of their lives and had at least one spare horse with them. The British Army were severely short of mounted soldiers and to meet this demand the Imperial Yeomanry were recruited from civilian life and shipped to South Africa with but the slightest preparation. However, although Lord Methuen said 'They bought experience rather expensively at first,' they performed quite well, being on the whole passable shots and good riders. As mounted infantry the men were technically privates organised into companies and battalions, but most units chose instead to adopt cavalry practice and referred to themselves as troopers in squadrons and regiments. They were mainly employed in small detachments to protect column flanks or escort convoys but were also found in some of the major actions. Due to their temporary terms of service no drafts were sent out, and so in early 1901 they were sent home with next to no overlap with the second contingent.

This second 'lot' of the Imperial Yeomanry, the New Yeomanry of 1901, had even less training, were poorly officered and their performance was unsurprisingly inferior. Most had been attracted less by the patriotism of the year before than by rates of pay. At 5s a day this was five times what infantry and therefore those in the Volunteer Service Companies (VSC) earned. Some men who had been medically rejected for the VSC went to London to sign up and, rather uncreditably, 'got into a 5s a-day corps'.[9] There was also the prospect of emigration to South Africa. This last was particularly true of Scots, 60 per cent intending to emigrate. Less than a quarter of the contingent were drawn from the Volunteers, men who could at least shoot, though very few from any source could ride. In fact two-thirds of the New Yeomanry had no military experience when they sailed for South Africa from 1 April 1901. Much of the blame for their lack of training rests with Kitchener of Khartoum, known as K of K, who had called for volunteer mounted infantry as a matter of urgency. Many units were even shipped without all of their officers.

On arrival at Cape Town some Yeomen were diverted to operations before any training at all at the main Yeomanry camp at Elandsfontein, near Johannesburg and as such many would only have fired the twenty-one rounds of ammunition the War Office had graciously provided them with at Aldershot, before exchanging shots with those expert marksmen, the Boers. The New Yeomanry promptly earned the undesirable nickname of '*De Wet's Own*', after the commando leader they were supposed to be defeating. Much of the discontinuity would have been alleviated with a steady programme of training and drafts. Nevertheless, all units improved, but this never erased the considerable criticism of the 'humbugs who declare that Volunteers are a useless crowd... Can a civilian rapidly become a useful soldier?'[11] The answer is given with reference to a company of 'Sharpshooters' steadfast to the 'last' at Tafelkop.

A score of the Ninth served with the Imperial Yeomanry, some with the 22nd Battalion of Imperial Yeomanry, known as the Rough Riders; three with Lord Fincastle's Horse (31st Imperial Yeomanry). One man of the Ninth joined the City

Imperial Volunteers (CIV), an almost private venture raised and equipped by the City of London. Ten men served with Tullibardine's Scottish Horse, also created outside of existing military structures. Finally, eight men were with the South African Constabulary.

Private George Watson of B Company was a clerk for an Australian wine importers on St Andrew Square when he quit both his battalion and his job in January 1901 and enlisted with the Lothian and Berwick Imperial Yeomanry. On one occasion in South Africa he became lost for four days on the veldt in a thick mist and his only food for that time was the raw flesh of a goat he had shot. Of the Ninth's forty-five men he was the only fatality. He died aged 20 in Charlestown on 7 May 1902 of enteric fever (typhoid), the major killer of the British Army.

Trooper Watson.

Volunteer Service Companies

ON the outbreak of war the 2nd Battalion Royal Scots were overseas at Poona, India and the 1st Battalion mobilised in Belfast, Ireland on 9 October 1899 to serve in South Africa. The battalion strength was 1,038 of whom over 700 were called up from the Army Reserve; it was announced in Parliament that they were the first unit formed up with their reservists fully accounted for. Following a month at sea aboard the SS *Dictator* they arrived at East London, South Africa on 3 December.

To reinforce the regular army, an Army Order was issued in January 1900 for Volunteer Service Companies (VSC) to be formed from the affiliated volunteer battalions amid 'a great outburst of national warlike enthusiasm'.[12] The first Volunteer Service Company of the Royal Scots sailed before the Ninth had been formed; in fact the lists of men were submitted from the eight Volunteer Battalions to Colonel Gordon in December 1899. A second, replacement company was called for in January 1901, before the year's service had expired on the first, and finally a third service company was requested in January 1902 which was in time to see the last months of the war. The Volunteer Service Companies, men with some volunteer training and the steadying influence of their regular regiments, rendered useful service. Attached to the line battalion, they were paid and equipped as regular soldiers, but wore their volunteer battalion shoulder titles.

The 1st Volunteer Service Company, of 112 men, left Southampton in February 1900 having been training in camp for a month. They joined the battalion on 23 March 1900 and were designated as L Company, 'a very fine body of men'.[13] In their midst was an anomalous soul, one Private Simpson who somehow served in the 1st VSC and appeared in the Ninth's roll of honour, probably Robert Simpson 8167. As D Company 1st Royal Scots had been formed into mounted infantry, L Company brought the battalion back up to strength with eight companies. They operated in the Boer Orange Free State (which became British Orange River Colony in May 1900) until joining the main army at Pretoria in August and moved on to Belfast (Map II).

River crossings by infantry and transport, September 1900

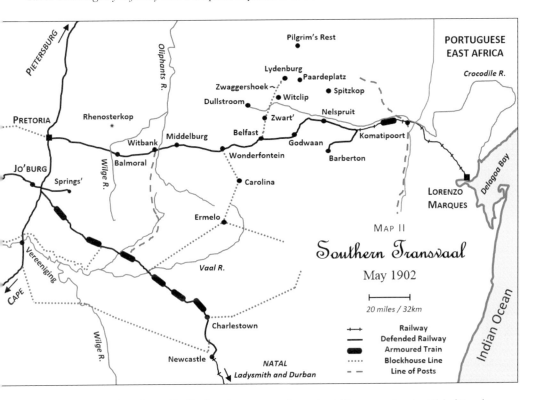

PORTUGUESE
EAST AFRICA

Crocodile R.

Pilgrim's Rest

Lydenburg
Paardeplatz
Zwaggershoek
Spitzkop
Dullstroom
Witclip
Nelspruit
Zwart'
Rhenosterkop
PRETORIA
Belfast
Godwaan
Komatipoort
Witbank
Middelburg
Wonderfontein
Barberton
JO'BURG
Balmoral
Springs'
Carolina
LORENZO
MARQUES

Ermelo

MAP II

Southern Transvaal

May 1902

Vaal R.

20 miles / 32km

	Railway
	Defended Railway
	Armoured Train
	Blockhouse Line
	Line of Posts

Charlestown

Newcastle
NATAL
Ladysmith and Durban

Indian Ocean

With General Redvers Buller's advance north against Commander-in-Chief Louis Botha at Lydenburg held up, the battalion, as part of Sir Ian Hamilton's force, left Belfast on 3 September 1900 and marched north on Buller's left. A Royal Scots officer reported:

'As we neared Zwarteskopjes, our advanced mounted men came in contact with the enemy. We pushed on, and presently – and I must confess to every one's surprise – 'bang', and a Long Tom 6-inch shell burst 200 yards from us – a bad shot. The Boers were in position on our right front. We at once opened out the companies and moved to the left behind the brow of a spur, changing front so as to face the Boers.

11

The men did this splendidly, and though we were shelled throughout the movement, at a range of about 5000 yards, never a man was hit. Two were knocked down by a shell that burst between them, and another had his helmet plugged, and a shell fell in the middle of the band, but no skin was broken.

Our guns came into action; four of our companies attacked in front, two to the left to seize some kopjes. The Boers decamped, and we bivouacked on the position won. Next morning we were off again, found our friends, the Long Toms, which greeted us, but our "cow" guns (5-inch naval guns) were up, and the Long Toms made off, we after them. We were in the mountains now. The scenery was magnificent, quite Himalayan; but it was awful work for men and animals.'[14]

The battalion made their way onto Dullstroom. On the night of 5 September the Royal Scots climbed onto the left side of the Zwaggershoek Pass, which Hamilton described as being 'like the Khyber, but shorter', putting them behind the Boers' right flank at Witclip and causing the latter to retire to Lydenburg, thereby making the Royal Scots the most advanced unit of the British Army. On the following day they worked their away along the pinnacles of the pass to the exit.

A picquet of Volunteers from L Company on the high ground, consisting of six rifles under Sergeant Bruce, was attacked by superior numbers. The Boers set fire to the grass and the six were forced to retire to stony ground. When the flames had passed they rushed back to their original position, reached it before the enemy and held it until reinforced. The British marched into Lydenburg on the same day and the Boers retired east toward Spitzkop. On 8 September the Royal Scots charged enemy positions at Paardeplatz after a hard climb and Botha's army began its drawn out retirement to the east.

The Royal Scots were part of the sweep heading steadily east along the railway and Crocodile River, arriving at the border of Portuguese East Africa, modern-day Mozambique, at Komatipoort by the end of the month. A number of Boers were driven

Paardeplatz, the battalion under shell fire and awaiting orders to advance, 8 September 1900.

over the border, others dispersed and a Long Tom was destroyed. The Long Toms were four French Creusot 155mm (6.1") guns bought by the Boers to defend Pretoria. Though garrison artillery, they were skilfully deployed across very difficult terrain and the British were forced to counter with their siege train and, most famously, by bringing naval guns ashore.

The 1st VSC left for home from Komatipoort on 7 October 1900 but were some months protecting the lines of communication in Orange River Colony before sailing for Britain.

Meanwhile, in late November the battalion moved to Barberton, but did not escape malaria, and thence onto Godwaan, guarding the Pretoria–Delagoa railway until 7 April 1901 or occasionally employed in mobile columns. This was a precarious time as 5,000-7,000 Boers operated between Carolina and Middelburg in their highly mobile *kommandos*. The guerrilla war, with both sides operating over vast areas, gave but temporary superiority in any given location, making gains impossible to consolidate.

It was into this new situation that the 2nd VSC marched. The Ninth sent detachments in both the 2nd and 3rd VSCs in 1901 and 1902, earning them the honours for South Africa, 1901-1902. However, the 1901 detachment included only Private George Ormiston, who therefore earned by himself this honour for the battalion. Replacement Volunteers had been called for on 25 January 1901 and M (Volunteer) Company joined the battalion in Eastern Transvaal in May 1901, where a large part of 1st Battalion earned distinction on the Bermondsey Heights.

Between July and October 1901 the battalion garrisoned Middelburg, until given command of the railway line between Wilge River and Witbank, with headquarters at Balmoral, to protect the vital supply lines of the British Army. Companies were also attached to mobile columns.

Middelburg.

Attacks on the Pretoria–Delagoa railway began in October 1900, shortly after the British had captured it. The Boer commander in this region was General Ben Viljoen (who thought the Irish and Scots the best fighters he faced), and within his commando was the expert train-wrecker 'Dynamite' Jack Hindon, a Scot who had deserted from the British Army in the annexed Zululand. Hindon was credited by Lord Kitchener as the Boer who had caused him most trouble, and personally too, as trains carrying Kitchener narrowly escaped destruction by Hindon on two occasions.

Boers sighting a British patrol.

Destruction of a train near Greylingstad.

Hindon wrecked three trains between Balmoral and Witbank on a single day on 17 January 1901. The British response was to build defences. The first blockhouses were built on the railway in January 1901, principally to defend stations and protect bridges. These masonry blockhouses cost £800-£1,000 and took three months to build.

Few, forgotten and lonely,
Where the empty metals shine –
No, not combatants – only
Details guarding the line.

Rudyard Kipling 'Bridge-Guard in the Karoo' 1901

Reading in a stone blockhouse, with a loophole betwixt Royal Scot and lizard.

In order to stretch the defences along the railway, a more efficient design was required. The Royal Engineers established a blockhouse factory at Middelburg, pre-fabricating circular blockhouses of corrugated iron, 13ft 6in in diameter that looked like water tanks. With the Boer artillery now rarely seen, blockhouses could be made safe against small arms fire by using two skins of corrugated iron, 6in apart, packed with shingle. Steel loopholes pierced the sides and the door led to an encircling trench, surrounded in turn by a barbed wire entanglement that extended as a fence between blockhouses. Alerted by automatic alarms and flares placed along the fence, and connected to each other by telephone, the sections of men posted within could, in theory, call up armoured trains when attacked.

These blockhouses cost a mere £16 and took about five hours to construct, with the barbed wire between blockhouses at £50 per mile. Nevertheless, the scale of the project became immense: some 3,700 miles were protected, initially with blockhouses 1½ miles apart, but reduced to ½ to ¾ mile intervals, employing over 8,000 blockhouses at a cost of £1 million . Between March and April they were extended along most of the Delagoa Bay line. These measures made attacks less likely to succeed, and by June even crossing the line had become an uncertain undertaking. Ben Viljoen turned his attentions to the north with only sporadic attempts on the railway. The Royal Scots were proud that none of the lines they protected had been destroyed or breached under their watch.

The Royal Scots' 'Fort Lorentz', named for Sergeant Major Lorentz, at Godwaan constructed February 1901

The success of the railway defences led Kitchener to devise plans to intersect the sub-continent with defensive lines of blockhouses, starting in June 1901. The Royal Scots provided the escort for the 25-mile line between Wonderfontein and Carolina. Commenced at the end of 1901 and completed in eighteen days, it consisted of fifty-five blockhouses and posts.

The extension of the British Empire, along the arteries of the railways and across open ground, now prevented the Boers disappearing into the night and allowed the mobile columns to sweep through as the hammer to the blockhouse anvil. The war of movement, that had so suited the Boer, was being partitioned and contained to become a static war, with clear consequences for 1914. The Boer was being boxed in and, in the worst excesses of the war, his farms burned and his family imprisoned.

Half of the 1st Battalion was attached to Urmston's mobile column, operating from Belfast, and half was garrisoned in Balmoral, controlling the railway between the Wilge River and Witbank. M Company was part of Urmston's column, which brought Ben Viljoen in as a prisoner in February 1902. They left the battalion in March 1902 and were in England a month later. Finally, after the third call on 9 January, the 3rd VSC with four men of the Ninth, joined the battalion as Q Company in February 1902 and garrisoned the defensive line.

It was known at this time that the Transvaal government was north of the Delagoa Bay railway, making its way west, but attempts to intercept them had failed. A mediation offer from the Netherlands was communicated to them and on 10 March 1902 acting state President Schalk Burger wrote to Kitchener 'desirous and prepared to make peace proposals' and wishing to confer with President Steyn and the remnants of the Free State Government. Kitchener granted them safe conduct and, doubtless to the surprise of those guarding the line, Burger arrived at Middelburg on 22 March 1902 and went on to Pretoria by train.

However, whilst negotiations continued, so did the war. The Royal Scots diary records the following noteworthy incident on 5 April:

'There was a splendid little fight at Balmoral, where Jack Hindon's Commando, 200 to 300 in strength, endeavoured to capture some cattle; this attempt was frustrated primarily by the gallant and intelligent conduct of three men... all of the Volunteer Service Company "Q", ...[who] were promoted corporals by Lord Kitchener for their gallantry.'[13]

The only officer of the Ninth to serve was J.C.C. Broun of B Company who had received his commission in October 1900. James Broun, an advocate of almost 40, was made temporary lieutenant in the regular army whilst serving with 3rd VSC between February and August 1902. He was the last officer to cross the enemy's lines having been sent with a message from Balmoral under a flag of truce to the remaining members of the Transvaal government at Rhenosterkop. He therefore had the 'interesting experience'[7] of spending the last night of the war at the laager of the South African Republic. Peace had been signed at Vereeniging on the evening of 31 May 1902, and each commando laid down their arms by 16 June 1902.

The 1st Royal Scots recorded casualties of: 19 killed or died of wounds, 65 died of disease, 36 wounded and 7 captured by the enemy.

The 3rd VSC, consisting of three officers and 106 men, departed South Africa on 25 June 1902 aboard *The Walmer Castle*. Back in Edinburgh, in the winter of 1903/4, Broun gave a battalion lecture on the 'Closing Scenes of the South African War'.

Volunteer Force 1902-1907
THE full-time professional soldier is something of a modern invention and most soldiers in history have been part-timers and charged with the defence of hearth and home. Edinburgh's volunteers were not always a force to be reckoned with, Scottish

enlightenment figures made up a mere forty-two men to turn out against the Jacobites in 1745. The more creditable rifle volunteers were created in 1859 during yet another French invasion scare and after the Crimean War had demonstrated how insufficient Britain's armed forces were with an expeditionary force overseas. Yet they were a grass roots movement, not created by government. Their rôle was codified in the Volunteer Act of 1863 and subsequently the Childers Reforms of 1881 affiliated county rifle volunteers to the local regimental district. For the volunteers in Linlithgowshire, Peebleshire, Haddingtonshire and Edinburghshire this was The Royal Scots (Lothian Regiment).

There were ten infantry regiments in Scotland: The Royal Scots (RS), Royal Scots Fusiliers (RSF), King's Own Scottish Borderers (KOSB), Cameronians (Scottish Rifles)(SR), Black Watch (Royal Highlanders)(BW), Highland Light Infantry (HLI), Seaforth Highlanders (SH), Gordon Highlanders (GH), Cameron Highlanders (CH) and Argyll & Sutherland Highlanders (A&SH). See Map III. The Scots Guards recruited throughout.

Ferguson had no doubt that his battalion was recruited 'from a superior and intelligent social stratum'[7], the very men whom he thought should be recruited to the volunteers, distinct from militiamen and the 'second lot' of Imperial Yeomanry in the Boer War. These men were also those who had difficulty attending camp every year.

The annual camp was the major feature of the year, for one or two weeks in July, with all volunteers expected to attend at least one in their first three years for essential training. Ferguson appealed to employers that 'the Navy and the Volunteer Force stood between the ordinary working population of this country and the burden of compulsory military service'[7] and they sometimes granted the volunteers holiday to attend, though of course this was unpaid.

As part of 1st Lothian Brigade, the Ninth's first summer camp was at Tyndrum in July 1902 where attendance was a gratifying 76 per cent. The day at camp started at reveille at 5am (6am on Sunday) and ended with lights out at 10.15pm, the sergeants' mess closing at 11pm. In their free time men could be seen climbing Ben More in red coats, though a service dress of khaki jacket and spats had just been adopted, and regimental sports were held. The terrain here was thought to resemble that around Ladysmith, Natal, by those who had been there. They practised crossing a river and the assault of a mountain position. The Ninth, marching from Tyndrum toward Crianlarich between the south bank of the River Fillan and the Highland railway,

The Camp at Tyndrum, July 1902.

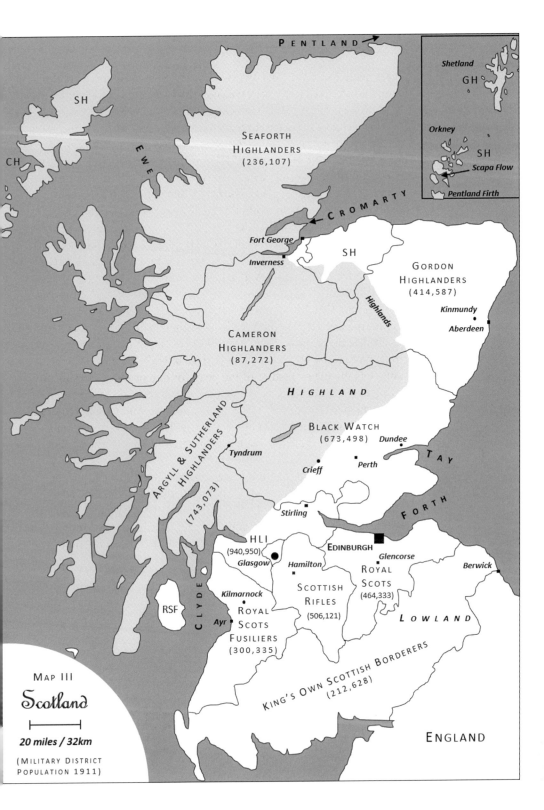

PENTLAND

SH

CH

EWE

SEAFORTH
HIGHLANDERS
(236,107)

CROMARTY

Fort George

Inverness

SH

GORDON
HIGHLANDERS
(414,587)

Kinmundy

Aberdeen

CAMERON
HIGHLANDERS
(87,272)

Highlands

HIGHLAND

ARGYLL & SUTHERLAND
HIGHLANDERS

(743,073)

BLACK WATCH
(673,498)

Tyndrum

Dundee

Crieff

Perth

TAY

Stirling

FORTH

HLI
(940,950)

Glasgow

Hamilton

EDINBURGH

Glencorse

ROYAL
SCOTS
(464,333)

Berwick

CLYDE

Kilmarnock

SCOTTISH
RIFLES
(506,121)

RSF

Ayr

ROYAL
SCOTS
FUSILIERS
(300,335)

LOWLAND

KING'S OWN SCOTTISH BORDERERS
(212,628)

ENGLAND

Shetland

GH

Orkney

SH

Scapa Flow

Pentland Firth

MAP III

Scotland

20 miles / 32km

(MILITARY DISTRICT
POPULATION 1911)

1911

1911

1911

1912

1912

1913

1913

1912

1913

21

encountered a defensive position set up by the 4th Volunteer Battalion Royal Scots along the Auchtertyre burn that flows into the Fillan.

In the way of these exercises, the defenders' Maxim machine gun opened up silently about 10am and the Ninth approached by crawling through the stream unaware they were enfiladed. Despite this, General Hunter must have been impressed for he selected the Ninth to be the volunteer battalion represented in a mixed brigade of regulars and militia at the new Stobs Camp in the summer of 1903. This two-week camp entailed some financial concerns, however Ferguson felt the honour could not be turned down.

In the major exercise at Stobs, 31 Brigade, including the Ninth, were the reserve and were not called upon until required to take a flank trench at night. General Hunter observed:

> 'Severe punishment would undoubtedly have been the fate of this attack, particularly to the leading troops from the fire of the right company, 4th Scottish Rifles, but, in view of the fact…that their attack was developed to close quarters before discovery was possible, that they overwhelmed in numbers by twenty to one (and more) any opposition that could be offered in the available time, and that the flank trench, once taken, more or less enfiladed or took in reverse the right of the defence, the assault of the 31st Brigade is held to be successful.'[7]

Hunter had seen for himself in South Africa how difficult it was to attack trenches defended by modern rifles. Yet he later said of the battalion that 'he was prepared to stake his life and risk his neck in the defence of this country with such men as they were'. With the hindsight of the Great War overshadowing these Edwardian summer camps, it is difficult to see them as true preparations for what lay ahead. The financial burden of trying to put the battalion on a two-week camp, without having the numbers to warrant higher allowances, meant the men were not paid, whereas others at camp were drawing 2s 6d, 3s or even 4s a day. Soon afterwards, from a strength of 713, the Ninth lost over 200 disaffected men and was only able to make up half of their number the following year. With recruitment weak, the 10s deposit was dropped in 1905 and they regained their earlier strength.

Stobs was again the location for the camp in 1904, where the Ninth fought a rearguard action against the other battalions. A major attraction for the volunteers was an evening visit to an immense marquee nearby for Buffalo Bill's show. Finally, the full eight companies had been formed. Ferguson had attended the Edinburgh Ross and Cromarty Association to encourage volunteers and the recently promoted Captain Angus Gregorson was entrusted with G Company (Ross and Cromarty). Many of the officers were Edinburgh alumni and there had always been a large number of university students in the battalion, including a section raised by Frederick Lucas, a medical student. Captain David Huie commanded H (University) Company, with Lucas as his colour sergeant, containing not only undergraduates, but clerks, apprentice accountants and young civil servants. The university authorities attempted, and failed, to get the students to boycott this new company.

Detraining Stobs 1904.

Many boys from George Watson's College, Edinburgh, went on to join the Ninth and the association was particularly strong during the Great War. However, under the headmastership of Dr George Ogilvie, the Rifle Club 'might sometimes have been seen stealthily leaving School with five or six boys carrying rifles which on no account were to attract the attention of the headmaster. The Doctor had a rooted antipathy to all things military, and Mr Sellar had practically to have recourse to weekly "gun running" to let the boys get decent practice.'[15] All of this changed in 1904 with the new headmaster, Dr John Alison, who founded a kilted Cadet Corps, affiliated to the Royal Scots, with a uniform modelled on that of the Ninth with dark green tunics.

By the end of 1904 the battalion had recruited 1,000 men, possessed a pipe band and buglers, organised an ambulance section, a signallers' section, a Maxim machine-gun section and owned their own headquarters. However, Ferguson's younger son died in February 1904 of influenza, aged 16, and his father died in September. Inheriting an estate of over 4,000 acres as sixth laird, Ferguson resigned his position at the end of the year 'for reasons of a private and personal character (due to) unforeseen circumstances'. Major James Wardrop assured the battalion he would not have relinquished his command if it had not been necessary. At the 1904 prize-giving, Mrs Wauchope giving the prizes, James Ferguson bid the battalion goodbye and wished it God-speed. His speech was followed by music and a gymnastic display. Ferguson's elder son,

Jimmy Ferguson.

23

James Ferguson junior, known as Jimmy, joined as a junior subaltern in June 1904 aged 18 and continued the family's service to the Ninth.

As civil commitments prevented Major Wardrop accepting command, it now passed to James Clark, who had been promoted major in the previous month. Clark was popular 'in spite of his manner'.[16] Educated at the Lycée in Pau, he was an advocate and King's Counsel. His military career began as a private in the 5th VB Gordon Highlanders and then in James Wardrop's mounted infantry of the QRVB.

Ferguson and Clark, KCs, were both members of the Conservative and Unionist party; Ferguson's 'views were of a strong Conservative complexion' and both were active in the anti-Home Rule campaign over Ireland. Like his father before him, Ferguson believed he represented the agricultural portion of the community. In 1884 he referred to Gladstone as a dictator and said the Conservatives were not 'endeavouring to resist the extension of the franchise. They are resisting... an attempt to jockey the Constitution and to "doctor" the representation.'[17]

Having been at Stobs again in 1905 and the Royal Review, the 1906 camp was at Gosford Park, East Lothian on the southern shore of the Firth of Forth. Special attention was paid to the training of scouts and included cyclists:

James Clark.

'Machines, which must be provided by members, must be rear-driving safety bicycles, front-steering tricycles, or tandem tricycles... The following articles will be provided by the Battalion: Patrol jacket, knickerbocker breeches, spats, hose tops, active service caps, rifle covers, and fittings for carrying rifle and ammunition.'[7]

Royal Review 1905.

Edward VII inspects the Ninth at the Royal Review, King's Park, 1905.

The Ninth were now equipped with large marquees and a cooking wagon. The following year, at Stobs, the brass band made its first appearance at the prize giving and flag signalling was especially praised. An unusual honour was welcoming Prince Fushimi of Japan at Waverley Station in 1907 with a guard of honour, the band having learnt the Japanese National Anthem.

'As up-to-date as Germany', the patent steam cooker of the Ninth.

Territorial Force 1908-1913

WITH origins in the *levée en masse* of the French revolutionary wars, French and German conscription required men aged 20 to serve for two years and then enter the reserve. Without conscription Britain had a limited reserve of professionally trained soldiers, a deficiency that had been exposed in the Boer War, and so reform had been brewing for some years since. The Norfolk Commission of 1904 considered that the volunteer force 'is not qualified to take the field against a Regular army'. The simple fact was that the one week of unpaid annual leave offered by most employers was insufficient for the training of a modern army. Colonel Clark had witnessed the cost to the battalion of attempting to exact more time from the men at Stobs in 1903, his view was:

> 'Compulsory camp was a very good thing if they could get the men who could be "compelled" to go into camp. But compulsory camp would deplete the ranks of the Volunteers, unless the object were to do away with Volunteering altogether.'[18]

The Haldane Reforms of 1907 created an expeditionary force for the regular army and attempted to create a suitable force for home defence that could be mobilised in the event of the British Expeditionary Force (BEF) serving overseas. A Territorial Force (TF), combining the Volunteer Force and County Yeomanry, was formed, to be funded by central government. Although watered down from the original proposals, in order to increase professionalism, the burden of training was increased: regular drills and fifteen days of annual training were required. The changes had particular effect in Scotland as at this time 1 in 36 Scotsmen were enrolled as volunteers, about twice the level found in England and Wales.

At the instigation of the Territorial Force in April 1908, all of the battalions of the Royal Scots were numbered in sequence. This entailed renumbering the Volunteer

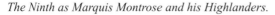

The Ninth as Marquis Montrose and his Highlanders.

Battalions to become 4th to 10th Battalions. Only the Ninth retained their number, pushing 8th VB to the more junior position. This may have been because the identity of the unit as the *Dandy Ninth* was now well entrenched. For a time the threat of amalgamation hung in the air; the rumour was reported in the press, whence too came a warning that if 4th and 9th Royal Scots were combined 'there would be trouble'.

Table 2. Battalions of The Royal Scots (Lothian Regiment)

1907 Regular Force and Volunteer Force	1908 Regular Force and Territorial Force
1st Battalion Royal Scots RF	1st Battalion Royal Scots RF
2nd Battalion Royal Scots RF	2nd Battalion Royal Scots RF
3rd Battalion Militia	3rd Special Reserve
1st QRVB	4th (Queen's Edinburgh Rifles) Royal Scots TF, HQ at Forrest Hill
2nd QRVB	5th (QER) Royal Scots TF, HQ at Forrest Hill
3rd QRVB	
4th (Edinburgh) VB	6th Royal Scots TF, HQ at 33 Gilmore Place
5th (Leith) VB	7th Royal Scots TF, HQ at Dalmeny Street, Leith
6th (Midlothian and Peebleshire) VB	8th Royal Scots TF, HQ at Haddington
7th (East Lothian) VB	
8th (West Lothian) VB	10th (Cyclists) Royal Scots TF, HQ at Linlithgow
9th (Highlanders) VB	9th (Highlanders) Royal Scots TF, HQ at East Claremont Street
No 4 Coy QRVB and H Coy 9th Royal Scots	OTC Officers' Training Corps

Special Reservists began with six months training, sustained by annual camps, and were to supply drafts to the line battalions. The QRVB ceased to bear the title brigade given to them by Queen Victoria. H University Company was intended for the new Officers' Training Corps, but it seems was subsequently reinstated.

Therefore, on 1 April 1908, the Ninth became a unit of the new Territorial Force, designated 9th Battalion (Highlanders) The Royal Scots. During 1907 the Ninth lost 160 men, 10 joining the regulars and 60 having gone to Canada; but also gained 170 recruits, and their capitation grant was 35s per man based on their strength on 31 October of 636 men. As anticipated by Clark, the new conditions of service meant that not all of the men transferred and only 413 re-attested under the new Territorial regulations. Major James Wardrop resigned his commission and Captain Blair was promoted to major in his stead. A regular officer, Captain William Green from the Black Watch (Royal Highlanders), became adjutant.

On formation the Territorial Force as a whole was only a third of its intended size. Rather understrength, the first TF camp of the Lothian Brigade was at Corrie Camp, Hillend in the Pentlands, under Colonel Sir Robert Cranston.

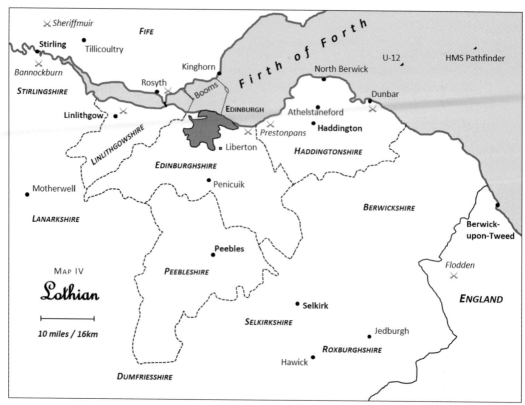

Members of D Company at camp, 1909.

To obtain the necessary strength a major recruitment drive was undertaken in early 1909, helped in no small part by an invasion scare. In February the sergeants recruited at one of the rugby internationals, in which played the likes of nimble centre James Pearson. In March 1909 the numbers leapt from 549 to an impressive 1,023 with about 30 recruits coming in every day. The Ninth was the only battalion in the city to attain full establishment on 31 March 1909, 'with two men to the good'[7], wrote Ferguson.

By this achievement the Ninth secured the great honour of receiving their colours from King Edward VII on 19 June 1909. The detachment to Windsor was limited to twenty-five, and Lieutenant Frederick Lucas commanded the colour party. When the Princess Royal presented new colours to the 7th/9th (Highlanders) Battalion in 1955 as colonel-in-chief she remembered, as a child, being present at this ceremony.

Just as they had for Edward VII in 1905, the Ninth were among those lining the route on the occasion of the royal visit of his successor, George V, in 1911. The following year Colonel

Alexander Blair.

James Clark retired; he was already chairman of the Edinburgh School Board and became chairman of the City of Edinburgh Territorial Force Association. He was replaced as CO by Major, now gazetted Lieutenant Colonel, Alexander Blair, previously of D Company.

As an undergraduate at Oxford, Blair had won the quarter-mile race against Cambridge and played for the first XI and the first XV where he was a very fast back, part of the new 'scientific' rugby game. He became Secretary of Scottish Rugby Union, through the controversial period when the International Board was founded without England, and became president in 1909. One of the original company commanders, now 47, he was an advocate and Writer to the Signet (senior solicitor) in Edinburgh.

Machine Gun Section, Riccarton 1911.

As a more suitable locale the battalion moved to 89 East Claremont Street (telephone no.7945) in 1913, due in no small part to the generosity of Colonel Clark who matched the government's financial commitment. Purpose built for the battalion at £7,000, it comprised three floors with a lecture hall, two billiard rooms (officers and men), a wagon store and a 100ft drill hall. Here, among more martial activities, they held an indoor football competition organised by Sergeant William McLeod Black. The Territorial Force in the last months of peace was, however, in decline with numbers falling steadily from a peak in 1909 and fewer still attending camp. In 1909 the annual camp was at Balmule Camp, Aberdour in Fife, followed in 1910 by Slipperfield Camp at West Linton, Peeblesshire; 1911 Riccarton, Ayrshire; 1912 Stobs; 1913 Monzie Camp at Crieff and 1914 Stobs.

Bobby Johnston was a 'son of the regiment', born in Glencorse Barracks, his father being a sergeant in the Royal Scots. With an education at garrison schools in Bermuda and Stirling, he was a 14-year-old Boroughmuir High School boy out cycling when he first saw territorials at camp in 1909. The following March he joined the Ninth as a drummer boy on a pay of 8d per diem. As bugler he sounded commands such as cease fire, recalling that there were 'no wireless sets in those days!'[19] He commenced his 'man's service' aged 17 and at 17½ passed out as proficient, appearing as a private in full dress uniform before Sir Ian Hamilton. In 1912 the requirement was to pay annual subs of 2s 6d, and efficiency was achieved with ten one-hour drills (forty for recruits), musketry and camp.

In addition to the regular adjutants, the professional soldiers who made up the permanent staff were senior NCOs, most of whom had seen service in South Africa. The first regimental sergeant major was James Morrison in 1900, joined soon after by

Crieff 31 July 1913.

Colour Sergeant Instructor James Mackay. Both had been Gordon Highlanders and awarded Distinguished Conduct Medals: James Morrison receiving his for conspicuous bravery at Elandslaagte and James Mackay for gallantry at Dargai. J. Duncan became the sergeant major in 1905 when Morrison was discharged. From 1905-1913 the battalion benefitted from the experience of Colour Sergeant Alexander Stephen, once again a Gordon Highlander with a DCM to his name, ready to share his recollections of storming the Dargai Heights on 'the Frontier' and of South Africa. As a strict disciplinarian he ruled the sergeants' mess with an 'iron rod'[19] where there was little drinking and no swearing, though in his youth he himself had been charged with drunkenness a number of times in India. Yet he was also encouraging to the young and most attentive to marching and shooting. Stephen was made regimental sergeant major in 1910.

James Mackay, died unexpectedly in 1903 and was carried to Warriston Cemetery on a gun carriage.

At Stobs camp in 1912 a live fire exercise was conducted which involved going forward at the double in stages from 400 to 200 yards to fire upon 1ft-square targets. Sergeant Major Stephen constantly upbraided the men for not maintaining the correct spacings for skirmishing. One section hit none of the targets and they were lambasted 'with some strong language, that this was a repetition of the battle of the Modder River in 1899, when poor musketry had contributed to disaster. Despite it all,' remarked Bobby Johnston 'we thought that this must be what war would really be like.'[19]

In 1913 James Buchanan, formerly 1st Cameron Highlanders, became sergeant major, a position he held until commissioned in March 1915. The sergeant-instructors were also from the Camerons: Alexander McKinnon with a Distinguished Conduct Medal from Khartoum and Peter McLachlan, who was to become sergeant major in

1915 and win a DCM in 1917. The value of these men to a territorial corps would be hard to exaggerate. Nevertheless, it was not unknown for veteran-trained recruits to proceed to France with a Boer vocabulary of *kopjes*, *veldt* and *donga* which did not equip them well for the Western Front. However, once there they were soon picking up supposedly Hindi words from the regulars returned from India, such as chatting, the pesticidal habit of crushing lice between the finger nails, and blighty from *bilayati* for foreign or European, now meaning *home* or a wound resulting in repatriation. This was the language used by 'Pukka fighting soldiers'.[20]

Tom Lowe.

James Buchanan, later MBE.

The establishment had a further eighteen staff including Bandmaster Herbert Laubach, Sergeant Shoemaker A. Campbell and the Sergeant Cook and Caretaker, who resided at HQ, Bob Tait. Gymnastic Sergeant Tom Lowe seems to have led an interesting life. Born in Manchester, he was stabbed in a scuffle aged about 16, joined the Gordon Highlanders under a false name and went to India. Wounded at Doornkop in South Africa, he was laid out for dead, but recovered and returned to Britain in 1900, became PT instructor at the Royal High School and joined the Ninth.

A little sibling rivalry is shown in David Bell's postcard to his brother Ian, of 7th Royal Scots, from Stobs in 1912: 'This is a better looking lot than the Swiss or even the 7th.'[21]

Stobs 1912.

At this time the battalion consisted of eight companies, each with a captain, two lieutenants, a colour sergeant and four sections, with each of these under the command of a sergeant. As well as the commanding officer and two majors, there was the adjutant, the machine-gun officer, the quartermaster and two medical officers.

Chapter 2

Defence of the Realm
1914

AT the end of June 1914 Archibald Gordon reflected on Archduke Franz Ferdinand's 'cruel end'.[22] A few years previously, in his rôle as private secretary to the Duke of Wellington, he had played host to the heir to the Austro-Hungarian Empire and found him a lover of flowers and champagne, but not of England. Now this life spark fell upon the kindling Balkans, soon to raze Europe, reach around the world and in time consume more than 16 million lives before it finally burnt out. The Germans invaded Belgium, Brialmont's forts did not long withstand Krupp's and Škoda's howitzers, and the Belgians retreated, eventually flooding the land in their traditional defence against the fire of war.

On 4 August Britain entered the war. The Royal Scots reached peak size in the Great War of 1914-1918 with thirty-five battalions, eighteen seeing active service. The 2nd Battalion were sent with the British Expeditionary Force in August 1914 and the 1st Battalion, recalled from India, arrived in France in December.

Gordon was hard at work fundraising to save the battlefield of Waterloo from property development when war began. He immediately diverted the funds and his efforts to the unfolding Belgian refugee crisis. However, this work came promptly to an end as the German advance neared Antwerp. Gordon, restored to the rank of major, Royal Scots, by his account helped command the Royal Naval Division (RND) out of the trenches, was jumped by two spies who were subsequently shot, personally led the column through the blazing streets of Antwerp and across the River Scheldt, which was alight with petrol, and then passed over unknown country to Saint-Gilles-Waes where the RND entrained for Bruges. Gordon had bought tinned goods for 10,000 men of the RND in Antwerp on account and, as the city was now occupied, a Dutch friend had to settle the bills on behalf of the Admiralty.

Mobilisation 1914

'On receipt of the order to mobilise, all members of the unit will at once report themselves at Headquarters in Marching Order. Those not reporting themselves within twenty-four hours will be treated as deserters.'

Standing Orders

34

David Huie, Alexander Blair and Robert Dudgeon on mobilisation.

With the printing presses prophesying war, the battalion completed their summer camp 'with two days of brigade exercises over the heather covered hills of the Lowlands'[19] at Stobs. They came home by train on Sunday, 2 August 1914 and two days later they were at war. At 5.30pm on the Tuesday, mobilisation orders arrived at their East Claremont St HQ and notices were sent out to 767 men, Captain Robbie Wallace's car being employed to deliver them. An exception to mobilisation was Lance Corporal Charles Park, officially told to stand fast at his government work as a telegraph operator. The men arrived throughout the following day and at 10.30pm, all accounted for, the final party marched to billets at St Ann's Maltings in Leith, their first 'war station'. Given the wild rumours, this was considered a rather 'tame'[2] destination.

Each of the large rooms at St Ann's Maltings, owned by the brewer Robert Younger Ltd, held 250 men, but they were not entirely suitable with several hundred men attempting to wash from two taps. High jinx led two men to fall into the 'ammoniated'[2] sump in the yard. Dod Fraser tried shaving with 'Kola'.[2] 'Squeak' Wallis bashed his head on a roof beam and, it was said, wore his bandage long after it was needed because civilians thought he had a war wound. Sadly, the first death occurred less than a month after mobilisation when Lance Corporal George Ledingham, a woollen warehouseman, fell from one of those wooden beams and died the following day on 1 September.

New recruits also began to arrive, beginning on the day of mobilisation. One of these was James Quinn:

35

Arrival at St Ann's Maltings, 5 August 1914.

'Even yet, I can remember that night. The Adjutant calming the crowd, the hurrying and bustling etc. and the 'Fall in'… Next day I was one of the DANDY NINTH and felt, and likely looked, a 'muckle gawky'. I was one of about fifty or sixty recruits and we were handed over to Sergeant [William] Hannay of the Camerons, who made us sweat blood almost actually. But he made us passable soldiers in the time allowed him.'[23]

Bobby Johnston agreed:

'My heroes at that time were the two Colour Sergeant Instructors – both Cameron Highlanders who had four war medals each (the Sudan, Atbara and Khartoum plus the South African War).'[19]

Recruits were drilled morning and afternoon, and a miniature range was established behind the Maltings. The noise at lunch was 'like the lions at the zoo'.[24] They ate sitting on the floor, though the last to arrive went hungry, and a thousand men washed their plates in a 6ft bath.

An exceptional number of recruits came from George Watson's College, in fact more Watsonians volunteered for the Ninth than for any other battalion, with 122 serving as at 9 March 1916. The entire first XV are said to have enlisted with the Ninth, including rugby internationals James Pearson, Eric 'Puss' Milroy, J.Y.M. Henderson

At the Maltings, 1914.

and Alex Angus. Apart from anything else, this gave the Ninth's rugby team a formidable back division. Some masters also joined, such as John Nisbet, also of the Fabian Society. Many officers were recalled and many more were commissioned from the rank of private within a month or two in October 1914, including Private William Cullen, son of Lord Cullen, who sadly died of pneumonia in Edinburgh in March 1915, David Kydd, later Machine Gun Officer and Charles Marburg, a rugby player later wounded at Gaza.

Defence of the Realm

> *The Scottish coast is the most convenient point of attack for Great Britain... Not a ship could leave either Rosyth or Cromarty without an immediate cable being sent by me to Berlin... it is no ways impossible to blow up the Firth of Forth Bridge and bottle all war vessels concentrated at the Rosyth base.*
>
> Armgaard Karl Graves, 1914

THE Ninth formed part of Scottish Coast Defences, which were responsible for the Forth, Clyde, Tay and Aberdeen. They were also under the aegis of the Territorial Force Association (TFA) for Lothian, which had, as chairman, their former colonel, James Clark.

Table 3. Scottish Coast Defences, part of Scottish Command on mobilisation

Scottish Coast Defences (Infantry)	
Major General Frederick C. Heath-Caldwell	
Black Watch Brigade	**Lothian Brigade**
Brigadier General A.deS. McKerrell	*Brigadier General H.F. Kays*
4/Black Watch	4/Royal Scots
5/Black Watch	5/Royal Scots
6/Black Watch	8/Royal Scots
7/Black Watch	9/Royal Scots
-	-
5/Argyll and Sutherland Highlanders attached	6/Royal Scots attached
	7/Royal Scots attached
	8/Highland Light Infantry attached

Scottish Command had their headquarters at 22 North Bridge, Coast Defences at 30 Rutland Square, and Lothian Brigade at 23 Rutland Square, TFA was at 53 Hanover St.

Coastal defence had been intended for the Royal Scots Volunteer Battalions since the 1880s. Defence of the realm was, after all, the main purpose of the Territorial Force. However unlikely the threat of invasion, it appeared real in 1914 and Kitchener, Secretary of State for War, held back two of the six infantry divisions of the BEF against such an eventuality. The Germans also held back IX Reserve Corps in Schleswig-Holstein against the possibility of a British amphibious landing.

> 'We have been buoyed up with the hope that a serious invasion of these shores was impossible, but we must remember that that has never been the opinion of German army and navy experts... As soon, therefore, as men are available the German project of invasion of these shores will, in all probability, be tested.'[25]
>
> Lord Kitchener, 20 October 1914

There was an invasion scare within a week of mobilisation, the Ninth spent much of the night of 7 August lying in King's Park (Holyrood Park), which was the war station for the brigade reserve.

The strategic value of the Forth lay not only in the threat of a landing, but in the vital importance of Rosyth naval base. With anti-submarine defences still under construction, plans were made for the Grand Fleet to reside at Cromarty and Scapa Flow and the dreadnoughts of the Grand Fleet were located thirty hours from the North Sea at Loch Ewe in the west of Scotland. Isle of Ewe – Edinburgh is about three-quarters of the distance from the German naval port of Wilhelmshaven to Edinburgh.

War came quickly to the Forth. On 2 September the U-boat *U-21* passed under the

The glengarried Ninth defending the dunes (or golf courses).

Forth Bridge where her periscope was fired upon, and three days later she sank HMS *Pathfinder* off St Abb's Head, the first ship ever lost to a submarine torpedo. The surface ships of the the Imperial German Navy were also at sea and bombarded the east coast towns of Scarborough, Hartlepool and Whitby in December 1914 causing 592 casualties, nearly all of them civilians, of whom 137 died.

Even in July 1915 potential recruits for the Ninth were being urged to join because Edinburgh 'might yet have to be defended. The German Emperor would not hesitate to sacrifice a hundred thousand men for the honour of being able to say that he had invaded the shores of Great Britain,' so urged Harry Rawson of the TFA. 'If the Germans were to land in this country,' added Captain Frederick Lucas, 'Belgium would be put in the shade.'[26]

The Ninth trained daily at King's Park and Leith Links, with frequent route marches. These went to Longniddry, Joppa, Musselburgh, Pinkie and Seafield. On one route march they ate at Loretto School, where both Alexander Blair and adjutant Robert Dudgeon had gone to school. On another, G and H companies bivouacked at Dalkeith. The machine-gun section also took the gun limbers over Arthur's Seat. Yet another scare, which conjured up submarines in the Firth of Forth, rushed them all back from Malleny on a tiring march.

At the end of September the battalion moved billets (Map V). The left half-battalion (E, F, G and H companies) moved to Bruntsfield School, on the corner of Marchmont

An airship over Inchcolm watches the fleet at anchor in the Firth of Forth.

Road and Crescent, 'a hotel after the Maltings'.[24] The swimming bath was filled twice a week. The 1,265 pupils were relocated to Boroughmuir School in Viewforth, or Sciennes School.

The right-half were at Redford, described below, until they rejoined in October when D Company went to Bruntsfield School, whilst A, B and C companies went to Warrender Park School under Major John Taylor Cameron. The MG Section ensconced themselves with a gramophone in the 'little sweetie-shop'[2] at Bruntsfield and 'worked the oracle'[23] running rumours between the half-battalions.

At Bruntsfield many of the men had their photographs taken by the eastern steps, and sadly many of these pictures subsequently appeared in the papers the following year, when those depicted were wounded, killed or missing.

The 'athletic CO' Blair and Dudgeon, during 'an al fresco lunch on a route march.'[27]

At Christmas 1914 bunting brightened the halls, turkey was on the menu and leave granted where possible in the afternoon. At Hogmanay they were confined to billets expecting orders for France, which were again cancelled, but a fine New Year's dinner was laid on. Inevitably the canteen was soon dry and men went first footing over the back wall at Bruntsfield in foraging parties. Men who returned late at night, singing, tired and emotional, ran the risk of falling into gun pits dug in the Meadows. Despite these disturbances, the neighbours took to them well; a Mrs Middleton of 1 Warrender Park Crescent, held a dance for the Ninth and they raised £5 for the Belgian Relief Fund to which Captain Dick Moncrieff added another £5.

Nevertheless, the imposition of military law would surely have grated on officers and men alike, they were constantly under orders, 'weekend warriors' still stationed in Edinburgh but unable to go home. Robert Ker fell foul of his superiors, causing a disturbance after 'lights out' in December 1914 that resulted in his being confined to barracks for three days. By the end of the month he was commissioned into the King's Own Scottish Borderers and rose to command 9th KOSB in the war. Lieutenant Thomas Wilfrid Bennet Clark, known to his

The Adjutant, Robert Dudgeon and Sergeant Major James Buchanan at Bruntsfield School.

family as Wilfrid, and to his men in the MG Section simply as 'BC', was a 27-year-old Writer to the Signet living at 11 Charlotte Square, Edinburgh. He joined the Ninth

Armoured Train.

in 1911 and was now machine-gun officer. At the end of 1914 he was asked to furnish an armoured train detachment to operate the two Maxim machine guns on Great Britain's first armoured train.

The train conversion was carried out at Crewe in December 1914 with half-inch armour plating, loopholes for rifles and Maxims and a 12-pounder at each end. No.1 Armoured Train 'Norna' underwent its trial trip on Boxing Day between Crewe and Chester. It was then stationed at Craigentinny, in east Edinburgh, and made frequent runs east along the coast. BC went out on one such patrol, that well-known hazardous run to Dirleton. The detachment remained with the armoured train until the battalion was ordered to France. An ambulance train was also put into service for coast defences soon after the outbreak of war, and a second armoured train, No.2 'Alice', was ordered early in 1915 to serve in Norfolk.

Freddie Paulin.

Although training continued in the Pentlands and Braid Hills, the battalion, which had been brigade reserve, was now given a sector of the landward defences to construct. The battalion divided its time equally between drill and defence, each half-battalion week about. Much of the defence work was digging the trenches intended to protect Edinburgh from invasion, with the men billeted for the week in farmhouses.

'As we have been digging trenches in rock most of the time, I am quite a competent navvy', wrote the Oxford classics scholar and poet John 'Jock' Brown, 'When we get out it will not be so dull, but the censor will make it impossible to write about it, so I shall not be able to tell you anything of interest till it is all over.'[4] However from

LEGEND	10. Wemyss Place (drill hall 1901-1911)	20. Arthur's Seat (King's Park) with Hunter's Bog rifle range marked
1. Granton Harbour	11. Royal Scots Club	21. Bruntsfield School
2. Leith Harbour	12. Calton Hill	22. Warrender Park School
3. Leith Fort	13. Princes Street Station	23. Duddingston Loch
4. Leith Links	14. Edinburgh Castle	24. Royal Observatory on Blackford Hill
5. Craigleith Hospital (Western General)	15. Waverley Station	25. Hallhead Road
6. East Claremont Street (drill hall from 1912)	16. Scottish Command	26. Redford Barracks, Colinton
7. St Ann's Maltings	17. Holyrood Palace	27. Liberton Tower
8. Olympia	18. Craigentinny Depot	28. Meadowhead Farm
9. Marine Gardens	19. Forrest Road (drill hall 1900)	

Addresses 1902
- ○ Officers
- ○ NCOs

MAP V

Edinburgh

1 km / 0.6 miles

Zeppelin L.14
Approximate route
2/3 April 1916

✿ Areas bombed
by L.22

Landward Defences

43

Belgium he wrote that the drudgery of digging was getting on his nerves and that the war's motto should be, 'The spade is mightier than the rifle.'[4]

Edinburgh's landward defences were organised in three main sections. To begin with they mostly consisted of barbed wire entanglements but developed into complex trench systems. An additional, forward line of defence ran from Marine Gardens, where the 5th Royal Scots were billeted, across the top of Portobello High Street and on to Craigentinny railway depot.

The northern, Section 1, ran from Seafield, on the coast at Marine Gardens, to Duddingston Loch. Section 2 continued the line, near the 4th Royal Scots' billets, to firing positions along Hallhead Road, which at that time overlooked fields. Here Mayfield Road defined the boundary to Section 3 (Map VI). This section, dug and defended by the Ninth, initially went west to the fortified farmhouse at Liberton West Mains, before heading south over what is now Craigmillar Golf Course and where some features remain, to cross the Braid Burn at Blackford Road Cottage, provided with firing positions. The line then climbed uphill to Liberton Tower. Redoubts with machine guns flanked the road here. The line of defence terminated near Meadowhead Farm, near Mortonhall, in a strong firing position and westward sweeping flank, near a possible Cromwellian army camp. Here the Ninth were 'right of the line' looking out at the Pentland Hills. The Section HQ was at the Royal Observatory on Blackford Hill, connected to the four strongpoints and Leith Fort, by telephone lines.

The recruits were temporarily attached to E Company and were sent digging trenches beyond the Braid Hills for a week. One man of E Company got a pick in the seat of his civilian trews.

The emplacement at the fifteenth-century Liberton Tower, alongside the Braid Hills, took weeks to build in the rocky earth; years later they wondered whether it was ever finished. The tower was 'principally inhabited by bats and rats'.[28] In daylight the sentry post on the roof afforded views of Edinburgh and the Forth, where the Ninth 'looked for bodies of the enemy's troops'[4] and at night were amongst the wheeling bats. One of their duties was to knock on doors in the district if they were showing a light. This, they were told, was on the rather unlikely assumption that they might be signalling to German ships but was probably a sensible blackout precaution.

Such patrols were halted that winter by a thirty-six-hour blizzard that closed the roads with up to 8ft of snow and the section had to dig themselves out of the tower.

Liberton Tower.

One unpleasant duty was in the city itself:

'On Saturday nights we have to take our turn of picket duty in such unsavoury districts as the High Street and Cowgate. Each picket numbers eight men under an NCO, and usually we have a pretty tough time with drunks.'[28]

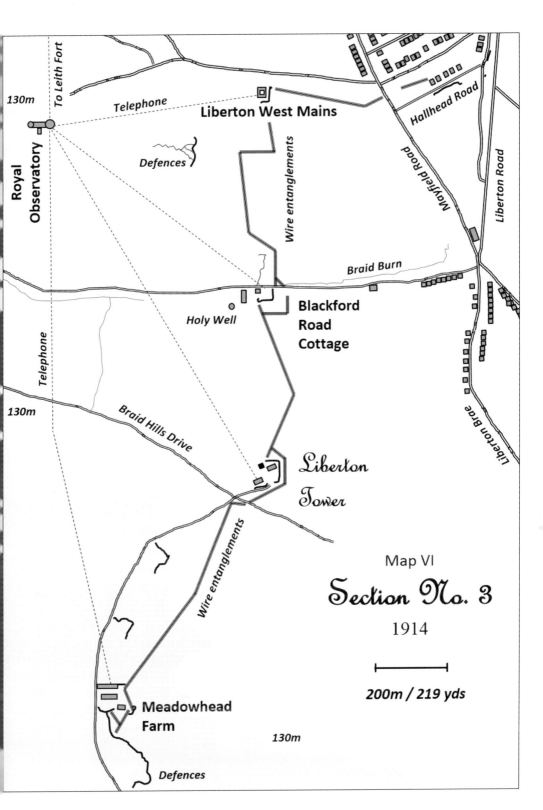

130m

To Leith Fort

Royal
Observatory

Telephone

Liberton West Mains

Defences

Wire entanglements

Hallhead Road

Mayfield Road

Liberton Road

Braid Burn

Holy Well

Blackford
Road
Cottage

Telephone

130m

Braid Hills Drive

Liberton Brae

Liberton
Tower

Wire entanglements

Map VI

Section No. 3

1914

200m / 219 yds

Wire entanglements

Meadowhead
Farm

130m

Defences

Trenches at Meadowhead Farm 1914.

Some of these men were on a short spell of leave and were taken directly to their trains rather than the police station. However, later, the reserve battalion found picket duty at Overgate, Dundee far worse, needing at least fourteen in the patrol.

An important duty was protecting Leith docks, where only those with special passes were permitted entry, and to guard ships brought in on suspicion. Night duty here was cold and miserable, without lights or fires and even smoking forbidden, unless they found themselves snug in the galley of a seized vessel. Arthur Anderson describes:

> 'One of us, complete with loaded rifle, must always accompany the customs officials in their examination of an arrested ship… some of the others have been fortunate to be present when contraband has been unearthed and have had the pleasure of putting the officers and crew under arrest.'[28]

Corporal Forsyth faced genuine danger on a 'dark and stormy'[6] night in December. Leaving the SS *Nigel* to do the rounds, the ship 'rocked at the pier of Leith' and he lost his footing on the gangplank and fell about 15ft into the dock between the ship and the quay. There was a real risk the 1,400 ton ship would crush him against the quay. He was rescued from drowning by Lieutenant Kenneth Mackenzie who dived in and held him up until ropes could be got to them. Mackenzie, 'a strong and big man, [who] in 1905 threw the hammer for Oxford against Cambridge,' was awarded the unit's first commendation, the Royal Humane Society's Bronze Medal. Writer to the Signet and Justice of the Peace for Lanarkshire, he was commissioned in October 1914 and killed in action in August 1918.

The Royal Navy were bringing into harbour a number of German trawlers and within a few days of the outbreak of war there were 300 men in detention at Redford

Barracks, mostly Germans, with a minority of other nationalities. Consequent to the Aliens' Restriction Act of 5 August 1914, 624 'enemy aliens' were registered in Edinburgh in the first month, though most naturalised as British citizens were unaffected, and men of military age (17-45) were told to report routinely to the police station. One night they were suddenly transported to a camp and handed over to the Royal Scots, without possessions and with bread left leavening. The camp population doubled by the end of the month and reached a peak of 1,400 in September and October.

Kenneth Mackenzie.

Austrians arrived at the camp immediately Britain declared war on 12 August, as an Austrian ship had been held up at Greenock, but these prisoners immediately fell out with their German allies. Redford German Prisoners' Camp, a central Scottish transit camp, had been created at Redford Barracks at Colinton. Bell tents were erected to the south of the barracks, each with a wooden floor and a dozen men to a tent. They were surrounded by barbed wire with 'made in Germany' labels on it. The prisoners complained of the cold, sleeping on straw palliasses with two blankets to each man. Their guards were also under canvas, on the other side of the wire, with three blankets between two men. However, the morale on either side could hardly have stood in starker contrast. Nevertheless, a great favourite among internees for passing the time was leap-frogging, 'as one frequently witnesses schoolboys engaged in during their play period.'[8] Reports that someone in the camp was signalling to the outside merited a special operation that discovered the signals were merely the dealing of poker cards in a candlelit tent.

The right-half of the Ninth Battalion (A, B, C and D companies) was posted to guard the camp under Major David Huie from early September and remained for six weeks patrolling the wire with elevated sentry stands at each corner. James Quinn thought it 'cushy'[23] and from the photograph of the guard officers Major Huie was probably not as dour as he might otherwise appear.

Captain Davie Bell, part of the guard at Redford, may have had to guard his father's business partner, August Bieberstedt. At the outbreak of war their seed business had been impounded and it was only able to continue after Bieberstedt dissolved the partnership at the Hotel Oranje-Nassau, in neutral Arnhem, in 1915. Rupert Bieberstedt, son of August and schoolmate of Davie Bell, changed his name to Beverton and served in the RAF.

The German cruiser SMS *Mainz* was sunk at Heligoland on 28 August 1914. HMS *Lurcher* put herself alongside, at some risk, to take off the survivors, for the *Mainz* rolled over and sank suddenly. Ninety survivors were brought to Leith the next day

Redford Guard Officers (Undress Uniform).

'rather like drowned rats'[29] and were issued with knitted jerseys. The wounded went to Edinburgh Castle by motor ambulance and the fit 'marched briskly along the pier to the train between the files of the armed escort'.[6] The soldiers on the train to Gorgie were seen trying to communicate with the prisoners by gesticulations. Among the officers at Redford was Oberleutnant Wolfgang von Tirpitz, son of the German Naval Secretary.

The City of Edinburgh Police wrote to all enemy aliens, regardless of age or sex, on 26 October 1914, informing them to remove themselves from the new prohibited area, including most of Lothian, by 2pm on 29 October. The nearest unprohibited area was Peeblesshire, though most went to Glasgow or London. Throughout this period the police were handing civilians over to the Royal Scots for internment.

Stobs Camp, where the Ninth had spent many a summer camp, began taking prisoners in November 1914 where huts were built as winter quarters. A wild, but unfounded rumour circulated that Tirpitz had led an escape, but instead he had merely been escorted by char-a-banc to Slateford Station and sent south. Internees also found themselves transported under territorial guard to the Isle of Man, where Britain's biggest camp was expediently created by putting barbed wire round Cunningham's holiday camp, which may say more about holiday camps than prison camps. The camp at Redford closed soon thereafter.

Charles A. Inglis, travelling on an American passport, mentioned the Royal Scots to his contact in Stockholm: 'The fear of espionage is very great and every day I see some Germans going to Redford barracks under the escort of a soldier.'[30] Inglis had arrived from Bergen and stayed throughout the month of September. He took lodgings as a neighbour of Colonel James Clark, rented a bicycle and toured the area. However, he studiously avoided the Royal Scots sentries at Leith docks and his reports to Stockholm were duly forwarded to Berlin, because Inglis was a German spy named Leutnant Carl Hans Lody. He attempted to report to the German Admiralty on the movements of submarines and ships, the laying of mines from Berwick and the gun defences at Berwick, North and South Queensferry, Inchgarvie island, Kirkcaldy and Kinghorn, getting much of his information on Leith and the Forth by standing on Calton Hill.

Lody was tried and shot at the Tower of London on 6 November 1914, the first execution at the Tower since the Jacobite Lord Lovat in 1747 (captured, Ferguson tells us, by his relative Captain John Ferguson RN). In this atmosphere, guard duty may not have seemed so far removed from the war.

The Ninth had, if briefly, at least one recruit of German descent: Fritz Klingler, a chartered accountant, attested on 5 August 1914. His overbearing Bavarian father was a brewer and the 'father of Scottish lager brewing'[31] who toasted the German army with champagne and advised his sons to go where the German bullets would knock their brains out. They did not see their father again. Despite having had four years' service with the Lothians and Border Horse, Fritz's current service lasted only three months until he was discharged under regulation 156(6) 'who cannot be discharged under any other heading'.

Perhaps this is unsurprising, given the intense anti-German feeling prevalent at the time, the relationship with his father and possibly a requirement to guard people he knew at Redford; but the exact reason is not known. He left for the USA aboard the SS *Lusitania* in December 1914 and became a Brooklyn accountant. It may not be coincidence that nine days after Fritz arrived home on a visit to Edinburgh in 1916, his father was interned. Fritz eventually succeeded in joining up in July 1917 (by this time he was Fred Klingler) by crossing the border to Toronto. He served in the 1st Tank Battalion of the Canadian Expeditionary Force.

Imperial Service

ALTHOUGH the Territorial Force was intended for home defence, the scale of the war and losses in the regular army serving in the British Expeditionary Force in late 1914 and early 1915 necessitated the service of TF units overseas. Territorials had long been invited to sign the Imperial Service obligation, committing themselves to service overseas in event of national emergency, though only 7 per cent had chosen to do so. This had proved a source of friction within units, particularly between married and unmarried men. Territorial units as a whole were under no statutory obligation to serve abroad, but Kitchener agreed at the Army Council of 9 August 1914 that any territorial unit volunteering *en bloc* for foreign service would be accepted. There was widespread concern that asking units to volunteer was tantamount to compulsion, though this did not always prove to be the case. Early in the war a territorial explained to Walter Nicholson, a staff officer with the 51st (Highland) Division, that 'the Territorial Force was only a last resource, in his opinion; it was not meant to come into a war until all the Regulars had been killed'.[32]

Kitchener's disdain for the Territorial Force as a 'Town Clerk's army' was partly based on the disappointing performance of the yeomanry in the Boer War, something for which he himself bore some responsibility. Lloyd George noted Kitchener thought of the TF 'in terms of the Volunteers who were the joke of the Regulars – a few hundred thousand young men officered by middle-aged professional men who were allowed to put on uniform and play at soldiers'.[25] Kitchener knew, however, that the war would be 'long and doubtful'.[33] As Secretary of State for War, he therefore faced the monumental task of raising the largest British Army ever fielded. Perhaps mistakenly, he created an alternative New Army, but winning over foreign service volunteers in the Territorial Force was also essential. By 25 August over 70 territorial battalions had volunteered; in all 318 saw overseas service.

Back row: James Robertson (actuary), George Strachan (Writer to the Signet), William Lindsay (coal exporter), Simon Fraser (solicitor), Alexander 'Daddy' Taylor (Sheriff of Forfar), Bob Lindsay (Writer to the Signet), Jimmy Ferguson (advocate), Basil Yeats (theologian), Pat Blair (accountant), Norman Macdonald (advocate), Dick Moncrieff (accountant), Frederick Lucas (doctor), Patrick J. Blair (advocate 1921)
Middle row: Davie Bell (seed merchant), David Huie (accountant), Alexander Blair (Writer to the Signet), Robert Dudgeon (army officer Camerons), John Taylor Cameron (advocate)
Front row: John Smith-Grant (distiller), Aymer Maxwell (medical student), Arthur Aitken (pharmacist), Willie Urquhart (solicitor), George Cowan (Writer to the Signet), Andrew Gordon (solicitor)

Colonel Blair raised the question of Foreign Service with his officers on a route march in September and asked for volunteers. According to Lieutenant 'BC' Bennet Clark, critical of the CO, the battalion were not all that forthcoming, but the company and platoon commanders were far more successful. Twenty of the twenty-five men of the machine-gun section volunteered. By the week ending 7 November 1914, an above average 993 officers and men had signed for Imperial Service. The battalion was divided into Service and Home Service battalions on 12 September 1914. On parade the Imperial Service group found themselves to be 'The Fine Fellows on [the] Right'[23] and when the billets were divided between them, this, the men said, separated 'the goats from the sheep'.[2]

In November, because of the First Battle of Ypres, the battalion was placed on 48-hour notice for the front and had even been marched out in the middle of the night. 'Short final leaves'[8] were granted on 4 November in readiness for departure and on 5 November Captain George Cowan married BC's cousin Marjorie 'quietly, in view of the impending departure of his regiment'.[34] Bernard Holmer 'had tea with Minie at 19 and said goodbye then. She was very brave, the sweetheart.' They had previously agreed that 'the last had been the best year of our lives'.[24] However this but proved the first of many false calls. Only from late January 1915 did men begin to receive Embarkation Leave prior to their actual deployment.

Dear 'Dandy Ninth' we'll miss you when from Bruntsfield you depart,
And you will leave behind you full many an anxious heart.
We've watched you doing sentry, and seen you on the march.
Egad! But there's a difference since the days when you wore starch.
The days when you wore starch, my boys,
And socks of varied hue,
Soft Homburg hats and yellow spats,
And fancy waistcoats, too.
But with it all there's been brave hearts beneath each fancy vest;
With bayonets fixed, you're ready now to exterminate 'a pest!'
Here's luck to every gallant lad who leaves this shore, for why, sir?
He wants to have a little sport in cornering the Kaiser!
In cornering the Kaiser, boys,
And won't he quake with fear
When he sees the boys of the 'Dandy Ninth'
From Scotland drawing near.

The 'Dandies' – A Metamorphosis[26]

Chapter 3

France and Flanders
1915

*I send them a hearty God-speed. We know the stuff of which they are
made, and the stock from whence they come, and are confident that they
will distinguish themselves, and bear the name of old Scotland with glory.
May I be there to see when Edinburgh welcomes them home, crowned
with laurels and victory. (Cheers.)*[6]

Lord Rosebery

THE Ninth were impatient, they had been on standby to join the BEF since November
1914 when the First Battle of Ypres was underway, but the line had stabilised and the
east coast looked no less secure and so the battalion had languished in expectation.

'On the 23rd February we were wakened by reveille, and looking at our watches found
it an hour too early [it was 5am]. We had a vague feeling that this meant something,
and then we heard – we were leaving that night.'[4]

To William Young of B Company they were 'The always-
never-going-battalion...the laughing stock of Edinburgh!'[35]
At last on the evening of Tuesday, 23 February 1915 they
marched through the snowy streets of Edinburgh via the
Links, Tollcross and Lothian Road to Princes Street Station
and embarked upon three trains, departing between 7.20 and
9.50pm. The gathering crowds meant that the last
detachment had to fight their way down Lothian Road.
General Ewart sent them off and Colonel Ferguson must
have had mixed emotions: pride in seeing the battalion he
had created go to war and understandable concerns for the
men he knew, including his only surviving child, Captain
Jimmy Ferguson.

Cadell's 'The Parting'

The next day dawned with all the fields white with snow
under a bright sun. A rumour that they were going to
Winchester for divisional training was scotched when they steamed straight through
the station and men posted notes home at stations *en route* as thoughts now turned

The Ninth cross to France.

more firmly to France. So it proved, as they pulled into Southampton docks on Wednesday afternoon.

The battalion boarded a large cattle ship, crewed by 'Hindus', now the transport ship HMT *Inventor*, which slipped her lines at 6pm but remained in the Solent that night and all the following day awaiting escorts, a 'scunner'[23] of a wait. They had plenty of time to consider the fact that the week before the Germans had announced unrestricted submarine warfare. The tender took off their last postcards.

The overnight crossing was calm and quiet, escorted by three destroyers whose crews played melodeons and smoked, whilst strict discipline was imposed on the Ninth. They eventually arrived in Le Havre in the early hours of Friday 26 February, in possession of at least the numerical strength to serve on the Western Front with 30 officers and 987 other ranks.

Le Havre, or Havre as it was then written, was the usual port for disembarkation, and later TF units usually went for training near St Omer, but the following morning the Ninth marched, now on the right-hand side of the road, to the railway station to be sent to their division. The MG Section had a poor start when a machine-gun limber ran away from them down the hill into town. Entrained in wagons labelled 'Hommes, 40; Chevaux, 8', typically mispronounced 'forty homs or eight she-voos',[36] the men who only had space to sit, kept their spirits up with a sing song, which did not endear them to those who had room to sleep. They travelled for twenty-six hours with but few clues as to their direction: Rouen, then Calais, St Omer and Hazebrouck appearing among the unknown station signs. There is no disguising that this was Jimmy Pearson's attempt to locate them: 'None to whom we shouted, whether our would-be linguist

53

(with a reputation more solid as a Rugby three-quarter than as a French scholar), with his "*où êtes-nous, monsieur?*" or in plain English, would or could tell us where we were going, so on we went mystified, but knowing we must be getting very near "the front".'[35]

They detrained at Cassel – with her stepped gables familiar to visiting Scots and long cited as the hill of the Grand Old Duke of York – and had a march of 12 miles on straight continental roads. With the colonel ahead on horseback accompanied by an interpreter, they arrived at L'Abeele near Boeschepe, nicknamed *Bo-peep* in the Ypres Salient area. The Ninth had gone 'up the line' to join 81 Brigade, 27th Division. They were the first of the Edinburgh TF units to go to the front, and one of forty-eight territorial battalions in France by the end of February. Now some 8 miles from the front they were 'within sound of the guns'.[37]

No.9 Platoon was in a hay loft which had previously billeted German and French soldiers. The men were told these leaky billets would be considered 'Buckingham Palace to Huns'.[24] Men were allowed into the village in small parties but had to carry their rifles and five rounds; they found that the village accommodated a number of refugees who only spoke Flemish. Clarence Gibb adapted quickly, had his hair cropped very short and reported that the water was not safe, so had to be boiled or they were 'reduced to beer and light wines... It is rotten stuff, but quenches the thirst.'[37]

The 27th Division had, in January 1915, taken over from the French 32nd Division, extending the BEF line northward to St Eloi, with the 28th Division in turn taking it north to the Ypres-Menin road. The Official History records that the trenches were shallow and not only waterlogged but regularly flooded out. The French had maintained them merely as outposts and expended considerable 75mm ammunition in defending them. The British had an allowance of only four rounds a day per field gun and were forced to fully man the trench lines, resulting in increased casualties.

Table 4. Infantry Brigades of the 27th Division as at April 1915

27th Division		
Major General Thomas D'Oyly Snow		
80 Brigade	**81 Brigade**	**82 Brigade**
Brigadier General WEB Smith	*Brigadier General HL Crocker*	*Brigadier General JR Longley*
2/King's Shropshire Light Infantry	1/Royal Scots	1/Royal Irish Regiment
3/King's Royal Rifle Corps	2/Gloucestershire Regiment	2/Duke of Cornwall's Light Infantry
4/King's Royal Rifle Corps	2/Cameron Highlanders	2/Royal Irish Fusiliers
4/Rifle Brigade	1/Argyll and Sutherland Highlanders	1/Leinster Regiment
Princess Patricia's Canadian Light Infantry	–	–
	9/Royal Scots (TF)	1/Cambridgeshire Regiment (TF)
	9/Argylls (TF)	

The 2nd Glosters were known to them as 'English Jocks'.[2] Harris, as sentry, challenged men of the PPCLI and told them 'I don't want your b..... alphabet, who are you?'[2]

The division consisted of regular battalions, 'old sweats', brought back from overseas service, to which were added territorial battalions as they arrived. Only in 1916 did the Ninth join a TF division and before then they had much to prove about the abilities of a territorial corps, especially as they were brigaded alongside 1st Royal Scots returned from India. Also in their brigade were the 9th Argyll and Sutherland Highlanders who had crossed to France the week before, making for an exceptionally large brigade. These two 'Ninths', the two territorial battalions in the brigade, were from the east and west of Scotland, 'whose speech proclaimed them as Glasgow as we were Edinburgh'[35] and met frequently on roads in the relief of trenches. On that first march they passed their old colonel, James Clark who had retired in 1912 but had been recalled the previous August to command the 9th Argylls. He was the first member of Edinburgh Town Council to join up, the second was Lieutenant Robert Bathgate of the *Dandy Ninth*, whose total service ran 1902 to 1921.

The first week was spent at L'Abeele, where they had to cope with the mud and

the rations. 'Even the best parts of the best roads were ankle deep in mud,'[37] wrote Gibb, 'thick mud all the way,'[38] adds Walter 'Wattie' Scott of B Company.

The territorials had a three-fold deficiency to overcome: first, they were undertrained compared to the regulars, second training does not account for the realities of war and the regulars had been present some months, and third the war was evolving very rapidly such that the lessons of 1914 were insufficient for 1915. Nevertheless, by February 1916 the Germans recognised that the territorials could begin to be compared favourably in efficiency to the regulars and Field Marshal Viscount French, speaking at Edinburgh in August 1916, went as far as to say that the territorials 'went out and practically saved the country'.[6]

At this stage, any sense that they were professional soldiers was doubtless dispelled as they rubbed shoulders with their brethren in the 1st Royal Scots, although Gibb wrote home that the regulars 'consider us one of the best of the battns. out here'.[37] They were given lectures on trenches and periscopes and began to be inculcated in the art of trench warfare. Disturbingly, three-quarters of the rifles were found to be fouled with caked oil. For some they were genuinely the brother battalion, for example A. Watson's brother was a sergeant in the 1st Royal Scots.

Wattie Scott.

The companies were taken out for training by Lieutenant Norman Young, formerly a law student and a private in the Ninth, but since 1913 a regular in the 1st Royal Scots and serving in India, 'the most popular officer the 9th ever had'.[16]

They still found the training more amusing than frightening:

'At intervals the officer in charge fired his revolver in lieu of a star-shell, and down we flopped, hoping for a dry spot, as often as not on top of the man in front, in silent convulsions of laughter.'[35]

Norman Young.

It made John Brown think of musical chairs without chairs. Liberally coated in mud they were inspected the next day by Brigadier General Macfarlane who considered them a fine body of men, 'I suppose it was the men he was looking at not the clothes,'[39] wrote James Lawson Cairns of No.5 platoon. James Quinn had misplaced his rifle on the last night in Edinburgh, whilst he had been loading limbers, and ended up with a long Lee-Enfield which his bayonet did not fit. On inspection he was 'fair shaking in case it would come adrift'.[23] They spent a good deal of time cutting willow branches and making them into fascines for repairing roads and revetting trenches, as well as longing for their post and parcels.

Table 5. Officers of the Battalion proceeding on Active Service, February 1915

1/9th (Highlanders) Royal Scots	
CO Lieutenant Colonel Alexander S. Blair	
2-i-c Major John S. Taylor Cameron	
A Company	**1-4 Platoon**
Captain Pat A. Blair (formerly OC E Company)	Lt William Liddle (Signalling Officer)
	2/Lt Freddie W. Paulin (2 Platoon)
Captain Alexander Taylor (from Territorial Force Reserve)	2/Lt Robert S. Lindsay
	2/Lt Robert Menzies
B Company	**5-8 Platoon**
Captain Jimmy Ferguson (formerly OC D Company)	2/Lt Aymer D. Maxwell
	2/Lt Hew M. Wardrop
Captain Davie Bell	Lt Willie M. Urquhart (7 Platoon)
	2/Lt Cyril Falconer Stewart (8 Platoon)
C Company	**9-12 Platoon**
Captain Dick H.F. Moncrieff (formerly OC G Coy)	Lt Norman Macdonald
	2/Lt Charles G. Melrose (10 Platoon)
Captain George D. Cowan (formerly OC C Company)	2/Lt Patrick J. Blair
	2/Lt Edgar A.G. Robb
D Company	**13-16 Platoon**
Captain Frederick R. Lucas (formerly OC H Company)	Lt David A. Ross Haddon
	2/Lt Simon Fraser
Captain George H. Green (formerly OC F Company)	Lt William C.S. Lindsay (15 Platoon)
	2/Lt William R. Richard
Captain and Adjutant Robert M. Dudgeon, Cameron Highlanders	
Machine Gun Officer Lieutenant Thomas Wilfrid 'BC' Bennet Clark	
Quartermaster and Honorary Major Mr Andrew Gordon	
Medical Officer Captain John M. Bowie, RAMC	

As of 1 January 1915 battalions were reorganised from eight companies down to four 'double' companies. A&E became the new A Company, B+D=B, C+G=C, F+H=D Company

The senior officers were advocates. Alexander Blair was a Writer to the Signet and John Taylor Cameron an advocate and Examiner in Law, to confirm his Highland connections he 'resumed' the family name of Cameron. The company commanders were mainly lawyers and accountants.

Alexander 'Daddy' Taylor, born in Carrickfergus, was an advocate.

Davie Bell, a partner in his father's seed merchant firm in Leith.

Pat Blair, chartered accountant, was a senior partner of Macandrew and Blair.

Jimmy Ferguson, second generation Ninth, was admitted to the Bar in 1913.

George Cowan studied law at Oxford and was a Writer to the Signet.

Frederick Lucas, a doctor, in 1913 he had been a ship's surgeon to Australia.

Richard Henry Fitzherbert Moncrieff (also Moncreiff), a chartered accountant.

George Green, who transferred from 4th Royal Scots in 1913, worked in insurance.

The battalion had three officers named Blair: Alexander Blair, the CO, Patrick Alexander Blair and Patrick James Blair. The two Patricks were cousins. Pat A. Blair being then 33 years old and P.J. Blair, 'Young Blair' or 'yon long lad', ten years his junior.

P.J. Blair.

A family with close ties to the battalion included a pair of serving brothers: Willie and Douglas Urquhart. Lieutenant William Macduff Urquhart, solicitor, amused No.7 platoon when ordering them from a trench with 'Get out and fall in'.[35] His younger brother Douglas, known as Twinkle to his society friends in Edinburgh, was Private No.1389 but was commissioned in the Seaforth Highlanders in the middle of March. Their sister Helen was engaged to 'Pussy' Milroy, scrum half and captain of the 1914 Scotland rugby team and also a Ninth until commissioned into the Black Watch at Christmas 1914. He was tragically killed at Delville Wood in July 1916.

Voormezeele and Ypres

> *'The predominant features of this country are the mud and the cafés – everywhere mud is conspicuous by its presence while every second house appears to be a café, without any 10 o'clock opening or closing'*
>
> Clarence Gibb, *'Somewhere in France'*[37]

B COMPANY were the first in harm's way, much to the annoyance of A Company who had fallen in with their parcels hung about them. Moving up to yet more mud, now ankle deep, at a wood at Dickebusch (Map IX) on Saturday 6 March, for eighteen days, the company was on nightly fatigues. Marching out toward Voormezeele, 'a mass of ruins',[24] about 5 miles, the last mile open to rifle fire; digging a complete line of reserve trenches, filling sandbags and erecting barbed wire, sometimes in snow, with bullets flying about in the dark. They had to 'work like fury'[37] in digging the trench to afford them some protection. Not being able to see what they were doing, most of the men received some nasty tears on the wire and in heavy fire had to lie down for half an hour. 'While bullets fly about, you have no one to shoot back at, which is very annoying.'[26]

Russell 'Cherry' Thin was part of a carrying party:

> 'Had to wade through a field of liquid mud and flop every now and then, with spent bullets whizzing overhead all the time. Didn't feel exactly funky but was sweating like a pig by the time we reached the trench.'[3]

In the early hours they retired along the exposed road to their 'mud-hovel' of tarpaulin-covered huts in the wood 'à la Wild West'[24], and their rum ration. They were issued with twelve cigarettes to last them a week and 5 Francs. With twenty men to a hut they were so crowded the men had to lie on their sides.

Whenever an unknown aeroplane was spotted, a whistle was blown and they had

Benny Irvine (centre) 'Drumming Up'.

to rush for their shelters. The first casualty came about when, as noted by the colonel 'a young lad accidentally shot his foot cleaning his rifle. It was not serious, I am glad to say,'[6] it was the 'usual fool game – didn't know it was loaded'.[23] Digging a trench near Vierstraat on the fourth night, 10 March, Private W.C. McMillan felt a whack in his leg. 'Who hit me, you blighters?' he said, and only realised he had been shot when he felt the blood and the hole. 'The hero of the night,' wrote William Young, 'Oh, for a cushy wound!'[35]. He was carried away on a stretcher to a dressing station half-a-mile to the rear. McMillan was the first casualty of the Ninth to enemy action, but they were nightly occurrences thereafter.

A Company came up to the camp the day after B and were first into the trenches. All of the companies were put into the trenches for 24 hours' experience attached to a line battalion. Inexperienced and moving in darkness they unsurprisingly flinched at the crackle of far-off rifle fire and threw themselves down into 'terra-aqua'[26] at distant shell bursts whilst their guides stood stock still. In these early experiences, shells falling a long way behind them were described as 'pretty close'.[6] They soon developed the experience and the 'fey' fatalism of their chaperons who had been several months in Flanders with phrases such as 'if a shell's got your name on it...'. William Young thought they sounded, on the surface, 'completely pagan'; but then they had left their life and loved ones 'far off in another world'[35] and now inhabited a strange world, passing the remnants of a destroyed London bus on the roadside on their way up.

Entering and leaving the trenches was the most dangerous and introspective time, silence and a ban on smoking were strictly observed, for there were no communication trenches to allow men to safely move up to and away from the front line. A fortunate soul wrote to a friend in Edinburgh:

> 'For 200 yards before entering we were under fire, and very hot, too. When close to the trench I had a miraculous escape. Mother sent me a metal mirror, which I received that Sunday morning, and it was this that stopped a German bullet. I was hit in the left breast, the bullet lodging itself in the mirror, which was in my left pocket.'[40]

The newspapers were fond of these tales, but the bullet must have been near spent before it struck.

Jock Brown of A Company had an inauspicious start, 'We filed along, and, before we realised where we were, found ourselves falling into a pool, which was the door of the trench we were to hold.'[4] Typically there were three territorials to two regulars in a post and there they found a willingness to share information and small luxuries, contrary to what they had been led to expect. A Company 'had a very quiet but monotonous time and have no wish to go back'.[39] In the early hours they were told to show more activity, put their heads over the parapet and open rapid fire. In daylight they surveyed the enemy lines through periscopes and noted the dead Frenchmen in front of the trench, looking like their forebears of 1870 in red trousers and blue coats. In this stint Beaumont Beatson had his left arm fractured by a bullet.

When it came to their turn, B Company similarly scrambled in at the double and not at the steady pace they had practised. They found themselves in No.8 trench, attached to the 1st Argylls, and 130 yards from Bavarians in front of a wood. Nonchalance set in immediately, 'It is wonderful how cool one becomes. I go into the line now as cool as if I were coming into the office at ten o'clock.'[26] A drummer wrote home to say, 'When the shells came way overhead they would simply grin and ejaculate "Thumbs up; nothing doing." As for bullets – well, they just took their chances with them, that was all.'[41] On their first experience in the line, the Machine Gun Section had their 'gun pointed at a loophole which was <u>not</u> to be opened till Sir John French wrote and told us!'[23]

C Company had their turn on Saturday 13 March going into trench T6, except David Lang who was shot through the thigh on the way up. The night was quiet but cold. The men had greased their feet and legs against the cold with whale oil and dressed in cap comforters, less conspicuous than Glengarries, or else Balaclavas, and multiple socks, sheepskin 'furries', gloves and mittens. They were just going to take tea around 5pm on the Sunday when:

> 'There were three terrific explosions, which shook the ground tremendously, rapid firing was started by both sides and the German guns fairly belted us. Then ours

got going. The latter were wonderful, and miles better than theirs. The Germans came over until about 200 yards from us, and from that point came some further way. They did not come over opposite us – I will say no more.'[6]

C Company unexpectedly held the line on the southern flank of a German attack. Heavy fire followed through the night with a counter-attack going across to their left in the small hours. They could not be relieved as planned, though No.14 Platoon got water and provisions to them.

The men in the fire trenches fired nearly 500 rounds each, engaging in rapid fire once when an attack was expected. Here the battalion discovered an important fact, as explained by Clarence 'Gibby' Gibb writing home to his fiancée Annie Logan:

'The first night was quiet but Sunday was something awful, German and British attacks off and on throughout the day and night. The bullets were not so bad and being in the support trenches we were under German gun fire – the actual fire trenches being too close to allow them to be shelled. All we could do was to take refuge in bombproof shelters expecting every moment to be our last.'[37]

The support trenches were 500 yards from the enemy and subject to artillery fire, but the fire trenches were too close to the Germans at about 100 yards, yet unforgivingly close for rifle fire.

The Adjutant, Captain Robert Dudgeon, cycled to headquarters and on return ordered the rest of the battalion back to the huts and to stand by through the night. The MG Section, 'too excited to take our rum',[23] had to manhandle their limbers across fields. C Company were forty-eight hours in the trenches and returned to camp at 1am on Tuesday. It was 'exciting'[35] reported William Young, but the battalion did not know it had been an attack on the 30ft mound at St Eloi, that recalled 'a familiar landmark in Edinburgh'[6] two miles to the left, until they got week-old papers from home.

'It was a great experience for our first time,'[6] wrote a young Morningside man to his mother. Gibb wrote honestly to his fiancée, 'I am glad to say that I am keeping splendidly fit here and if I could control my nerves a wee bit more would feel much better.'[37] He later wrote in apology, 'You must excuse my last letter. I was absolutely shaken up… I had a man on my left-hand side shot – the bullet whistled jolly near my forehead. However, everything is better now.'[37] A week later 'Gibby' was wounded in the jaw and was told it would take two years to heal. His mates called him a 'Lucky Dog' when they heard he had his discharge papers. Clarence and Annie were married in 1917 and had three children. After the war, he worked as an accountant in Glasgow, smoked a pipe to exercise his jaw and wore a Royal Scots tie every day until he died in 1980.

In this action the first man was killed, long-serving Sergeant Thomas Crichton, No.27 of 12 Platoon, from the Leith branch of the Co-op. He had been 'too confident'[26] and was shot by a sniper, who in

Tommy Crichton.

turn was killed by a sergeant from the Argyll and Sutherland Highlanders. Tommy Crichton was buried behind the trench where he fell.

The Medical Officer, Dr John Bowie, invited D Company's officers to dinner on their return from the trenches. He served stew and steak and tinned fruit he had received from home, followed by coffee, cake and cigarettes. His staff, Ambulance Sergeant William Millikin and Medical Orderly James Lawson Cairns, who had just been assigned to the doctor, were pleased to get the same. A typical day involved going around the billets in the morning with sick parade at 12 noon. These three travelled with the ambulance wagon, were billeted apart from the companies and often shared a room. They lived relatively comfortably, the NCOs contributed 2/6 and the doctor 5/- a week to keep them in liver, pork chops and the like and on occasion Bowie treated them to a bottle of red wine. From time to time Colonel Blair also contributed kippers for breakfast or a boiled ham. The colonel made the rounds and looked in on people who had lost friends or had difficulties at home. He rather surprised the Machine Gun Section, when they were delousing, with a cheery, 'Well, boys! Had a good catch this morning? Got eight myself today.'[5]

Among the wounded of this period, 18-year-old Robert Stewart had been shot through the spine and sent to No.3 General Hospital at Le Tréport. After a week the matron planned to send him to England by the next ship, but about 4am he called the night sister and said, 'Sister, I feel so funny; something's happening,' and died.

At the end of March 1915 the Ninth found themselves billeted in Ypres, already famous to them for the halting of the German advance on Calais in the 'Race to the Sea'. The ancient city had yet to feel the full force of German artillery but was perilously located in a Salient with enemy forces to the north, east and south. A and B companies were billeted in the Abbaye des Dames Irlandaises d'Ypres, vacated by Irish Benedictine nuns some of whom, by coincidence, had been evacuated from Antwerp with the help of Major Archibald Gordon, and included *Sœur* Gordon from Aberdeenshire who made a point of introducing herself.

Major Archibald Gordon was a frequent visitor to Ypres, even bringing the Prime Minister's wife, Mrs Margot Asquith, to view the Salient. Their differing accounts suggest he thought he had left her peacefully in the car whilst he attended to a grave. She, however, had climbed a hill to see the

Our first resting place in Ypres.

St Martin

Cloth Hall

Grand Place

100m / 109 yds

Porte de Menin

Rue de Lille
(Rijselstraat)

St Jacques

Abbaye

Ypres

Map VII

Rue des Riches Claires

Rue Saint Jacques
(Sint-Jacobsstraat)

St Pierre

N

Porte de Lille

The Abbaye from the city ramparts, Saint Jacques on the scaffold.

German guns firing. Gordon became a King's Messenger for King Albert of Belgium, titled *Attaché à la Maison de Sa Majesté le Roi des Belges*, whilst his brother William Gordon VC was *aide-de-camp* to King George V.

The improvement over their muddy huts was remarkable: 'How comfortable we were! a sacrilegious horde of kilted heretics! The days we lay within the high-walled garden in the sun; the afternoon teas we gave when some of us "struck it lucky" with parcels.'[35]

The choice of words seems strange, for William Young, writing as an anonymous private, had been a missionary in Livingstonia, Nyasaland (Malawi) and was home on furlough when war broke out. His published account of B Company included rifling through the nuns' possessions and, notwithstanding that the Abbaye was destroyed, was perhaps the reason why the nuns, now in Ireland, attempted to sue for damages. Francis Patrick, 6ft 2in, who had postponed his studies in Indian agriculture to join up, could be found if you 'go to the roofless library or convent ruins and there you will find him rumaging amongst the old and shell-torn books, smoking his pipe'. He was the first Watsonian to fall, on 12 April.

D Company were in the Convent School, two platoons to a room. Some of C Company were in a part ruined and drafty hall – the windows had all been blown in – with hard stone floors to lie upon. The rest of C Company were in evacuated and partially ruined houses, also devoid of glass, in the Rue des Riches Claires (Rijkeklarenstraat). No.10 Platoon was in house number 16 and soon had a 'ripping'[24] fire going beside which they fed. The refuse went into a 15-foot shell hole in the garden. However, they were awoken one morning by water pouring down on them. The sergeants on the floor above had lit a fire on the floor, and unsurprisingly the floorboards had caught fire which they were hurriedly attempting to extinguish. Some of the boards had to be pulled up. At first the men made their own fires to 'drum up' and fry ham and eggs, but Sergeant Cook Bob Tait soon arrived and established his field kitchen in the yard of the Abbaye. Later Notre Dame Hospital was also used as billets.

Some Yprois, understandably, barred their doors to billeting troops, in contravention of Belgian law dating back to 1887. There was scarce opportunity for the gendarmerie to open the doors before German artillery had flattened the houses.

However, the Ninth received a very warm welcome from the local population. On their rest night they were given a pass for an hour to make for a café. 'Cherry' Thin fed very well, for 1½ francs, but the townsfolk were also 'making hay'[37] by selling provisions at elevated prices. At Ypres the Ninth 'accustomed only to the Scottish method of cooking eggs, which affords little variety, had their first extensive experience of Continental resources in the preparation of omelettes'.[6]

Russell 'Cherry' Thin.

James Quinn remembered being told by locals *'Allemand, boom! boom! – Anglais, boom! boom! Guerre fini!,'*[23] to which he adds 'True in the end – but a mighty long way off in those days of March and April 1915.'[23] Wull Grossart conjured from his memory: 'Ypres estaminet sing-songs, first a Jock with "Annie Laurie", then a Belgian swaddie with his counterpart, to be followed by the Ypres lassie at the counter and a Froggie.'[5] 'Cherry' Thin managed to get to a concert where a 'man murdered Kipling's Mandalay'.[3] James Quinn recalled, 'There was one estaminet there I mind, where one of the girls in it had picked up a lot of English and some songs. One, she sang regularly – *'After the Ball'* – half in Flemish and half in English. Plenty comic!'[23] James Beatson found the cafés charging double and that, perhaps on a different tack, 'Disease is rampant in Ypres; some half dozen cafés have been put out of bounds for us. I suppose lack of doctors prevents proper supervision.'[42] Walking home after a few drinks was not without hazard as there was much debris and not a light in the town.

Then there was work, with nightly fatigues now in two four-hour shifts, rather than the nine hour stretches they had occasionally suffered at Voormezeele. The promises of the adjutant were kept: they were building breastworks on wire frames a mile from the Menin Gate, but with no rifle fire, able to smoke and back by midnight. 'Fatigues at Ypres were rather a picnic' was our unanimous decision.'[35]

In early April the BEF took over a further 5 miles of the French front, to the Ypres-Poelcappelle road to a total of 30 miles. The 27th Division relieved the French occupants, French 17th Division, and 28th Division and the Canadians successively extended the British line north. This left two French divisions between the British and the Belgians at the canal. The trenches were poor with many breastworks above ground. The Germans agreed, capturing a French position that it was: 'A primitive sandbag parapet, hardly bullet-proof, miserable shelters.'[43] It might be noted that these high-power service rifles were capable of penetrating 18in (460mm) of sandbags and that modern assault rifles deliver a little over half the muzzle energy. News of the trenches to the east circulated and rumours with it, one being that a four-poster bed had been seen in one of the dug-outs.

A and B companies left the relative comfort of Ypres on 4 April, Easter Sunday. Standing quietly in the square beneath the damaged Cloth Hall that night, they quietly sang the twenty-third Psalm *The Lord is my Shepherd*. Marching 3 miles east on the road and a mile over fields they came to isolated dug-outs that formed the support position, recently vacated by 'the Froggies'.[24] 'We passed through what had once been a beautiful estate with a large pond, wooded and shrubbery round a ruined chateau close to Hooge. Then a little further to the Sanctuary Wood where our dug-outs were located.'[42] A Company were carrying such a number of wooden knife-rests for wire entanglements that a wit along the way asked if they were going to trap the Germans. 'I hope the Germans only got half as tied up with them as we did,'[4] thought Jock Brown. Similarly, marching up with the rations Bill Robertson fell his length into an old trench full of water, reaching their destination thoroughly drookit, he had to be sent back for the ration bag he had been carrying.

They had now replaced fatigues with duties in the line, and accordingly losses began to mount. Arthur Lawson wrote to his sister (adding 'Not for Press Publication'):

'The day before yesterday the Germans commenced putting shrapnel into the wood in which our dug-outs were. The first shell came over a rise of ground opposite occupied by a lot of other men who were walking about. They heard it coming and the next minute there wasn't one of them to be seen, they had all gone into their huts. After that we lay pretty close in our huts for a while only popping out after each shell to see how near it was. We were just starting tea when this happened and after about the first half dozen one of our lot said, "Ah to H— I'm not going to eat my tea... inside this hut," with that he went out. The next moment one burst about 200 yds on his left and he came into the hut again with the greatest speed and celerity.'[44]

Robin Marcel, whose father was still in Brussels, was wounded on 6 April, and was later discharged to join the French Army.

The next day officers and sergeants inspected trenches in the brigade's left sector at Glencorse Wood, prior to taking over. The wood had been part-renamed from Nonne Bosschen, or Nun's Wood, scene of fighting in the First Battle of Ypres, and named instead for the barracks and depôt at Penicuik. The support positions were dug-outs in the wood; largely unobserved, they were 4ft high and covered with branches and earth. Moving forward, the trenches were 'uncomfortable short ditches'[2] and as Sergeant Reginald Rogers leant over a tea dixie, a bullet came through the parapet and passed through his collar and under the skin at the nape of his neck. He was blind and deaf for three days but recovered and expressed satisfaction that he had 'bagged two that morning' before they got him. The front had trenches numbered 68 to 73, right to left.

From trench 73 they could see the enemy trenches about 200 yards away. The trees that had been in no man's land were largely destroyed, and here, once again dead *poilus* could be seen. Despite all this a lark rising up from no man's land at 4am could be heard amidst the rifle fire.

> 'Men were torn from their environment and put together indiscriminately, "in bundles of ten," more or less. They had thereafter to live together in the closest possible human companionship... The superficial markings of class and education, environment and opportunity, were gone, and the reality – the man himself – was left.'[35]

William Young got to know his section better than family. He recalled one getting drunk on Belgian beer and another of the section took his two-hour guard duty, and when called up before the company commander for smoking on guard said nothing, for the greater crime was letting your pal down. The slightest fellow was a 'hero' who always 'stuck it' and never fell out of the march from Sanctuary Wood, nor took a place on a 'bus if he thought another needed it; when the swaggerer and lance corporal slipped away to report sick. They all learnt unselfishness to the fullest degree, and only quarrelled over each other's over generosity.

A Company's first loss was Bertram Brown, shot through the head whilst carrying up supplies to the trenches. The following morning he was buried in a little graveyard to the west of the wood and, in the absence of a chaplain, the colonel read a short service. C Company marched past West Hook (Westhoek) and Bernard Holmer went into Trench 69. The enemy were only 100 yards away here but there was little return fire 'which is as well, as one can scarcely keep always below parapet'.[24] The trench was a mere 4ft 6in at the front but was screened by a hedge, and there were some inches of mud underfoot. At 3am shelling threw dirt on them, and Holmer heard that the company had nine casualties and James Brass in the adjoining Trench 70 had been killed while filling sandbags.

Sergeant William McLeod Black No.1001 of C Company, 'one of our best,'[26] 'went down the communication trench between nos.69 and 68 soon after daybreak on Saturday and was found sitting in it an hour or two later, with the top of his head blown off'.[24] He had worked for the City Chamberlain and was a popular member of the Civil Service football team. Colonel Blair chose to write to Black's mother that he had been killed instantaneously by a bullet 'and suffered little or no pain'.[26] He also had cause to write to the parents of Sergeant Charles Young, A Company, 'Poor fellow he kept his head a little too long above the parapet'.[26] On the day of his death a photograph of his baby daughter arrived, born the day after they left Edinburgh.

B Company were more fortunate, certainly 7 Platoon remembered Trench 71 almost fondly:

> 'By day, after the chill of dawn passed, we cooked and read our mail, slept, wrote letters, or did one hour's sentry-go in complete peace and delightful weather. Few

shots were fired on either side; their trenches were at least 200 yards away, and we let sleeping dogs lie; even through periscopes we hardly ever saw a movement. At night we went on ration-parties across the open, which we came to regard as safe – with care – or worked at trench-improving in the intervals of sentry-go. Behind the trench shallow pits were formed, where we dug earth for sand-bags, and these being found safe were used for siestas or tea-parties. Aeroplanes in the clear blue were idly watched, especially when shelled, and they soared triumphant with a trail of white puffs of smoke. Shells were most infrequent, and never very near. If trench life could ever be idyllic, Trench 71, on those bright April days, would have been. The only discomforts (once the wet places were boarded or dried) were the chilly hours from 1 to 3am, and the cramped sleeping-places in the back of the trench. But so long as we got plenty of food, plenty charcoal, plenty letters and parcels, and the enemy kept quiet, we were quite pleased.'[35]

Dr Bowie was based in the cellar of a house close to the trenches, where Cairns made the doctor a bed out of saplings and wire netting. This space had to be shared with the wounded until they could be moved on by ambulance wagon. The Ninth now fell into the pattern of trench life, typically four days in the front line, four days in support and four days at rest in billets to the rear, this now being camps at Vlamertinghe ('Vlam') to the west of Ypres. Beatson found, in good weather, the trenches preferable to the hard-labour fatigues of 'rest'. All the troops 'stood-to' for an hour before sunrise and for an hour at dusk, considered the most likely times of attack, and then they did two stints as sentries, doubled up at times of tension or poor visibility. By day they kept watch through a steel loophole or periscope, by night stood on the firing-step. A misty night provided an opportunity to go looking for 'souvenirs'.[28]

In Glencorse Wood they constructed a dummy trench and took amusement in seeing it mercilessly shelled by an enemy who had taken particular exception to it. The Germans also employed a dummy trench with dummy loopholes, and it is not clear whose was first. The 1st Royal Scots also told them that the Germans had marched a column in Cameron kilts down the Menin Road one morning, until they were fired upon.

Though D Company were billeted behind the lines at the Abbaye, they were still within artillery range. Wrote a sergeant:

'You could hear the shells shrieking over the building... we were covered with dust and dirt and the slates did scamper off the roof above us. We just had to stand by and wait until our shell came or peace reigned again. This shelling is a trying business; no cover avails one except when you are well underground.'[6]

About 8am on Wednesday 7 April, D Company's billets were shelled. The men were resting between night fatigues and going into the trenches, with some asleep and some up and preparing for the day, when a half-dozen shells fell about their billets at the convent school. At first 'we were inclined to joke at the whole thing. The first intimation that it was so close came when a man at the other end of the room was hit

A Dandy Ninth dug-out at Ypres (son of Tom Gray in cap).

in the cheek by a splinter of glass.' The next shell burst overhead, shattered the roof and wounded several. Lance Corporal Robert Lawrie was 'blown from one end of the room to the other'[6] and struck the far wall. The men hastily cleared the building in various states of undress when a third shell burst in the courtyard with fatal consequences. The field kitchen, about to serve breakfast, was located in a shed in the yard and was completely destroyed. John Spalding, coming down the stairs in just his kilt, was hit. Lawrie, now in the yard, was again lifted off his feet, falling 10 yards away, but was less lucky on this occasion, being wounded in three places, most seriously in his left shoulder. A shrapnel hole was also put through the ridge of his glengarry.

Robert Lawrie.

Private John Dalziel, formerly a student dentist, was on guard outside and was hit by a 'ragged piece of copper',[26] from the driving band of the third shell, which he later retained as 'an interesting souvenir'.[6] Those in the hospital building, adjoining the convent school, heard pieces of masonry rattling against their roof and walls. The NCOs soon established order and the wounded were carried to safety.

Six men had been killed outright: Gerard Frost, George Mackay, Charles Mackenzie, John Mathieson, Charles Newsham, Edward Walker. The war diary records a further forty-eight wounded. Gerard Frost and Charles Newsham were friends from Manchester who had joined up together and were killed by the same shell. Edward Walker had been five years in the battalion and was only 21 when killed.

Wilfred Thomson escaped harm having just crossed the room of the nunnery for a

Edward Walker.   *George Mackay.*   *Charles Mackenzie.*   *John Mathieson.*

shaving brush. The man he had been standing next to was fatally wounded.

Hugh Aiken and Robert Scott died of wounds the next day at 15 Field Ambulance in Ypres. James Burgess was taken to Poperinghe and then on to the General Hospital at Boulogne. He died of wounds on 10 April. Andrew Cheyne was also in hospital in Boulogne and Sister Robertson wrote to his mother Violet that he had every comfort. He died of wounds a week after the bombardment, bringing the toll to ten. Five of the wounded, including Lawrie, reached Edinburgh on 19 April by hospital train and went onto a hospital at Dalmeny House, home of the former Prime Minister, Lord Rosebery. Their injuries ran a random list of shrapnel wounds: left shoulder, thigh, left elbow, right buttock, left arm.

Robert Beveridge received twelve

Andrew Cheyne.   *James Burgess.*

shrapnel wounds, hit in the face and legs, and one bullet passed through his left foot. He was discharged in November 1915, a year to the day since he joined. Drummer Thomas Gibson, wounded and recovered, was killed by a bursting shell in August 1916. One lance corporal thought the three shells had come from different directions, there were claims that French officers taking an interest in the damage had been discovered as disguised Germans, and there were also rumours of a German gun hidden behind their own lines and of an Englishman spying for the enemy.

After acting as stretcher bearer, 'Cherry' Thin 'felt kind of dizzy over the whole business'.[3] The survivors all felt nervy, and when his section was washing in the greenhouse the door banged and they all jumped. The shelling also interrupted the funerals of two Belgian civilians, killed in houses almost opposite the billets, and they and D Company's eight dead were buried that afternoon on the ramparts next to the Lille Gate. There were many volunteers for the burial party. Every time they passed through the city it was significantly diminished by shelling, one platoon even witnessed a huge shell fall in the 'Square'[24] and much of the city was considered irreparable, yet it was rebuilt after the war.

Watching artillery duels may have been reported as 'better than a "Rugger" match'[26] or exclaimed as 'By Jove! it's not half exciting to hear the whistle of the shells as they come near and then burst,'[26] but the reality became rapidly apparent: the Germans possessed vastly greater quantities of guns and ammunition, especially an advantage in 'heavies'. Napoleon's verdict was that 'God is on the side with the best artillery' and artillery was the dominant weapon in this war. The Royal Army Medical Corps (RAMC) recorded that 59 per cent of British casualties were caused by shells versus 39 per cent by bullets. The French were reliant upon their *Soixante-Quinze* (75mm) field gun that had been revolutionary in 1897, the Germans had followed suit with 7.7cm field guns and the British were in the process of replacing their 15-pounders with 18-pounders (firing an 18.5lb / 8.4kg shell of 84mm calibre). For heavy field guns, British 4.7-inch naval guns, brought hastily ashore by 'straw-hatted sailors'[45] in the South African War, readily exceeded their 'average' life of 2,700 rounds and when worn had such a reputation for inaccuracy and shorts they were nicknamed 'strictly neutral'. These were steadily being replaced by 60-pounders. The Germans had 10cm (4.2in) High Velocity guns.

The Germans and British also employed light field howitzers firing at high angle: the Germans possessed 10.5cm howitzers and the British were introducing modern 4.5″ howitzers to replace outdated and outclassed 5″ howitzers, 'a relic used at Omdurman in 1896'.[43] Particularly devastating, German 15cm howitzers were capable of firing a 40kg shell in excess of 8km. To feet-and-inches adjutants writing in the war diary these were '5.9s' or the 'five-nines' of Wilfred Owen's poem *Dulce Et Decorum Est*. To the men witnessing the black clouds of exploding shells they were Jack Johnsons or '*coal-boxes*...sending their smoke towering up like a huge heavy foliaged tree...we could feel the ground shaking beneath us as we lay.'[4] The British at this time fielded no equivalent, though an obsolete 6″ howitzer began to be replaced by a modern version in late 1915.

71

Bernard Holmer saw Ypres being flattened and wrote in his diary, 'I am absolutely sick of artillery, which while so cruel seems the safest arm as many from batts haven't lost a man since September.'[24] To James Beatson, 'The cataclysm evoked by a gunner utterly transcends his own muscles, perceptions or emotions. To dare serve a Krupp or Armstrong gun, one should be as tall as an Alp, as good as an angel, as wise as a god.'[42]

In contrast in mid-April a Zeppelin dropped six bombs on their camp at Vlamertinghe but only two were within 100 yards and caused no damage, nevertheless it was said Bob Tait climbed inside his own Aldershot cooker. The holes were 'simply huge',[3] about 30ft across, but 'made a handy hole for rubbish'[23] and resulted in lights out being enforced at 9pm. When camped at Busseboom the pond frogs kept them awake until a jam tin bomb was employed.

Colonel Alexander Blair wrote home to say, 'We are well, and have been very lucky these last few days in the trenches. We are shortly due for a few days rest'[6] and so Regimental Sergeant Major Peter McLachlan, newly arrived, watched his battalion come into Vlam in the early hours of 21 April 1915 for four days' rest.

Second Ypres

'It is especially prohibited (a) to employ poison or poisoned weapons'
Article 23, The Hague Convention 1899

ON 19 April 1915 the German bombardment of Ypres was stepped up with the employment of the famous *Big Bertha* 420mm howitzer, described as a '17" German beggar, which makes twice the hole of a J. Johnson'.[24] At the close of the First Ypres battle the opposing lines had stalled, surrounding the ancient city in a great arc (Map IX). This Salient was now defended by two French divisions on a 5-mile front to the north and British V Corps with a 10-mile front, consisting of the Canadian Division to the north-east, 28th Division to the east and 27th Division, to which the Ninth belonged, to the south-east. However, the Ninth were not on the division's front having been relieved by the 9th Argylls the day before. Instead they formed part of the divisional reserves, along with the 4th Rifles and 2nd Cornwalls, and as such were in huts south of Vlamertinghe, where they were to have four days of rest.

There were a large number of Belgian civilians still living in Ypres, but soon the fleeing refugees flooded the Poperinghe ('Pops') road heading west. The Ninth watched the civilians pass their billets as the city was bombarded. The poet Walter Scott Stuart Lyon, a lieutenant in the Ninth, wrote:

So lies this ruined city. She hath heard
The rush of foes brutal and strong and proud,
And felt their bolted fury. She is ploughed
With fire and steel, and all her grace is blurred.

'Easter at Ypres' excerpt, W.S.S. Lyon

Walter Lyon.

Unknown to the Ninth at the time, the afternoon of 22 April saw the introduction of a new and frightful weapon, gas warfare. The Germans had been waiting for a northerly wind and at 5pm, accompanied by furious howitzer fire, two greenish-yellow clouds could be seen passing on either side of Langemark. The French 87th Territorial Division and 45th Algerian Division, nicknamed Turcos, stood in the path of 180 tonnes of asphyxiating chlorine gas, producing a burning sensation and capable, with a sufficient dose, of causing lung damage and death. The French divisions fell back in disarray, increasing their exposure as they moved with the gas cloud. The Germans, possessed of little more protection against the gas cloud than the Allies, tentatively followed into what became an 8,000 yard gap between the Belgian 6th Division at the Ypres canal in the west and two French battalions and the Canadian Division to the east, who held firm. The door seemed to have been left wide open for the enemy to make the Salient untenable: to cut-off V Corps, gain Ypres and develop a decisive breakthrough.

The terrain here consists of gently undulating ground, formed by spurs of the Ypres ridge as east-west ridges named Pilckem, Mauser and Hill Top. As regimental historian John Ewing notes, 'The ridges were really inconsiderable elevations, but in the low, flat country of Flanders they were of supreme tactical importance.'[33] In fact the changes in elevation never exceeded 100ft. To Jock Brown, 'The country is annoyingly like Oxford.'[4]

The German 51st, 52nd and 46th Reserve Divisions soon passed their immediate objective of Pilckem Ridge and on to the limited-objective of Mauser Ridge. Fortunately, most began digging-in with the onset of dusk about 7.30pm, in accordance with their training. This provided a vital respite to rally a defence. Nevertheless, the situation was grave with 17½ British and Canadian battalions, including reserves, facing 42 German battalions, with an unfavourable ratio of artillery of five to one; this making itself felt as enemy gunfire made important roads impassable.

'Turco soldiers with eyes wild with fright… were the first victims of the poison gas that the Royal Scots saw.'[33] Wull Grossart had not been long in an estaminet across the road from their huts when he saw 'Zouaves foaming at the mouth running down the street.'[5] Bill Hay 'heard them say it was gas. We didn't know what the Hell gas was!'[46] At 8.45pm on Thursday 22 April the Ninth received orders to march toward Ypres and their first major encounter.

St Jean (Gravenstafel Ridge)

'Although they have borne a brilliant part in several sanguinary actions they have had casualty lists so comparatively light that they are known by the happy title, "God's Own Highlanders."' [6]

Colonel the Reverend William Beveridge

THE Ninth advanced *au pied* to Ypres, with a fair proportion of legal brains and rugby brawn, following 'the tall figure of the C.O.',[4] Lieutenant Colonel Alexander Blair, himself advocate and three-quarter back, whose son had been missing in the Salient since the previous October.

'All along it we met old women with bundles flying from Ypres. In front was the glare of the burning city and the thunder of the guns... There were some cavalry beside us who called out to us: 'Give them hell.' We wondered vaguely how we would do it.'[4]

Among the westbound were D Company, making their way back from fatigues. They had had to 'double a bit'[3] through the Menin Gate and find an alternative road through the city to avoid the Grand Place and the parts of the city in flames. 'When we were about half way back and congratulating ourselves, we met the battalion proceeding in the opposite direction'[3] and had to pass back through Ypres.

Progress proving impossible against the flow of escaping families, they turned off the road and went along the railway. Even here, 'We met the refugees coming down the railway... all sorts of people, old people, young people and kids and parrots and goats and all the lot, running away from Ypres and the shelling.'[46] They could now 'see the dark mass of the Cathedral and Cloth Hall backed by the wall of flame.'[35] There were rumours that Ypres had already fallen to the Germans.

Reaching the city around midnight they found that the quarter they had previously been billeted in was burning.

'Sinister crashes betokened that the town was still being shelled, and in Indian file, with 50 yards between platoons, the Royal Scots hurried through the inferno. Hugging the sides of the ruined houses, the troops by some miracle passed rapidly through the town and out by the Menin Gate without a casualty.'[33]

Bill Hay, a coach-trimmer, now a company sergeant major's batman, was so convinced they would not get through, he discarded the CSM's kit into the flames. Quinn described the city as 'melting while we ran through the Square and all the Jerry shells in the world seemed to be chasing us'.[23] They turned to the left and on making 27th Division HQ at Potijze Chateau (*Pottige*) at 3am they took shelter in Potijze Wood in shallow scrapings known as *graves* that 'would not have given sanctuary to a grasshopper'.[23] What seemed like minutes after a 5.9″ coal-box hit the neighbouring field, a shell splinter struck Private George Hogg, a marine engineer, in the knee. He was bandaged and carried off on a door to a farm house containing the St Jean dressing station. A large number of Canadian casualties were waiting here, gasping as they described what it was like to be gassed.

They remained here, with occasional shelling, through the morning of 23 April as Corps reserve with Colonel Tuson's 2nd Duke of Cornwall's Light Infantry (DCLI) battalion. One recollection is that orders were issued to counter the effects of gas by holding wetted handkerchiefs over their mouths. The seriousness was perhaps not apparent, Cairns writing on the day, 'All the trouble was caused by the French leaving their trenches. Germans had been firing stink bombs & the smell was felt for miles around.'[39]

At noon they were sent north in double file with the 2nd DCLI but half an hour later half of the battalion were detached to the Canadians. Therefore, on reaching the Ypres

Menin Gate   St Jacques   Abbaye

– St Julien road near Wieltje (*Whichy*), the right half of the battalion, A and B companies under Colonel Blair, turned right to St Julien to support the Canadians, whilst the left half, C and D under Major Taylor Cameron, turned left to St Jean with the 2nd DCLI and found themselves part of a composite brigade under Colonel A.D. Geddes of the Buffs, subsequently killed on 28 April. He had attempted to attack the enemy that morning with heavy losses to Canadians and men of the Middlesex Regiment, who thought it impossible to close within 600 yards of the enemy without support. The Royal West Kents agreed that 'without artillery preparation and strong reinforcements it would be madness to assault'.[1] Up to this point the men had been 'as ignorant of why and wherefore as the "men" in a game of draughts'.[42] It was now becoming apparent that Geddes was about to make another attempt to fill the void.

Brigadier General Wanless O'Gowan's 13 Brigade formed the left of the attack, between the canal and the Pilckem-Ypres road. Geddes's detachment placed the 2nd East Yorkshire Regiment against the road, then the 1st York and Lancaster Regiment; 27th Division supplied the right of the improvised attack with the 2nd DCLI supported on the right rear by two companies of the Ninth (see map X). D Company was on the left under Captain George Green, with Major Cameron; C Company was on the right under Captain Dick Moncrieff.

Orders to advance through the line toward Pilckem were issued by Colonel Geddes at 3.15pm, each battalion on a two-company front of 500 yards, and each company in two lines 200 yards apart. This composite force was to advance north-westward over the gentle rise of Hill Top ridge – not some blasted heath but cultivated land, with

Turco Farm (left)   Algerian Cot (centre)   Morteldje

Turco Farm (left), Algerian Cot (centre) and Morteldje estaminet (right) from Hill Top.

Sketch of Colne Valley showing hedge lines with Fusilier Farm centre left and Turco Farm on the right.

farms and many hedge lines 'that closed our view'.[35] Between Hill Top Ridge and the Germans on Mauser Ridge lay a gentle valley, later called Colne Valley, of open country. The German positions could not be discerned, but later reports described them as parallel trenches about 300 yards apart on rising slopes to the north. The attack was to be at 4.25pm with the right following half-an-hour later, or ten minutes earlier, depending upon the source. The artillery had been told the attack was at 3pm and in just three minutes had already expended their limited ammunition.

Each man became distinguishable cresting Hill Top Ridge and C and D companies immediately came under heavy fire from Mauser Ridge opposite but continued down the other side into Colne Valley. 'We were told to advance in the late afternoon. This we did in the best Braid Hills fashion under pretty heavy machine gun, rifle, and artillery fire, practically without the support of any artillery.'[4]

Bernard Holmer: 'We advanced over the open under very severe rifle and shell fire and I was hit by rifle bullet in the left leg when we'd only been going half an hour. Cameron stayed to help me and I got back to a shallow trench where he bandaged me and I lay till dark.'[24]

Edwin Archer was shot in the hip, but found that the bullet had passed through a cigarette case in his lower tunic pocket, saving him from more serious injury.

Reaching a road, the attack paused. Lieutenant Walter Lyon of C Company noticed there was thick wire intertwined through the hedge in front making it impenetrable. Under machine-gun fire he 'very coolly stood up and taking his wire-cutters, began to make gaps'.[33]

'Cherry' Thin of D Company:

15/5/15

'At one point we lay down in a ditch at the side of the road. We thought we were going to be left here in support but a brigade officer got up and shouted "The Royal Scots will advance" so we got up and dashed on again over absolutely open ground.'[3]

The composite brigade moved toward the enemy, thinned by losses as bullets threw up dust and dropped men, until they reached dead ground where they could not be fired upon. After reforming they began to climb the gentle slope on the far side of the valley toward some farm buildings, approaching the German outpost line. By 7pm the attack along the entire front, with hand-to-hand fighting in farms and cottages, had come to a halt under heavy fire. At 7.30pm the Ninth commenced digging, making themselves some 'lead-cover,'[3] 2,000 yards due north of St Jean and a short distance short of the enemy positions atop the ridge. It is likely they had advanced as far as the German outpost line, now abandoned.

John Reekie, C Company, killed.

The 2nd DCLI came up through View Farm and reached the German outpost of Turco Farm at 8pm, with the German main line about 200 yards further on. They killed the garrison, including a man still speaking on a telephone. Exceptionally, men of the East Yorkshire Regiment got to within 30 yards of the enemy line. The improvised German defences were discovered to be three tiers of sandbags and barbed wire.

Meanwhile A and B companies had been off to support the Canadians. A Company crossed a dangerous gap in Wieltje, opened up by the road junction, and 'doubled across in small parties, wondering if we would suddenly be smitten down'.[4] B Company, following, were less lucky and twenty were hit.

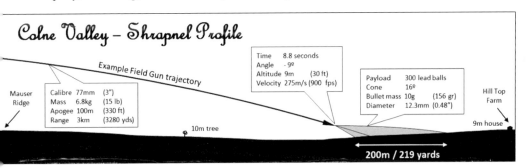

Colne Valley – Shrapnel Profile

Example Field Gun trajectory

Time	8.8 seconds
Angle	- 9º
Altitude	9m (30 ft)
Velocity	275m/s (900 fps)

Payload	300 lead balls
Cone	16º
Bullet mass	10g (156 gr)
Diameter	12.3mm (0.48")

Mauser Ridge

Calibre	77mm	(3")
Mass	6.8kg	(15 lb)
Apogee	100m	(330 ft)
Range	3km	(3280 yds)

10m tree

Hill Top Farm

9m house

200m / 219 yards

The German field guns fired a typical shrapnel shell, containing 300 lead alloy balls. The time fuze was set to burst in the air before the target, forcing out the bullets that then spread out in a cone of dispersion, striking the ground in a lethal swathe over 200m in extent and about 18m wide. With such shells, a six-gun battery could puncture the landscape with over 7,000 bullets a minute for prolonged periods, and perhaps five times this rate in extremis.

The two companies went up the road to the outskirts of St Julien and lay down. Jock Brown was able to reach out his hand and pick up shrapnel balls. Everyone kept their heads down, the signallers were like 'shot rabbits',[4] except Lieutenant Cyril Falconer Stewart who 'swanked along as if he were on Princes Street'.[4] 'A Canadian came down and he shouted to our captain, "The bastards have broken through; they've gassed us and they've broken through, so give them the bloody bayonet, Jock."'[46]

On the north side of the road, Bill Hay explains:

'We had to go into ditches and fire a few rounds, and go on a bit further and fire a few more, and come back again and fire again – and this was to give the impression to the Germans that there were plenty of troops there. There were a lot of Canadians lying there dead from gas the day before, poor devils, and it was quite a horrible sight for us young men... The first time that I've ever felt really terrified in my heart was when the Colonel gave us orders to fix bayonets... I didn't expect to be going bayonet fighting with the Germans. No, I didn't expect that. There was a temporary sort of cottage they were using as a dressing station at St Julien and I took a look round the corner of it and saw loads and loads of Germans, just like rabbits! There were thousands of them there, a good bit away of course. You could see at a glance that we were very much outnumbered.'[46]

Bill Hay is not only the most quoted Ninth, but one of the most quoted soldiers of the First World War, particularly as he describes this first experience of gas: 'The chaps were all gasping and couldn't breathe, and it was ghastly, especially for chaps that were wounded – terrible for a wounded man to lie there! The gasping, the gasping!'[46]

Brigadier General Richard Turner, Canadian Division, intended to use them in a counter attack, but did not want to move them up until nightfall. Long before that they were recalled by Geddes at 4.15pm. They made their way back through Wieltje, well spread out in single file, past shell cases and dead horses where a battery had been in action. Eighteen other ranks had been wounded.

B Company were told to lie down south of the village and A Company continued until they met elements of the 2nd DCLI near Wieltje Farm and then ascended Hill Top Ridge:

'We began to advance at the double in open order... Weariness had left us, the bullets were thick about our feet. After advancing over several fields we lay down behind a hedge. On our right was a hedge, and just over it the Germans dropped six 'coal-boxes.' We could feel the ground shaking beneath us as we lay.'[4]

They moved forward 100 yards and lay down on a road.

Cyril Stewart had a lucky escape:

'These stink bombs have only a local explosive effect, our Lieutenant Stewart being only bowled over by one bursting six feet away, but the fumes are horrible and hang in the air for a long time.'[42]

William Young provides a vivid description of B Company advancing right up the right of the line:

'Hardly had we got settled when a tremendous rattle of machine-gun and rifle fire broke out, with the crash of "coal boxes" for bass accompaniment, and we were ordered to advance. We stole down to the houses [at Wieltje], and at the opposite corner stood the Adjutant and the Colonel. "Keep going, boys, and you'll be all right," was their greeting, and we wondered vaguely what it meant. Round the corner of the house we saw.

An open field, perhaps four hundred yards in length, at the far side a blazing farm [probably Cross Roads Farm]... a string of men advancing on our left, "coal-boxes" screaming and tearing up the field, and over all the incessant rattle and crack of rapid, heavy fire. We went at the double; a "coal-box" on the left buried a bunch of the other lot, another just on our right quickened our flagging steps, but we got across. At the edge of the farm we got orders to dig in and keep well down. The scene was awful; the farm well ablaze, and shells bursting about it every second; yet men were there.

Before we had even dug cover the order to advance came again, and we rounded the farm, and in small groups dashed through the orchard... A gap in the hedge gave access to an open flat, over which, some hundred and twenty yards away, was a square hedge and gateway into a small field and cottage [perhaps Forward Cottage]. We advanced again, this time amid a storm of bullets from the right. We were well spaced out, and rushed it, and not one was hit, but we could almost feel the rain of bullets past our knees.

Once in the enclosure we lay close up to the hedge, gasping. War never seemed such a hateful thing as in these moments of reflection. The enemy were still invisible, but more than one "coal-box" landed in the enclosure, and some of us had narrow escapes. The bullets, too, were raining in, and we lay very low. We had not thought of time, but two hours must have passed, for the afternoon light was waning when we crept round the cottage and into the vegetable garden. We began to dig in, but a further advance was ordered.

We slipped out of the hedge and doubled as before across coarser grass pasture, with the bullets singing in the tops of the grass, till we reached a hedge and ditch thick with nettles two hundred yards ahead. There we lay till the sky grew dark and the stars began to shine out and the firing died down. In front was an open valley with a wooded ridge sloping from it. Ruined houses were there, but where the enemy were was still a matter of conjecture. Probably this was part of the ground left by the French, and the enemy had retired to the ridge on seeing our advance to gather his strength for the next attack. Our company officers held whispered consultations while we lay in the ditch and wondered.

We had had extraordinary luck so far, but disaster befell us by that hedge. "Coal-boxes" were still crashing about us; one in particular burst very near on the right. In the stillness after it we heard an "Oh – damn!" and in a moment came the dreaded whisper, "Pass the word for the stretcher-bearers." "Who's hit?" passed up, and back came the reply, like a numbing blow to us all – "Captain Bell". We had trusted him completely, and he had led us well; we would have followed him anywhere, had gloried in being his men, felt for him, secretly, the devotion all good leaders inspire; and now he was down with a great rip in his leg. Stretcher-bearers had got separated from us in the advance, but there were plenty volunteers to carry Captain Bell. His going left a never-filled blank in the Company.'[35]

Young is most likely correct that the enemy had abandoned their outpost line. Ewing describes the most northerly point of the attack as: 'There the men reformed, and in the gathering dusk the whole line swarmed up the far slope in the expectation of rounding off the day's work with a bayonet charge. But when they reached the ridge the enemy had vanished, and patrols despatched immediately could find no trace of him.'[33]

Bill Hay remembered that 'the Jerries ran back, they fell back, they didn't wait for us to get close enough'.[46] Wilfrid Bennet Clark wrote to his mother: 'In the afternoon the Bn carried out an attack which we have been told by troops on our right turned the Germans in front of us though we never saw one to fire at.'[16]

Whatever the situation, the Ninth were right of the line with a gap of 800 yards to their right to the Canadians. The losses for the day amounted to 4 officers wounded, 12 Other Ranks killed, 98 Other Ranks wounded and 10 missing, with much of the loss again exacted from D Company.

After sunset at 9pm, Geddes withdrew his force. The Ninth moved back to Hill Top Ridge with A and B companies digging a front line with Cross Roads Farm on their right, and C and D companies the support 150 yards behind. Some of these lines became part of the front-line defences for the next two years, facing north-east. 'Whether we were in the front line or not we never knew, but we supposed we were… Half-right (the direction of St Julien) there was the continual crackle of rifle and machine-gun and the sight of flaming houses, but we seemed to be out of it.'[35] 'During the battle not only houses but whole villages were ablaze and at night lit up the whole country… for 48 hours until all the houses were burnt out.'[16] In the words of the Official History 'it was a miserable night'.[43]

In the early morning Lieutenant Edgar Robb, C Company, told them to 'Dig!' and that if they knew how serious it was they would be more energetic![23] Further gas shells came over in a heavy bombardment about 5.30am. Most sections lay in unfinished trenches the following day, deepening them that night when some rations came up, the first for three days, and they sent postcards home. It rained heavily and they were thoroughly cold and miserable when Sunday 25 April dawned:

'It is not a pleasant thing, we found, to cower in a trench and hear coal-boxes come screaming at you, bursting with their peculiarly nerve-racking crash anything from twenty to one hundred yards away. And on Sunday afternoon, too! Still, it's an ill wind that blows nobody good; a herd of cows, startled by the racket, came out of the farm and ambled along the back of our trench, one or two of them agreeing to stand to be milked.'[35] 'It rained all day. 'Coal-boxes' came gurgling over us, and wounded were passing all day.'[4]

With their heavy Maxim machine guns left in the Glencorse Wood trenches with the 9th Argylls, Bennet Clark's machine-gun section was charged with bringing up ammunition with the transport on 23 April and came under shell and rifle fire. The shells were coming over four at a time and sweeping the ground with shrapnel bullets. Archie 'Pow' Ramsay got a crack on the chest from a shrapnel bullet that went through his tunic but whose energy was all but spent. He shouted out to BC, 'Please sir, I'm hit'[23] but realising he was not done for he carried on. Some of the section were armed with only entrenching tools. James Quinn had his rifle but at the order *Fix*, his troublesome bayonet would not. He tripped and choked the muzzle in the ground but found a branch to clear the barrel.

They stayed overnight in a farm that was unmolested until morning when BC decided to clear out. Writing soon afterwards:

'At one time I, with 3 of my men & 4 transport wagons were at a farm with absolutely nothing between us & the German lines. Needless to say, I only discovered this afterwards. That only serves to show that even when you are in a tight corner, as long as you have luck nothing happens. I had not even a horse hit there.'[16]

He managed to lose the transport for twenty-four hours as they did not go to the right place. The MG section dug in near two dead Canadians, their first sight of men killed in action. On the evening of 25 April BC received orders to move and fortunately found the transport, then followed two days in support 'while a great artillery battle was going on. The noise was terrific.'[16] Averaging two hours sleep in the twenty-four for a week with his boots never off, 'During the fighting I was doing Assistant Adjutant, Transport Officer, Machine Gun Officer with a section but without guns & several other odd jobs all at the same time.'[16] He reflected that 'the hours all count as days in this life'.[16]

The medical staff had been hard at work throughout. Losing the battalion when they had marched from camp apace, they caught up with them at Potijze, then worked alongside Canadians in a dressing station and later in a cellar. Three times Captain

Bowie, Sergeant Millikin, Corporal Cairns and Drummer Connolly (the doctor's servant) were shelled out of their dressing station but their work continued, even after other medical staff had left.

James Cairns wrote of 26 April:

'A convoy of about 24 ambulances arrived about 12.30 a.m. & we had loaded 2 & were busy on the 3rd when a stink shell burst in the middle of the road killing a few [seven] & wounding a large number including the doctor, sergeant & 5 stretcher bearers. We were busy attending the wounded when the first car went on fire & we had to unload it. It was an awful sight & we could hardly work because of the bad fumes. When the car went on fire the Germans sent over 3 more of these awful shells. We had to lift the wounded without bandaging them & get them away.'[39]

James Lawson Cairns from a tweed milling family at Langholm, was one of eight grandsons of Mrs William Wilson serving or prisoner. His citation for a Distinguished Conduct Medal (DCM) reads: 'He was assisting Captain Bowie RAMC (TF) and conducted the First Aid Post single-handed under constant and heavy shell fire after the officer had been severely wounded.' The Adjutant, Robert Dudgeon, having heard the news, sent men to collect Cairns and the stretcher bearers and bring them back to the battalion.

James Cairns.

John Bowie had been made Surgeon Lieutenant in the Ninth in 1906 and then became part of the Royal Army Medical Corps (RAMC) in 1908 with the Territorial reforms. Now 40, he was severely wounded in both legs below the knee, but managed to send a postcard off to his wife Jane that he was going to the coast, and was admitted to hospital at Boulogne. He went on to serve at Malta and Salonika.

Ambulance Sergeant William Millikin was wounded in the lower jaw, hand and shoulder. A cabinet maker, who had been with the Ninth since formation, he was sent to Netley Hospital, Southampton. Among the bandsmen, acting as stretcher bearers, Robert Templeton, also a trombone player in the Hallelujah Army Band, died of his wounds.

John Bowie.

Having been hit in the advance of Friday 23 April, Bernard Holmer had waited until dark and, there being no stretcher bearers, had hopped to the battalion dressing station about 9pm. He left there about 11pm by motor ambulance to Pops. His motor ambulance collided with a lorry, so they went on by horse transport and he was finally sent on board a hospital train on the Saturday afternoon, arriving in Boulogne early on the Sunday where he went into the Rawal Pindi Hospital. He remained there until 3.30pm, was then taken aboard the hospital ship HMHS *St Patrick* which departed at 6pm and arrived at Dover before 8pm. Another hospital train left at 9pm, arrived in Brentwood about 1am and he was in hospital at Great Warley, Essex on Monday 26 April. Holmer was a convalescent, but not walking wounded, so was taken out in a car most days. Playing down his injuries, he projects a gentlemanly life of ease: 'We spend our time between croquet, motoring and walking out,' he writes, 'Dinner with the skivvies is a big drawback, but one gets used to it.'[24]

Private William Calder was reported to have had a bayonet wound to his leg. It was also reported that some men had been hit by darts dropped from aeroplanes, with one witness seeing the leading rider of a gun limber killed by them.

Sergeant William Clark 'had a marvellous escape. A shell burst quite close to him, killing another sergeant and severely wounding a corporal. The force of the explosion blew Sergeant Clark into one of the trenches whereby he was injured in the stomach.'[6]

Captain Davie Bell (23) had been wounded in the leg but blood poisoning resulted in amputation. His parents visited him in hospital in Boulogne. He got a job at the Record Office at Hamilton, 'Of course it is a lot better than being dead.'[21] His nephew recalls: 'After that he was on the staff and used to pull all the girls by parading down Princes Street in a kilt and peg leg.'[21]

Edward Curtis Murray Gray died in an ambulance at 1am on 24 April, while being removed to hospital, of a bullet wound received when D Company were 'engaged on a bayonet charge'.[6] Six weeks earlier he had escaped the Abbaye shelling with a torn tunic and scratched elbow.

Robert Templeton.

Charles Mackay 'crawled into a ditch, where he lay for an hour and a half, with bullets whistling a few inches above his head'. Fred Hyslop was wounded and died in a military hospital at Norwich on 11 November 1915. He played three-quarter for the Watsonians and formerly for Selkirk. It was not until September 1916 that Ian McKinnon died of his wounds. A recurring feature is that of the man hit whilst attending to a wounded comrade. Alexander Lindsay, already twice wounded, was assisting a schoolfriend from George Heriot's, when killed; so too was William Kent.

Jim Elliot, John Laurie and Dishington had 'a jaunt between the lines' having been holed up in a cellar with the medical cart for three nights wondering if British or German shells would 'remove' them. When they turned up Robert Dudgeon, the adjutant, hailed them 'like long-lost brothers' as they had been reported 'missing, believed dead… and like Mark Twain, we wired home telling our people that the report of our deaths was grossly exaggerated!'[2]

William Clark.

Dudgeon told the men the enemy had retreated three-quarters of a mile. He was quoted in the papers saying: 'The Ninth did extremely well at the second battle of Ypres and during the attack we made they were as steady as rocks, and advanced with great dash and spirit.'[26]

It was a phrase repeated by the colonel: 'I can honestly say that the old Ninth did splendid work, and that the men were as steady as rocks, advancing in broad daylight in the open for nearly a mile under terrific shell-fire and enfilade Maxim and rifle fire.'[6] 'It was touch-and-go,'[41] he thought.

'An Edinburgh man' wrote: 'Most of us at the beginning felt a little nervous. Honestly I think we felt a little funky; but we were buoyed up by a strong moral resolution, and soon almost passed heroism.'[6]

Wattie Scott summed up the action very succinctly: 'Advanced from 4p.m. to 9.30p.m. Terrible fire. Trenches retaken.'[38]

For James Quinn, emphatic that he had seen Germans:

Robert Dudgeon.

'We seemed to be all alone in a world of shells and bullets and our biggest concern was to keep a straight line of men when advancing – and we did it all to the whistle too!... This was really the middle of Hades…For myself, I recall this time as the most elevating and spontaneously happy that I have experienced. The crusading spirit had not quite died out maybe. The same elated feeling never came again.'[23]

The way Jim Elliot saw it was, 'What a different story the war would have been if we had not made the show of strength between the 22nd and 26th April 1915.'[2]

Between 24 and 26 April the Ninth, 'veterans of two months'[35], endured heavy shelling as they held the ridge where they had dug-in. They were finally relieved in the small hours of Tuesday 27 April. Over a month later the rank and file of the Ninth discovered they had been in the 'Geddes Detachment'.[23] So synonymous was poison gas and the city that the French referred afterwards to *Yprite*, and later mustard gas was known to the Germans as *Yperite*. The use of gas contributed to anti-German rioting in Britain. The gas attack had opened a wide gap in the line and only throwing in the reserves and desperate resolve had closed it. Most accounts, written for others to read, speak of a stiffened resolve as much as horror. William Young wrote that gas was…'the devil's work…an utterly wrong thing. The enemy had burned their boats, and now it was war to the end, bitter and implacable... This was no clean war, it was devil's work, and had to be cut out of the world, an utterly wrong thing...'[35]

84

The Ninth had helped plug the gap. They were the undertrained and the untried, the citizen soldiers thrown into the breach. The attack was extremely dangerous, advancing over open ground, under observation in broad daylight and without artillery fire or reserves. The Official History states that an advance purely at night could have achieved the same at less cost. However, the fact that the enemy were not, in truth, poised to push through to Ypres was not known at the time.

Back in a shed at a large farm at Busseboom, the Quartermaster, Andrew Gordon, was chanced upon on 24 April by his near-namesake Major Archibald Gordon, who recorded, 'He gave me a vociferous welcome and got a tin mug and gave me a goodly tot of our Scots "wine". How we talked over old days when we fought sham battles on the heights above Tyndrum or on the wilds of windswept Stobs. We never dreamt of the real thing then. Blessed ignorance!'[22] They were still ignorant of the real thing, as at that hour the boys were being shelled.

Later the quartermaster wrote, 'We have had a dreadful week, and I never wish to go through the same again'[41] but the Second Battle of Ypres was not yet at an end.

Sanctuary Wood
'In behint yon auld fail dyke, I wot there lies a new slain knight,
And nane do ken that he lies there… The wind sall blaw for evermair'
Twa Corbies

AT Potijze at 11pm on 27 April the Ninth received orders to return to their division and proceed to Sanctuary Wood. The MG Section retrieved their guns from Glencorse Wood and at a roll call on 1 May, 472 answered. In the wood the Ninth were accustomed to being able to sleep by day and as the dangers faded with the light, steal out and bathe their feet in a woodland pool of spring water. They were, apparently, more concerned that a shell might take away their abandoned clothes. When Jock Porteous and James Quinn stripped to bathe in a shell hole, Porteous was blown into the water by a shell and received a crack on the shoulder, whilst Quinn retrieved his clothes and cleared off behind a tree in a state of half-dress. These two were sent out one night to clear bushes out of the way of the machine-gun position, 'Jock had the bill hook and I went forward as a "covering party". Did my heart beat? It did! Jock made noise for a dozen, but nothing happened, and I came back at his call.'[23]

It was decided that on the night of 3/4 May that V Corps would reduce the now dangerously acute Salient by withdrawing an average of 4,000 yards from the north-east and east (Map IX), leaving the Ninth's cemetery at Glencorse Wood in enemy hands, 'a bitter thought'.[35] The 27th Division, on the right, were to retire to Sanctuary Wood and hold from Hill 60 up toward the Roulers railway. All of the heavy artillery was withdrawn west of the canal, 5 miles away. The Salient however was not quiet. On 1 May, 'Cherry' Thin recorded that, 'To-night the Germans sent over some of their asphyxiating gas. It was chlorine. You could see the yellow haze against the sky. Fortunately for us we only got the edge of it but that was bad enough.'[3]

The following evening the Ninth and 2nd Cameron Highlanders were ordered to

Potijze, only to be sent back. On 3 May a heavy German attack was launched against Berlin Wood, despatching the Ninth out on another hard march through the shell zone to support the 28th Division. As the Germans were unable to advance, the reinforcements were marched back to their positions for the Corps withdrawal. This was particularly hard work for the MG Section, operating without mules. Unable to get back to their dug-outs before dawn, the battalion had to sit out a day of drenching rain under waterproof sheets.

With their positions on the edge of Sanctuary Wood suddenly becoming the front line, considerable improvement was required to the trenches which had been 'hastily constructed 400 yards behind the previous line',[42] often only 3ft deep and without wire or dug-outs to protect the men from the elements or bombardment. 'It was in part breastworks of earth and sandbags held up by stakes, wire and fascines (intertwined branches) and was open to the rear... There was no barbed wire at all. The trench was not continuous.'[19] No sooner had dug-outs been made

Benny Irvine.

when, with shells coming over 'fast and furious'[39] the men were told they had to dig separate dug-outs for each man. The dressing station had to be abandoned, with water oozing through the floor, and another started on 7 May. On this day, passing the colonel's dug-out James Cairns saw him making cocoa and was called in for a cup and some biscuits. Here he heard that Ambulance Sergeant Millikin had died in Edinburgh. He had received full military honours at his funeral, with the pipe and brass band of the reserve battalion in attendance.

The Germans, XV Corps (30th and 39th Divisions) being opposite, moved up and likewise dug-in about 500 yards distant and here had twice the numbers of the British with the ratio of a corps to a division.

At this time the youngest member of the battalion was killed, 16-year-old Private James Brown Morgan, born in Glasgow in February 1899; he should have been 19 years old before he was allowed to fight overseas. He died shortly after he had been shot by a sniper and his name is recorded on the Menin Gate at Ypres.

Protection against gas was under local manufacture, 'wet hankies'[23] of cotton wads held by elastic, issued two weeks after Second Ypres, and on 5 May the division warned all men to keep

James Morgan.

86

their respirators wet with cold tea, urine or water. Official Smoke Hoods, a bag placed over the head with mica eyepieces, were issued by June but the first batch of only sixteen per battalion went to the machine gunners. In July they were on parade to get their smoke hoods sprinkled with solution. Leather sporrans were discarded and a gas helmet satchel carried over the kilt apron. This type was succeeded by the box respirator in the second half of 1916, with development continuing through both world wars.

In April 1915 No.1471 Robert Bruce was commissioned into the 15th Highland Light Infantry (Glasgow Tramways Battalion), but in August, being a chemist, he was brought into the new Special Companies of the Royal Engineers, responsible for prosecuting gas warfare. He rose to command L Company, Special Brigade in March 1917, which became a specialist in smoke clouds. All men transferring to Special Companies became corporals and carried revolvers, and at least half a dozen Ninths did so.

A heavy bombardment on 8 May caused a considerable number of casualties, though on the Ninth's front no infantry attack was made. This was the heaviest they had yet experienced. Drummer William Simpson, 4ft 9in and 5 stone, received a bullet in his left shoulder. Lieutenant Walter Lyon became the first officer killed. Written less than a month earlier, his 'Lines Written in a Fire Trench' evoke something of the wood under bombardment:

'Tis midnight, and above the hollow trench,
Seen through a gaunt wood's battle-blasted trunks
And the stark rafters of a shattered grange,
The quiet sky hangs huge and thick with stars.
And through the vast gloom, murdering its peace,
Guns bellow and their shells rush swishing ere
They burst in death and thunder, or they fling
Wild jangling spirals round the screaming air.
Bullets whine by, and Maxims drub like drums,
And through the heaped confusion of all sounds
One great gun drives its single vibrant "Broum",
And scarce five score of paces from the wall
Of piled sand-bags and barb-toothed nets of wire,
(So near and yet what thousand leagues away)
The unseen foe both adds and listens to
The selfsame discord, eyed by the same stars.
Deep darkness hides the desolated land,
Save where a sudden flare sails up and bursts
In whitest glare above the wilderness,
And for one instant lights with lurid pallor
The tense, packed faces in the black redoubt.
WSS Lyon
Written in a fire-trench above Glencorse Wood, 11 April 1915

(He wrote this two days after censoring Arthur Lawson's letter to his sister, Rhoda: 'I remember you once told me that you liked the feeling of being frightened, if you were out here you would get quite a lot of enjoyment out of the shells which go overhead.'[44])

Lyon was an Oxford graduate and scoutmaster from North Berwick. He had resigned as staff captain so as to go overseas with his battalion and 'is believed to have been the first advocate killed in action since Flodden'[10] in 1531. Robert Affleck, a keen cricketer fatally wounded by a shell burst in his trench, and Louis Cowan, a strong swimmer born in Malay, were killed on the same day. The three bodies were brought behind the front line and laid in the heather under pine trees 'in what would be a most beautiful corner of a wood'.[16]

Into the mælstrom the first draft of replacements arrived from home on the evening of 8 May. Some seventy men from the second-line reserve battalion under Lieutenant John Burns had crossed aboard the paddle steamer *Duchess of Hamilton*, been taken by train to Cassel and marched to the transport lines and quartermaster stores at Busseboom. Making their way through Ypres they attempted to adopt the regulars' indifference to shells, and a few miles after the Menin Gate turned right to the woods, largely to make up the numbers in C and D companies that had been much reduced in the attack at St Jean. With them were four young subalterns: Second Lieutenants Basil Yeats, son of a vicar who divided his time at Cambridge between higher theology and hockey; Alastair Macfarlane, son of Lord and Lady Ormidale; Archibald Douglas, as captain of Edinburgh Academy's XI he scored a century in the last match of 1914, whilst his father had been a surgeon lieutenant of the battalion in 1900; Thomas Lawson, who started as a private soldier in 1907.

Two days after joining the battalion Basil Yeats was sent to hospital suffering from shock due to shell fire (shell shock was named in February). 'A pretty rough introduction to war,' was how BC saw it, 'As I thought [Yeats's] nerves would not stand the show and he has gone back. He ought never to have come out with nerves in the condition he's in.'[16] James Quinn recalled that 'he was wind-up mountains high'[23] and that every time a shell landed within quarter of a mile he threw clods of earth at it. He resigned his commission in October 1915.

Yeats's sister Monica had a rather different war service, as a driver with the Red Cross in Serbia and France with Dr Elsie Inglis's famous Scottish Women's Hospital.

Macfarlane, a keen motorcyclist, had abandoned medicine at Balliol to take a commission and had left home a fortnight before. He went into the front line on 11 May and was killed by a stray bullet the next morning having been twelve hours with his platoon. BC was sitting with him behind a dug-out, which had always been a safe place, when he was killed. 'It was so tragic, though we are hardened, and that night my nerves

Basil Yeats.

88

were quite gone. He was such a nice fellow and would have made a splendid officer. I am awfully sorry for his people and I know they were anxious to keep him at home.'[16]

Sergeant Bobby Johnston had come out with the draft and was assigned to B Company 'which had lost 6 NCOs in 6 days'.[19] He had only met his officer an hour before, though he records his death differently:

Alastair Macfarlane.

'Mr MacFarlane who had joined us for stand to, took Tam [Yeatts, Platoon Sergeant] and me along the Platoon's front... We halted for a moment beside a little stream which flowed through the wood across our front. As we stopped the officer was hit in the head and fell dead to the ground at our feet. It was a great shock to me to see sudden death at first hand and so early in my war service. The reality of war had become very apparent. We laid the body on the side of the trench covering the face and hands with sandbags and proceeded on our way, Tam now as Platoon Commander and I as his Platoon Sergeant. That night we buried our officer in a clearing near Battalion Headquarters.'[19]

At the outbreak of war Johnston left his job as a clerk in London and rejoined the Ninth as a private. Within a week he was promoted lance corporal, and in September 1914 became sergeant, aged 19 years and 4 months, when the Home Service men were separated. Tam Yeatts, 'an old man at 35',[19] did not remain in command of No.7 Platoon for long, he was wounded in the face by shrapnel and sent to hospital at Rouen.

Jimmy Ferguson, son of the first colonel, was the popular officer commanding B Company. 'He visited us twice each day and once by night speaking to every soldier. He was a member of the Scottish Bar and a delightful man in his early thirties.'[19] He was also very generous, and used to lend his men money but refuse repayment, so they stopped asking him.

Captain Jimmy Ferguson's B Company were in support when the 2nd Glosters, 150 yards away, were driven from a trench at the edge of the wood at 3.30pm on 9 May. Two platoons were sent to assist, according to Bobby Johnston:

Jimmy Ferguson.

'We were led along a footpath in the wood until we reached a place where there were fewer trees. The trench area was pointed out to us by the Gloster officer. We formed up into two lines astride the path and without any yelling and shouting or running made our way steadily forward with heads down and rifles and bayonets at the ready expecting to be fired on at any moment. It took us all our time to get across the ground – the noise of bullets overhead hitting the trees and shell-bursts of shrapnel fairly close to us but not overhead continued.

We suddenly saw bodies and a trench and jumped into it. I was with another man who turned to his left and I to the right. As I reached the end of the bay and turned into the traverse I came face to face with a tall Prussian Guard (who were known to be opposite us) with a long black beard and a small round cap, and a rifle and bayonet in his hands. My reflexes were quicker than his. I pulled the trigger and lunged at him with the bayonet but there wasn't room to get my rifle and bayonet clear from his equipment. As I struggled to do so his body was falling on me. I heard hurried footsteps coming round the traverse. I then felt a fear amounting to panic. Was it another Boche? Fortunately, it was Corporal Forsyth who helped me get clear and place the body on the fire-step. The Boche was dead.'[19]

This incident gave Johnston nightmares, especially upon the frequent occasions when he was exhausted. The Ninth had 'promptly ejected'[47] the enemy and held the position for an hour until the Glosters' own support arrived.

On 10 May the whole front of 80 and 81 Brigade was attacked, with gas being employed. Though the improvised respirators proved barely adequate, the British artillery decidedly did not, and the attack was repulsed by rifle fire. Jock Brown complained that 'we have had very little support from our artillery. In fact the troops there have been getting all the dirty work to do.'[4]

In contrast to the high level of ammunition consumption by the enemy, these attacks occurred in the midst of the shell crisis with almost no 4.5" howitzer ammunition remaining and the field guns rationed to four rounds per gun per day. Before the month was out the shell scandal contributed directly to a new coalition government.

Relying on small arms fire was also problematic as ammunition was scarce at 93 rounds per rifle, and rifles in short supply too as the New Army or 'Kitchener' divisions began to deploy. The draft carried long Magazine Lee-Enfield (MLE) rifles of the type that had been used in South Africa and were 'incapable of rapid fire'.[48] There was a degree of resentment among territorials that they were being passed over for the more modern Short Magazine Lee-Enfields (SMLE) issued to new Kitchener units, though K units reported the opposite. On arrival in France the draft handed in their MLEs in expectation of being given SMLEs; instead they received MLEs once more, but these rifles were modified for the more modern, high velocity Mk VII ammunition that complied with the Hague Convention. However, there were plenty of SMLEs to choose from now. Bobby Johnston picked up one from a wounded Gloster in Sanctuary Wood and carried it until the time he was commissioned.

Colonel James Clark of the 9th Argylls was killed leading a counter-attack along the Menin Road on 10 May, aged 56, and was buried in the yard of a school. Clark, Deputy Lieutenant of the City of Edinburgh and a chairman of the Edinburgh School Board, had a new elementary school in Edinburgh named after him. The Argylls suffered such losses that the battalion was subsequently temporarily disbanded. Colonel Blair pointed out in *The Scotsman* that actions by the 9th Argylls and 9th Royal Scots were sometimes mixed up, not least in Sir John French's eighth despatch.

Gas was used once more when the focus of the attack again shifted further south, into Sanctuary Wood and the positions of the Ninth and 81 Brigade on 11 May, but

this blew back onto the attackers with a contrary wind. After repulsing two attacks, the bombardment so destroyed the Camerons' trenches that they were forced to retire to the support line. 'An Edinburgh man' was again phlegmatic: 'The Germans are still continuing to use their asphyxiating gas, but if they expect a little gas blown from a pipe is going to stop the British or French advance, they are nursing a vain hope.'[6] Wattie Scott again was concise: 'Chlorine gas bombs burst near tent & all get nearly suffocated.'[38]

At one point the Ninth had to hold the adjacent part of the line as well as their own as the 1st Royal Scots had been called away. Each man was out of sight of his pals and was instructed to fire the occasional shot at the enemy. James Quinn 'felt like a god that time!'[23] On another occasion Jim Elliot got into a machine-gun duel with a German Nordenfeldt, 'damned foolish, but great fun at the time', until a bullet came through his water jacket, bounced off the feed block and hit his No.2 Dod Fraser in the side of his head. Fraser said, 'A'm deid, ma heid's aff'[2], but though he was bloodied and shaken up he was otherwise all right, but soon after got a job in a munitions factory.

The shelling inevitably held up the rations. Men ate under waterproof sheets, tied across the corners of fire bays and observed how, 'It was really ludicrous to see a worried sergeant reduced to working fractions – one-twelfth of a small tin of butter, one-sixth of a tin of jam…the obvious inadequacy of it gave way to the humour of the division'.[35] The transport officer was Lieutenant Aymer Maxwell, a medical student, who frequently brought up the rations at the gallop through Ypres under shell fire.

'Poor old Maxwell has a rough time of it just now. He has to bring up our ration transport each night along several miles of road which is being shelled. Luck has favoured him so far and he has only had one limber scuppered.'[16] The transport section dumped the rations in a clearing between Zouave and Sanctuary woods, quite close to battalion headquarters, and then they were brought in on foot to the dug-outs. By the end of their stint, the dug-outs were rapidly disappearing, the shelling knocked in some and others were flooded. Finally, the Ninth and their neighbours, 1st Royal Scots, were relieved on the stormy night of 22/23 May after thirty days in or adjacent to the trenches. Bobby Johnston did not see the east side of the wood until 1975.

Cairns reckoned on there being an average of nine casualties a day between 3 and 17 May, and the first day without a casualty was 19 May. A track in the wood was especially dangerous at night for it 'fairly hummed with bullets and several men "stopped one" in that place'.[23] On 11 May Jimmy Ferguson and Sergeant Walter Thomson were trying to locate a sniper who was 'rather troublesome', when the sergeant dropped dead from a bullet. George Russell Lawson had been hit in the thigh and was carried out by four bandsmen. When a salvo of shells fell nearby, as they crossed the glade between Sanctuary and Zouave woods, the four bandsmen got under the stretcher with Lawson on top. One man wounded here in both legs refused to leave the trench on a stretcher for fear of being hit again. The glengarry of one B Company man, who had been shot in the head, was carried by his pal Bobby Lunn for almost a year. Eventually Lunn got leave because his father had died and he took it home to the lad's parents. Lunn was later wounded in an 'old Jerry trench' where the dug-outs faced the wrong way, hit in the leg 'the piece of shell just came downstairs looking for him!'[23]

Among 28 deaths in this period, on the evening of relief, James Pearson was killed, shot by a sniper whilst heading out behind the trench to fetch water to make tea. The bullet hit him in the back and cut an artery. Unconscious almost immediately, he died in a few minutes. Jimmy Pearson, 'the most notable of the men still remaining in the ranks'[35] had twelve International rugby caps for Scotland between 1909 and 1913. 'For a centre three-quarter, nine stone fully clad is an absurd weight, and so this gallant Scot was always struggling against an overwhelming handicap when it came to International fray.'[49] At war, Colonel Blair wrote, 'He was as popular with the men of my battalion as he was at Myreside.' He had been a company runner, one of two men who carried messages between battalion headquarters and the company commander, Jimmy Ferguson, and excused carrying equipment except rifle and bandolier.

James Pearson.

'Sanctuary Wood has many memories, but there is one which transcends all others – the sight of the wee white face with the little smile as we filed passed the little athlete lying in his last long sleep, clad not in the panoply of greatness which he deserved, but in the common tunic and kilt of a private lying like a warrior taking his rest...– the resting place of Jimmy P, peerless three-quarter, private soldier and gentleman.'[15]

Bobby Johnston describes the funeral:

'At this early stage of the war we were most meticulous to ensure the correct burial of our comrades. We dug three shallow graves in a plot set aside as a Cemetery near Zouave and Sanctuary Wood, lined the foot with sandbags, placed the bodies on them with their hands crossed in front… The padre read the short service – a piper played "The Flowers of the Forest" which was interrupted by a salvo of shells which caused all present to lie down flat very promptly until the shelling ended. We heard the approach of the ration limbers i.e. wagons from Ypres and saw ourselves almost surrounded by Very lights and the fires in Ypres itself behind us and set off to our duties with many poignant thoughts.'[19]

'Myreside without Pearie – what a blank!' The Edinburgh newspapers were awash with hyperbole:

'He was indeed a man of grit, determination and courage, and there is no doubt that it is these qualities which make the fine soldier in the British Army of to-day. It has even been proved that the Rugby game is a splendid preparation camp for the bringing out of these qualities which make Scotland's sons the envy of the civilised world in the field of battle.'[26]

John Young, a schoolboy at Watson's, had stood at the Usher Hall with his mother and watched with pride 'the Dandy Ninth, the cream of Edinburgh's youth' march to war in February. Now 'I can remember exactly where I was at school, where I was standing… The word came that Jimmy Pearson had been killed… It brought home to a great gathering of schoolboys the real reality of war, we had lost our great hero.'[50]

The Ypres road must have been the epitome of modern war to the battalion. The city itself had been burning to the west for two weeks whilst they were in Sanctuary Wood. Now they marched out in one long line through the burnt-out city, lit occasionally by flashes of lightning, the battalion strength reduced to about 400. However, the actual number killed was the lowest in the brigade, perhaps giving rise to the optimistic title of God's Own Highlanders. 'It is now 27 days since I had my clothes off, changing only socks. When we left our rest camp 27 days ago we expected to be back in 6 hours!'[16] wrote BC. Most men had to cut their socks off and all found their equipment imprinted on their skin.

The next day Bobby Johnston's eyes began to water and the doctor thought it might be delayed reaction to gas until they received news that 28th Division were under attack in the woods, Johnston was thereafter nicknamed the Human Gas Alarm. The battalion was called into reserve. This meant pulling boots onto sore and swollen feet and marching once more. Their fatigue was evident and remarked upon by the Corps Commander General Pulteney (Johnston thought it was Sir John French). Not called on to go further, they bivouacked near Vlam, where the Quartermaster, Andrew Gordon, brought up cookers and bacon. Motor buses commandeered 'from the

Strand'[42] carried those whose feet were so blistered that they could not walk. Men were almost too tired to keep their feet, and Jock Brown left instructions to 'wake us up when peace is declared'.[4] At Busseboom the battalion was distributed among farm buildings, fires were lit with broken up hop-poles, to the displeasure of the farmer, and baths were taken at Pops brewery. At this time Johnston claims to have been almost run over by a Grenadier captain on a bicycle, the Prince of Wales. Similarly Bob Lindsay says he tripped over a man in a trench and told the future King Edward to keep his feet in before realising who it was. Lindsay, who became Brigade Intelligence Officer, had various problems to solve, such as camouflaging white horses with Jeyes fluid.

Alastair Shannon observed:

'We are "*the Dandy Ninth*" no longer; we have passed beyond that into something more solid and cruel... we have passed as it were, from a dream into life, and often here in the wood you may see men look into each other's eyes and say in the same breath, "This is the life." Strange that it should be so, but it is true.'[35]

For all the horrors of Ypres, in a short space of time it became a 'chord of comradeship retouched'[10] and old stories circulated for 'After all, these were the days.'[10] Quinn too saw beyond mud and destruction: 'Old Homer had nothing on us in those days!'[23]

The battalion was looking forward to a change, for the Salient was 'certainly a beastly hot corner'.[3] Marching south to their next sector they were dragging their feet, not least as their re-equipment meant many were in new boots, when the band of an English regular battalion welcomed them into Locre, and they smartened their march. 'After all, we had held the line at Ypres and survived and we had a fair conceit of ourselves!'[19] Next they passed a New Army unit that had been out three weeks, 'Like all Kitchener's Army they consider themselves regulars and were inclined to be a bit patronising towards us. What a difference from the real regulars!'[3]

Armentières and the trench

We '*shook hands with ourselves for having luck. We <u>were</u> in luck! Armentieres was a fine town and though the line ran just outside it, the war was a jolly sort of war.*'[23]

AFTER Ypres the Ninth were sent south to quieter Armentières on 31 May 1915 which 'compared with the Salient, seemed a veritable haven of peace'.[33] Just over the border into France, the town was largely intact and most hospitable. One Ninth even met his father, a Royal Engineer, on coming into town.

The billets were 'glorious,' even though much of the battalion were in the hospice (poor house), sleeping on the concrete floors. Rhoda Taylor, wife of Captain Alexander Taylor, had sent everyone in A Company a rubber inflatable pillow. On arrival D Company found 'it was quite a treat to see water flowing from a tap again'.[3] Soon enough the water was turned off and they 'had to send kids out to get it'.[3] When shelled, B Company found refuge in the cellars of a linen warehouse. They later moved to smaller buildings and houses. Moving 200 yards away to an old school had the advantage that the courtyard was 'small so that there will be less opportunity for drilling, which is decidedly pleasing'.[3] Others in the battalion 'languished'[2] in the railway goods sheds, 'rather a dirty hole'.[3]

The MG Section moved to the School of Music before being billeted in a doctor's house in the Rue de Fauberg de Lille. Having consumed much of the doctor's wine cellar, the adjutant made them all part with 20 francs each. This they thought very cheap, and the doctor probably agreed if ever he returned home, but it particularly aggrieved those of the section who had been in the trenches at the time. Headquarters was in a large manufacturer's house of twenty bedrooms and a large courtyard and where officers wrote letters whilst lying in the garden.

Having had their clothes on for 'six weeks' without a change, no baths 'up there', the colonel was pleased to report from Armentières, 'Here is a different story – clean trenches, wide and safe – very little danger, almost no firing, a charming part of France... as happy and merry as sand-boys.'[6] This prompted the characters in the depot staff at Glencorse barracks to enquire if others 'are also "as happy as sandboys?"'[10] The half-battalions had a day each at the baths. On heading out for his bath James Cairns heard a shell hit the building he was in, but fortunately it was a dud. A shell landed in the square about 3 yards from James Hutcheon (later OBE; he named his home in Dumfries *St Eloi*), it also did not burst though 'he got a bit of a start'.[3]

Church services were held at the beautiful St Vaast church. The Reverend Colonel William Beveridge gave a fanciful sermon in which he called for recruits to be new Knights of the Round Table. 'These splendid addresses I fear act on us spiritually like the passing brilliance of a star shell.'[42] There was swimming in the River Lys and concerts held in the recreation room. The famous Estaminet des Amis in Armentières was run by sisters Marie and Louise, serving grenadine, beer and coffee. These girls learned to dance the Schottische and, of course, were going to marry the boys of the battalion 'après la guerre'.[23] 'Cherry' Thin remembered dinner at Au Boeuf and Wattie Scott the old café at Rue Bayard. Madeline checked them for swearing in her estaminet, which she referred to as *blaspheme*,[23] and umpired the beer drinking contest, won by Johnny Black.

Some proclivities were also met; James Beatson had an encounter with a *nymphe du pavé*, who was a 'dark and handsome, jovish beauty'.[42] Bernard Holmer confided his indiscretions to his diary in French. After he was married his wife said: 'Don't write any more "*funny*" French things, Bernard darling.'[24] Later Duncan Geekie was hospitalised with gonorrhoea in January 1916. Geekie 'joined the Lewis Guns because he thought we got more grub than the men in the Coy, but came to like us for ourselves'[23] and joked in the shell holes of the Somme.

James Cairns' diary entry for Wednesday 9 June reads:

'We had a long lie till 8.00am & after breakfast spent all forenoon cleaning our new digs & arranging things to our own liking. We had spring mattresses to sleep on & a

stove to cook on & are most comfortable. In the trenches the fellows are also very comfortable with rainproof dug-outs. They have also a piano & other luxuries. We can go to & from the trenches at any time by a long communication trench. Everything goes on as if there was no war going on. Children running about & men & women doing their daily work. We can also get milk, butter & eggs. We have to attend the civilians here as they have no doctor. Sat reading till about 11.00 p.m. & then turned in.'[39]

To get back to the war they marched out to nearby Chapelle d'Armentières, half a mile behind the front line. After the relative excitement of Armentières itself, Beatson thought the place 'pretty dull, and dully pretty'.[42] A communication trench ran from Chapelle over a mile or a mile and a half of duckboards to the line and took thirty-five minutes to negotiate. At Sanctuary Wood the ration wagons had been able to get to within 400 yards of the reserve line, but here the flat country meant they only got as far as a level crossing and then everything was carried up. They could buy eggs from the bakers near headquarters, and an estaminet near to the trench entrance sold egg and chips, for a price, and so for the first time there were volunteers for the ration parties. This came to an end when a sentry was posted at the entrance. Anyway, Thin had found it difficult to get the eggs he had bought safely up to the line whilst carrying two sacks of potatoes. Other cumbersome burdens included four 20ft planks between two men. James Quinn carried a petrol tin half full of beer that 'weighed a ton'[23] only to find it was sour. So long was the communication trench that, Quinn tells us, on one occasion the ration party went on strike.

Bobby Johnston described the front as consisting of 'lovely trenches, had to sweep them out every morning... spotlessly clean'[19] and they were nicknamed 'Daily Mail' trenches after a photograph from earlier in the year showing them untouched by shells and its famously inaccurate portrayal of events. The empty tin cans placed in the wire as warning alarms had to be put in the fire first to try and keep down the number of flies and the rats that disturbed the sentries, and the trenches were kept clean for the same reason. They were 'the last word in comfort'[42] with 500 yards of wheatfield to

Panorama of the front between Armentières and Bois Grenier, probably showing the houses of Gris Pot.

the enemy, giving rise to names of trench bays such as *Poppy View*, alongside *Debating Club* and *Rest and be Thankful*.

No man's land varied from 400 yards to as little as 70 yards in places, with saps closing the distance. As Thin describes:

> 'There are three sentry posts on the sap, one at the mouth and two at the end. It runs about seventy yards in front of the trench. It is a beastly place to get out to. One has to stoop double and even then you get a terrific bump on the head every few steps. The ground in front of the trench has been an onion field at some time. It is covered with them.'[3]

On midsummer nights the poppies and grass in no man's land had to be cut by patrols from both sides, and on a memorable occasion a tall German was heard and then seen sharpening his scythe. Grass cutting was unpopular, with a covering party placed further forward and all anxious to get back into the relative safety of the trench. The mosquitoes were unbearable and the patrols came in stinking of onions. 'Cherry' Thin was fired at in no man's land when repairing the wire one night. 'We lay down double quick, even on the top of bits of wire. It was a good thing we did as the shots whistled right over us. It is wonderful what a feeling of absolute safety you get in a trench after you come in from the ground in front of it.'[3]

Further down the line a sign reportedly said 'Welcome Jocks, we are ready for you'[23] and Monday 14 June began with a German shouting across to No.8 Platoon 'Good morning, Scotsmen',[42] a reply being given with rapid fire and a piano recital. For their part the Germans usually responded to the piano with a rifle fusillade adding a 'staccato accompaniment'.[6] Though not all of the keys were working, Harry Hills knocked out a few tunes and he used to sing from the *Chocolate Soldier, The Merry Widow* and *The Arcadians*.

They also heard a piano in the German lines near Houplines:

'Our Jocks sat enthralled as in the quiet of the early evening, classic and popular music was heard across no man's land. No one on our side ever interrupted the concert but usually the end came by someone in a neighbouring sector opening fire.'[19]

The Camerons alongside made themselves unpopular by punctuating stand to each morning with a mad minute of rifle fire, that invariably brought an artillery retaliation along the front line. On one occasion a voice called back, 'For –'s sake, jock, stop that firing.'[3]

At night they used a pump against a wall where the support line ran through a cherry orchard, but in daylight you could see the wall was covered with bullet marks as there was line of sight to the enemy positions. Just before dawn cherries could be gathered from the trees, but as they were sniped at from the German lines some 800 yards away this also became prohibited and a sentry posted to enforce it. Although no longer allowed to pick cherries, there were still those which had fallen to the brick paved floor. Presumably because it was thought to be an observation post, the Ninth returned to the line at a later date to find enemy artillery had destroyed the orchard.

The MG position was in a trench cut at right angles through the railway embankment and looking at Pérenchies. One night they put the gun up on the destroyed rails and fired at an enemy patrol 'but Jerry never answered'.[23] Behind this position was a kitchen garden where they could crawl about the strawberry beds and raspberry canes.

When digging-in in Flanders water was usually encountered 2 – 3ft below ground level, therefore breastworks, 15-20ft thick, had to be laboriously built above ground, often all night, not infrequently to be demolished by enemy artillery fire within minutes the following morning. Trenches were the defining feature of the Western Front. Their use was as set down by Vauban, whose ramparts surround Ypres, in the seventeenth century for siegework, advancing toward the enemy's defences with saps, and then digging parallels called trenches. 'A well-traced, sufficiently manned, and well-defended entrenchment is, *as a rule*, to be looked upon as an impregnable point,' wrote Clausewitz in *On War* in 1832.

The first trenches, including those dug by the Ninth, were rudimentary, constructed in a night and deepened as time and enemy attention permitted. They were typically close to the enemy lines and often in an unfavourable lie of the land: overlooked and waterlogged.

The breastworks at Voormezeele had been made entirely of sandbags, some 4ft thick and 6ft high, in order to be bullet-proof. Using an ammunition box as firing step, the men became accustomed to taking quick shots at the 'Germs'[26] and getting their heads down in two-seconds. Beatson described the British breastworks as 'childish in comparison'[42] to those of the enemy, offering only 6ft of cover and no loopholes, forcing them to fire over the parapet. Only later were breastworks added behind, as a parados, to protect them from shells dropping to the rear.

These structures took a lot of material. No.9 Platoon had been looking forward to an easy job carrying wood, as D Company had had a similar job the day before. However, they found sixteen timbers 22ft x 1ft square, to be taken up the communication trench. They finally got back to billets at 4am, only to be up again at 7am with sore shoulders. The German 'evening hate' started as D Company wended their way along the communication trenches, which included Leith Walk and Cowgate.

'Cherry' Thin: 'I think a machine gun is about the most horrible thing in war. It is strange to hear it as it sweeps along the parapet, getting louder and sharper as the shots get nearer the part you are in and then dying away again.'[3]

To provide protection dug-outs were essential, 'without these the daily casualty list must be heavy'.[51] Contemporary German defences were better sited and better constructed, many 10 – 11ft deep and revetted with planks. The dug-outs at Ypres, when they first went in, were simple affairs called 'trench shelters'. The best were 6ft x 10ft but only 3 – 4ft high, sandbagged on three sides, open at the rear, and roofed by corrugated iron and earth or a few sandbags. Simple holes in the wall of the trench became known as 'funk-holes'.[28] There were no shell proof structures in this part of the line.

Cairns laboured all day adding earth to the top of his dug-out in order to make it a little more proof against shrapnel. He had just stepped back to admire his work when the new medical officer asked him to do the same for his shelter and was then asked to build up the parapet in front. 'Doc'[39] David Ross Haddon RAMC had already been out with the Ninth as a lieutenant in D Company and had been wounded in the jaw by shrapnel at Second Ypres. He now returned as the doctor and treated his section as Dr John Bowie had done, including the occasional partridge for tea.

Ross Haddon.

Arthur Anderson remembered a dug-out made home from home by a picture postcard of Princes Street tacked to a support. The men were allowed to write one letter or postcard a day, but these had to be read by their officers acting as censors, so various terms came into use, 'the historic city' meaning Ypres for example. Though daily talk was of trenches and wounds, Bernard Holmer thought carefully about what he put in his letters home. It took about five days for letters and parcels to reach them, 'Our mails and parcels reach us here, so nothing else matters.'[6] Having been almost a month in Sanctuary Wood the men were treated to a vast quantity of parcels from home, though many cakes were beyond eating. In few wars can mothers have provided their sons overseas with scones, testimony to the efficiency of the Post Office. Men even managed to get items home for laundry.

The quality of food was most variable, ranging from delicacies sent by relatives to being sustained through counter-attacks by iron rations of bully beef and hard biscuit. Arthur Anderson thought the cooks' efforts were to ensure they were hardened internally as well as externally and certainly William Rosbottom was discharged as unable to cope with army rations. Bob Tait and his cooks were frequently cursed by men out on 'rest' but welcomed by the hungry coming out of the line. In the trenches the men had to make do themselves. The Germans found that, 'The British in general show more interest in good food and accommodation than in the make-up of their formations, the identity of their neighbouring forces or the names of their commanders.'[63]

On their first trips in, the Ninths had been bemused to see the regulars carrying all manner of rations, in addition to their personal kit and the stores of ammunition and wire they were required to carry from the dump. These included loaves of French bread stuffed into their tunics, parcels under their arms, firewood and bags of charcoal. They soon followed suit; excess kit, however, was frequently abandoned, 'on the march, every ounce counts'.[37] Clarence Gibb wrote to his fiancée Annie that, 'Our caravan experience is very useful as we have to fend for ourselves. Fry our own bacon, cook tea etc.'[37] It even dawned on the officers that the mess required rather more organisation than 'a somewhat prolonged picnic,'[36] though BC seemed well supplied:

> 'Today I am spending a lot of time eating! Breakfast at 5.30am consisted of a hard-boiled egg, half a dozen sardines (I don't know where they came from), bread & butter & jam and cocoa. Next meal was luncheon at 11am consisting of oxo & bread & butter & jam. Next dinner at 2.30 pm of cold fresh meat, bread, butter & cheese, an orange & aerated water. At 5 pm I shall have tea consisting of cocoa and cake (a present from Dudgeon) & I shall finish up with supper consisting of cocoa, potted ham & turkey, bread, butter & jam. Not bad that is it!'[16]

Jock Brown bought himself a pork chop on coming away from trench digging, but it took him about an hour to cook it. He also noted that *skean dhus* seemed to have been used principally for eating. An incident well remembered was when a frantic 9th Argyll ran up to them asking 'Whaur's Jock?', and on being told he was dead the man wailed and rushed on saying, 'Weel, living or deid, he must be found for he has our Section's Maconochie.'[35] Mac 'of Boer War fame'[24] was a tinned stew. Tinned food was in good supply, 'next to a good rifle, one needs a good tin-opener,'[26] but locally cost two to three times that sent from home. A further advantage was to keep it from the rats. A trench occupied by Arthur Anderson was visited by a tame rat they called Archibald. He would allow them to stroke him 'and there is a sort of gentlemen's agreement between Archibald and ourselves that he won't pinch our rations if we feed him regularly. I don't know that we would trust him after dark, however.'[28]

At Dickebusch water had to be boiled a mile away at a creamery and then brought over by a 100-gallon cart three or four times a day. To get water to the trenches it was brought in 2-gallon petrol tins tasting of petrol or chloride of lime. Hughie McKenzie

Jackdaw mascot of the cooks, allegedly taught to say 'What the deil are you looking at?'.

100

(who later flew RE8s in the RAF) pinched a goat from the Lahore Division, just after Second Ypres, and promised his mates milk, but was 'chaffed'[2] when he discovered it was a billy. Arriving in February, the men suddenly found themselves consumers of *vin rouge chaud*. Less palatably, strong lime juice had to be consumed in front of the platoon commander. Then there was the rum ration, an eighth of a pint a day (71 ml).

Bobby Johnston recalls the almost continual efforts to boil water by burning rifle oil, 'drumming up,' and achieving merely hot water after two hours for tea or Symington's pea soup. Douglas Howard was breaking up wood with a pick axe when it set off a cartridge that had been left by a previous battalion. No sooner had the fire started than another went off. A little later, at Maricourt, a cartridge in a brazier went off and burnt Tommy Lamb, giving him quite a fright.

Bobby Johnston received a Christmas pudding in June 1915 and this was cooked in an ammunition box half filled with water, behind the parados for two hours. They were about to serve up when they instead received a salvo of shells that hit the trench, parados and pudding. Accused of drawing fire with their smoke, the section spent the night rebuilding the position. Similarly, Norman McCaskell lit a fire in the support dug-outs at Glencorse Wood, raised 'a trifle of smoke' and brought down the colonel with a 'hell of a wrath'.[24] The names of the six men in the section were duly taken and they cheerfully talked of six months prison at Le Havre. McCaskell was wounded soon after, the bullet had to be carefully removed from near his spine and he rightly considered himself lucky and was commissioned in the Argylls in September.

Fires were not permitted in trenches until dark because of aeroplanes. Conversely smoke was not permitted by day and Cairns found it very hard to get

Lunch at Dragon Wood December 1915 (and shadow of William Geissler, photographer).

coke lit without coals if his fire went out overnight. The result was three meals of bread, butter and jam.

Primus stoves were much sought after, but expensive, and paraffin was on regular issue. In April Colonel Blair asked the Lord Provost's Comforts' Committee for 300 'Tommy's Cookers... They cost about one shilling each, I think'[6] that burnt methylated spirit (later solid alcohol came into common use for cooking in outposts). The committee duly sent off 154 socks, 108 shirts, 500 respirators (£10 10s for the thousand and urgently required), 990 Tommy's cookers, 7 periscopes, 60lb tobacco and 24 gross pipes. Quartermaster Gordon in turn sent his thanks, 'You ought to see how the men enjoy their cigarettes.'[6] As well as the comforts' committee, a committee of ladies was formed in 1916 and took charge of woollen goods, under the presidency of the Hon. Mrs Mildred Moncrieff, mother of Dick and Adrian Moncrieff of the Ninth. The blanket committee allocated 500 donated blankets to the Ninth, The Royal Scots Tobacco and Cigarette Fund was generously subscribed to, sending 40,000 cigarettes a week to the front, the Organisation for Socks for Edinburgh Territorials promptly sent a thousand pairs; and a parcel scheme accepted parcels up to 7lb for despatch every Friday.

A pitifully small number of these items were returned to loved ones as the possessions of the deceased, a razor, sometimes a photograph or bundle of letters. It became accepted that parcels intended for men who had been wounded or killed were divided up amongst his section.

Ration parties were 'a deadly affair'.[23] On dark nights they easily got lost or fell in water-filled holes. Jim Quinn hated carrying the Huntley and Palmers biscuit tins for they gleamed in the light of star-shells or cigarettes. One night his tin received two bullet holes and, preferring soggy biscuits, he elected to stop carrying it on his shoulder and to drag it into the trenches on the end of his belt instead. The lumbering transport had to work its way along congested roads, with the horse-drawn wagons falling up to their axles in ditches or 'Jack Johnson' holes. Working back, divisional lorries supplied the 'refilling points' from the railhead that connected the Expeditionary Force to Britain.

Away from the line far better things could be bought if you had the money and means of communicating, rations remaining the main preoccupation. The Scots and French bartered jam for *vin ordinaire*. Of the halfway words that bridged the linguistic gap, the most used was 'napoo',

Cadell's *The Desired Menu*.

from '*Il n'y en a plus*' ('There is no more') but taken to mean none, finished or even dead. This was no mere corruption by the British, it was used as freely by the French to make themselves understood. Two civilians fleeing home, in their Sunday best as was usual, were found sheltering in a shell-hole and summed up their situation to a Brit as 'No bon!'

The Jocks were always on the scrounge for grub with a cheerful 'Bong swarr, wifie!'[36], but David Rorie RAMC found, when he asked the said 'wifie' if the men troubled her, that they were in fact gentlemen who drew water for her from the well and washed down her doorstep. Wheras a Flemish lady claimed no need for translation from the 'Doric' Scots, these *courte jupe*, 'petticoated men', but did not understand the English at all. Whisky, of course, always helped to win over 'hosts' upon whom the soldiers were billeted; though when too freely consumed it was liable to re-labelling as 'paraffin'[52] by the owner. Aymer Maxwell would sit in his tent in his pyjamas and dispense whisky to all comers, perhaps for medicinal purposes.

After 'omelettes and chips, and café avec rum',[23] Quinn and his mates settled up for theirs, and for others in the division who had cleared off without paying. They were known thereafter by the mother and daughter owners as *'Bon cinque Sergeants Ecossais'*.[23]

Bobby Johnston picked up a French and Hindi patois from the regulars *'Qu'est ce que vous dites?* became Coquidit? ... A trench brazier became Sigri; water became Fani; we demanded *'oeufs and pommes frites'*, but used Ek Dum (at once), Rooti (bread) etc., to show that we understood the Bat (language).'[19]

Tommy (to Jock, on leave): WHAT ABOUT THE LINGO? SUPPOSE YOU WANT AN EGG OVER THERE, WHAT DO YOU SAY?
Jock: YE JUIST SAY, 'OOF'
Tommy: BUT SUPPOSE YOU WANT TWO?
Jock: YE SAY 'TWA OOFS,' AND THE SILLY AULD FULE WIFE GIES YE THREE, AND YE JUIST GIE HER BACK ONE. MAN, IT'S AN AWFU' EASY LANGUAGE.

There were thankfully few casualties at this time compared to the preceding sector, though the relative pleasures started to tire to boredom 'in fact if it had not been for the occasional shot, we should have thought the war was over'.[39]

In the middle of June, on the centenary of Quatre Bras, Lieutenant Norman Macdonald, Private William Ross and Private Malcolm Matheson went into no man's land in front of Grand Porte Égal to place propaganda 'newspapers'[33] in the German wire.

Norman Macdonald.

Macdonald was a third generation advocate and volunteer: his grandfather, Lord Kingsburgh, had been a founding officer of the QRVB and Lord Advocate of Scotland, and his father had been one of the original company commanders in the Ninth.

The War Diary reads:

'Lieut. N. MACDONALD & Ptes. W. Ross & [M. Matheson] went out on patrol about 11p.m. to examine the enemy's wire entanglements. While close up to the German trenches a stray shot hit Pte. W. Ross, which made him give a shout. The Germans turned searchlight on to the spot and opened rapid fire. Pte. [Matheson] returned about 12.25a.m. 17/6/15 & stated that when rapid fire was opened on the patrol, they scattered by rolling over in the grass. He lay still for about 15 minutes, when the rapid fire ceased. He then crawled about looking for Lieut. N. Macdonald & Pte. W. Ross but could find no trace of them & in his opinion Lieut. N. Macdonald is unwounded and a prisoner, & Pte. W. Ross wounded & a prisoner.'[1]

Most of these patrols consisted of an officer, a sergeant and three men; and most went out to a ditch parallel to the lines, halfway across. On this night, a German patrol were in the ditch before Macdonald and his men got there and they were fired on from close range. It was reported that Ross's leg had been broken, he himself recorded that a bomb wounded him in both thighs. Macdonald bandaged his knee and was attempting to rescue him when they were both captured. Matheson, accompanied by Sergeant William Leslie, made a search for them the following night but they could not be found. A week later the *Edinburgh Evening News* reported Macdonald as 'missing believed taken prisoner'.[8] Through the International Committee of the Red Cross, it was confirmed a month later that he had been captured *en patrouille* and was now a prisoner of war. *Leutnant* Macdonald was sent to the *Gefangenenlager* (prison camp) at Gütersloh in Westphalia. To add insult to injury he was recorded as an *Engländer*.

William Ross had worked for a grocer in Gilmore Place and was a member of the Northern Harriers. He was treated at a dressing station at Lomme where his left leg was put into traction. From there he was moved to Valenciennes and then to Reserve Lazarette (hospital), Remise No.2, Ingolstadt in Bavaria. 'I do not think the doctors were very skilled,'[53] he stated, but here at least his parcels arrived, he could write once a week and he had no complaint about his general treatment:

'There was one sister for the whole hospital and three orderlies for every 60 men. The nursing was quite good. The lodging was not at all good. The hospital before the war had been a wagon shed. The rooms were about 10 feet high and the atmosphere was, on the whole, pretty good. It was, however, very dirty. I was there five months and the floor was only washed once during that time. The food was bad. For breakfast we got some very bad coffee, but enough. We were issued out about 250 grammes of bread, which had to last us 24 hours. For dinner we got a very watery soup, sometimes potatoes, carrots, &c., and a small piece of very tough meat. At 6 p.m. a small piece of sausage only… A favourite punishment was to put us on bread and water for two or three days.'[53]

Ross's left leg was permanently shortened by 9cm. He was one of the 185,000 British prisoners captured by the Germans during the war.

A replacement draft was received in July and at the end of the month ten men went to Cadet School at St Omer to become officers. One of these was Tom Perry and he held a farewell supper the night before with toasts until 10pm. He was commissioned in the Camerons in August, killed within a month at Loos and interred in a mass grave with his platoon near to where they had stormed the enemy lines.

Their place taken by Canadians, the Ninth retired to a rest camp with classes of instruction. The Machine Gun Section received instruction in the Vickers MG from the 1st Royal Scots. Grenadiers or 'bomb' throwers were trained, during which John Sexton was wounded. They were also visited by Sir Douglas Haig, then in command First Army, who made a favourable impression by informally strolling about the camp and chatting to the men. He was accompanied by General Pulteney, who complimented 'the good behaviour of the Battalion, the proof being that there had not been a single Court Martial during the six months the Battalion had been on service.'[1]

Beatson's response was that he 'sort of patted our baby curls and called us good boys; of course if we stray from the straight path there's a big stick in the corner.'[42] A common misdemeanour in the summer of 1915, with short, frenetic nights and quiet hours of sentry duty, was for sentries to fall asleep standing at their posts. Bill Hay was 'dead beat' on sentry duty having been awake for four days and found himself being woken by Sergeant McGill and warned 'You could be shot'.[46]

Early one morning Bobby Johnston heard Lieutenant Aymer Maxwell 'from far away': 'Sergeant Johnston, are you asleep?' Johnston had had his head resting on his hands looking out at no man's land, but quickly recovered himself. 'No, Sir, I think there is a Boche on the wire.'[19]

It had been a shock and he was careful not to rest his head again. The new General Officer Commanding (GOC) General Milne conducted courts martial for this offence and soon had about twenty men of the Camerons and Argylls sentenced to death, none confirmed, and succeeded in stamping out the 'dangerous practice'.[19] Sergeant James Mitchell took exception to Archie Pow, on sentry duty, getting a cup of coffee from the wife of the billet, and promptly arrested him. The MG Section's lusty singing brought the CO to their estaminet after hours. The next morning, hauled up on charges, they managed to explain that it was also their billet.

Men lost stripes for various reasons. One, who lost his for leading his men over the open past a flooded part of a communication trench, felt misused. The following year a man from B Company burnt his foot with an overturned mess tin of tea and was sent home to Blighty. There was quite an investigation to determine if it was intentional and the War Diary records it as a 'self-inflicted wound'. Another man just back from a self-inflicted wound the year before was suspiciously shot in the shoulder during Lewis gun training as there was unexpectedly a live round in the drum. A Company had a man who reported sick and they never saw him again. 'While on sentry one night he went 'loopy', and began seeing things. Several times he called me to look for 'deil kens what' – coming through the wire. For a while I believed him shamming and now I'm almost sure he was.'[23]

Despite these infractions Colonel Blair could state: 'These lads of mine are simply splendid. I have no trouble, no crime, no drunks, no complaints and not a single court martial since we came out nine months ago.'[6] Shortly after however, news reached him that Arthur Annandale, formerly private 2158 of the Ninth, was to be court martialled at Mailly-Maillet. Annandale was from a paper manufacturing family connected to James Lowson of the Ninth. Since November 1914 he had been a lieutenant in the 9th (West Belfast) Royal Irish Rifles, a battalion formed from the Ulster Volunteer Force, whom their Commanding Officer Frank Crozier described as his 'orange-blooded revolutionaries... my Shankill Road boys'.

Now in France, Crozier explains 'Everything is shaken, including [Annandale's] nerves... Now the trench mortaring is too much for him. He rises, pushes past me, and bolts down the trench in front of his men as fast as he can go. After daylight he is discovered in a disused French dug-out behind the lines, asleep – apparently a deserter.'[54]

Colonel Blair provided him with a character reference that may have saved him from the firing squad as the General Court Martial of 1 February 1916 determined the man should be dismissed on grounds of health. A medical board subsequently found Annandale was suffering shell shock, his muscles in tremor, his speech hesitant and jerky. He became an equipment officer at the Central Aircraft Repair Depot, Chelsea. The case gained notoriety because later that month Crozier sent a rifleman to trial, and whereas the officer had been shown leniency, the other rank was found guilty of desertion and shot.

The Ninth actually had the opposite problem. Arthur Blaylock was tried in the field in January 1916. Colonel Blair submitted that: 'I should like the case disposed of without punishment as Pte Blaylock has rendered good service since he joined the Battalion under my command on the 7th September 1915 and his character during that period has been exemplary. I am desirous of retaining Pte Blaylock in the Battalion under my command.'

The man's statement runs as follows:

'I, Pte Arthur Blaylock, now being No. 3291 of the 1/9th Battalion (Highlanders) The Royal Scots (TF), do hereby confess that I was a private, (number unknown), in the 10th Seaforth Highlanders, having enlisted at Manchester on 1st May 1915 and being sent to the depot at Fort George on 3rd May, that I absented myself from that Corps on 5th May, and that I fraudulently enlisted in the Territorial Force on the 6th day of May at Edinburgh.'

Blaylock died of wounds in July 1916 at High Wood on the Somme.

As well as physical training and drill they enjoyed swimming and football and a day of regimental sports. B Company defeated A in the tug of war for Captain Lowson's Cup, though A Company won the relay race. There was a good deal of football, the men easily beating the lieutenants, but the battalion lost to the Camerons. There was also flat racing and boxing.

Arthur Farrimond, a keen runner, won the 1½ mile race. Despite being wounded twice he planned to take part in the 1916 Berlin Olympics, cancelled by circumstances beyond the control of the organisers. Discharged in 1919 he had insufficient time to train for 1920 but he was able to compete for Britain in the marathon at the 1924 Paris Olympics.

One Sunday a heavy thunderstorm gave way to a glorious afternoon and a sombre service was held before they went back into the trenches, 300 taking communion with 86 new communicants taking bread from the colonel and wine from the adjutant. Of this a man wrote to his mother:

Arthur Farrimond.

'Away somewhere to our right sharp reports among the clouds where the Germans were firing upon one of our aeroplanes kept us in mind of the war. A communion out in the battle-area is a terribly sad thing, for it almost seems so futile... How are living conditions in Britain? I feel like an old campaigner now whose country is almost foreign to him. Has it become necessary to pawn my gold ring? Are you keeping this tragedy from your affectionate son?'[6]

Cairns notes, 'We had rather an amusing experience today. The Catholic minister came & asked if he might leave his horse. While he was away it bolted!'[39]

Late August saw them in trenches at La Vesée, where the medical orderlies were able to dig potatoes and leeks out of the garden of their dressing station farm and from where Dr Haddon could reach the trenches by bicycle. However, there were canards afoot. 'This calm backwater,' wrote Beatson in September 'of the greatest war the world has known, but the rapids are not far ahead...'[42] Popular rumours ran of St Omer or Bangalore; pessimistic ones spoke of Ypres or Arras. 'A world tour was nothing to what we were going to do!'[23]

One morning the Germans were flying a kite. The Germans opposite D Company kept throwing up flags for them to shoot at – and let them know the score. 'Cherry' Thin also admired the shot at 300 yards that destroyed his periscope. Sniper activity was 'red-hot' here, and their experiences of 1915 make for uncomfortable reading. Sergeant Hills in the MG Section was filling sandbags when a bullet passed through his hand and the shaft of his spade. That same evening Alexander Farquharson, a sentry from B Company, was killed, 'fell beside us, shot in head, a sniper's bullet through his brain'.[5] The next day the 1st Argylls got this sniper. Beatson blamed the death on the poor quality of the trenches and therefore upon the officers.

'Downie Grant kept gazing through the periscope all day, spotting imaginary snipers. At one time we all had to get up and fire at a man he said he saw peeping over the German trench. Half the men didn't know where they were firing. He saw such wonderful things he refused to come off sentry duty.'[3] On one occasion the 'Saxon Snipers'[2] were teased with the skin off a cooked ham. A sniper's bullet went through Walter Chisholm's left hand, passing through 'broadwise'[6] without touching a bone except a small chip to his little finger. Freddie Paulin had a narrow escape when a sniper's bullet swished between his legs when he was examining a drain pipe in the trench with his electric lamp. Duncan McLeod Campbell was wounded in the thigh by a sniper and rescued by Harold Hutchison, both men from North Berwick with sequential numbers. However, Hutchison was also wounded, perhaps by the same sniper, and this bullet killed another man outright, probably Archie Fraser. Campbell died of wounds shortly thereafter.

Sergeant Jock Tod, 'a sniper who had much success in shooting Boche', usually operated at dusk. Early on the morning of 28 August, however, he was himself sniped and there was speculation that the early morning light had reflected off his telescopic sight. 'He was a very brave man and one of the nicest men one could meet, and never without a smile on his face. His orders were always carried out cheerfully, as his platoon liked him awfully much.'[26] His brother James was in the same battalion but had been wounded at Second Ypres and the King and Queen had visited him in hospital. Before the war, the brothers had worked for their step-father at the Royal Botanic Gardens in Edinburgh.

Another of the battalion's best snipers was George Gibb, wounded a fortnight later with a gun shot wound (GSW) to the head but not seriously. He was a farmer from Fife, with previous service in South Africa with the Imperial Yeomanry; he had been 32 when he enlisted for the Boer War and was now 48.

One sergeant made light of the sniping, 'Once, when I was sitting in the trench laughing at the shots which landed behind me, the German sniper in question struck the sandbag on the top of the parapet, and down it came on to my head. It was no light weight either.'[6] 'Cherry' Thin kept score on a sniper hitting the parapet and parados just above their heads, 'His "bag" so far consists of a mess tin, a water bottle and an entrenching tool.'[3]

Armentières was the 'cushiest'[2] of all the sectors they served in, a 'pleasant interlude in warfare'.[19] Yet there were moments of heavier action, such as a 'sham attack'[38] on 13 July and at the end of the month a house that formed part of the German line near Rue de Bois was destroyed. An 18-pounder was also dragged across – at some risk, as the Germans made much use of searchlights – to be built into the parapet. At the end of their stint Bruce Dymock wrote home to say that the brigade held the record of the British Army, occupying trenches and close supports for 4½ months on end.

Forrest Road

Wemyss Place

East Claremont Street

Royal Scots Volunteer Battalions 1859-1907

1st- 3rd VBRS (QRVB)   4th VBRS   5th VBRS   6th VBRS   7th VBRS   8th VBRS   9th

Uniform of the 9th Royal Scots

Field Officer, Review Order (mounted)

Company Officer, Review Order

Company Officer, Levée Dress

Field Officer, Review Order (dismounted)

Officer, Drill Order

Officer, Mess Dress

Officer, Regimental Duties

Officer, Marching Order

Private, Review Order

Private, Service Order

Uniform: The private in review order wears a glengarry of Royal Scots pattern with diced border of red, white and blue. The swallow tails on the glengarry and the diced pattern itself are vestiges of the ribbon that was threaded about the rim of a bonnet to draw it tight. The Royal Scots cap badge has St Andrew and cross in the centre, in gilt; surrounded by the star and cross of the Order of the Thistle, in silver.

He wears a scarlet doublet with royal blue facings (gauntlet cuffs and collars) denoting a royal regiment. Collar badges, at thruppence a pair, were gilt thistles. A buff waist-belt is worn with a Pattern 1888 knife bayonet. The Lee-Enfield rifle is fitted with a buff sling. As well as the kilt of Hunting Stewart or Stuart (dark green and blue, with an alternate yellow and red stripe), a plaid is worn in review order from the left shoulder, but is not clearly visible here. The sporran is white with two long black tassels, a black glazed top with white metal thistle and mount, adopted from the Gordon Highlanders. Hose tops are black and red diced and turned over the garters, showing the scarlet garter flash. He has white gloves and spats. In marching order Slade-Wallace equipment, introduced in 1885, buffed with pipe clay, was worn. The private in khaki wears a colonial pattern helmet, khaki drill jacket and spats, and brown leather service sporran. Ferguson has labelled this as service dress, introduced in 1902.

The glengarry provided next to no protection from the elements and to wear one might even be to dice with death as the chequered border and reflective cap badge were a gift to snipers. More appropriate khaki balmorals (later tam o' shanters, with a separate crown stitched on) were issued in 1915, but 'steel bonnets' were not forthcoming until the following year. Jock Brown lost his glengarry in May 1915 and wrote that he would have to 'swank home in a balmoral'.[4]

Archibald Gordon claims to have suggested Hunting Stewart for the battalion. 'Stuart hunting-tartan' was possibly invented by the Welsh 'Sobieski Stuart' brothers in the 1830s, and at least one of the first recruits thought it a 'fanciful pattern of comparatively modern origin'.[6] Instead he proposed an ancient tartan, such as the early hunting tartan worn by the Appin Stewarts. 'Surely when we Edinburgh Volunteers are about to don the kilt once more, we should adopt a tartan which is not the invention of yesterday, but some pattern – let it be Stewart or any other – of some antiquity.'[6]

The QRVB's Highland companies, until disbanded due to expense, wore the government tartan of the Black Watch. This was 'called by the scornful Highlanders McChilder's Tartan'[18] after Hugh Childer's army reforms of 1881 when Lowland regiments were put in government tartan trews, Highland doublets and 'German' helmets so that the Royal Scots were now 'sham Highlanders'.[9] The Royal Scots applied, instead for Hunting Stewart in 1886 and were refused until July 1901. They adopted it on return from the Boer War.

The Royal Regiment of Scotland completed this 'Highlandification' in 2006 by placing all its infantry in ceremonial kilts.

The Somme Valley
THE tranquil River Somme, popular with Impressionist painters, runs from St Quentin, by Amiens to Abbeville and the English Channel, and at this time represented the

The Reserve Trenches at Fontaine-lès-Cappy.

boundary between the British to the north and the French to the south. In September 1915 the division, and hence the Ninth, left Third Army, with adieus from General Pulteney, and went into the valley of the Somme. There they were surprised to detrain south of the river and marched with skirling pipes to Lamotte-en-Santerre, 'a hungry village'[42] where the villagers had nothing to sell but apples. For the remainder of the month they trained in the attack at company and battalion level in preparation for a breakthrough at Loos to the north. As this never materialised, they were engaged at the front near Fontaine-lès-Cappy from October.

The front line had stopped in this sector in September 1914 and was very quiet. Bobby Johnston remarks that, 'The French had lived more or less in peace with the Boche except for occasional bursts of shellfire. The infantry on each side ignored the other side and there were few casualties.'[19]

However, the underground war was very active with no man's land 'honeycombed with mines' and with frequent explosions. The battalion was principally employed in mining operations under the supervision of the 2nd Wessex Field Company Royal Engineers.

James Beatson assisted French sappers, whom he thought so slow at their gallery that everyone else would be in Berlin before it was finished. Given the Ninth were supposed to be 'Hush-hush'[23] troops, so as not to disabuse the enemy that the French were still in full possession, it came as a surprise one night, whilst Beatson worked the air fan at the sap head, for a German to call out, 'How do you like your job tonight, Jock?'[42] For his part Jimmy Quinn remembers a mine going up further along the line: 'Gee Whiz! Yon is a funny feeling – all the ground moving sideways. Of course, he shelled us too.'[23]

The line was thinly held because of the mining and was also under direct observation from the church at Dompierre-Becquincourt opposite. Universally this was considered an awful place, swarming with rats, and the services of a professional rat-catcher in the ranks were much sought after. The trench 'in the usual French fashion was just a trench – no revetting, posts or bags and certainly no duck boards'[23] and much hard work was required to convert them into 'first class trenches'.[19] Jock Dowie was a time-expired Terrier who had just returned from a month's leave having signed on again. He was sleeping in one of the dug-outs when it collapsed on him; no one heard him calling out and he was only rescued when it was discovered he was late for sentry duty.

'Sentry go' was very cold as they approached another winter, despite theft of coal from the nearby sugar factory, the Sucrerie. One night Wull Grossart said to Jimmy Quinn 'Stick it, Jimmy – we will get rum at five o'clock,' to which Jimmy replied 'Rum at 5? I'll be a bub-bub-bloody cor-r-pse long before that,'[23] a phrase that lived on in their section.

Life in the villages was pleasant and 'not too exacting'.[19] They were now billeted nearer the front line at Chuignes ('Sheens') and at Chateau Fontaine-lès-Cappy. The battalion headquarters was on the ground floor of the chateau, where French officers were introduced to whisky, and two companies were accommodated in the cellars. The MG Section was billeted in the tool shed of the chateau garden. Jim Elliot was rudely awoken one morning when John Laurie disturbed the sandbag of rations, hung on the rafters away from rats, and a tin of bully beef left a permanent mark on his head. 'Dr. Haddon patched me up and dilated on the benefits of hard wooden heads.'[2] The tunneling resulted in many men reporting on sick parade suffering from 'chalk fumes'.[39] Here the battalion were joined by a draft of 105 men, about a dozen of whom were returning having recovered from wounds.

In November the 27th Division, consisting mainly of regulars with foreign service experience, were ordered to Salonika. General Milne, the divisional commander, had requested that the Ninth accompany them, saying they had 'worthily maintained the character of their race',[41] but was refused, and Brigadier General Croker spoke highly of them. For their part the battalion, on the whole, regretted not going with their division. The Ninth therefore also parted company with their friends in the 1st Royal Scots. Sergeant Bobby Johnston however, did not. He had just returned to France from leave and being mistaken for 1/RS rather than 1/9RS, was entrained for the troopship at Marseilles. Having spoken to Regimental Sergeant Major Joseph Williams (killed in January 1916), 1st Battalion, a friend of his father's, he waited until they were at sea to point out the error. He served a year in Salonika and witnessed the battle of Struma, before being sent to cadet school and his commission. Throughout the 1950s, as part of the UK's NATO delegation, whenever he passed Amiens he looked out for Longeau Sidings where he had entrained for Marseilles and changed the course of his life.

The Ninth, least far-flung battalion of the Highland diaspora, now began a diaspora of their own. Commissioned into other units, Scottish and English, and including the Royal Engineers (RE) and the Royal Flying Corps (RFC), by the end of 1915 they were far and wide. Before he had left Edinburgh, Jock Brown wrote 'it is hard to believe that one will be put out of the action of life without having done anything, I have a hope that there may be something in the poems I have written,' and having been in France he told his father, 'I am putting away a fine lot of stuff to write about afterwards.'[4] 'I am beginning to feel that I shall come through this, though of course I may be knocked on the head at any time.'[4] Less than a month from arrival Jock Brown was suggesting to his father, 'I am not at all sure I don't wish I had taken a commission.'[4] At the end of March he took up the subject again, 'Do you think there is any chance of my getting a commission either in a regiment out here or coming out quite soon?'[4] Letters on the subject followed to his mother, even his letter following Second Ypres is more interested in a commission than the battle he has survived.

> *Killed lay Achilles, yet for a short time*
> *Love held both life and death within his breast;*
> *No more for him the kindly sun would climb.*
> *Yet as he lay he watched it as it sank*
> *Below his home, the ever restless crest*
> *Of the wild wavering sea.*
>   Excerpt from Achilles (1911) by John Brown (1891-1918)

By April he was speaking of his 'right to a commission after sticking nearly three months of it out here as a private… Down pride, I say, and let's take a commission!'[4] He wrote to his Oxford tutor and urged his parents, 'You must get a Colonel.'[4] They made more than one visit to headquarters on his behalf. Admitting it was obsessing him, and that he particularly wanted a Highland battalion, he also made it clear, 'I don't want to miss any big fights.'[4] Jock Brown received a severe wound in May 1915 when a stray bullet knocked out his two front teeth. Writing home from hospital in Leicester, he devotes one paragraph to his condition, that he is unable to eat solids, before taking up his theme again, 'Now about the commission…'[4] It was frequently the case that wounded men, at home, were able to get their 'pip', and Brown was in hospital in Edinburgh when he was gazetted to the 3/6th Seaforths in August and was with them by the end of the month. He was killed in April 1918 and buried at Voormezeele, very near his first days of war.

Jock Brown.

Reginald Price Cole was a medical student serving in H Company, when he sought a commission in the Royal Field Artillery (RFA) in January 1915. In writing to a prospective CO at Porthcawl he stressed he was 'pure Welsh', though born in Scotland, and mentioned friends of the family who wished him to use their names in his application. Price Cole served in France with the Ninth, obtained a commission with the HLI that October, and was killed while leading the first wave of his company in an attack on the Hindenburg Line in May 1917.

Bobby Johnston, after his sojourn in Salonika, was one of 120 cadets sent to the 9th Officer Cadet Battalion for four months, based at a golf course at Gailes, Ayrshire. Here a model trench system had been dug; though they thought the mock cemetery was in poor taste 'we did have to admit that some of the crosses had amusing entries – "Here lies Captain Collett accidentally drowned in a rum jar" and another "Lieut. Hamilton – Died of hernia in an attempt to speak the truth".'[19] Typically the instructors had not been in France since Mons in 1914 and had seen far less of trench warfare than their cadets, as Johnston says, 'I remember one lecture opening with the remark "This is a sandbag. Its use etc." The audience howled the lecturer down.'[19] Johnston passed third in his course and was gazetted second lieutenant a few days later. After leave, a couple of weeks at Catterick and Étaples, he was posted to 16th Royal Scots. Bernard Holmer benefitted when John D. Davidson was commissioned as he got a new kilt by swapping Davidson's for a smaller one.

Arthur Lawson was another man injured and promoted. He fell into a well at Lamotte-en-Santerre

Arthur Lawson.

and was posted to officer training in November 1915. Commissioned in the Gordon Highlanders, he was killed in Salonika in 1916, attached to the Scottish Rifles.

Of the 1,186 men on the 1915 Star Medal Roll, being those who were in France and Flanders that year, an impressive 27 per cent became officers. This number would, naturally, have been higher but the battalion also lost 81 of its number in 1915 and a proportional number of casualties could have removed over 300 men from the strength. For example, John Haddow had been nominated for a commission and was expected home when he was killed. A far higher figure is obtained looking at the first 500 men of the British War Medal and Victory Medal Roll, this records the men in serial number order and as such includes the older, experienced territorials. Such a sample produces a truly remarkable figure of 43 per cent commissioned. Many of these men had been to good Edinburgh schools, but many also broke through class divides to gain their commissions. Pre-war the battalion had a good many officers come up from the ranks, but this was probably less a case of social mobility than that many NCOs came from the same social class as the officers, and some were even younger siblings.

Table 6. Infantry Brigades of the 5th Division, November 1915

5th Division		
Major General Charles TMcM Kavanagh		
13 Brigade	**14 Brigade**	**15 Brigade**
Brigadier General LOW Jones	*Brigadier General CW Compton*	*Brigadier General MN Turner*
2/KOSB	1/Devonshire Regiment	1/Norfolk Regiment
2/West Riding Regiment (Duke of Wellington's)	1/East Surrey Regiment	1/Bedfordshire Regiment
1/Royal West Kent	1/DCLI	1/Cheshire Regiment
2/Yorkshire Light Infantry	2/Manchester Regiment	1/Dorset Regiment
–	–	–
9/London Regiment (TF)	9/Royal Scots (TF)	6/Liverpool Regiment (TF)
		6/Cheshire Regiment (TF)
5/Cheshire Regiment (TF) (Pioneers)		

KOSB King's Own Scottish Borderers, DCLI Duke of Cornwall's Light Infantry

The Ninth remained on the Western Front, being transferred on 24 November 1915 to 14 Brigade, 5th Division, another regular army division with service from 1914 at Mons and La Cateau. The division presently held the British right, immediately north of the River Somme, having taken over this part of the line from the French in August. Divisional headquarters was at Étinehen; 14 Brigade was on the right, lying between the river and Maricourt with headquarters at Suzanne chateau; 13 Brigade was in the centre and 15 Brigade on the left, the front held by all three brigades (Map XI).

When the division first took over this part of the line it was so quiet they could fish in the millpond. The relative peace and quiet was partly due to a system of artillery retaliation they inherited from the French. The Germans were allowed to fire two shells in any sector, but on a third being fired the infantry informed the artillery and rapid field gun fire commenced. Likewise attacks on villages were responded to: shells falling in 'British' Vaux resulted in the shelling of 'German' Curlu. The British policy of offensive spirit, with sniping, trench mortars and trench raids, made the place steadily more 'lively'[55] and the Germans introduced 5.9s to the area.

The Ninth arrived at Suzanne in heavy frost, the horses having difficulty keeping their feet, and in December went into the line at Vaux, the extreme right of the British line adjoining the French. However they were not strictly adjoined. The British trench line ran as far as Moulin de Fargny and the French trenches began at Frise. Between the two were marshes that meant that trenches could not be established, only posts, and these posts and contact with the French were maintained by patrols day and night.

The River Somme presented the Ninth with a very different kind of war. With 6-mile visibility up the valley, they could see the smoke of the German train going to Péronne, peppered with the artillery's attempts to stop it. They could engage German parties afloat on pontoons in the reeds, and at night punt a boat upstream themselves with a machine gun in the bow. 'The Germans used to come out on patrol on pontoons with muffled oars, and we did the same, it was an exciting place to be, a bit adventurous and we enjoyed it all.'[56] *The Scotsman*'s 'special representative' claims, 'There was all the excitement of a Red Indian stalking adventure in these episodes.'[6] Even in 1933 Quinn wrote, 'I can mind the thrill of it yet.'[23]

The Ninth were initially disposed as follows: battalion headquarters and A Company were in Vaux, from the relative heights of which the German positions in Curlu could easily be seen, and the same must have been true in reverse. B Company were in reserve, C Company in Vaux Wood and D Company in Royal Dragoons Wood, which the War Diary calls Royal Dragons Wood. Vaux Wood slopes steeply down to the river, a cliff of pure chalk that turned readily to glue. As orderly sergeant, Bill Hay

A section at Vaux in goatskin 'furries', December 1915.

visited the posts in front of Vaux, the Church Post, the Forge Post, the Ville Post, 'ensconced in the drier parts of the marsh',[33] on an old bicycle, and on one occasion, receiving unwanted attention from a machine gun, had to continue his journey by crawling in the ditch. At Fargny Mill a man named MacBlack went into no man's land and collected 'grisly souvenirs'.[23]

The four machine guns of the battalion were positioned thus: two were on the high ground to fire across the marsh, one in a cave overlooked the mill and one was placed by the riverside. It suited the section just fine to be kept out of the front line. On their first night the gun section were led to their post by the guides of the outgoing 5th Cheshires, 'the water's edge fringed with willows, low trees and what looked like a sort of bullrush'.[23] They were told to be quiet, and to keep being quiet. The Maxim was set up between pegs and, using a clinometer to set the elevation, they fired at an unknown target 1,200 yards distant, firing sporadic bursts throughout the night. A sentry was posted to look out for a boat or raft, which would mean a German raid, but as often as not he was spooked to shooting at wild ducks or 'ghosts'.[23]

The section's job, seemingly without further details, was to fire 2,000 rounds down the Péronne road every night. Frequently the gun in the cliff cave was moved into the woods at night to fire two belts (500 rounds) along the Curlu road. At daybreak it was moved to a cartwheel hub set in a pit as an anti-aircraft gun. Shifting the gun one morning, Jim Elliot in the pit slipped and grabbed both of the firing handles, firing off a good burst. This singed the sleeve of Jimmy Quinn who had just handed him the gun, 'That was as near as I want to be to the wrong end of a machine gun.'[23] Later Bob Tait, the sergeant cook, complained at bullets dropping into his cookers. One morning their luck was in, an aeroplane came over low in the mist and Roddy McKenzie was confident he must have scored one or two hits, but when the CO asked if he had 'got' him, all he could reply was 'I've fired 2½ belts, Sir.'[23]. Much of the day was consequently spent refilling belts but the arrival of a belt-filling machine made them all the more eager to fire off ammunition.

The battalion's first function was to maintain contact with the French by patrols. It was thought by some that the Scots formed the true liaison between the British and French armies, for the Auld Alliance and because 'many of the English had never got away from the "d—- foreigner" idea of the Napoleonic wars'.[36] Patrolling the islands in the river made quite a change from trench warfare. These patrols typically crossed the causeway from Vaux to Lodge Wood, passing their own post, and edged out toward Curlu seeking like-minded German patrols. Sluices on the Fargny causeway were demolished, as were poplars lining the routes. They usually returned via Frise to make contact with the French left. On moonlit nights up to a dozen owls watched the returning patrols from Vaux Wood.

The Germans held a similar post in the loop of the river, at the extreme end of a causeway at La Grenouillère, which in December had been reconnoitered by Second Lieutenant James R. Black. The previous August, Black had been commissioned from the ranks, and for his readiness in volunteering for patrols was awarded the DCM. On 3 January 1916, Black and six men attacked the post and thirty-three bombs (grenades)

Somme near Frise, William Geissler: 'Taken from the bridge, which at this time formed the linking up of the French and British armies. Bosche had their trenches on rising ground in distance'.

were lobbed into the enemy position. In this action Private Charles Gray Templeman, of Leith, was wounded and probably evacuated by barge. He had previously been wounded in April 1915 at St Julien, but was less fortunate on this occasion and in April died in hospital.

Next to the river at Fargny Mill was a chalk bluff called the Chapeau du Gendarme, after the cocked hats of Napoleon's police. The Germans held the summit but opposing listening posts on its side were 'less than 5 yards' apart 'almost like the mythical position where the British and Germans took it in turns to use the same loophole'.[55] The most extreme of these posts was called the Crow's Nest and could only be reached by ladders and ropes. This was large enough for a few men, who were switched out at night, but they had to lie still throughout the day, more for fear of falling out than from the attentions of the enemy.

Charles Templeman.

Further to the left was sap T11 with a listening post, and two days after the raid on La Grenouillère the Germans attacked it. They got round behind the post and threw in fifteen to twenty bombs, wounded two men and captured Private Thomas Rutherford, one of a number of men who worked for the biscuit firm McVitie's, who was subsequently imprisoned at Giessen. The Ninths in T12 opened fire and believed they hit one German. A German helmet was recovered and taken home on leave as a souvenir. This action of 4/5 January 1916 was also the night when Lieutenant Arthur Eaton RE, was decorated for reconnaissance behind enemy lines. He made to return by the Chapeau but hearing the fighting, continued on to the marshes and swam back to the Ninth's lines.

Thomas Rutherford.

Panorama from Vaux Wood, white with bombardment and digging of the chalk.

Fargny Mill and Chapeau du Gendarme beyond.

North from Moulin de Fargny, the trenches ran either side of a ravine and the conditions deteriorated markedly toward Maricourt. It was a 'mud bath with trimmings',[23] a desolate place, wading knee-deep in a water-filled trench, 'the war was a sort of sideline now – water and mud held our interest and activity'.[23] A company sergeant major of the 12th Gloucestershire Regiment, a newly arrived battalion, would probably have agreed after he became stuck in the soon infamous Somme mud, carrying a rum jar. He was sober when he got stuck, nevertheless the Ninth found enough left in the jar to reward them for rescuing him.

An unpleasant distraction was a 60-pounder trench mortar firing 'footballs on a shank'[23] from their position. After firing, the crew would 'clear' and the Germans instantly responded with artillery. One morning Jimmy Quinn was shaving when a whizz bang hit the parapet, he was completely deafened and his soap, razor and cup

German front line

Fargny Mill

Chapeau de Gendarme

Crucifix

vanished. Cleanliness was proving all too close to God, as at Armentières he had previously lost a new cake of Pears Soap to a sniper.

Christmas was quiet, though the men had plenty of orders of what to do if the Germans started to make friends. However, in contradiction of the commander-in-chief's orders, Jock Porteous danced in no man's land from the gun position at Fargny Mill, and 'Jerry waved back'.[5] Hogmanay certainly saw the line weakened by intoxicating substances, enlivened as it was with saved-up rum rations, the result summed up as 'I don't know where our bullets went that night!'[23] Johnny Black, known for singing Scots songs, was accidentally stepped on and 'Schank you, Scorporal'[2] was his barely recognisable response.

At Suzanne the 5th Division had an impressive set-up with a regimental canteen, recreation rooms and a picture house in the chateau, south of the town. Here the Ninth had their first experience of wartime cinema, and hanging candelabra tinkled in reply to gunfire. The 5th Division were generous with rum, food and equipment, so the men were 'in clover'.[23] They were, however, also within range of

Fargny Mill, Trench 10, Christmas 1915.

German artillery, and on one occasion were shelled with gas whilst under canvas.

The advent of a new light machine gun meant that the machine-gun sections of all battalions in the division were given a three-day course on the Lewis gun at Suzanne. In due course they handed over their four 'ancient, trusty, heavy, much-loved and frequently cursed Maxims and received new Lewis Guns in exchange'[23] but these 'developed all the faults and "stoppages"... whenever we set out to try them... I damned... the gun and Haig and the B.E.F. and likely enough the rest of creation too!'[23]

The weapon refused to more than 'cough' when Quinn was told to demonstrate it to the battalion's officers. A new return spring sorted it out and David Kydd, the MG Officer, took Quinn back to the billets, but instead of a dressing down he was offered a drink and that was that. A new lad to the section received burns to his face as the cartridge cases were ejected to the right, rather than in front as with the Maxim. Unfeelingly, the section thought this rather funny. A reorganisation later distributed the Machine Gun Section amongst the companies, so that they had a two-gun section apiece. At this time the Machine Gun Corps (MGC) was being formed and they were given the choice of transferring. In a single batch, thirteen men left the MG Section to join the new corps on 3 June 1916.

Jim Elliot claims to have been trained on a Lewis gun near St Omer in early 1915 and goes as far as to say that he and an 'old sweat' were standing by it when they were inspected by no lesser personages than Kitchener and Asquith. Kitchener said to Asquith: '"No damned good!" Even the great make mistakes but I remember wondering at the time, did he mean the gun or my half-section or me?'[2] The 13kg (28lb) Lewis gun was certainly heavier than an SMLE at 4kg (9lb), but was mobile enough for sections to carry it forward, to enfilade the enemy and to consolidate captured positions. The German response was to lighten their Maxim, the *Maschinengewehr* 08 *Spandau*, to make the *null-acht fuffzehn* MG 08/15 at 21kg (46lb) including water.

Shaving with bayonets...perhaps.

Suzanne Chateau.

The Ninth were only a short time with the 5th Division as the brigade was transferred to the 32nd Division. On departing on 11 January 1916 the whole battalion gathered at Suzanne chateau when 5.9s 'started bumping'[23] the village. Of the thirty to forty shells, one fell into the chateau courtyard and one just outside. The courtyard and village green were littered with dead mules, smashed limbers and injured men from the incoming and outgoing battalions.

Two were killed: Willie Caldwell, a bricklayer from Redford who had just returned from leave, was killed outright by shrapnel and Eddie Grenville's leg was nearly severed at the knee and he died that evening. The Transport officer, big Bob Menzies, an accountant, was carried into the cellar of the chateau; he met Jim Elliot at the Caledonian station in 1917 and thanked him for taking him to safety. Jock Dowie received the first of his four wounds and was so 'broken up' by the death of Caldwell he was never the same again. Poor Tam Muir, a fruiterer from Leith and in his forties, was found sobbing behind a tree by Jim Elliot. 'One or two of the boys laughed at it, but honestly I saw no humour in it even though his bare hindquarters did present a ludicrous picture. I remember threatening anyone to relate it outside the section.'[2]

Robert Dudgeon, the popular adjutant, left on 12 January to become second in command of 16th Warwickshires. The Ninth rejoined Third Army, but for their only time in the BEF they were Army Troops and not a front line unit. This made it, for a month, the safest part of the war. As Army Troops the battalion was split into detachments, many under Royal Engineer supervision, and some had it easy, 'grooms without horses',[23] while others had long and back-breaking work unloading trains, such as at the railway siding between Arras and St Pol, without 'even the risk or excitement of shells'.[23] Still, there were jaunts to Amiens and lots of apples lying in orchards to be stewed. Henry Kiely, however, had a difficult month; his testicles were replaced in his scrotum at a Casualty Clearing Station.

Chapter 4

Highland Division
1916

ON 29 February 1916, an advance party of 100 men of the Ninth joined a brigade on the line of march to Mirvaux. This was 154 Brigade of the 51ˢᵗ (Highland) Division, a Territorial Force division. They were to remain from 1 March 1916 until 1918, during which time the division gained an enviable reputation for tenacity. The Highland Division, with their HD badges, had been labelled 'Harper's Duds', (after General Officer Commanding George Montague 'Uncle' Harper) having been hastily made up from various units and rushed to the Western Front in an undertrained condition. In 1916 they were intent on disproving this and worked tirelessly at new tactics that were key to the success of the division in the days and months ahead.

The division was the principal formation in all armies, an independent fighting formation, on the principle of a *corps d'armée*, with infantry, artillery and communications of its own, plus field ambulances, logistics, trench mortar batteries and machine-gun companies, numbering almost 19,000 men.

Table 7. Infantry Brigades of the 51ˢᵗ Division (at the Somme)

51ˢᵗ (Highland) Division		
Major General George Montague Harper		
152 Brigade	**153 Brigade**	**154 Brigade**
Brigadier General HP Burn	*Brigadier General AT Beckwith*	*Brigadier General CE Stewart*
1/5 Seaforth Highlanders	1/6 Black Watch	1/9 Royal Scots
1/6 Seaforth Highlanders	1/7 Black Watch	1/4 Seaforths
1/6 Gordon Highlanders	1/5 Gordons	1/4 Gordons
1/8 Argyll and Sutherland Highlanders	1/7 Gordons	1/7 Argylls
1/8 Royal Scots (Pioneers)		

A significant change was the replacement of the battalion's commanding officer. Lieutenant Colonel Alexander Blair was appointed Commandant at Abancourt, which he described as 'a big supply depot',[26] in April 1916. Though Abancourt before and

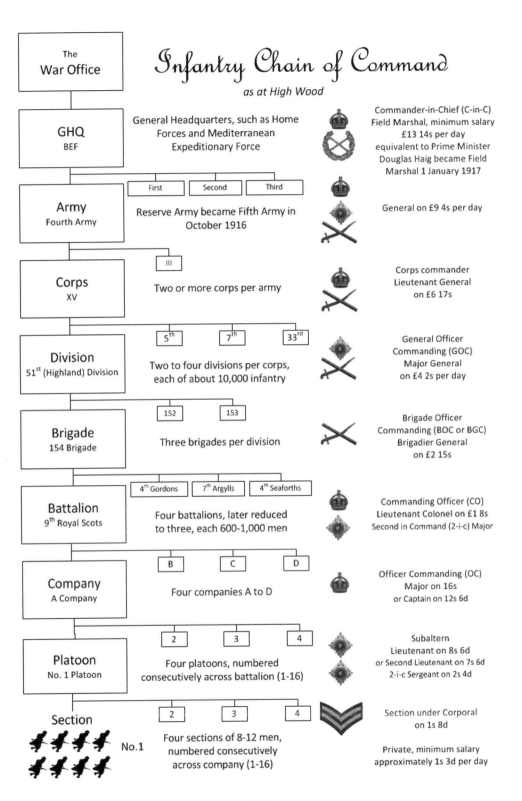

Infantry Chain of Command
as at High Wood

The War Office		
GHQ BEF	General Headquarters, such as Home Forces and Mediterranean Expeditionary Force	Commander-in-Chief (C-in-C) Field Marshal, minimum salary £13 14s per day equivalent to Prime Minister Douglas Haig became Field Marshal 1 January 1917
Army Fourth Army	First Second Third — Reserve Army became Fifth Army in October 1916	General on £9 4s per day
Corps XV	III — Two or more corps per army	Corps commander Lieutenant General on £6 17s
Division 51st (Highland) Division	5th 7th 33rd — Two to four divisions per corps, each of about 10,000 infantry	General Officer Commanding (GOC) Major General on £4 2s per day
Brigade 154 Brigade	152 153 — Three brigades per division	Brigade Officer Commanding (BOC or BGC) Brigadier General on £2 15s
Battalion 9th Royal Scots	4th Gordons 7th Argylls 4th Seaforths — Four battalions, later reduced to three, each 600-1,000 men	Commanding Officer (CO) Lieutenant Colonel on £1 8s Second in Command (2-i-c) Major
Company A Company	B C D — Four companies A to D	Officer Commanding (OC) Major on 16s or Captain on 12s 6d
Platoon No. 1 Platoon	2 3 4 — Four platoons, numbered consecutively across battalion (1-16)	Subaltern Lieutenant on 8s 6d or Second Lieutenant on 7s 6d 2-i-c Sergeant on 2s 4d
Section	2 3 4 — No.1 — Four sections of 8-12 men, numbered consecutively across company (1-16)	Section under Corporal on 1s 8d Private, minimum salary approximately 1s 3d per day

after was a minor stop, it had become a vitally important hub of the southern line of communication sending out over a thousand railway wagons a day to provide for over a million men. An Advanced Supply Depot responsible for rations, ammunition and engineers' stores, it connected the BEF to Le Havre and Rouen and hence home, and required a huge effort of organisation. Blair regretted 'that though he still remains on the 9th's roll, he will be, in future, merely a name to them. His personal interest, he says, will always be with them, and his prayers for their safety and good luck.'[26] Blair was described by the Earl of Haddington as a good soldier, with a record of proficiency, a good sportsman, who knew how to play the game and thirdly a good business man.

The relationship between the colonel and Bennet Clark, does not appear the most harmonious. BC was critical that even under fire in Flanders, 'More fuss was made in Edinburgh "standing by" with the Germans a hundred miles away than here with them one hundred yards away.'[16] He thought of any temporary absence of the CO as a holiday, 'We are enjoying ourselves with Jimmy Ferguson as CO. Although I expect our fellow... to be back tomorrow.'[16] In the hotspot of Sanctuary Wood he complained that the colonel and adjutant were never seen, but became daily visitors at quieter Armentières, prompting a final brush-out of the trenches before 11am. In May 1915 BC believed his seniority made him due his captaincy and he was still frustrated in July at not yet having his third pip, when he went home on health grounds. He had an argument too with Murrayfield Golf Club, insisting they repay his membership, which they did. In contrast Private J. Ferguson, pigeon fancier, had his fees paid for him at the ornithological society and his birds looked after.

Lieutenant Colonel Percy Westmorland held the command for a few weeks until he left to command 151 Brigade, at which point his second in command was promoted to the colonelcy. Major William Green, Black Watch, former adjutant of the battalion, became the commanding officer, one of those officers 'almost worshipped by

William Green.

their men'.[33] Green had served in South Africa and in France since August 1914, alongside Blair's son, and he had already been wounded twice. Jimmy Quinn describes the new CO:

'As a fighting soldier he was first-rate with 'Efficiency' as his watchword; a dead Jerry his greatest delight. The whole battalion improved greatly when he took over... The war had ceased to be a joke to us now and we were much more serious in our outlook. Of course, the part of the line we held was not conducive to gaiety.'[23]

The Labyrinth

> *'What Labyrinthine dug-outs too,*
> *Ye're making in oor kilts the noo'*[57]
> 'To a Louse' by an unnamed Ninth

ON 1 March the division received orders to take over a part of the line north of Arras from the French, who were becoming increasingly committed in the battle for Verdun. The French Tenth Army was removed from the line and the British Third Army extended north and the First Army south, meeting near Vimy. Soon afterward 51st Division transferred from First Army to XVII Corps, Third Army; 154 Brigade replaced the French 46 Brigade, 23rd Division about 1,200 yards in front of Ecurie and a New Zealand Tunnelling Company took over from their French counterparts (Map XIV).

The maze of trenches astride the Lens road had been called by the French the *Labyrinthe* and lay between Roclincourt and Neuville-Saint-Vaast. Major Frederick Bewsher, 51st Division historian, writes that the sector 'was overlooked by the enemy in an astonishing degree'.[51] The German trenches were between 25 and 200 yards distant, with saps almost within bombing distance. Some even connected the Allied and German lines such that some lost working parties were taken prisoner. There was continual patrolling up to the enemy's wire at night and much work was undertaken to improve the condition of the trenches, the parapets not being bulletproof and there being no traverses. Indeed, a new main line was dug approximately along the line of the French support line and was duly withdrawn to. In some places the men were wading up to their hips in muddy water, so gum-boots were discarded and they instead resorted to wagon grease as a preventative to trench foot.

Many French trench names were left on signs. The names *Boyau Fantôme*, anglicised as far as necessary to Avenue Fantome, and *Rue de le Morgue* were soon appreciated when French dead started to emerge from the parapet. A spade could not be used for long without uncovering more and the Lewis gun sections found plenty when seeking gun positions away from the trenches. Rows of dead also lay out in the open to the obvious interest of the rats. Ernst Jünger, German officer and author, also observed that the French lived in close proximity to their dead. The Ninth lost Harold Hampson to a sniper on their first morning. The Royal Engineers, meanwhile were busy placing dummy figures mounted on frames in Bonnal Trench and Saphead 22.

With dug-outs in short supply, men from incoming companies were sometimes able to 'wangle' a place in exchange for a tin of cigarettes. Anderson felt these provided 'moral'[28] security, but would not offer any protection to a direct hit. However, the alternative was sleeping on the firestep.

Into the disorientating Labyrinth returned BC, now a supernumerary captain in his old company:

'I arrived in the end and found the place very different from what I was accustomed to in the north. We live literally inside the earth, it seems as if a little digging would bring us outside at the other side of the world... one has to be careful not to get lost. I was doing a wander round today and time after time got mixed up, it is difficult to keep a sense of direction.'[16]

His 'wonderful little dug-out', he supposed, had not long before been occupied by Huns, and required candles day and night. However, it was not only the precariousness of trench life that occupied him:

'I still occupy an indefinite position. The Coy is commanded by young [PJ] Blair who is of course my junior by a long way… Have an idea I am not to get command of this one, nothing for some time unless something unforeseen happens.'[16]

A typical tour consisted of eighteen days in the line, six each in front, support (Écurie) and reserve (Étrun) lines. They might hope to get out once every two months on 'rest' (fatigues) as the brigade's reserve battalion. Any live and let live system such as found at Armentières or in the Somme valley, was swept away for one of offensive spirit in the 51st Division. They developed a reputation for being uncomfortable opponents, and comparisons were made, which may not have been received favourably, with the Prussians. The German 4th Guard Division were on their left front and 1st Guard Reserve Division on their right front.

Big Jim Elliot won Third Army's bayonet fighting competition, against 240 other NCOs. He found this particularly amusing, because as a machine gunner he had not carried a rifle for eighteen months. Colonel Green was pleased, saying that Elliot had shown the Army what the *Dandy Ninth* could do. He was seconded from the MG Section because 'Pat Taylor thought I was the biggest fool,' he was promoted 'Sergeant in charge of No Man's Land'[2] attached to C Company and spent his nights crawling about saps and listening posts, following orders which came direct from the adjutant. On one occasion, Elliot claims, he was tasked with taking a man through the lines to Thélus; this man was a spy with a Cambridge MA. On another occasion about the end of May 1916:

'I was nearly scuppered one night… three Jerrys and I met near their wire, and I fought like a devil and used my '*tatie champer*'[club] to the best advantage, and dragged their Sergeant very dead into the line of the 7th Gordons.'

For this he was sent down to see Brigadier General Charles Stewart:

Stewart: Why did you bring in a dead Hun?
Elliot (stuttering badly): I killed him between the wires and thought I would see if I could get a 'souvenir'.
Stewart: Ah! Ever thought of taking a commission?
Elliot: No Sir!
Stewart: Do you want one?
Elliot: No Sir!
Stewart: Don't be a damned fool – here's your papers. Goodbye![2]

'Commissioned in the Field', he was given two cotton stars and told to report to the 7th Gordons. 'I walked back into the line, collected my pack, spoke to nobody and got along into the trenches on our left and reported to C.O. 7th Gordons and so finished my connection with the finest Battalion of infantry in France.'[2]

The brigadier general clearly favoured offensive spirit. In September he complained to Aymer Maxwell, now trench mortar officer, that he was not being aggressive enough, and the next day the brigadier was hoisted by a shell, possibly retaliatory, and killed.

A patrol on 17 May did some 'good work' on either side of the Lille road, twice firing on working parties and twice bombing trenches. On the evening of 3 June a German guardsman came over waving a white flag, but was killed by the Germans before he made it to the brigade's line. A fortnight later two deserters made it across, but one was wounded and died. In return an enemy raid captured a man on the night of 23/24 June. The divisional front was extended to the north on 21 May, leaving the brigade and battalion with greater frontages to cover.

The mining meant that there were frequent large explosions accompanied by enemy incursions. Every battalion was therefore required to have a platoon ready to consolidate craters. A Company occupied a German mine crater that seems to have gone off prematurely, but were soon bombed out by a German plane. A small mine in July, soon after the Ninth had been relieved, created a crater 30ft broad and 20ft deep and pushed the inhabitants out of their line.

Arthur Anderson, now a month with the battalion, describes such a German attack, but the date is difficult to determine. In the evening soldiers appeared through the smoke of a barrage, in places they were bunched up making good targets for steady firing from the front line and support line. However, the front line troops were forced to abandon their position and doubled back in the open to the support trenches, after which the division's artillery got the range of the front line and shelled it for two hours without dislodging the new occupants. A counter-attack went in at 10pm:

'It is still twilight when the signal is given and we go over the top, advancing across the open ground with difficulty, as two lines of trenches have to be 'jumped' by means of narrow bridges, which causes much congestion. Everyone is in the charge; stretcher-bearers, signallers and Lewis gunners, and we make our way blindly forward through a chaos of bursting shells and machine-gun bullets. It is only possible to see one's nearest neighbours in the smoke, the sense of direction is entirely lost, and there is an awful feeling of being very much alone.

The noise, which at first was deafening, is hardly noticed after a few minutes, shell splinters and bullets are practically ignored, and dead and wounded lying in the way are only looked upon with a sort of mild interest. The sole idea seems to be to keep on until something happens. It appears as though it would be impossible to get through such an inferno, but at last we reach the trench. The Germans have put up a stout resistance but we manage to get about sixty prisoners before they break away for their own lines.'[28]

The prisoners' rifles were pitched over the back of the trench, and the prisoners themselves were largely ignored as the recovered trench was put into a state of defence. Anderson thought them 'lucky devils'[28] for being out of the war. In daylight they were escorted back down the communication trench to St Catherine; they were talkative and confident Germany would soon win the war. On 3 May the Germans proudly displayed a board in their line reading 'Kut el Mara captured, 13,000 Englishmen made prisoners'.[1] The next month, after Jutland, the Ninth were assailed by a French newsboy shouting out two seemingly juxtaposed headlines – 'Good news for the British – Lord Kitchener Drowned.'[23]

Out on rest in ruined Marœuil, Arthur Anderson's section had billets in a mule stable. A rickety ladder brought them to a long, low room under tiles which jumped to the firing of a nearby howitzer battery, hardly helping to keep the place watertight, and it was infested with rats. The rats, they speculated, had come from all the surrounding destroyed buildings. They slept in the men's blankets or across their necks and trying to move them usually resulted in being bitten so they were left alone. One night the floor collapsed onto the mules below. One man, whom Anderson calls Henderson, had his face split open by a kicking mule, and others suffered broken bones. An officer had to shoot a dozen of the mules who were badly injured. In the cold light of day, the bruised men had another problem, in that all of their kit was suspended from nails in the rafters 20ft above them, but a long ladder was eventually found. Henderson later died of his wounds.

The whole of the Scarpe valley was under direct observation by German balloons. Arthur Anderson describes the 'fine view' from the wood above Bray where he could count eleven balloons behind Vimy Ridge:

'The whole of the Ridge lay in front with Mont St Eloy rising abruptly on our left. In the valley the network of the Labyrinth was spread out like a map with the German trenches beyond, whilst five miles down the valley to the south, Arras could be made out faintly in the haze. Most striking feature of all perhaps was the desolate, bare appearance of the battle lines gradually giving place to trees and green fields in the back areas.'[28]

Near Ransart, Ernst Jünger too looked out on Arras and St Eloy [Eloi], but from the south:

'The tightly woven web of trenches spread its little white and yellow links, secured by lengthy communication trenches. From time to time, there was a puff of smoke from a shell, lobbed into the air as if by a ghostly hand; or the ball of a shrapnel hung over the wasteland like a great white flake slowly melting.'[58]

Men could get a lift to Mont St Eloy by lorry but from there, on foot now, were split into threes and fours to make their way along the overlooked roads. Here the landscape changed dramatically as they passed into desolation, the roads lined with but the stumps of trees until eventually they made battalion headquarters up the valley at Étrun. However, even here a French estaminet was prepared to run the risks and sell *bière* to the British, albeit at an extortionate one franc for a small glass.

A cinema on the Anzin road was also under observation and therefore the queue was behind a wall on the other side of the road and men hurried across two or three at a time to the pay box. The best part of the show was always the 'loud-voiced interpretations by the troops'.[28] Church parade was held in the open air in one of few fields hidden from the enemy. There were hard frosts and John Wilson and 48-year-old William Carter suffocated from coke brazier fumes in reserve billets at Étrun with two others made seriously ill. Even in late spring, swimming in the River Gy was very cold, but made a change from the irritation of lice, and the local washerwomen ignored them.

One fatigue duty was transporting supplies up to Anzin by pushing bogie trucks on the light railway. On the return journey the men would joy-ride downhill to Marœuil, hoping the brakes would scrub off enough speed for the corners. More typically they marched past the sawmill at Louez, where they were treated to the sight of hundreds of freshly made wooden crosses, and utterly ruined St Aubin to get to Anzin. Supplies were brought up to Anzin at night in very dense traffic, the horse harnesses muffled, the hooves deadened with sacking and the wheels with old motor tyres or else on a 'sea of mud... each motor transport that passes showers us from head to feet with brown slime'.[28]

Men in fatigue parties met the transport at Anzin and then bore the burden to Roclincourt along very long communication trenches. One of these, Boyau d'Anzin Montant, started grimly in Anzin graveyard and ran 2½ miles to the reserve trenches. These were often knee deep in thick mud, with submerged duckboards as likely to tip up as to provide firm footing. The chalk was sticky and made a terrible mess of everything, it was 'infinitely worse than ordinary mud'[28] and made everyone unrecognisable to each other. Repeatedly carrying 60lb (27kg) mortar bombs, one apiece, along these trenches was extremely tiring. Separate parties brought up ammunition from the cellars at Roclincourt every night, to carry them on to the trenches. This was especially hazardous under a full moon and crossing the Lens road was dangerous at any time as it was sporadically under fire. Anderson tells us the man in charge of the cellars, Old Watt, was over 60 and refused to leave the army. He had 'a spectacular end'[28] when a German shell detonated the ammunition dump, it burned for two days amidst showers of flares and coloured rockets.

A 'shock raid,' a trench raid without artillery support, was planned for C Company and, according to Anderson, everyone made it clear they did not want to be chosen. Colonel Green explained the raid in battalion headquarters by means of diagrams and maps to the three assembled parties involved, each of a subaltern, a sergeant, a corporal and five men, making twenty-four in total. The night before the raid the route through the wire was marked with tape, though crawling on their stomachs gave them no clue whatsoever as to the lie of the land. An anxious day followed waiting to be away at 10.40pm, before the moon came up. Dressed in slacks and puttees, their badges and identification handed over to the company sergeant major, some carried bombs, others rifles and bayonets and the sergeant and lieutenant, revolvers and bombs. Finally, they gathered in a saphead, had their rum and their officer, 'looking a bit scared',[28] passed word along to climb over the parapet. Following the tape as well as possible, for in places it had been wiped out, they regrouped at the British and German wire and prepared for the final dash.

Arthur Anderson wrote:

'I found myself in the German trench... and everything marvellously quiet. Lieutenant Gordon [probable pseudonym] with two men in the next bay got hold of a German sentry without any fuss and we just had time to throw a couple of bombs each down a dug-out before the whistle went for us to get back. The German was hustled over the parapet, and we all started on the way back with the sole object of reaching our own trench in the shortest possible time. Before we were half way across, the inferno commenced and the Germans began sweeping the place with rifle and machine-gun fire which seemed to come from every direction.'[28]

Anderson was 'mighty thankful' to get back, his rifle butt had been splintered by a bullet which had also torn his tunic. The whole raid lasted less than fifteen minutes and resulted in four German sentries captured, for a loss of three missing, probably dead, near the German line.

To disguise the fact that only one division held the corps front in May 1916, the kilt was not worn and trousers were issued instead. The workload entailed long stretches in the trenches and short rest periods, and so by the time the division moved they were thoroughly tired. Furthermore, the division to date had been largely on the defensive and had taken efforts to excel at their work. Now, with a minimum of preparation, they were to take part in a large-scale attack.

In mid-July, with the Battle of the Somme raging to the south, they marched to Chelers, the divisional band playing cheerily as the dusty column marched by. 'Well, we left the Labyrinth and all of a sudden became precious to Somebody who wanted us badly, and we had to hurry night and day to them.'[23] Over the course of a week by train, motor lorry, bus and foot they arrived at Mametz. The artist Francis Cadell wrote home:

'It is so funny to get on a London Bus here. Such strange and mixed sentiments crowd one's brain. Its placards, associations and memories. It's very small, seen so far away from its present surroundings. I could not but think of Piccadilly as I switchbacked along on damnable roads towards the firing line. So in the end the old Bus won – triumphed over its entourage and transported me for a very pleasant half hour to our old pre-war London.'[59]

The Somme – High Wood

'Should God spare me, this country will see me again. I want to hear wooden shoes clattering over its cobbles and see the avenues with the homeward bound workers in the evening and its 'estaminets' brilliantly lit and peopled with a noisy debating group such as only villages produce. Children and mothers at the doors or in the gardens. See it at daybreak, noon, evening and moonlight and you'll feel the peace of the country. May the day soon come when its ruins will be restored and its people return to it.'[42]

James Beatson, No.8 Platoon, killed in action 23 July 1916

THE Somme offensive, 1 July – 18 November 1916, is etched upon the collective memory of the nation. Intended as a joint Anglo-French battle with little to recommend it other than a convenient division of forces along the line of the river, it was necessitated by the need to save the French army from destruction as they were being bled white at Verdun. A particularly bloody obstacle was diamond-shaped High Wood (Bois des Fourcaux, Map XII), the highest point in Picardy, which lay at the apex of a Salient in the German second line. The 7th Division, and a famous cavalry action, had failed to take it on 14 July and the 33rd Division had failed there on 20 July.

At midday on Friday 21 July Harper's Highlanders were ordered into the line where so many had failed before them and the Ninth and 4th Gordons of 154 Brigade drew the short straw. Harper was convinced that a special bombardment by heavy artillery would be required to carry the objective, but his superiors believed the enemy were faltering and time was of the essence. However, by this stage Paul von Hindenburg, about to replace Erich von Falkenhayn as German Chief of Staff, saw the British command as resorting to nothing better than 'battering-ram tactics'.[60] It may also have been ordered, as Ewing concedes, to prevent enemy reinforcements being sent to Pozières. It might be noted that the 1st Australian

Relaxation at Fricourt – Jack Brebner and men of D Company.

Division were ordered, on 18 July, to take Pozières with a day's preparation, but after a fierce argument the attack was delayed until 23 July and was successful.

A prior lesson for the army had been the effect of losing too many officers and NCOs for a unit to continue efficiently, and so only twenty officers were with the battalion, eight in the attack. The 'stand-backs', typically 10 per cent of each rank, remained at the transport lines that moved to Bécordel. Overlooked by balloon, the approach from the south, nicknamed Happy Valley, was routinely shelled day and night and as a consequence made for an extremely dangerous route for advance, for supplies and for evacuating the wounded. A census of traffic, interrupted by gas shells, through Fricourt between 9.15am 21 July and 9am 22 July included: 26,536 troops, 63 guns, 568 motor cars, 95 buses, 3,756 horse-drawn wagons, 5,404 horses (riding), 330 motor ambulances and 1,043 cycles.

The Ninth came through on the evening of 21 July and placed A and D Companies into the line.

'As we plodded up the dusty road to Fricourt we passed a battery of howitzers firing and I, for the first time, noticed that the shell is visible as a black blur when it leaves the gun's mouth. Next we passed the old front line trenches now all crumbling and ruined by bombardment with torn and twisted barbed wire entanglements still standing between. Of Fricourt village nothing remained but heaps of ruined bricks and rubble. We were now in what had been since 1914 German territory and looked around us with strange feelings.[61]

There was one particular place just before we got to High Wood which was a crossroads, and it was really hell there, they shelled it like anything, you couldn't get past it, it was almost impossible. There were men everywhere, heaps of men, not one or two men, but heaps of men everywhere, all dead...[56]

Expecting every minute to be blown to atoms, with shells bursting all round and on every side, we continued our rapid advance and at length with a sigh of heartfelt relief found ourselves beyond the barrage near the comparative safety of our fire trench. This was a shallow ditch at the foot of the banking of a sunken road broken down by shell fire in which crouched the survivors of the preceding division whom we were to relieve.

We filed along the trench exchanging whispered questions and answers from which we discovered our predecessors were Worcesters and that they had made an unsuccessful attempt to occupy High Wood and had suffered terrible losses. Then they disappeared in the darkness and left us to settle down in our new position.'[61]

Thus when the sun came up on 22 July 1916 the Ninth could see for the first time the ground ahead of them. Their position lay between the windmill and crucifix corner. There had been waist-high corn rising up to the ridgeline ahead earlier in the month, before the attentions of artillery from both sides. Now the shell holes had begun to merge into each other. Air reconnaissance during the day identified a trench half-way between the Switch Line and the British, called Intermediate Trench; it was observed to be 'full of men'. It became the first objective of 19th Division, on the left, but the information does not seem to have been passed to the Ninth.

To the right of 154 Brigade, 5th Division were to assault Wood Lane. The brigade objective was High Wood itself, up to the northern edges of the diamond, and the connected Switch Line trench for 600 yards to the north-west on the reverse slope. Hard fighting had previously pushed the enemy out of the southern corner of the wood, though they occupied an exceptionally strong position, a redoubt, on the eastern corner. The 4th Gordons were to occupy the wood, with a preliminary attack on the redoubt at 10pm on 22 July. The Ninth, on the far left of XV Corps, in a two-company attack were expected to work up the west of the wood and up a shallow valley to take the immensely strong Switch Line, almost a mile distant. There was no time in which to study the ground and enemy dispositions as this would have required patrols by night.

They spent the day deepening the shallow front line trench of joined-up posts dug by the previous occupants. B and C companies were to make the attack and readied themselves at the south-west edge of Bazentin-le-Grand Wood. The men stowed their remaining rations and prepared their kit, including rifle, bayonet, 120 rounds of ammunition, haversack, waterproof sheet, mess tin, cleaning kit, entrenching tool and steel helmet. Helmets were issued extensively in the spring of 1916 and reduced the average rate of head wounds to less than a quarter, 'It is not a thing of beauty,' remarked BC, 'but gives one a great sense of security.'[16] Captain Robert Ross, 7th Gordon Highlanders, was in Happy Valley with his brigade in reserve and observed men sheltered in 'precarious recesses among the tangle of roots'.[62] As Ross wryly remarks, the artillery were *ubique*.

Bazentin-le-Petit.

The inimitable Bill Hay gives his views in these well-known quotes:

'That was a stupid action, because we had to make a frontal attack on bristling German guns and there was no shelter at all. ... You were between the devil and the deep blue sea. If you go forward, you'll likely be shot. If you go back, you'll be court martialled and shot. So what the hell do you do? What can you do? You just go forward, because the only bloke you can get your knife into is the bloke you're facing. There were dead bodies all over the place where previous battalions and regiments had taken part in previous attacks. What a bashing we got... Even before we went over, we knew this was death. We just couldn't take High Wood against machine-guns. It was ridiculous. There was no need for it. It was just absolute slaughter.'[46]

It was a stupid attack because it was made across open ground from these trenches, a thousand yards nearly to go, some sections had to do that, under heavy machine-gun fire, completely uncovered... There's a relationship that you have with your officers, in the Territorials particularly, where the lieutenants and up to captain, even up to major you were on terms of Christian name familiarity, because we knew each other in civilian life. So you're talking to these people and these men went into action with you, what happened above in Brigade Headquarters and above there, an ordinary soldier has no idea what's happening because he's only moving flags.'[56]

The preliminary bombardment began at 7pm and 'undoubtedly put the enemy on his guard'[43] ahead of a moonless night. The two assault companies came up at 10pm over ground pitted with shell holes and under counter bombardment. 'When we reached the road at Bazentin village we turned left and moved up the road. We were in extended order right up that road and, oh, the German guns were knocking us down wholesale and the same with these machine guns.'[46]

B Company on the right, under Major Jimmy Ferguson, and C Company to the left, under Major Dick Moncrieff, lay on the road behind the trench with shells falling and waited for the off. They were to go over in four waves on a platoon front. The British had made no attempt at surprise: the bombardment, the earlier attacks on the flanks by the 19th and 5th divisions, then the redoubt was attacked and finally at 1.30am on 23 July, the British artillery lifted, the brigade went over and 'suffered accordingly'.[43]

The Gordons' attacks on the redoubt and in the wood were completely defeated with heavy losses, facing very heavy going in the wood and uncut wire. This meant the Ninth could still be swept with fire from the east. At the whistle and immediately after No.6 Platoon had been directly hit, they went 'over the top'.[61] The companies were immediately exposed to shot and shell and soon lost touch.

David Watson's section in B Company ran down the slope to the dip for a few minutes rest:

'We were to form up about fifty yards from High Wood to rush it. The corporal and three of us, three privates, we reached the fifty yards spot, but no order came to charge the wood. The corporal decided to go and see what had happened but we saw him knocked down about fifty yards from us. And he had given us an order, "Don't move from where ye are until I get back." But we couldn't move because we were pinned down with machine-gun fire. Bullets were flying all roads and men were dropping on each side. In fact, I saw Sergeant [Dugald Thompson] who was badly wounded being helped by a lance corporal who had gone down on one knee and had the sergeant sitting up against him, and a big shell splinter came across and sliced the sergeant's head off. That poor corporal, he was nearly demented. He was inches away from him.'[46]

The German 165th Regiment at High Wood observed that 'all at once the curtain of a deadly barrage descended in front of our entire position, cutting down the enemy by whole ranks… But the British are persistent! Again and again they attacked… in some places as much as four or five times over. Everywhere they failed, and not a single one of the British reached our regimental positions.'[63]

C Company ascended the open slope under shell fire when unexpectedly flares went up from the left. They came under close-range machine-gun fire from the well-wired Intermediate Trench, manned by II and III Battalion 93rd Regiment. Their objective was still half a mile onward, with machine guns to the right, to the left and in front of them.

Major Dick Moncrieff was advancing with Corporal Andrew Blyth's No.11 Platoon in the third wave, when shell fragments hit him in the neck, shoulder, face and hand. He fell into a shell hole, managed to stand in order to see the progress of his company but lost consciousness. Blyth continued until he received gun shot wounds (GSW) to both legs and became a prisoner of war.

Jock Dowie carried one of the B Company Lewis guns in the second wave, and Jimmy Quinn the two panniers of drums:

'The whistle went and it was '*Up and over*,' and then began one flaming nightmare. Everyone was loaded to the limit and at best we could only walk, and slowly at that… Of course, before we were any distance a barrage blasted through us and Dowie, who had my gun, cried out… It felt like a kick, he said, but 'no blood', so we carried on… M.G. fire caught us and we had to dodge about. Soon we heard rifle shooting from the first wave and then bombs. Ahead of us we could see our fellows near what we took for the Jerry trench – there was wire though – this I was told later – and no opening – in spite of the shelling. Some of our wounded came back and as I was near Ellis, the C.S.M., I learned how things were – a '*fizzle*'.[23]

Gordon Ellis, Company Sergeant Major of B Company, known as the 'Sairgint', went forward saying he would call for the Lewis guns, but was wounded soon after and carried away. The runners were constantly out in the heavy shelling, trying in vain to keep communications open. Having lain in the open for a while, Sergeant Hugh Oliver came back saying all the officers and most of the NCOs were gone and that he was rounding up all the men he could find to make their way back. David Watson was also thinking about getting back:

135

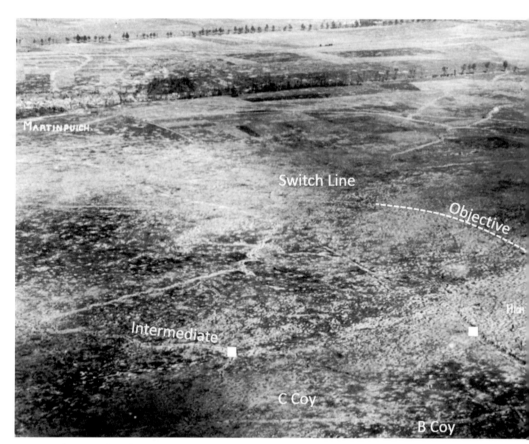

Looking north with High Wood (right) and Martinpuich (left), September 1916.

'One lad lost patience with the strain of waiting, just got up on to his feet and ran away and he went down. He was hit. You saw the flashes coming out of the machine guns, pointing directly at us. They knew where we were but hit everything bar the two of us. We could hear the bullets going into the ground in front, behind and at the side. Just never seemed to get us. We decided the best way was just to lie still because it was level ground and the bullets were whizzing over and hitting the earth all round about us.'[46]

This may have been the action when Corporal Thomas Sumner's platoon commander, in C Company, was wounded near the enemy trench and he brought him in. Sumner died of wounds on 6 August. John Turnbull, wounded in the leg, took shelter in a shell hole that was later seen to be hit by another shell, probably accounting for his disappearance.

Meanwhile for Dick Moncrieff 'everything remained a blank till he realised that he was digging furiously with an entrenching tool in a shell-hole'[33] with three men from B Company. He must have staggered about half-a-mile from where he had been wounded, diagonally across the battlefield, and was now, about 2am, only 30 yards from a German sap. Under the illumination of flares, 'Boche snipers were potting

136

vigorously at the semi-fortified shell-hole.'[33] The four of them waited for the Germans to stop sending up flares and then crawled out fan-wise back to their own lines. Corporal Alexander Baxter failed to make it; hit in the belly, he was taken prisoner. Moncrieff received another injury, a bullet to his elbow, before he reached safety.

Most of the survivors were back in the British trenches by 3am where A and D companies, in defence, had also been mauled in the shelling. Alexander MacPherson described the aftermath:

'Dawn was now breaking and as the light strengthened we could see stragglers of the attacking companies coming in through the wrecked barbed wire and across the waste land now pitted with shells and strewn with bodies... The dead had to be stripped of valuables (pocket books, rings, watches, etc.) kept for sending home later, and then were carried in waterproof sheets across the road, placed in shell holes and covered with loose earth. This makeshift burial performed, rude crosses made of pieces of ration boxes with the name, number and regiment of the dead soldier, were erected to mark the place. Though the burial was carried out without any service or spoken prayer, nevertheless the uncertainty of life will be more strongly felt in such circumstances than with all the pomp and ritual of a Church Service.'[61]

It took David Watson two hours to make it back to the assembly trench. They made it into the dip of the valley and to the crucifix at the crossroads, then along the road to Mametz Wood before climbing the hill behind Bazentin Wood to their starting position. 'Of the 232 of us who went up, only 11 came back. I was the ninth of those 11. The wood was lined with German machine guns... Yes, I suppose I do feel bitter about that.'[64]

In the evening the Ninth retired to the east of Mametz Wood. Lieutenant Andrew Nicoll, formerly the MG sergeant, directed his gun sections to 'souvenir' some stray mules to pull their barrows, but the brigadier put a stop to it and they had to continue man-hauling their heavy loads. Dowie and Quinn slept in a howitzer gun pit as the only bit of shelter they could find, but were kicked out when the crew had to get to work. That night gas shells meant they slept with gas masks on.

On 24 July Captain Rowbotham, Sergeant Bill Hay and three men marked out the line of a trench with white tape in broad daylight from High Wood to the windmill, and were astounded that they were not fired upon, Hay concluding that the enemy were biding their time. That night 8th Royal Scots (Pioneers) started to dig the trench.

The battalion only moved on to relative safety on 26 July at Bécordel. What remained of the Ninth, 'a shadow of its former self,'[46] were led out by a piper playing *The Flowers of the Forest*.

A draft of 105 other ranks was brought in from nineteen different battalions on 28 July in an attempt to maintain effectiveness, and in early August officers were attached from various battalions of the Royal Scots to fill the vacated posts, whilst others were promoted. The battalion's strength was 21 officers and 645 other ranks.

At High Wood it was next the turn of 153 Brigade who were also badly handled. Finally, Brigadier General Pelham Burn's 152 Brigade were in the line intent on a siege tactic: they successfully 'jumped' a trench 200 yards forward, digging in overnight 3/4 August and suffering no loss. The Ninth were in support trenches in Mametz Wood at the time and supplied carrying parties for the attacking brigade; 154 Brigade also dug a new communication trench up to High Wood whilst being shelled.

The Royal Army Medical Corps were forced to use horse-drawn ambulance wagons from the Quarry Collecting Post in Happy Valley due to the badly shelled road at 'Death Corner', near Mametz. Colonel David Rorie RAMC tells us of one wagon overturned in a shell hole, with wounded on board in a valley full of gas, and how, unsurprisingly, few had time to help. Having got their wounded away in relays in another wagon, they eventually righted their own with twelve horses, all the time under shellfire.

B Company commander, 30-year-old Major James Ferguson junior, son of the old colonel, was wounded, missing and never found. It is possible that a cigarette case found recently in the east of High Wood was his. Second Lieutenant Robert Gibson, also of B Company, was also missing. Gibson, a joiner, was a battalion original. He had been at Windsor in 1909 for the Colours and came out on the transport ship *Inventor* as No.98 company sergeant major. Commissioned in November 1915, he returned to the battalion as a junior officer on 6 June, aged 39, and within seven weeks was dead. Sergeant Herbert Eagar was also killed; born in Hong Kong he had been orphaned and joined the Ninth around 1910.

The casualty estimate at the time was 11 officers (9 wounded, 2 killed) and 142 ORs (89 wounded, 46 missing, 7 killed). Although the number of missing decreased, the death toll for the day eventually rose to 40. Further casualties accumulated to 224 by 28 July.

Among the survivors were Arthur Anderson, hit by a machine-gun ricochet and who celebrated his twentieth birthday at the Casualty Clearing Station (CCS). Andrew 'Bally' Ballingall, wounded, had been a private in the Ninth in 1914, commissioned, fought in Egypt and returned to his old battalion on 5 July as a lieutenant of C Company. William Macaulay of D Company was wounded in the chest, hand and left leg by a shell. Having had his leg amputated, he made it to Aberdeen by ambulance train on 11 August and his stump was promptly operated on but he died of a secondary haemorrhage.

Lieutenants Hew and North Wardrop were sons of Major James Wardrop. Both had been commissioned from the rank of private in October 1914 and both became casualties at High Wood. North joined for duty on 6 July 1916, and on 25 July he was reported a casualty of shell shock. Modern wars have found Post Traumatic Stress Disorder rates of 10-18 per cent, with higher levels found after multiple tours and when separated from the parent unit.

Robert Purves, a law clerk from Prestonpans, had joined the Ninth in early 1916, but on being sent to France in July he was separated from his battalion and transferred to the 5/6th Cameronians (Scottish Rifles), an unusual figure in his kilt. At Fricourt

Wood, early on the morning of 29 August, he wrote in his paybook: 'I have shot myself as I cannot stand the hardship & suffering of this life any longer, and there is no chance of getting home again to see my parents whom may God bless & comfort in their trouble... Goodbye & good luck to everyone.' He fitted a lanyard to the trigger of his rifle, placed the muzzle in his mouth and shot himself through the head, dying shortly thereafter; his death was recorded as Killed in Action (self inflicted).

Nor was such a distressing course of action limited to the inexperienced thrown into war. James Kinna was a Scots-Manchester lad who was commissioned from a private in the Ninth into the Lancashire Fusiliers in January 1916. Soon after he was awarded the MC for his courage and cheerful example, but died in September 1917 of a self-inflicted wound.

As well as the wounded returned through British lines, about a dozen injured men fell into enemy hands. Among them was Sergeant Andrew Blyth No.975 C Company, who had led No.11 Platoon. He had been subject to court martial 'in the field' on 6 July 1916 under Section 40 of the Army Act, 'Conduct to prejudice of military discipline', and reduced to corporal, then at High Wood he was shot in both legs and was interned until April 1918. Both Allan Aitken and Henry Logan were wounded in the neck and taken to Göttingen. Aitken survived but Logan, a golf professional, must have remained critical for he died in January 1919 and was buried in Germany.

Private Andrew Lees, an apprentice engineer, who had been injured once before in May 1915, was severely wounded in the attack on High Wood. His captors reported his injury to the Red Cross as *Schädelfraktur*, skull fracture, he was also wounded in the shoulder and left hand. Lees was in Courtrai hospital for a couple of weeks but neither of his field postcards made it home to let his parents know he was alive. He was then taken on a two-day train journey

Göttingen Lazarett.

Andrew Lees.

to Göttingen Lazarett (hospital), where he was given a pair of trousers and a pair of wooden clogs.

At the end of October he was moved to Kassel. When interviewed on his treatment as a prisoner of war he described the conditions as satisfactory (abridged):

'We were lodged in wooden huts, about 200 French and English in a hut. I do not think there was any form of heating. The latrines were open troughs in a shed and were very evil-smelling; they were washed out once a week. The food in the camp was quite good. There was a canteen in the camp at which we could buy fruit and vegetables, &c., but everything was very expensive. Letters and parcels arrived regularly and the parcels were opened in our presence by a German N.C.O. Nothing was taken out of the parcels.

We were allowed to write four postcards and two letters a month. I have no complaint to make of my treatment in the camp. I was not long enough in Germany to notice any difference in treatment of prisoners. The guards were changed to older and older men and were reduced in number. When I first went to Cassel there was a sentry to every sentry box, but when I left there was only one sentry to every two sentry boxes.'[65]

Here he was examined by the Swiss Medical Commission and at the end of 1916, as part of a new scheme benefitting seriously wounded British and German combatants, he was moved via Konstanz to the mountain resort of Mürren in neutral Switzerland. He ceased to be a prisoner and became instead an internee. He was not the first Ninth in the country as William Ross, captured in 1915 at Armentières, was at Chateau d'Oex, in the first batch to cross to Switzerland in May 1916.

About 600 men were interned at Mürren and arrangements were even made for family members from Britain to visit them on two-week excursions. Although in far better circumstances, money was restricted as experience proved that boredom soon turned to alcohol excess. A bobsleigh run was cleared and caused a few injuries of its own. Lees was repatriated to the UK in March 1918 and admitted to the King George Hospital on Stamford Street, London.

The Reverend John Sclater arranged for parcels to be sent to all the prisoners. Each was 'adopted' by a lady at the Royal Scots Association who sent them a parcel fortnightly, but not weekly as hoped, for about 3/6. These parcels supported fourteen PoWs (one address unknown) in October 1916. William Ross wrote his thanks, saying he enjoyed the contents very much. Sclater, chaplain to the Ninth, was clearly a man who preached sacrifice:

'A sergeant in a base camp some time ago was returning to his unit after being wounded twice. He was, as we have it in Scotland, "fey". A presentiment was upon him that he would not come back; and to all optimistic prophecies he turned a deaf ear. "But," he said, "I don't mind. It's going to be a better world for the kiddies afterwards." What is this but religion in a very pure form?'[66]

'Our Interned Ski-Club Tour'.

On 7 August the 51st Division was finally relieved having suffered over 3,500 casualties, the Ninth's portion being some 300 and having failed to carry the enemy's positions.

A few days later Walter Schubert, German 134th Regiment, recorded at High Wood:

'A filthy stench of corruption lay over our position. There were dead, decayed Scots, and a skull with a helmet crowned the parapet. The shells buried the bodies, then ploughed them up again. Thousands of fat black flies.'[63]

The redoubt in High Wood was finally removed by a mine, dug at the suggestion of young 'Odyssian' Brigadier General Burn, and the wood was captured on 15 September after two months of bitter conflict that left the small area the last resting place of over 8,000 dead from both sides. It is difficult to see that the attack on 23 July had any realistic prospect of success. Against a strong position with uncut wire, they were reduced to mere *Kanonenfutter*; a wanton waste of men.

The Lys – Armentières encore une fois

ON the day following relief the division's troupe, the *Balmorals* gave an open-air tailgate performance with 'Stanley' and 'Gertie', attended by almost all of the infantry. In the middle of August the division moved north. The heat and the packed trains caused a number of men to fall out of the march from the station, though they were only permitted to ride in the horse ambulances with the written permission of the Medical Officer. They arrived once more in 'tranquil'[33] Armentières, where the Ninth already had experience. In fact, they were recognised by some inhabitants from the town and given a warm welcome, including the estaminet where Johnny Black had won his beer drinking contest, though by this time Black had been commissioned into the MGC.

The line was in a nearby sector and at Touquet was reported to run at right angles through an abandoned train which had been stationary for months. They took over breastworks from the 3rd New Zealand Brigade; the Ninth took over from the Auckland Battalion. Patrols were carried out by night, when the Germans used searchlights, with snipers lying out in no man's land through the day. Arthur Anderson was assigned the duties of a sniper in the breastwork, but these hardly employed his skills as a first-class marksman. The rifle was fixed to uprights and aimed at a point in the German line through a 3ft tube through the sandbags and covered by a piece of wet sacking to conceal the muzzle flash. He had but to cycle the action and pull the trigger.

The weather was good and the enemy quiet, except for machine guns at night, and it was 'described by the Jocks as bon'.[51] The most famous estaminet in the town, though still in range of enemy field guns, was the indomitable Lucienne's, who ran her restaurant in spite of the shelling.

> 'I grant you there were interludes,
> When life had somewhat cheerier moods,
> And memory calls up nights of song,
> And wine in merry Amiong,
> Where, o'er a bottle of Pomard,
> We swapped choice lies about the war;
> Some night, mayhap, we'd chanced to drop
> Into the famous oyster-shop,
> Kept by that lass, on profits keen,
> The dear tempestuous Josephine;
> Or else, when on another track,
> We supped with Marguerite at Acq,
> Where, in old billet thirty-seven,
> We gloried in a transient heaven
> Of omelettes and good pommes frîtes
> With drinks that warmed our hearts – and feet!
> Or, harking up the trail again,
> Our hostess next was Lucienne,
> That maiden famed of Armenteers
> Who did us all so well (Loud cheers.)'[36]

However, the town was shelled daily and inflicted some terrible injuries on the civilians who clung on to the place. Tom Mather from Congleton 'went west', hit in the head by shrapnel. One shell caused only sore heads by frightening the horses of a brewery dray, sending it away at a gallop and causing the driver to fall off. He chased after his charge as the double row of barrels rolled from it, and curious Anzacs and Jocks appeared from their billets. The drayman returned to find the street empty of soldiers and barrels. In September the troops were shown the film 'The Battle of the Somme' and a divisional horse show was held where the officers' jumping competition was won by the General Officer Commanding, 'who knew, or loved a horse better than

"Uncle" Harper?'[36] At this time of 'rest' the Ninth were supplying 200 men daily to the Royal Engineers as working parties.

A Company were in the right subsector, close to the north bank of the River Lys and north-east of Houplines, when Alec Wright and Johnston Hood were killed by a *minenwerfer* (trench mortar). In one account their dug-out was collapsed; in Bill Hay's recollection they were working their way on a long laden trek down a communication trench to company headquarters when a *minenwerfer* shell dropped nearby. Bill Hay ran down to check on his best mate, Wright, and found him lying at the side of the trench badly mutilated. Hood, he says, 'was blown to bits, his kilt was still hanging in the trees, bits of it, for weeks afterwards'. Hay promised Alec he would go to see his mother true to their 'boyhood pact' and Alec died soon thereafter.

'I went to my Captain, [Pat] Blair and asked for permission to go and put some flowers on his grave, and he said I couldn't go because we would be moving soon. So I ignored his remarks and I committed a terrible crime, I went and borrowed a Signals bike and cycled away and put some flowers on his grave. So I was Absent Without Leave in the face of the enemy.'[56]

Hay did not face a court martial but was transferred to C Company and lost his stripes. In Edinburgh on leave Hay told Alec's mother that he had been shot through the heart, which she did not at first believe but accepted. 'I was devastated,' remembered Hay, 'I lost my pal, I didn't care what happened to me then, whether I lived or died… even today I still remember Alec and wonder what he would be like if he lived as long as me.'[56]

From the beginning of September Lance Corporal Thomas Merrylees patrolled ceaselessly in preparation for a raid against a machine-gun emplacement. Merrylees had been working in Nigeria when war broke out and enlisted in April 1915. On 16 September the Ninth carried out what was considered a successful trench raid, though it met with heavy rifle fire from the enemy support line. The men had blackened faces, electric torches attached to their rifles and carried a number of bombs (grenades), and some wore Dayfield body-shields. To cut the wire they employed long, sometimes 75ft long, Bangalore torpedoes. Lieutenant Archibald Douglas was shot dead at the enemy parapet whilst leading this raid. Second Lieutenant Findlay Ross, born in Manchuria, was temporarily knocked unconscious but took over command, 'rallying his men he headed them in a wild charge into the trench and the garrison fled before them'.[33] At least three of the enemy were killed and one taken alive.

They were unable to take the machine gun off its mountings, so it was destroyed, and they recovered papers and equipment of the 156th Regiment. Douglas's body was brought back. The prisoner started to fight half-way back and was also brought in dead 'an interesting exhibit until morning'.[23] Stragglers were guided back through the night with the oft repeated password 'Marmalade'.[23] Merrylees was awarded the Military Medal for the determination he had displayed in the raid, and Findlay Ross the Military Cross. The cost was 1 officer killed, 1 wounded and 13 ORs wounded.

The Ancre – Beaumont Hamel

'Beaumont Hamel was the first occasion when the Highland Division was able to prove that, given a fair chance, it would certainly be successful against the enemy. Here was a fortress defended by every artifice of which the Boche was a past master...When I went to those Divisions that had attacked in order to try to get some tips, I was told, "You have not a dog's chance." '[36]

Major General Harper

AT the end of September the division was relieved by Australians and headed south again by train in preparation for an attack on Puisieux, subsequently cancelled. Instead the division's attention was directed toward the capture of Beaumont Hamel, the site of a village at the centre of an extremely well-defended system of trenches including many dug-outs, caves and tunnels, extensive wire and the infamous Y Ravine (*Leilung Schlucht*, map XIII). These positions had been 'assaulted in vain on 1st July'.[43] This northern part of the Somme offensive had barely budged and now the offensive was almost at its bitter end. The ensuing nineteen weeks of trench warfare had pushed the British line forward so that in some places no man's land had been halved to less than 250 yards. However, the unbreached enemy defences were recognisable, with, in addition the enormous crater on Hawthorn Ridge, blown by a mine on 1 July, now stoutly entrenched. Harper wrote:

'The Highland Division is about to undertake a most important but difficult task. The gallant deeds performed by the Division in the past inspire the General Officer Commanding with confidence for success in the coming engagement. He feels sure that every man will worthily uphold the traditions and honour of Scotland. He desires to convey to all officers and men his heartfelt wishes of good luck.'[1]

Orders came through on 23 October that the target was to be Beaumont Hamel with 'Z' day originally set for 25 October but subject to many delays. The Ninth were still gathering their strength after the trauma of High Wood, with a draft of 163 in mid-October. As such 154 Brigade formed the divisional reserve on the day of attack, though for a time they believed they would be in the thick of it. As part of the preparations, despite days of pouring rain, the Ninth carried out patrols and in the run up to the attack were patrolling most nights, one or two fights in no man's land winning Military Medals for the participants. Lewis guns were employed to prevent the enemy closing gaps in the wire, each gun firing 1,500-2,000 rounds a night. On 29 October they had found a 100 yard stretch of front line trench to be empty; but in early November it was well-defended.

A detailed trench raid was organised by Colonel Green for the night of 7/8 November. The objective was 'To inflict material damage on the enemy, capture as many prisoners as possible, and obtain identification marks.'[1] A box barrage would isolate part of the enemy system involving five artillery batteries, trench mortars (Toc Emmas in the phonetic alphabet in use at the time) and all of the division's machine-gun companies, lifting only over the area of the raid so as to cut the garrison off from support. A feint bombardment to the south was also included.

Commanded by Captain Alexander Taylor, who was in a forward dug-out, the raid was organised in three groups. One group was to hold a defensive line in no man's land with Lewis guns on the flanks. A second group was to enter the German front line and block it to the south. Then the third group would cross over to a communication trench, work along it and south along the front line, bombing any dug-outs and taking prisoners, until they rejoined the second group. The groups comprised Second Lieutenants James R. Black, Alex Moir, Ian MacLennan and fifty-two men. They were lightly equipped, dressed in shorts, with no identification of their own unit upon them. Their rifle, with wire-cutters attached, was to have one round in the chamber, nine in the magazine and they carried fifteen in their pocket, as well as up to six Mills bombs.

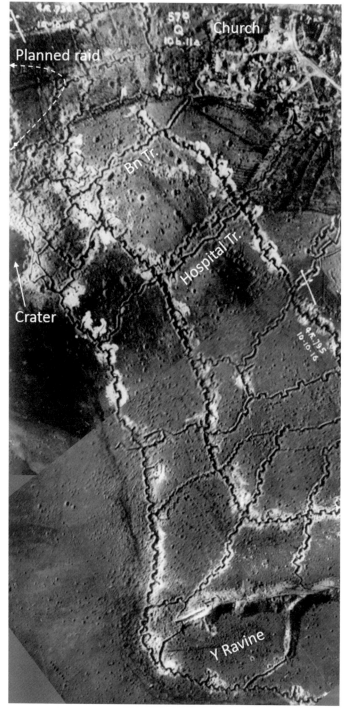

Runners went with the parties, and stretcher bearers were ready to cross no man's land. If captured, 'the man will have a concocted story to tell'.[1] It had rained all day

145

and the trenches were sloughing in. Bayonets were fixed and dulled and their faces, hands and knees were blackened.

They crept out at Zero minus ten minutes and waited for the barrage to lift. The artillery was described as excellent, allowing a party to approach within 25 yards of the German lines. At Zero hour, 5.45am, they got up and made a dash for it, but the ground was so cut-up they were up to their knees in mud. 'Consequently, the rush was an excruciatingly slow process'[1] and 5-10 yards from the German fire trench they came under attack from bombs and rifle volleys. Unable to move with any rapidity, several men were hit. The officers agreed the attack was hopeless and withdrew, once more struggling through the mud to regain their own lines. There was vigorous artillery retaliation onto the British lines. Five men had been wounded and two missing, and they had failed to get into the German trench at all. One of the missing, John Inch, was eventually reported as a prisoner of war wounded in the lower back. The Ninth relieved the 7th Argylls during the day but the trenches were in such a bad state after all the rain that some Argylls had to be dug out of the mud.

The preparation for the major attack was thorough. To deal with the fortified crater, a new 30,000lb (13.6 tonne) ammonal mine was prepared at the same site. In contrast to the partly obsolete and entirely inadequate artillery of 1914, the critical shortage of ammunition in 1915, and the rushed advance of guns at High Wood in 1916, dense and carefully planned artillery was available to V Corps which was to prove crucial to success. Wire cutting ammunition was 'unlimited', though the instantaneous fuze was not in widescale use until the following year. Identical bombardments were delivered daily so that the day of attack was not announced. There would be no preliminary bombardment, apart from the usual night firing, until at zero hour an intense barrage would begin as the infantry left their jumping-off positions.

The infantry were trained to creep within 50-60 yards of the barrage, with the warning that at 3,000 yards range one in a hundred shrapnel shells could be expected to burst 60 yards short. In training the barrage was marked merely by coloured flags. The infantry were also to employ Harper's 'leap-frog' system, each unit stopping at its objective to consolidate and 'mop-up' whilst the next, fresh wave passed through to a further objective. The first objective (Green Line) of the division was the far edge of the village and, due to the converging divisional boundaries, the second objective (Yellow Line) consisted of 2,000 yards of Frankfort/Frankfurt Trench between Leave Avenue and Glory Lane. As the reserve, the officers of 154 Brigade were instructed to acquaint themselves with the whole divisional front in case they were called upon to support the imminent attack.

The brigade dump had extensive stores laid in, including 200,000 rounds of small arms ammunition, 14,800 Mills No.5 hand grenades, 800 shovels, 2,400 emergency rations (bully beef, biscuits, jam, tea, sugar etc.), 20 gallons of rifle oil and 48 gallons of rum, plus four boxes of quicklime for the inevitable use of burial parties.

Orders were also issued to prepare concealment pits 16ft x 32ft and 6ft deep with ramps; it transpired these were for six tanks. Parts of communication trenches and support trenches were filled in to permit them to cross; yet orders specified: 'It should be impressed on Infantry that they <u>should on no account</u> wait for tanks.' Alexander Macpherson first saw tanks as they prepared to support the assault. 'On emerging from the trench we saw strange lights on the ground near Auchonvillers and on passing these found they came from chinks in the sides of the tanks.'[61] On the day of the attack they did not progress well in the mud, 'We could see the tanks still not far in front of the village slowly pushing forward over trenches and earthworks like snails.'[61]

Heavy rain delayed the attack in stages, often a day at a time, from 24 October until 13 November 1916 and with the uncertainty 'all ranks had passed through a time of great tension'.[43] Eventually the Ninth were relieved on 12 November by the attacking units. At six minutes before zero on 13 November the leading battalions moved clear of the British wire in only 30 yards of visibility due to fog. At zero hour, 5.45am, the Hawthorn Mine was detonated for a second time and the creeping barrage began, advancing at 100 yards over five minutes. In the front line the men of the German 12th Division had been kept safe by their deep dug-outs with 6-8m of overhead cover, but were too slow to stand-to and were immediately engaged in hand-to-hand fighting. The division fought on to the first objective. However, they were stopped before their further objectives; Munich and Frankfort Trenches remained in enemy hands.

Hamilton's 154 Brigade, as the reserve brigade, were in Mailly Wood, over 3 miles behind the front line and on a quarter-of-an-hour's notice. Just after noon the Ninth were ordered forward in support of the attack. Having assembled along the railway south of Auchonvillers ('Ocean Villas') station, in the afternoon Colonel Green was ordered to move two companies in support of 153 Brigade along St John's Road; the rest of the battalion followed at 6pm. The picture then becomes increasingly blurred. The Ninth were asked to despatch two companies to 152 Brigade but this was revoked. These overnight movements were not accomplished seamlessly as MacPherson recalls:

'Various rumours were afloat. One that we were going back to Auchonvillers; another that these two companies were for White City [a chalk face into which dug-outs were cut] Orders were passed up and down and great confusion prevailed. "Pass the word up if there are any of 10 Platoon in rear." "Is 'B' Company in front?" and so on. At last the order was given for the two companies to turn about and advance again [along Tipperary Avenue] to Brooke Street in our old front line and take up our quarters in dug-outs there. Luckily the shelling had died down though we could see its results by frequent miniature landslides of the parapet into the trench.

St John's Road, along which we had to pass, was particularly damaged and in the bottom of the trench was a ghastly reminder of the night before, i.e. what remained of a body of a man lying half buried on the duck-board. As we stepped over it our first thought was that above it on the parapet lay a German stretcher bearer with his stretcher, evidently killed while assisting in taking back our wounded. We hurriedly pressed on past these gruesome sights and, guided by our officer's runner, reached the old front line which showed little signs of bombardment but was in a bad state of mud and water.'[61]

Quinn explains that they were kept moving back and forth all night in the communication trench to limit the damage of the 5.9s. He only found in daylight that the 'bumpy corner'[23] was the dead man of the stretcher party. Early on 14 November, Captain George Deas Cowan's D Company worked along Tipperary Avenue, across no man's land and into the warren of trenches to support a half-battalion of 7th Argylls, arriving at 7am. He was probably short of a Lewis gun as MacPherson had decided that without specific orders he might as well wait up the communication trench. D Company were later joined by Pat Blair's A Company, reporting at 12.15pm and possibly moving to Beaumont Hamel.

The composite unit from 154 Brigade, with D Company on the right, at 7.30am moved up Beaumont Alley and Leave Avenue and an hour later Cowan led his company uphill in a 'brilliant charge which carried Munich Trench'.[33] They found it had been badly damaged by the British heavy artillery. However the next trench, Frankfort Trench, which was the Yellow Line objective and was beyond the range of 18-pounders, was strongly held by the enemy with active machine guns. By 1.30pm the composite unit had to vacate their position as they were being shelled by their own guns. They withdrew to Leave Avenue and into shell holes. Cowan reconnoitred Munich Trench at 4pm and found it still unoccupied by the enemy. A plan to attack that afternoon could not be put in place in time.

At 6pm the 8th Royal Scots (Pioneers) came up to consolidate Munich Trench and discovered that it lay unoccupied in no man's land, instead they would have to dig a 'New' Munich Trench, which they did overnight with the help of the infantry and Royal Engineers. In the early hours of 15 November instructions were received that this was now to be a jumping-off point, so instead of cutting a fire step, steps to the parapet were made. Biscuit tins were placed as markers so as to help the artillery observers. The companies were relieved at 4.30am and withdrew to Beaumont Hamel. It seems the new attack may have involved the other half-battalion of Argylls and D Company 9th Royal Scots once more. Haig's intervention came too late to cancel the attack.

Zero hour was to be 9am commencing with a field artillery barrage on Munich Trench, followed by three lifts to Frankfort Trench (the Yellow Line) and a fourth lift clear of the objective, all at five-minute intervals. Every man was to carry two or more bombs and the bombing parties were to work along any trenches encountered. They were warned once more to stay close to the barrage. To those on the ground, the barrage once more fell short, falling on the jumping-off trench. However, moving on they got ahead of the barrage which inevitably caught them up. Some parties entered Frankfort Trench, despite opposition, and bombed some dug-outs. As the flank attacks 'did not mature'[1] and were not as far forward, the companies were forced to return to New Munich Trench, which continued to be the advanced British line. D and A companies returned to battalion headquarters in Fethard Street in the afternoon.

In a post-mortem of the attack, the division reported that the artillery plan had to suit 2nd Division on the left, who employed 50-yard lifts, whereas 51st Division had trained with 100-yard lifts (100 yards in four minutes). Therefore with 'impetuosity'[1] they were caught up in the barrage, incurred severe losses and became disorganised. General Hubert Gough did not agree that the training of infantry to certain lifts was

relevant, stating, 'It is only necessary for the infantry to know that they are to keep close to the barrage.'[1] Regarding the shells falling short, Brigadier General Henry Burns suggested that Very lights be used to inform the artillery, a method used by the Germans. In truth, by this time the enemy reserves had been brought up and it was hard to maintain the momentum.

To the south, on 15 November, B and C companies helped to clear dug-outs in Y Ravine. A great many shrapnel shell fuzes were found on the edge of the ravine,

Beaumont Hamel church (centre).

testimony to consistent British artillery work. Investigating the double storey dug-outs, there were few 'souvenirs'[23] left, but some men did find automatic pistols. David Watson stated some years later that the floors of the concrete bunkers were lined with cement bags which he thought were of British origin. Though no evidence was found, reports of this kind prompted a parliamentary investigation, after which cement could only be exported under licence.

Lieutenant Colonel Rorie, RAMC made his way through the mud for the clearing up. Despite a wartime career and inured to unspeakable horrors, this left a lasting impression upon him. Descending forty-steps into a dug-out 50 feet in length, he found it full of German dead and injured, rats and a gas-gangrenous stench.

On 16 November B and C companies relieved the 4th Gordons in the Green Line, consolidating it with two strongpoints and wire, whilst A and D companies moved in turn to the Y Ravine dug-outs. Even now the British artillery were dropping short. However, they also received a 'gracious telegram' from His Majesty the King:

> 'I heartily congratulate you upon the great success achieved by my gallant troops during the past three days in the advance on both sides of the Ancre. This further capture of the enemy's first line of trenches under special difficulties owing to the recent wet weather redounds to the credit of all ranks.'[1]

The whole divisional front was taken over by 154 Brigade and held until 17 November, when the foremost positions were relieved. The division left two days later, and the battalion returned to Mailly Wood.

Casualties for the period were 6 ORs killed, 38 wounded, 1 died of wounds and 11 sick to hospital. Lieutenant Richard Morison Ireland had been invalided home from Gallipoli, now with the Ninth he was wounded on 18 November. He later became an intelligence officer with the RFC. Hugh Oliver was hospitalised but had evidently been saved by his entrenching tool for it had an enormous dent in it.

The division had not reached its second objective and incurred losses of nearly 2,200 officers and men. Nevertheless, Beaumont Hamel was a great success for the 51st who took a square mile of densely defended territory and over 2,000 prisoners, including remaining members of I Battalion 23rd Regiment. Harper attributed the complete turnaround in results to being able to prepare and fight their own battle. The artillery fire was, on the whole, well managed: much of the wire cut and the infantry had kept as close as 50 yards to the barrage, able to rush the enemy trenches when it lifted. The value of surprise was also recognised, Harper stating afterwards, 'I consider that the decision to have no preliminary bombardment immediately before the attack was a very wise one.'[1] The poor weather had forced General Gough to exercise uncharacteristic patience.

The Germans, recognizing that immensely strong defences, developed over two years, had been overcome, ascribed defeat to the weeks of heavy bombardment, the failure of the defensive barrage on account of the fog and the poor performance of the 12th Division from Upper Silesia. It might also be said that they had simply been too

German prisoners.

slow to the fire step. Erich Ludendorff, head of operations, admitted that the loss of Beaumont Hamel was 'a particularly heavy blow'. He issued instructions in December to employ elastic tactics in a deep battle zone of some 2,000 yards in depth, part of the very serious lessons learnt by all participants in the Somme.

Whether or not the loss of this stronghold prompted, or merely contributed to the German withdrawal in 1917 to the prepared lines of the Siegfried (Hindenburg) Line, the belief that it did was a substantial basis for the *esprit de corps* of the division, built on through the following year. Haig was certainly able to take news of a victory with him to conference at Chantilly. In such circumstances, it suited British and German high commands, as well as the Highlanders themselves, to promote the division as an élite corps. Bewsher describes Beaumont Hamel as 'the foundation stone on which the reputation of the Highland Division was built'[51] and quotes a Jock saying, 'Onyway, they winna ca' us Hairper's Duds noo.'[51]

Courcelette and the kilt

'The first move for Courcelette was to dump the kilt and put on breeks, and very funny we found them.'[23]

Jim Quinn

IMMEDIATELY following Beaumont Hamel, instead of a well-earned rest, the division was sent to an unpleasant part of the line and wintered in trenches north of Courcelette, the scene of fierce fighting in September. Courcelette proved 'the most awful wilderness possible to conceive... Everything was a nightmare vision of mud... The experiences here were as good an imitation of "The Inferno" as anyone may expect to find on this earth.'[6] Trenches could not be cut here; with the water table at a mere 3ft, the liquid mud drowned horses and the men were issued with ropes to extricate themselves.

The communication trenches were rendered impracticable as they took hours to slog through and the men arrived exhausted. As such the men could not move during the day so were utterly isolated in shallow, wet posts. The only communication in the hours of daylight was by telephone and the wires were frequently cut. There were also great difficulties in getting supplies in. 'At night-time, going down on a ration party, it was a hell of a job to get down without slipping into a shell hole and be drowned.'[56] An unnamed major of the Ninth led parties to the Royal Engineers dump and gave them instructions that if challenged they were to reply that they were 'Warwicks',[23] they came back with a quantity of duckboards for the camp.

This area had been recently captured and raids or a major counter-attack were expected but did not materialise. However, on the first day in the line, Jim Quinn tells us, 'Speaking as a machine gunner I got my best target of the war as day broke. A party of 10 or maybe 15 carrying dixies on poles – hot soup for breakfast maybe – the Lewis coughed merrily – a whole drum – and traversed the line of them – never saw them anymore!'[23] The following night two more Germans were brought down by rifle fire; it was not certain if they were deserting or a bombing party.

Once more overlooked by the enemy, even single men would be sniped at by howitzers, and on that first day, Company Sergeant Major 981 Jock Davie, an Australian, was killed by a shell. Guides often lost their way and all of the battalion orderlies were sent out to reconnoitre the routes. Such noncontiguity meant that a lost German, returning to his post with filled water bottles, walked straight through the British line to be captured near brigade headquarters.

To make matters worse a severe winter set in throughout the northern hemisphere and there followed trench foot, frost-bite and dysentery.

The immediate measure to mitigate the conditions was to limit the time they were expected to man the posts. A 'Method of Holding the Line with 4 Companies Only' was issued with three-day reliefs between the front and reserve line, the limit of endurance. On the seventh day they rested, coming out as 'a miniature Napoleon's retreat from Moscow'[32] and spending a week in the support area where they received baths and a change of clothing. Even then three days might result in seventy cases of trench foot in a battalion. Considerable work was undertaken to make improvements, foremost was the construction of corrugated iron shelters in the shell holes, and tommy cookers were issued to allow hot food to be cooked by the isolated sections of men.

A divisional gum boot store was established but these did not work well with kilts, the top edge of the waders causing chafing; and feet kept in rubber *gutty* boots for too long also led to amputations. Hay understood that General Plumer cried to see the morass the kilties were being put into, who were so *guddled* that 'they took pity on us'[56]

'That Astronomical Annoyance, the Star Shell, which momentarily enables you to scrutinize the kind of mud you are in.'

and, on 3 December, kilts were temporarily discarded in favour of trousers.

The kilt, 'garb of old Gaul'[7] as Ferguson would have it, was certainly worn with pride and distinction, a symbol of Highland *esprit de corps* and a direct link to Scotland's past. Long famed in martial story, the Scots have held a reputation for discipline and dash throughout Europe since the middle ages, and throughout the world as empire expanded. After Waterloo, the Russians even called Highlanders 'The English Cossacks'.[67]

Tartan probably came from Flanders, via the Lowlands, by the sixteenth century; the kilt is more recent. During the seventeenth century, the plaid (*plaide* is Gaelic for

153

blanket) came into use, in the Lowlands as a cloak, and in the Highlands as the belted plaid: a length of cloth wrapped around the body, held with a belt and often raised over the shoulder. It provided untailored economy and could be rearranged for sleeping out in the open. The evidence suggests that the kilt, a skirt of sewn pleats, was invented and first worn by Englishman Thomas Rawlinson about 1730, and first made by the regimental tailor in Inverness. Following the '45 rebellion, the Disarming Act (1746, repealed 1782) allowed only the regiments to wear Highland dress; civilians risked imprisonment or deportation. From their uniforms perhaps came the differentiation of tartan or 'setts' that in the nineteenth century was falsely and retrospectively ascribed to clans. The first Highland regiment was the Black Watch, formed from the earlier independent companies in 1739; though John Hepburn's Royal Scots in France of 1633 derived from Lowland Scots and Mackay's Highlanders previously serving Gustavus Adolphus.

William Pitt the Elder, in need of troops for the Seven Years War, authorised the raising of Highland regiments in 1757, which included many men who had fought at Culloden for Prince Charlie – the Royal Scots of course had fought for the government. These Highlanders, permitted a kilt of government pattern, also wore the scarlet tunic of the British Army's *Saighdearan Dearg* 'red soldiers' and, as the very embodiment of Union, made a notable attack at Abraham Heights in Quebec and built a reputation for 'gallantry which those hardy mountaineers had evinced in America'.[68]

Scots, Lowland and Highland, Protestant and Catholic, served most visibly and with distinction in all major British campaigns and actions, playing a significant rôle in the creation of empire. In a couple of generations, from George II to George IV, they were transformed from reviled *teuchters,* as in the sixteenth century poem '*How the first Helandman of God was maid of ane hors turd';* by way of the *noble savage* associated with Rousseau (who himself masqueraded as a Jacobite); to the revered, to be immortalised as the *thin red line* derived from Russell's Crimean despatches. The Highland battalions after 1746 are responsible for much of modern Scottish identity, and also the regrettable conflation of Scotland, Highland and Jacobite.

There was also precedence for kilted Volunteers outside of the Highlands, notably the London Scottish Regiment, though they had had to relax their rules on Scottish ancestry. There had been kilted companies in Edinburgh between 1859 and 1875 until required to conform to the uniform of the QRVB, partly through expense.

The War Office stripped some Highland regiments of their kilts in 1809 after fifteen years of war and due to dwindling Highland populations, but returned some of them over the remainder of the century. Colonel Alan Cameron of the 79th Highlanders famously defended 'our native garb in the field' against 'the buffoon tartan pantaloons... sticking wet and dirty to the skin' not least 'as levelling that martial distinction by which they have been hitherto noticed and respected... will prove a complete death-warrant to the recruiting service.'[69] 'The kilt was alright,' agreed our own Bill Hay, before adding 'a bit hot in the summertime, we had no pants on of course, quite heavy, you can imagine what it is like when it gets wet in the trenches.'[56]

154

There were still supporters in 1915, such as this private in a Highland regiment, admitting kilts were cold to wear on guard duty but that, 'It's no uncommon thing for a trousered section who've stood shivering on their platforms with their wet things clinging to their legs for twenty-four hours to see with a feeling of envy their kilted comrades coming up through the water to relieve them with their kilts tucked up.'[26] In truth, 'The kilt was a useless dress for flooded trenches,'[23] thought Quinn, but he cited it as a reason to remain in the Ninth when he was asked to join the MGC. In flooded conditions he discarded his and put his legs through the sleeves of his cardigan. Private McCord was wounded in the legs working one night without his kilt and his mates wondered what the hospital thought of him arriving soaking wet in just tunic and boots. Anderson's knees suffered a touch of frostbite lying out at night. Kilts and mustard gas, which caused severe burns, were the final, unacceptable combination. As a military garment, the many disadvantages of the kilt ultimately resulted in its replacement with trousers, but only on the eve of the next war.

The 15th (Scottish) Division discovered from the outset in August 1914 that 'the glamour of the kilt was irresistible'[71] for there is no recruiting sergeant like a kilted recruiting sergeant, and indeed in the eighteenth century some recruiters had even falsely attired themselves as Highlanders in order to win over recruits.

If impractical, the kilt did provide for that great prize amidst uniformity – identity – a struggle John Brown thought of in terms of Dostoyevsky's *House of the Dead*. Lord Salvesen noted that, 'With all battalions a mass of khaki, Lowlanders were as much inclined to adopt the kilt as the mark of a Scottish soldier, rather than be mistaken for members of an English regiment.'[6]

Regimental reputation passes readily to new recruits and, although not absolute, it can be self-fulfilling, both positively and negatively; but it is doubtful how much is transmitted to the enemy. Once more our 'private in a Highland regiment' writes 'in actual fighting the moral[e] effect of the kilt is of value, and its associations with hard and terrible fighting are so well known and appreciated among the enemy that the very sight of bare knees and waving kilts in an advance have the effect on them that our battlecruisers have on German raiders.'[26]

The kilt was known to the Germans and Kaiser Wilhelm II had worn one as a child, but it may not have been seen as the same the badge of honour it was to the wearer. Indeed, raiders appearing with blackened faces (and knees) in kilts sometimes gave rise to surrendering cries of 'Kamerad Kaffirs!'[51] as they were mistaken instead for colonial troops. Ernst Jünger recognised them:

'We raced past stout figures, still warm, with strong knees under their short kilts, or we crawled past them. They were Highlanders and their way of fighting showed us that we were dealing with real men.'[58]

Of their prisoners, a German view of the Scots was that, 'The most typical of them wear just as hard an expression as do the English, but there is a reflective look in their eyes which indicates a fundamentally different mentality.'[63]

Nicholson wastes little time on the subject: 'the General [Harper] had sound views where sentiment should begin and end. He entirely agreed with the wish of the division to abolish the kilt. It was in fact inconceivable that in such a war a kilt should be worn... The War Office flatly refused to look at the proposal.'[32] He was adamant that as much sentiment could be attached to a hackle, just as Napoleon asserted, 'A soldier will fight long and hard for a bit of coloured ribbon.' True as this might be, all identifying marks were being removed from the men but, 'While higher authority suppresses numerals and crests which might reveal troop dispositions to an enemy spy, local pride replaces them with new distinguishing marks.'[20] In the case of the Ninth this was a pale blue silk bar 'battle flash'. Again, in the Second World War badges of distinction, swept away in total war, were reintroduced for 'their value in the maintenance of morale'.[70]

The subtle distinction of setts was particularly irrelevant, especially given that khaki aprons were worn over the kilt, but in a surprising way mattered behind the lines at Bougainville. An animosity had grown up between the 6th Argylls from Paisley, and the 8th Argylls based at Dunoon, possibly started over a Gaelic remark about 'real Highlanders'. Their fights resulted in them being billeted well apart and banned from cafés. Beatson records, 'The folk clearly regard us as a horde of thieves, with some justification from the scum of a sister battalion. Hitherto we have been able to correct the impression and make the Hunting Stewart tartan respected.'[42] Clearly some locals knew their setts; but other Frenchmen mistook Highlanders for *vivandières*, the women traditionally attached to French regiments, but then saw they were 'great burly men in petticoats'.[71] Joseph Joffre was critical: '*Pour l'amour oui, mais pour la guerre non,*' though Parisian fashion and a 1917 Mary Pickford film helped the civilian sartorial resurgence of the kilt.

It may well have been true that at the time of the Clearances many Highlanders were sturdy, outdoorsmen, and subsequently ghillies would have had keen eyesight, been a good shot and accustomed to wearing a kilt. George Anderson of Kelso, killed in 1917, was gamekeeper to the Duke of Roxburghe, one of five gamekeepers. There was also John Law Wilson, a shepherd at Kingledoors in the Tweed valley. However, in 1914 few Ninths came from outside of Edinburgh, many may not have been north of South Queensferry and some new recruits would not have set foot in Scotland until they followed the drum. However, for all the wild individuality that may exist in a recruit, on adopting a uniform they take on the history and reputation of the unit, and hence the responsibility for their upkeep. Most new recruits, especially English, would never have worn a kilt before, it might be said to have exacerbated the discomfort of southern drafts. Indeed, a kilted Englishman in the 7th Cameron Highlanders cited the inadequacy of the kilt in winter among his reasons for deserting to the Germans. 'One of the boys' of the Ninth asked in the battalion magazine if his 'English cousins were 'kilt' wi' the cauld or cauld wi' the kilt'[10] and 'if it is the case that special lectures have been given to our English "transfers" on the subject of "*Caeskilohr*," and how many of them can pronounce it.'[10]

For all the trousers and tin roofs, the winter at Courcelette did nothing to revive the division, 'iron is beginning to enter our very souls'.[35] Levels of sickness were high and consequently in the space of the last month of the year the battalion lost a third of its strength and fell to its lowest ebb yet. Among them Patrick Dignan from Roswell had frequently been in trouble in the 3rd Royal Scots for being in possession of bottles of beer when on guard, striking his superior officer and resisting arrest. Sent to France, he was shunted over to the Ninth through the squalid winter and rapidly deteriorated from tough coal miner and recalcitrant soldier through rheumatic fever to heart disease and discharge from the army.

A well-deserved rest was hard to come by and leave was typically short. Seven days leave amounted to four days and three nights at home, less for those resident further north for it was fifty hours to Aberdeen, and Walter Nicholson describes an islander who had to turn back no sooner had he set eyes on his own shores. By December 1915 it was extended from seven to

'Xmas Day. Usual Firing. No attempt to fraternise was made by the enemy.'[1]

nine days for Scots. Most men were sent mid-week to avoid the weekend delays in London, a typical week gave the battalion one place on the leave train on a Saturday and seven on a Tuesday. A typical schedule had them away by train in early afternoon and on the overnight ferry, the leave clock starting on leaving the Channel port.

When Jim Elliot went on leave from Chuignes in late 1915 (abridged):

'The news of my leave arrived one night at dusk so, of course, I did not stand on the order of my going, but 'got'. I waded down that communication trench to the crucifix, then off across country minus boots which I had cut myself out of in the mud, and arrived to find the limber had gone. I plodded off to Méricourt and the train which was just starting I managed to catch, and cooped up but happy we got to Havre the next day arriving at Southampton early the next morning. What a mud heap I must have been. On arrival at Waterloo I was asked if I was London Scottish, for the kilt was covered in mud.

Then to St Pancras and again we caught the train on the move, and I settled head first in a lady's lap in a first class compartment. My companion was a titled lady, I was to meet her nearly two years later at Leeds when she actually recognised me as the Lance-Jock who had shared her meal about Xmas 1915. I arrived at Hawick at 5.30 a.m. It was a glorious ten days and I spent Xmas at home and it was a great time. Hogmanay saw me back at Vaux on the river edge a mile or so further on.'[2]

The leave train from Méricourt-sur-Somme.

Bobby Johnston got to London in time to see the Lord Mayor's Show, still dressed in his kit and goatskin coat, with the mud of trenches on his boots. Jimmy Quinn went on leave in January 1916 and was given a binge of a send-off on real champagne at 5 francs a bottle. His mate 'Jules [Neilson] came in after 'lights out' and by way of excuse offered Sgt. Davie 3 or 4 champagne corks complete with wire! (He got three days' pay stopped next day though).'[23] Next day the 5 or 6 kilometres to the station felt like a mere 100m, despite the weight of the souvenirs he was carrying. The train carriage was occupied by Royal Engineers who had plenty of wine and so they drank all the way to the boat. Leave, though enjoyable, was strange: 'Everything and everybody was different – really it was myself that was different I suppose.'[23]

Bill Hay, on leave in early 1917, was walking alongside the Union Canal in civvies when a pretty girl pressed a white feather upon him. He was soon back with the battalion and fighting at Arras.

Chapter 5

The Home Front
1914–1918

'Did you see the Ninth leaving for the front? Ask yourself if you experienced no thrill at that scene. No regiment has done better work ANYWHERE in France.'

Recruiting poster

Recruitment

THE SS *Glitra* left the Forth on 18 October 1914. She was a Christian Salvesen ship on the Grangemouth-Stavanger route, principally carrying coal. At noon two days later, approaching the Norwegian coast at eight knots, and fourteen miles WSW from Skudenes, she hoisted the signal for a pilot.

From the bridge a long, low vessel was observed 3 miles to seaward which closed on them with superior speed. She was the submarine *U-17* from the Baltic Flotilla, and a shot from her 5cm deck gun compelled the merchant ship to stop. At a ship's length the U-boat launched a collapsible boat and sent over an armed party of five to search the ship. The crew were given ten minutes to take to their lifeboats, the fireman still in his singlet, and the Germans scuttled the uninsured ship in deep water. She went down by the stern and had become the first merchant vessel sunk by a submarine.

Among the seventeen men pulling east on the oars that afternoon was 2nd Engineer Bertram Brown from Warrender Park Terrace, Edinburgh who had not long finished his apprenticeship. He returned to the city by passenger steamer and promptly joined the *Dandy Ninth*. He was one of many men to come 'home' to Edinburgh.

Bertram Brown.

James Sholto Bowhill was born in Tobago and was resident in British Guiana as a chartered accountant before joining the Ninth. James Boswall had settled in Pretoria after the Boer War as a farmer and inspector of police, he joined the Ninth in August 1914, and was commissioned into the Seaforth Highlanders. Leo Butlers was born in Brooklyn, Louis Cowan in the Malay States; William Meek Falconer returned from

James Bowhill.

159

holidaying in Switzerland. Then there was a refugee from Brussels, John Cant. All of these men were killed.

They came too from the vast émigré population in Canada, the US, Australia and the smaller outposts of empire, Jamaica and the Straits Settlements. Bethune Ingles Annandale, resident of German Samoa, was a civilian member of the Samoan Expeditionary Force which took control of the colony at the end of August 1914. Annandale sailed for the UK and took a commission in the Ninth, subsequently serving with the West African Frontier Force. Some men came less far. It seems likely that Sergeant John Campbell, of the Ordnance Survey and 9th Royal Scots, persuaded three of his colleagues to walk the hundred yards from the Ordnance Survey Office on Claremont Crescent to HQ and enlist. Tom Brown came no further than Traquair, but as a postman he could not be spared until after Christmas. Charles Smith came later still, he had already signed up once, to the Natal Mounted Rifles, and seen through the campaign in German South-West Africa, when he joined the Ninth in 1916. Others came back to the colours: it seems likely George Ormiston – he who held the South Africa 1901 honour – rejoined. Alf Ruxton joined in September 1900, went to South Africa with the Scottish Horse and was now 41 years old; Robert Johnston was 42. Bandsman Thomas Cruickshank, with service in India and South Africa, served until 1916 when he was aged 51.

Then there were the young. Visiting the King's Park on the day war was declared, John Young, a 13-year-old Watson's schoolboy saw the Ninth at drill:

'To my surprise I saw, among them, being drilled several of my older schoolmates, eighteen year olds, who'd immediately joined up… There was this great rush to the recruiting offices… joining the Royal Scots, and the sort of the élite battalion to get into was the 9th Royal Scots… It attracted all the outstanding sporting men in Edinburgh… they rushed to join the 9th Royal Scots, the Dandy Ninth.'[50]

At the outbreak of war some 400 men volunteered to form a new Manchester Scottish regiment, along the lines of the London and Liverpool Scottish. However, the War Office declined the offer. According to Private John Fidler, someone tipped off the Ninth, who sent an officer and a sergeant to the city in November, and 'pinched the 400'[72] from under the nose of the Manchester Regiment, and sent them north aboard a special train. Certainly, the Royal Scots had great success in Manchester from mid-October when Mancunians were 'invited to enquire'[73] at 4 Chapel Walks and later 27 Oxford St to the seven-strong recruiting party, including the Medical Officer.

The 4th Royal Scots were recruiting men with a minimum height of 5ft 3in, and the Ninth 5ft 6in (they had accepted men an inch shorter in September). So many joined the 15th Royal Scots that the label Manchester Scottish was soon attached to them; and by the end of the year the Gordon Highlanders were there too. At the end of October up to seventy names a day were being taken until the 220 strong Manchester Company of the 9th (Home Service) Battalion Royal Scots were given medicals and 'joined for the duration'. Those 'who walked along Oxford Street, Manchester, in that drizzly

*'During the past few days about seventy recruits have been obtained by the "Dandy Ninth".
The men are seen leaving for their training camp.' 24 November 1915.*

month of October 1914, to sign our names for The Royal Scots'[10] were instructed that at 9am on 14 November 1914, they would parade at Albert Street Police Station, march to Exchange Station and proceed to the depot at Edinburgh by special train. The Manchester recruiting authorities, 'in need of all the recruits they can get,'[8] protested that a thousand men had gone to Scotland, about 900 of them to the Royal Scots.

The battalion found the Mancunians spoke in a 'foreign tongue to us'[23] but the feeling was surely mutual. When they were issued with their kilts they, of course, asked the question 'What about pants?' to which came the inevitable reply 'You only wear what the army issue you with'[72] and that was that.

Arthur Anderson enlisted in Edinburgh in October 1914, passed his medical, was sworn in at the same time as about thirty others and received his first official 'uniform': a plaited cord of green, yellow and red, the tartan colours, to wear on his coat. They paraded in a mix of mufti and khaki and it was not until the end of November that most had full uniforms, and not until January 1915 that their own coats were replaced with khaki greatcoats. Rifles were also in short supply, about a dozen obsolete patterns per company, these being replaced with SMLEs from January 1915.

Reveille was at 6.30am, the pipe band ensuring the local populace were also awake. Then began the day of work: drills and manoeuvres in city parks or upon the Braid Hills, fatigues and guard duty until roll call at 9pm; though once or twice a week there were night marches. Friday was payday when they received a shilling a day, sixpence extra proficiency pay for passing their firing tests, plus 2d kit allowance, less 2d per week for breakages etc. On Sunday afternoons they had an opportunity to go home.

In keeping with other territorial units, the Ninth were below their establishment strength of 30 officers and 972 men at the outbreak of war. However, recruits were pouring in during these first months, peaking in September, with Scotland having the highest proportion of enlistments in the UK. To bring them up to strength the battalion were asked to accept two companies of the 8th Royal Scots, but on being told it would not hasten their deployment to the continent, they refused and continued to recruit. Instead 200 men were transferred from the 8th HLI to the 8th Royal Scots and they were the first to France. The 9th and 5th battalions were the first territorial battalions of the regiment to reach establishment.

The recruiting power of a unit was, and remains, the prerequisite of their military power, and the *Dandy Ninth* were favoured in this regard with a good reputation. After the recruiting rush in September, by November 1914 the numbers had fallen and the Synod Hall held a recruiting meeting on behalf of the Highland regiments, stating that many men in the north had enlisted and that the gaps could only be filled by the Highland diaspora. This struggle for numbers led some in the north to object to their young men joining Lowland regiments; whilst those in the south felt equally unhappy at the idea of Highland regiments 'raiding the Lowlands'[6] for recruits. The Ninth, of course, were well placed to offend both parties.

Colonel Ferguson appealed firstly 'to those young men who had come from the Highlands direct, or were of Highland descent, and so enable them to maintain the Battalion as a Highland regiment, and not let them deteriorate into sham Highlanders.'[6] In these speeches exhortations grew and history was thoroughly raked over, mentioning Montrose, the Forty-Five and the 'death-withered squares at Waterloo' that had halted 'that other arrogance' of Napoleon a century before. So said the Lord Advocate:

'When "the fiery cross" sped in the month of August through the straths and glens in the Highlands, the harvest fields emptied and the Highland regiments filled, and from all parts, from castle and cottage, from village and town, from the fastnesses of the hills and from the shores of the sea, the manhood of the North flocked to the Colours in their thousands'[6] as the 'Ingathering of the children of the Gael'.[6]

Lieutenant Kenneth Mackenzie attended a meeting of the Edinburgh and District Trades Council to appeal for army recruits in May 1915, informing them that not enough recruits were coming forward to fill the gaps in the battalion in France and saying that if a young man enlisted with them 'he would never regret it. No matter what the future might bring, he would feel in his own

September 1914.

162

'Cultured German (going into action): 'I must find a few civilians to go in front, then I shall be ready to fight the treacherous barbarians.' Private Andrew Wylie, wounded Second Ypres.

conscience that he had done his duty by his country and his God. (Applause).'[6] The Chairman responded that 'It would be a record in history that the "Ninth" was one of the finest fighting forces that ever left Edinburgh, and every man should be attracted by the battalion.'[6]

As for the enemy, 'There was no man dourer than the German,'[26] preached John Sclater. A Manichaean division of the world into good and evil was well underway. In February 1915 Dr John Kelman, on behalf of the Ninth at the United Free Church Assembly Hall, preached the war 'was not merely a fight of Britain against Germany but of love against hate, or Christ against anti-Christ... certain ancient paganisms had arisen... and it was the war of the ancient gods again – Thor against Jesus Christ, the Hammer against the Cross.'[6]

Those at the front could only despair at what was becoming common currency at home. Clarence Gibb advised his kin against believing a lot of what was written in the newspapers. BC learnt of Edinburgh rumours that the MG Section had been wiped out before they had seen any action. 'The people who start such stories at home should be shot.'[16]

William Young, the missionary, had been awarded the Distinguished Conduct Medal for his work as a guide. Badly wounded in June 1915, he came home but returned to the army as a chaplain with the Seaforths and was taken prisoner at

Cambrai. He knew the majority of men were 'dead off'[35] organised religion which did not speak to them in the fear and loneliness of action. He himself had found his true faith lying at a hedge after the rush over the crest at Second Ypres, 'reaching out over the abyss to God'.[35] After the war he became chaplain at Gordonstoun School.

Recruits were accepted at headquarters on East Claremont Street, where medical examinations were held every evening at 7.30pm, at the Edinburgh Recruiting office at 63 and 65 Cockburn Street, a Temporary Recruiting Office at 71 Princes Street, at 2 Castle Street and in 1918 at the new Main Recruiting Office at the Music Hall on George Street. Not all recruits, however were successful. In September 1914 Gordon Cameron was turned away on account of being short-sighted by the Cameron Highlanders on Cockburn Street, he then tried the HLI in the same building, then the 16th Royal Scots at Castle Street, the Ninth at Claremont Street ('The doctor is inexorable'), back to Cockburn Street to try for the Seaforths, and then to Dundee and the Black Watch in the High Street. Finally, in 1916 he was accepted by the RAMC. Victor 'Spiggy' de Spiganovicz was rejected on medical grounds but became a recruiting sergeant; after the war he established the Scouts in Scotland.

At his medical examination, William Soles, a carter from Nottingham (conscripted in group 33), was recorded as having a poor physique. He was at the minimum height of 5ft 3in, but under 7 stone and was soon in hospital with colic. Sent to the Cameron Highlanders depot in Inverness, the Substitution Officer soon moved him to 'W Class', to perform civilian tasks of 'national importance' but under threat of military discipline. He was given work as a porter at Inverness Station for the Highland Railway Company, thereby freeing a fit man for service. After five months Soles was 'not giving satisfaction' and was dispensed with. He duly took a train south, not realising he had not been discharged from the army. The police searched for him, found him at home in September 1917 and sent him back to the army. Disembarking in France in April 1918 he was posted to the Ninth and was soon in hospital again, this time with a fever classified as Mild PUO (pyrexia of unknown origin). He rejoined the battalion on 1 July and was killed a month later on 1 August 1918.

Another Nottingham lad killed on 1 August was Horace Knight, who had succeeded in enlisting with the Sherwood Foresters when aged only 15. 'My mother sent a claim up to the War Office for my discharge being under age… and the Batt is ready to proceed overseas on Saturday or Sunday and the Major is waiting to discharge me when they hear…' He was returned to England as under age, sent out again to the Ninth in April 1918 when he was 18, and was killed four months later. Frank Culley had a similar story: from Nottingham, sent home under age, transferred to the Ninth and killed 1 August 1918. Seventeen young men, below the age of 19, are recorded as killed prior to 1918.

William Whitehead, the manager of Edinburgh's Theatre Royal joined up. A dozen architects enlisted, among whom George Reid designed about 1,800 houses in Edinburgh after the war. John Craigie Bone and his brother William were both architects and artists and

John Bone.

164

joined at the outbreak of war. John's watercolours of the front were exhibited in Edinburgh and 'attracted much public attention'. He was commissioned and soon after returning to France in 1917 was killed in action with the 8th Royal Scots.

William Geissler, the grandson of a German immigrant, followed his cousin Paul to France with the Ninth in March 1915. Both transferred to the Royal Engineers, Paul to a Field Survey Company and William as a map draughtsman. After the war William became a much admired watercolourist of The Edinburgh School. He was unusual in that very few German descendants kept their names, including, of course, the royal family.

Bill Geissler, 1915.

Other artists included George Galloway and the sculptor Charles Ogilvie Rhind, part of the famous family of Edinburgh sculptors. Francis Campbell Boileau Cadell, who had studied in Paris and Munich, was already an established artist but was to find further fame as one of the Scottish Colourists after the war. He was a friend of Jim Henderson-Hamilton, of Dalserf, who had been a lieutenant in the Ninth before the war. Attempting to sign up with the Ninth in 1914, Cadell failed his medical so abandoned his pipe, built his strength up with farm work at Kirkconnel in Dumfriesshire, and in 1915 he was with the Colours, having passed his second medical.

Bill, the Artist c.1922.

Meanwhile his 1915 sketches were sold for the benefit of the Red Cross, and then reproduced as a book, *Jack and Tommy*. By the end of the year he was in the trenches, fit and well attired, doubtless the only member of 13 Platoon in a tailored private's uniform. Certainly a character, this dandiest of the Ninths (he wrote that in the absence of water he was going to bathe in *vin ordinaire*) the 32-year-old artist, who was almost certainly gay, would have stood in stark contrast to many of his comrades. The same would be true at home too, if it is to be believed that on leave he regularly dined at the Savoy wearing a blood-stained kilt. Taking the train north, 'Bunty' Cadell gave parties at 130 George Street, at which his fellow artist Samuel Peploe might appear.

FCB Cadell, 1932.

The strong recruitment of rugby players gave the battalion team an edge and in September 1914 they beat Edinburgh University OTC 22-5 (though they in turn trounced the Ninth in November 30-0). The following day the paper reported that £34 8d had been raised for the National Relief Fund. A similar match 7th v 9th Royal Scots raised £7 14s. H Company with Jimmy Pearson, Eric Milroy and captained by Arthur Thomas (shot dead trying to locate a sniper in 1916) only managed a draw with Loretto. Most of Dalkeith's first and second cricket teams had enlisted, including Robert Affleck who was killed by a shell in May 1915. Footballers also signed up, the Heart of Midlothian roll of honour includes John Allan, John Wilson and George Miller, who scored twice for Hearts against Clyde whilst a sergeant in the *Dandy Ninth* in April 1916. David Pool played for Bo'ness.

Three Manchester brothers by the name of Broad – Jimmy, Leonard and Bill – signed up with consecutive numbers: 3288, 3289 and 3290 in May 1915 and went into the same company. All were sportsmen and competed amongst themselves for the podium places in battalion games. Jimmy was a professional footballer for Manchester City, Manchester United, Oldham and, in 1914, for Morton. After the war he returned to the game.

Jimmy Broad.

Certainly D Company of the reserve battalion managed to win the Brigade Cup at Fermoy in 1917, and at least Bill went on to serve with the BEF, bolstering the inter-platoon football there and becoming a sergeant. James Roy, from Leith, became a professional footballer for Penicuik before transferring to Everton in 1913 for £3 a week. At Christmas 1914, Lord Derby was promoting a census of men willing to enlist and was able to boast of his success in securing promises from the Liverpool and Everton players. Roy was killed at Arras.

Lord Derby next organised a National Register of eligible men and in the autumn of 1915 introduced a scheme whereby men could attest and be put in the Army Reserve until called up. This gave them some assurances about when they might be called up and allowed them to wear an armband proving their commitment. The scheme failed to produce enough recruits and in March 1916 the Military Service Act introduced conscription. This broke the direct, voluntary enlistment into a battalion of your choosing, a system that had already been under pressure. As early as May 1915 the Edinburgh Territorial Force Association had voted in favour of compulsory service. Men could, however, appeal their conscription.

Manuel Berman, a tailor's presser on Hanover Street, voluntarily attested at Cockburn Street and was placed into Group 6 which began mobilisation in February 1916. He applied for exemption stating that he was the sole support of his parents, to the tune of £2 a week, who would 'be left at the mercy of local charity'. In addition he had himself been laid up in bed with influenza and neuralgia in the head, and his hammer toes would be unable to cope with military marching.

His appeal was finally dismissed on 9 May 1916 on 'insufficient grounds' and he joined up shortly thereafter. Berman went missing on 28 March 1917 when the battalion were providing carrying parties and working on assembly trenches at Arras. Although it was not known until July, he had died the following day of wounds in St Clotilde, a German military hospital in Douai, suggesting he had fallen into enemy hands either by a raid or accident. For some reason it seems his grave was lost as he is commemorated on the Arras Memorial. When his death was officially accepted, his parents received his pay and £3 as a War Gratuity. Similarly, Samuel Goldstein's appeal, that his

Manuel Berman.

166

rheumatism made him unfit, was dismissed after he had been medically examined at Cockburn Street; he was killed two weeks after Berman.

A member of the "Dandy Ninth" for four years in the piping times of peace, and posing as a British subject then; When Britain called you to the colours, you were an American subject, and escaped military service by a fluke. If you are a man, join up at once. If you don't join up, then remain what you are, *A damned Coward & slacker* & unfit to breathe the same air as decent men, let alone to live amongst them.
                    Yours contemptuously,
                              Scotsman.

Old accusations of cowardice taking new turns: 'Yours contemptuously, Scotsman'.

Leonard Hywel Evans, an estate agent, told his tribunal 'I am a socialist and believe in the Brotherhood of Man and regard war as being morally wrong and a crime against humanity... I am prepared to pay the death penalty for my conviction.' He was sent to the Ninth and died of pneumonia in January 1918. Another sobering case relates to painter William May (Group 30), who had prior service of four years with the 9th Royal Scots. When called up he declared himself a Conscientious Objector, as he was quite entitled to do under the terms of the Act, and refused his medical. He had been living with his uncle at Forrest Road, Edinburgh, an elder of the International Bible Students Association (Jehovah's Witnesses). The sons of this household had joined the No-Conscription Fellowship and refused military service, his cousin stating at his tribunal: 'Christ himself showed how wrong it was for a Christian to fight when he condemned Peter for smiting off the High Priest's servant's ear... I would rather be shot than change my allegiance.'

May followed suit and in June 1916 the army sent him to the 2nd Scottish Company of the Non-Combatant Corps (NCC), a military labour corps. Refusing to obey 'a lawful command', which may simply have been refusal to go on parade, May was court martialled and sent to Barlinnie Prison. This demonstrated considerable courage on his part as the army had recently transported thirty-five conscientious objectors in the NCC to France where such disobedience could, and did, result in the death sentence. These sentences were confirmed all the way up the chain of command to Sir Douglas Haig but commuted to ten years' penal servitude (hard labour), seemingly at the intervention of the Prime Minister.

From Barlinnie a tribunal transferred May to the W Class Army Reserve. In reality this meant punitive labour and he was sent to a number of gruelling work camps, finally at the Cawburn Chemical Works at Uphall, West Lothian. Meanwhile his younger brother Alexander, Black Watch, died as a prisoner of war from a fractured clavicle at Cambrai in March 1918. At the end of October 1918, Joseph King MP asked questions in the House of Commons about the severe conditions the COs were living under at Uphall. Such an intervention did not help May however, as he had been killed at the beginning of the month. May, aged 26, had been shovelling animal bones into railway wagons when the manager told them to shunt the wagons down the incline. He squeezed between a wagon and the platform to release the brake and was crushed between a hanging door and an iron upright. He remained true to his principles unto death.

To families left at home, state provision was slight and the great efforts of Chaplain John Sclater and his assistants can only have helped those most in need. There was some expenditure on medicine, occasional help with rent and gifts of Christmas stockings to a few families. Still he was able to report, 'In these ways we are trying to keep the home fires burning.'[10] Miss Mary Ritchie, 'to whom the Battalion owes a deep debt of gratitude,'[10] did much of the visiting of dependents and by the end of 1916 had made about 750 visits to 400 families.

The fourth and last of the Edinburgh TF week-long recruiting campaigns in July 1915 involved speakers on every night at such venues as Morningside Station, the bandstand in Portobello, Calton Hill, in front of the observatory and the Synod Hall. This last was attended by about 2,000, and more were turned away when the hall was full. A guard of honour was formed by soldiers looking even dandier, dressed in Royal Scots uniforms from the Waterloo period (William Richardson, killed at Arras, was incidentally great-grandson of George Richardson who served in the Peninsula War). Frederick Lucas gave a 'lantern demonstration'[6] of places visited by the battalion on the Western Front. Just as Norman Macdonald was a third-generation volunteer, so Lucas was a third-generation doctor, his father having been Royal Scots medical officer and Surgeon Major to the volunteers. Frederick Lucas later served as medical officer on White Star Liners before becoming a consultant in London.

Dudgeon had written from the front in support, 'We want men badly, and you can rub it in with some of those slackers at home… I am afraid those 'standbacks', as we call them, will not be able to hold their heads very high when those that are left of us come home.' Colonel Blair wrote in agreement, 'For Heaven's sake send us some more men.' Captain Arthur Aitken reassured those present that their training would be thorough, and that the battalion 'had an exceptionally good stamp of man'.[26] Patriotic solos were given by Miss Olga Z. Russell, contralto, and pianoforte recitals by Lance Corporal Rodgers; followed by a procession, including clan societies and some of the wounded, led by pipes and the battalion brass band.

The pipes and brass band made an important contribution to recruiting events, playing at the Usher Hall, the Synod Hall with Madame Clara Butt, and also at Bruntsfield School fundraising for the Ninth, at Central Hall, Tollcross in aid of the Belgium Relief Funds and at a Hearts game where the ball hit the bass drum (a boot had gone through it at Stobs). The Ninth provided the pall bearers, firing party and pipe band for the funeral at the Dean Cemetery of Black Watch Lieutenant Nigel Boyd, fatally wounded on the banks of the Aisne when a bullet bounced off his claymore. The bands of the 5th and 9th Royal Scots also paraded with 200 school children, the girls dressed as nurses and the boys with paper helmets and the banner 'The Chicken Battalion'; later the 9th played the 5th Royal Scots out of Portobello on their way to Gallipoli. It should be said that Colonel Blair spoke of 'whatever our little rivalries and jealousies were in peace time, these things are now all sunk in our respect and admiration…we shall not forget the glorious example of the 4th and 5th at the Dardanelles'.[26]

The first pipe major in 1900 was Duncan Kerr No.221. His brother Gilbert was also a Ninth volunteer piper, and a polar explorer. He took part in the Scottish National Antarctic Expedition of 1902-04 and is half of the famous photograph consisting of himself and an emperor penguin at 74° 1′ S.

Gilbert Kerr.

As well as the members of the pipe band, a number of the officers also played. The battalion marched in to 'O gin I were where Gadie rins', but for marching past and off 'Logie o'Buchan' was rearranged by Pipe Major Kerr as 'O wae to Kinmundy, Kinmundy the Laird'. Given the personal efforts of Ferguson to establish the battalion, he can be forgiven the occasional appearance that it was *his* battalion, and the song was adapted for them (excerpt):

'Though in khaki my lassie, he now gangs awa,
He'll come back an' see ye in scarlet an' a'.
Though in blue ride the gunners and red the dragoons,
Yet the braw kilted laddies for me are the loons;'[7]

Pipers, Drummers and Buglers, Pipe Major Thomas Porteous (left), Drum Major J. Small (right).

By the start of the war the pipe major was Thomas Porteous. He was still playing the pipes into his 60s, picking up tunes like 'I've Got You Under My Skin'. Charles McKinley was the pipe major with the battalion when they went to France, he was wounded in May 1915 and William Reid took his place.

In France and Flanders, the 51st Division's massed pipes had ninety pipers and seventy drummers. However, 'The band was kept out of action as far as possible as it was regarded as an invaluable asset on the march and in billets.'[74] Instead the men marched to songs accompanied by penny whistle or mouth organ; or were led by pipers: 'Who does not recall the response of the French cow to the shrilling of Caledonian music?'[36]

The Brass Band had been established in 1907 under Frank Waddington, who emigrated to Canada. The Ninth had the good fortune to recruit Herbert Laubach as No.491 B Company in 1908 and soon found they had secured the services of a talented bandmaster; he was promptly promoted sergeant. Laubach came from a German family famous in Edinburgh as music teachers and performers and known for their Matinée Musicale, indeed his father had been bandmaster in the QRVB. ('I have now thirty years here been, and I feel kvite Eenglish. Ven I go home to Chermanie they say to me, "Vat? your name Laubach, but you are not a Scherman; you are an Eenglishman."') [9] Herbert Laubach changed his surname to Bourne in 1916.

When the second-line battalion, of which more presently, split between Home Service and Imperial Service groups in May 1915, Laubach marched his band into Dundee joining the 5th Scottish Provisional Battalion. The Imperial Service second-

The band at Witham, Essex.

line battalion was forced to find a new band. Thankfully James Grieve, from Peebles, not only signed up himself, he encouraged other musicians to do the same. A curious priority came from the Edinburgh Town Council meeting in July 1915: second only to the appointment of a War Emergency Committee, was that £150 should be voted to Bandmaster Grieve of the second-line battalion brass band for buying instruments. With this money, and by the kind loan of band instruments by Innerleithen Town Council, the band was reformed.

Second- and Third-Line Battalions

COUNTY Associations had been given authority to form a second-line Territorial unit for every battalion that had volunteered and been accepted for foreign service. Men declining overseas service were transferred to the new battalion for Home Service, and rapid recruitment took place for Imperial Service. Therefore, barely a month after mobilisation, on 12 September 1914, a Reserve Battalion was formed at headquarters, as a 'rib' from the Service Battalion. They consisted of 5 officers, 42 NCOs and 395 men plus 36 recruits from the depot *told off* into five companies. To their number were added a Recruits' Company on 3 October, and another of trained men at month's end, followed by the final, eighth company, as well as the 220 men from Manchester. A week after formation Captain Arthur Aitken handed over command to Colonel James Ferguson, called back from retirement at the outset of war after a ten-year absence. He was one of sixty advocates on active service at the end of the year, and one of two commanding battalions; the other was James Clark.

Table 8. Officers of the Reserve Battalion, 15 November 1914

CO Lieutenant Colonel James Ferguson Majors Thomas G. Clark and Charles T. Gordon		
A Coy	Lieutenant Charles S. Matley	Second Lieutenant David G. Kydd
B Coy	Captain Angus M. Gregorson	Lieutenant Kenneth Mackenzie Second Lieutenant Alastair H. Macfarlane
C Coy	Lieutenant Robert Bathgate	Second Lieutenant John C. Bruce Second Lieutenant H.S. Ramsden
D Coy	Captain Hugh S. Hope Gill	Lieutenant John G. Burns Second Lieutenant Ian M. Robertson
E Coy	Captain Alastair M. Campbell	Second Lieutenant Archibald H. Douglas Second Lieutenant North D. Wardrop
F Coy	Captain George S.G. Strachan	Lieutenant Robert Hendry Second Lieutenant George A.A. MacGregor
G Coy	Captain Arthur C. Aitken	Second Lieutenant Charles L.H. Marburg Second Lieutenant William G.L. Cullen
H Coy	Captain George F. Deas	Lieutenant John I. Falconer Second Lieutenant Donald B. Sinclair
Captain and Adjutant James L. Robertson Quartermaster and Honorary Lieutenant Henry P. Huie Medical Officer John Cumming RAMC		

As of 14 January 1915 the battalion was reorganised from eight companies down to four, each of four platoons. A and B became the new A Company under Major Charles Gordon, C and D became B under Captain Angus Gregorson, E and F became C under Captain Alastair Campbell, G and H became D under Captain Arthur Aitken. Robert Bathgate became the Transport Officer soon after, an MG Section was formed in May 1915. Absent: Second Lieutenant Edward Fiddes, prominent in the establishment of the battalion, he later joined the Sudan Political Service in Khartoum.

Sergeant Major Alexander Stephen was 40 when the war broke out and signed on again with the Ninth the day the Reserve Battalion was raised as Private 2336. He immediately became their first regimental sergeant major. The young men found themselves under the stern but encouraging instruction of the 'excellent'[19] RSM.

Originally at St Ann's Maltings they moved to headquarters on East Claremont Street on 27 September 1914. Then the battalion, 600-700 strong, was split in half, one half accommodated in Olympia (a skating rink turned cinema on Annandale Street) on 19 October and the other half in the nearby London Street School. They became a new battalion in the Lothian Infantry Brigade, as part of Scottish Coast Defence Forces. The main duty was the Leith Dock Guard (Captain Aitken, Second Lieutenants Matley and Fiddes, 14 NCOs and 101 men). Two smaller guards were furnished, each of a corporal and three men: one to the Scottish Command Office, and the other assembled on the Castle esplanade and marched the length of the High Street behind a piper to become the Holyrood Palace Guard.

The reserve battalion moved from Edinburgh to Kilmarnock on 18 December 1914 with half the battalion billeted at Loanhead School and the other half in an old school on Union Street. Additional halls had to be found as the battalion's strength increased. The route marches became increasingly longer, until they were marching the 30-mile round trip to Ayr. George Robertson kept falling out with a pain in his side and was discharged with heart disease. George Walpole-Varo, at 18 stone, was also unable to keep up and was discharged. Training included the digging of trenches on Riccarton golf course, and sometimes being called out to occupy them at night. On one rainy occasion the battalion was filmed at drill and the men watched it the following week in the cinema.

John Clapperton attested in January 1915 and having been sworn in and given a plate and bowl at East Claremont Street in the morning, he was put on the train and joined the battalion at 'Killie' that afternoon. He wrote to his mother: 'I met one or two chaps at tea who belonged to Leith & I think I will not want for pals. After tea I had a wash, we are allowed out every night... There are a number of fellows here from the West & they are very free.' Clapperton transferred to the Machine Gun Corps and after training at Belton House served in France in 1918 where he was wounded when a shell hit his billet and his arm had to be amputated. Even as he went to France with the MGC in 1918, his father told him, in letters full of affection and concern, to 'Stand fast as a Royal Scot'.[75]

From 8 February 1915 the original Service Battalion was designated as 1/9th Royal Scots (*First-Ninth*), the new Reserve Battalion becoming the second-line 2/9th Royal Scots. Members of 1/9th took to filing off part of the Territorial 'T' on their shoulder titles to make them look like a number one, part of their transformation into the seamless khaki army of the BEF.

The 2/9th Battalion contained both Home Service men from the old Service Battalion, Imperial Service men under training for active service and those under 19 who could not be sent overseas, such that there was an ongoing exchange of personnel. On 19 February 1915, A and B companies became the Imperial Service Companies with 379 NCOs and men having taken the Imperial Service obligation, and C and D became the Home Service Companies.

On the 1/9th going to France, the 2/9th returned to Edinburgh in February 1915, having been warned for a move the week before, and took over the sector of landward defences as part of Lothian Brigade. On 18 February an advance party of three officers, ten NCOs and forty men, had taken over the trenches at Liberton and other guard duties. The rest of the battalion moved to Edinburgh on 24 February and took over the billets of 1/9th, four companies going into Bruntsfield School (where there was an outbreak of scarlet fever) and four into Warrender Park School.

In the press, officers of 2/9th, perhaps Ferguson, complained of the title *Dandy Ninth*. Alexander Blair robustly defended it saying:

> 'None of the officers and men of the real *Dandy Ninth* object to it in the least; in fact, we are proud of it, and try to live up to it. We are the real 9th Royal Scots, and no others have any right to speak for us… Apropos of the nick-name, you will be amused to hear that the other day I had a letter delivered to me in Flanders addressed "The Colonel of the Dandy Ninth, France". It had been delivered first to the Colonel of the 9th Lancers, who also are out here. He sent it to me with the following delightful letter: "Dear Colonel, - We never aspired to such a noble title, and so I think it must be for you."'[6]

James Ferguson 1857-1917.

At the end of February Ferguson was supervising training on the Braid Hills when his horse slipped on the ice and the old colonel broke his leg and was carried past the guard of the Ninth into Craigleith Hospital.

By May 1915 the 2/9th had provided 15 officers and 448 ORs to the 1/9th battalion. The Home Service and Imperial Service halves were split on 20 May 1915. The two companies of the Imperial Service group, now under Major Charles Gordon, left for Peebles on 23 May as a depleted 2/9th Battalion, yet by the end of July they were preparing themselves to be sent overseas with a strength of 508 all ranks. They remained there in camp until 6 October 1915.

Major Thomas Clark, commanding in Ferguson's absence, took the Home Service group (80 NCOs and 363 men) to become part of the 5th Scottish Provisional Battalion at Dundee (Tay Defences) under Lieutenant Colonel William Lachlan Forbes, Black Watch, headquartered in Dudhope Castle. Here the Ninths were described as 'a contingent' forming 'a detachment'.[76]

Arthur Anderson, too young for active service, was nominally with the 5th Provisional Battalion but found instead he was practically attached to the Royal Naval Air Service (RNAS) guarding the Stannergate Seaplane Station at Broughty Ferry, helping to put the aircraft in the water, even sitting in the comfort of a cockpit for night watch. As a precaution against fire they were searched for matches before going on duty and had to wear canvas shoes. A Zeppelin sighting off Berwick in June meant the machines were readied for launching, but at the last minute the Ninth guard and aircrews were taken by naval tender to wheeled machines at Barry. The Zeppelin was not found and the aircraft returned in the early hours of the morning having, according to Anderson, lost one of their number, the pilot and observer drowned.

On 30 October a visit to the theatre was interrupted by a stage announcement of another Zeppelin alarm, so they were marched out on the Forfar road, only to be recalled in the wee small hours. Similarly, the air raid on Edinburgh on the night of 2/3 April 1916, when Zeppelins *L.14* and *L.22* dropped 23 bombs and killed thirteen, had them stand-to at Selkirk, worrying about their families. One bomb fell near the drill hall at East Claremont Street and smashed windows, one on George Watson's College and another close to Warrender Park School.

The 5th Provisional guarded Dundee docks overnight from 7pm to 6am. Unfortunately, one member of the Ninth came into the guard room at Camperdown Dock Gatehouse, placed his rifle in a corner, it accidentally went off and shot dead customs officer Patrick Stuart asleep in the room above.

From time to time guards were taken out by motor boat to ships in the Tay and remained on board until they had been examined. The crew of the Swedish SS *Marthe Sorensen* locked themselves below decks, and a Ninth had to be lowered down a ventilator on a rope to open a hatch. In due course, contraband was found and the crew arrested.

A big trench system was dug at St Fort, Fife. Due to the huge demand for sandbags, a company was also pressed into service at Caird's jute mill, taking the bales of bags to the docks by horse-drawn wagon. The Ninth also furnished a firing party for the military funerals in the district, mostly from the hospitals. On a merrier note, they beat Dundee High School at rugby.

Early in November the Ninths in Dundee had been so depleted by drafts that they took over guarding the Tay Bridge as their sole responsibility. On the occasion of a parade for Provost Inches, for example, they were only able to muster about 250. Billeted in wet and noisy arches beneath Esplanade Station, a 'little humorous red-tape'[28] required all southbound trains to be stopped so that every compartment could be inspected and blinds checked.

'Night patrols on the bridge are particularly unpleasant and the four mile walk to the south side and back on the narrow footway, with trains rushing past only a matter of inches from one's face, is attended with a certain amount of risk, especially in a strong wind. At times the disaster of 1879 is vividly brought back to mind… added to which there is always the risk of being hit by a loose wagon rope or flying lumps of coal.'[28]

In bad weather, with ice on the footway, it took two hours to make the journey and the return to solid ground was most welcome; but on a bright morning it was a pleasant walk with fine views across the *Silv'ry* estuary. Finally relieved in Dundee by a third-line Black Watch battalion, the Ninths in the 5th Provisionals were at last returned to the Royal Scots from January 1916.

As early as November 1914 orders had been issued that when a battalion went overseas and was replaced at home by the second-line battalion, a third should be raised. In June 1915 the second reserve, 3/9th (Reserve) Royal Scots was formed in Peebles with Colonel Ferguson, just returned to duty following his accident, again taking command. Ferguson brought with him Captain Arthur Aitken as his adjutant and Sergeant Major Alexander Stephen, who was replaced in 2/9th by Tom Lowe, also of the Gordons, and long the gymnastic instructor of the Ninth.

This unit was to train and supply men to the first- and second-line battalions,

Second Reserve Battalion practising a bayonet charge in the Braid Hills

allowing the 2/9th to prepare for active service. The nucleus of 3/9th consisted of 104 men from 2/9th transferred on creation, and direct recruiting for the 2/9th ceased. By the end of July they were 400 strong. Later, because of losses in the 1/9th, a further 7 NCOs and 65 men transferred via the 3/9th. The second- and third-line battalions remained in camp together until the 2/9th went to Selkirk on 6 October.

At the end of 1915 there were therefore Ninths in four different battalions: the Service Battalion 1/9th on the Western Front, 2/9th (formerly Reserve), 3/9th Reserve Battalion and 5th Scottish Provisional Battalion (Home Service Battalion). In addition, many of the men in the Machine Gun Sections had transferred to the new Machine Gun Corps (MGC), a good many of them being drafted to France in just two weeks, and a similarly high number being wounded over the following months.

At Peebles the 3/9th had quarters in a big marquee. A number of drafts reduced the unit 'leaving the camp beastly quiet'[24] and in November they went into private billets (Bernard Holmer, for example to 2 Gibson Place) 'leaving the camp a quagmire'.[24] Life was not too onerous, they were allowed out between 5 and 9.30pm nightly. Ferguson presented 'war badges'[6] to boy scouts at Peebles, each of whom had done at least three hours work for the cause.

The 2/9th were only a few weeks at Selkirk before the 3/9th replaced them, A Company taking residence in the UFC Hall. Their mascot in 1916 was a dog called Dandy, and, by 1919, a pony named Sandy. In January 1916 the 3/9th welcomed back the detachment from the 5th Scottish Provisional Battalion and new companies were formed, including the thirty members of the band. The billets in Victoria Hall were so overcrowded that meals had to be taken in the courtyard, even when it was snowing, whilst at night those whose straw mattresses were near the centre of the hall had to

ROYAL SCOTS. NO. 45. R.C.

turn in first. The drafts, those under notice for service overseas, were put into intensive training: digging trenches, out on forced marches, gas drills in PH helmets and taking part in tactical exercises.

The *Supernumeraries* among them often had wounds from active service and were examined by a doctor periodically for fitness to join drafts. In February 1916, on the anniversary of their crossing to France, the Supernumerary Company, numbering ninety, had a dinner at the County Hotel in Selkirk. There were piano and cornet solos, and songs from the actor Harry Hobson, killed the following year, and Lieutenant Willie Urquhart's rendition of 'Pinkie Dinkie'', before Sergeant Major Clarke lowered the tone with an unnamed song. Following a toast to the senior battalion, the 1/9th Royal Scots, 'at "Lights out" some of the guests had great difficulty in finding their way to their respective billets – owing, we understand, to the new lighting regulations. Nevertheless, all seemed to thoroughly enjoy themselves, and many of the grim struggles in which they had fought in on the soil of Flanders were again fought over.'[77]

Ferguson, as colonel of the reserve battalion, 'was officially invited to go over and see the trenches in France, a visit which was to him a source of the highest satisfaction'.[6] In likelihood he would have visited the Ninth, Colonel Blair and his son Jimmy Ferguson; he was there for a week in March 1916 and experienced coming under fire. The 3/9th served at Selkirk, Stobs and, from November 1916, Catterick, where their colonel left them. James Ferguson, Sheriff of Forfarshire, founder of the battalion and first colonel of all three lines of the Ninth, predeceased by both of his sons, retired in March 1917 and died in Edinburgh the following month of lung cancer, aged 59. The University of Edinburgh Roll of Honour records that he had 'trained over 2,000 officers and men'. He was replaced by Lieutenant Colonel Claude Doig, who had a good colonial career and whose active service had been brought to an end by a

Second-line Territorials, members of 2/9th Royal Scots.

fall from a horse. All the third line battalions of the regiment were amalgamated to become 4th (Reserve) Battalion Royal Scots in July 1917, commanded by Doig.

When last mentioned, 2/9th Royal Scots were at Selkirk in October 1915 under the command of Major Charles Gordon, promoted to lieutenant colonel. At the end of November 1915 they were reassigned to the newly formed 195 Brigade, created from the 2nd Scottish Rifles Brigade, as part of 65th (2nd Lowland) Division, and relocated to Tillicoultry. Battalion headquarters was at Devonvale Mill with brigade at Stirling. Hopes of active service had to be postponed however, A Company and the MG Section worked on the construction of a camp at Cornton, Bridge of Allan. Between November 1915 and January 1916, they were temporarily renamed the 20th Battalion. A and B Companies which had formed the Imperial Service group, expanded to four companies on 29 January 1916.

Table 9. Infantry Brigades of the 65th Division, March 1916

65th (2nd Lowland) Division		
Major General Theodore E Stephenson		
194 Brigade	**195 Brigade**	**196 Brigade**
Brigadier General	*Brigadier General*	*Brigadier General*
FA Macfarlan	*PA Turner*	*HF Kays*
2/7 Royal Scots	2/4 Royal Scots	2/5 Highland Light Infantry
2/8 Royal Scots	2/9 Royal Scots	2/6 Highland Light Infantry
2/4 Royal Scots Fusiliers	2/5 Scottish Rifles	2/7 Highland Light Infantry
2/5 King's Own Scottish Borderers	2/6 Scottish Rifles	2/9 Highland Light Infantry

The 65th Division was transferred to Eastern Command, later Southern Command, and as such the 2/9th left Scotland for Brentwood, Essex on 22 February 1916. They were billeted in homes for the first time, the Town Hall afforded central messing and the White Hart Hotel became headquarters. For the first time they were also required to mount a 'Zeppelin picquet'.[10] On 21 March they moved to Witham and were more scattered: headquarters at the Constitutional Club, B Company in private billets, Temple Villa occupied by the Transport and The Retreat Villa (a lunatic asylum on Maldon Road) by new recruits (who nicknamed it the 'Retreat of Mons'). A, C and D companies formed detachments in the villages of Wickham Bishops and Great Totham.

Large drafts from other regiments now began to join them and included men from Yorkshire, Lancashire, Durham and Northumberland, Leicester, Staffordshire and Lincolnshire, as well as men from the 3/9th. It was not possible to equip them all uniformly, so many retained their original regimental dress. At least three setts of tartan could be counted, and both spats and puttees were on parade; but an attempt to issue plain black glengarries was rejected and the men bought their own Royal Scots versions with the diceboard-pattern. There were also issues of American made ERA rifles.

Transport Section.

Billets in Totham.

Marching along Newland Street, Witham, past The George.

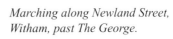

'Opposite the "Retreat" of Mons, we parade here at 7 each day, by order AL Wainwright Pte.'

On 8 June 1916 they moved out of billets to camp near Terling along with the rest of the brigade. Three days later Lieutenant Colonel Arthur Egerton became commanding officer. They were inspected in Terling Park in July by the Inspector General of Infantry who said: 'The 2/9th Royal Scots have the makings of a very good Battalion. It is the Edinburgh Kilted Regiment, and gets a good class of men, but has lately received a large number of English recruits.'[10]

Two days after this His Majesty King George V drove by and the division lined the road between Witham and Chelmsford. Other distractions included a Highland Gathering held at Hylands Park in August, and on the same day the band of the 2/9th RS played at an open tennis tournament at Easton Lodge.

From the summer of 1915 the 2/9th seemed increasingly likely to be sent on foreign service as a separate unit, and trained at Stobs in October, although they had already sent 15 officers and 433 men to the 1/9th. However, on 30 July 1916, in the wake of the terrible losses sustained on the Somme, over 300 NCOs and men were drafted, going first to Aldershot for special musketry practice, which ended any such prospect. The whole of 195 Brigade was similarly affected.

'All ranks had striven so very hard to perfect themselves in drill and manoeuvre these last two years, and in many individual cases had sacrificed their businesses and interests willingly, in order to become efficient, that this Order, virtually cancelling, for the time at least, their chance of going to the Front, struck the Battalion very hard.'[10]

181

Most of the drafts went to the 1/9th but, 'what a heartrending scene one conjures up in one's mind of the scene at the Base the day the boys had their kilts taken from them and were drafted into other battalions!'.[10] Thirteen of the best NCOs were interviewed by the divisional commander at Boreham House on 2 October and were recommended to be Officer Cadets at Gailles.

Spirits revived, naturally enough with a boisterous sergeants v officers football match where 'Mr [Ralph] Rhodes displayed a greater tendency to take the man in preference to the ball,'[10] nevertheless the sergeants won 9-2. Herbert Windle 'positively pranced home' in the gas helmet race. A battalion concert was also held with music, song and impersonations, sometimes 'at the expense of some of our noble instructors'.[10] The 'Scotch' violin performance ended promptly with the snapping of a string. A healthy rivalry developed between D Company *the Guards*, C Company *the Canaries*, B Company *the Brownies* and, what, asked the battalion magazine, is the *nom de plume* of A Company?

The 2/9th had a good view of three burning Zeppelins, conceding that they had nothing to do with it. The Depot staff wanted to know 'what the duties of a Zeppelin picket are, and if they are supposed to "run in" any stray Zepps they may see on a charge of "being without visible means of support!"'[10]

In January 1917, far from heading east they went to Ireland as part of the larger British Army presence in the country after the Easter Rising of 1916. The 65th Division relieved 59th (2nd North Midland) Division, which had been rushed to Ireland to deal with the Rising, had fought in the streets of Dublin and formed the infamous firing squads in the aftermath. One of the executed leaders, James Connolly, was born in Edinburgh and had served in the Royal Scots.

Divisional headquarters was at the Curragh under Irish Command; 195 Brigade were stationed variously at Fermoy, Tralee, Limerick, Moore Park and Kilworth, all in the south-west. Donald Sutherland had to leave his new wife in Witham behind, she gave birth to a son whilst he was in Ireland. The Royal Scots made themselves popular in Tralee, with massed pipe bands playing on The Green. In May 'The Royal Scots were all heartily sorry to leave Tralee, but they hoped to be sent back again. They had been fairly treated in Scotch towns and they had been fairly treated in English towns, but their warm-hearted reception in Tralee won all their hearts, and would be a life-long memory to the Scots,'[78] said the Bandmaster John Ross, who had been promoted to the dizzy height of unpaid acting corporal.

Men of the second-line arguably had more time for misdemeanours. There are five recorded trials in Essex and fifteen in Ireland, for drunkenness, insubordination, theft, violence to superiors, absence without leave, and most frequently, desertion. This typically attracted six months' detention. At one end of the scale Drummer William Stokoe, celebrated middle distance runner, was summoned for riding a bicycle without front or rear lights at Witham, pleaded guilty and was fined 5s. Toward the other, William Etherington, a former policeman, was detained for a year for desertion. John A. Brown, with the 3/9th at Selkirk in 1916, was given 28 days detention for fraudulent enlistment under the, perhaps joking, alias of J. Riddle. He was wounded the following

2/9th at Strand Barracks, Limerick 1917.

year and served subsequently with the Labour Corps. Another serious case was that of Owen Clarke, who already appears to have deserted twice from the HLI and to have absconded from the Ninth in September 1918. He was thereby dismissed for misconduct and forfeited his medals. A mysterious W.J. Hunter seems to have been commissioned into the Gordons and then suffered forfeiture. Disturbingly, Colonel Egerton was a member of the court trying officers of the 3rd Royal Munster Fusiliers for keeping men back though medically fit.

The Royal Scots Regiment had spent a considerable amount of time in Ireland since 1679 and were certainly in Limerick in 1700. In July 1917 they returned, with battalions based at Castle Barracks and the Strand Barracks.

Gladys and Alice Turnbull.

At least one man decided to settle in Ireland. Corporal John Turnbull of Edinburgh married local girl Miss Mary O'Mara at Limerick in May 1917, moving to Bishop Street. A daughter, Gladys, was born to them on 2 April 1918. Tragically he never saw her as he was killed in France on 1 August of that year. Mary raised their daughter with the help of her sister, Kay, and they made a point of visiting Scotland over the years so that John's parents and sister, Alice, could meet the young Gladys.

There was little overt military activity in 1917. Many Irish Volunteers had followed the Irish Parliamentary Party's Willie Redmond into the British Army. The 'City Regiment' in Limerick complied with the requirement to hand over their arms, but the resentment this caused led to a new 2nd Battalion being formed in early 1917 with about

183

100 men and some arrests were made. Politically, the region in 1917 remained active. When Éamon de Valera was released from prison he spoke passionately at Bruree and, following the death in action of Willie Redmond in July 1917, won the East Clare by-election for Sinn Féin.

With the Great War still foremost, a great deal of training was undertaken by the 2/9th and courses were run in physical training and bayonet fighting, musketry, sniping, anti-gas, bombing and platoon command. Corporal Ernest Barnes, bomb instructor with the Brigade Bombing School, was accidentally killed by a rifle grenade in September.

The route marches required considerable stamina. The weight expected to be carried by an infantryman in 1914 was:

Clothing	7.4kg
Arms	4.8kg
Ammunition (150 rounds)	4.1kg
Entrenching Tool	1.2kg
Accoutrements (1908 Pattern webbing)	3.7kg
Articles in pack, including greatcoat	4.6kg
Rations and water	2.7kg
Marching order	28.4kg (63lb)
Fighting order (less pack but plus 100 rounds small arms ammunition)	25.9kg (57lb)

The unconsumed portion of the day's ration was carried plus an iron ration for a day, consisting of biscuit, bully beef, tea, sugar, salt, cheese and meat extract, plus two pints of water.

William Dennis with MLE rifle.

As the war progressed the amount of Small Arms Ammunition (SAA) carried was typically reduced to 170 rounds, but this weight saving (2.2kg) was more than offset by the Brodie steel helmet (0.9kg), Small Box Respirator (1.5kg), waterproof sheet (1.2kg), Mills bombs (0.8kg each), aeroplane flares, tommy cooker with solidified alcohol, sand bags and, among the section or platoon, proportions of picks, shovels, wire cutters and such. By the end of 1916 each man could be expected to carry at least 30kg (66lb).

Despite all of the training, the men of the 65th Division were not to go to war with their present units. Notification that the division was to be broken up was given in January 1918, by mid-March the headquarters were closed and by 15 May 1918, the 65th Division ceased to exist, all its men transferred or drafted.

The first draft, back in March 1915, knew they were for France when their Highland shoes and spats were replaced with boots and half puttees. They marched along Princes Street behind a piper and Bobby Johnston was seen off by his father, who went to Egypt the following month. The draft crossed by the Clyde paddle steamer, the *Duchess of Hamilton*.

Samuel Gillespie carried in his sporran a teaspoon. This teaspoon had been used at the Wedgewood Café, at the New Picture House on Princes Street, in Edinburgh by a young Margaret Kerr when they first went out, and whom he married in 1921. In fact, the teaspoon went through two world wars. He was commissioned in the Gordon Highlanders, and the teaspoon was still in his dress sporran when he died in 1971.

Samuel Gillespie in theatre (right).

When Arthur Anderson's draft of twenty-four men left in April 1916 both bands were playing (though he was not convinced by their choice of *Will Ye No Come Back Again*) and the platform was thronged with people. He remembers that 'the perspiring station master has an anxious time making sure that none of the Selkirk girls is sent off to France by mistake'.[28] Their route was by night train to London St Pancras, then a march through deserted streets to Waterloo, and thence by train to Southampton. About 700 drafts were present from different regiments and old precedence was observed with the Royal Scots marching at their head.

The draft crossed overnight to Le Havre, anchored a day and a night and then proceeded up the Seine to Rouen. *En route* they passed a ship of German prisoners of war, some of whom grinned at the new draft and drew their fingers across their throats. Ashore at last they marched to their camp, 50 miles from the front. First impressions were favourable, because the food was better than on Home Service, but this was before they reached the horrors of Étaples. This vast camp, staging point for the front, succeeded at times at making the latter seem preferable. Drills were performed day and night with the men expected to grab the odd meal and a few hours sleep in overcrowded tents. Further, route marches to Boulogne and back, some 28 miles/45km in full kit, took fourteen hours. There were long defaulters lists and executions for desertion.

Without regrets Anderson and the draft joined the 1/9th Royal Scots at Arras.

'The colonel appears up the dug-out steps and wishes us good luck, saying that perhaps we mightn't find things so bad as we expected. In any case we are fortunate to arrive when things are comparatively quiet. The Boche must have overheard this last remark as a 'big-one' burst over the parapet not many yards away. I certainly am now feeling a bit weak at the knees. If this is a sample of 'quietness', what is it going to be like when they get busy?'[28]

Lectures at home that artillery needed a ton of metal to kill a man, did not provide the necessary reassurance. Quinn remembered a regular sergeant who used to scream at them, '"Stand up you shower, you won't all be killed at once." Cold comfort!'[23]

Now they were finally amongst their platoons under the searching eye of a sergeant.

'You've got to remember there was something like a thousand killed in the 9th Royal Scots, over the period…so there were very few of the original ones there… so then out comes a draft of new men and you've got to get to know the new men, the ones that are what we call windy, the ones that are reckless, you've got to try and know their characters, and they're not trained like we were.'[56]

Chapter 6

Offensive Spirit
1917

ON the Western Front, Scotland was about to field her largest ever host and face her biggest battle. At their lowest ebb, from the nightmare of Courcelette, the 51st Division was at last relieved and 154 Brigade moved to Rubempré, north of Amiens, on 12 January 1917. After nineteen days rest and training in marshy ground they were moved to Arras on a six-day march, of between 8 and 22 miles per day, during the coldest period experienced on the Western Front. The brigade was stationed around Acq on the River Scarpe, west of Arras and beneath the famous landmark of Mont Saint Eloi. The Ninth found their rest billets at Bailleul-sur-Cornailles, suitable for 33 officers and 1,300 ORs, were already occupied by cavalry, and half of them had to squeeze into billets at Chelers and Tincquette instead.

Just before dawn, at 5.30am on 16 February, a hostile aeroplane came over, dropped a couple of bombs and flattened two houses in the village, killing two civilians. Rifle fire had no apparent effect and the guard had a Lewis gun with them after that. On another morning an aeroplane destroyed an observation balloon with a rocket, the observer jumping clear with a parachute and the balloon turned to 'just a few rags of flame'.[23] This balloon had been spotting for an ex-Naval railway gun that 'was noisier than any shell bursting'.[23]

The outskirts of Arras were found to be in ruins, but in the centre many buildings were largely intact, less parts of their roofs, and the more precarious were roped off. The railway station had been reduced to twisted metal, but a uniformed station master was still on duty. Notices posted in French and English warned that looters would be shot on sight, and there were a good many Military Police 'red-caps' with revolvers 'capable of carrying out the law on the slightest pretext'.[28] The YMCA canteen was near the sandbagged cathedral and sold a lot of tinned food, cooked for no extra charge, and offered free tea and coffee.

Arras
ROBERT Nivelle replaced Joseph Joffre as French C-in-C after the failures of the Somme and his own successes at Verdun. He was convinced that an artillery bombardment in depth would achieve a breakthrough and planned to attack on either side of the Somme battleground: the French at Chemin des Dames, preceded by a supporting attack 80 miles north around Arras by the BEF. Famously the Canadians,

'Chambres pour Voyageurs' at Arras, 'the hub of the universe'.[32]

those 'bonny fechters',[36] were to take the northern part of Vimy Ridge. The 51st Division, sited north of the River Scarpe (Map XIV), was tasked with securing the southern shoulder of Vimy Ridge, an operation Ewing describes as 'one of vast difficulty'.[33] The attack would pass over onto the reverse slope of the ridge. The progress of the artillery's wire-cutting efforts here could only be assessed from aerial observation and at this time the Germans possessed a high level of air superiority.

The division took over the Corps' left sector on 11 February and Harper's preparations began, in three selected areas: improving the trenches they inhabited, reducing the enemy's defences opposite and on tactical training to rush the gap. The state of the trenches was described: 'The frost is breaking slowly, the effect on the line when the thaw does really set in is not pleasant to contemplate, as most of the trenches, though excellent now, are merely held up by the frozen state of the earth.'[1] Despite the ongoing snow, the trenches did indeed begin falling in and turning to mud. Poor trenches meant more casualties and Old 'Arper made the answer clear to his men, '"Dig 'undreds..." He was decidedly the right man for this somewhat feudal gathering of the clans.'[32] With his battalion commanders he discussed raids, and on 20 February spoke with Colonel Green and Colonel Unthank of the Ninth and 4th Seaforths.

However, to the south between Arras and Soissons, on 24 February the enemy began to retire and strong patrols were sent out every night to establish contact. The Germans were retiring to the Siegfried Line, known to the allies as the Hindenburg Line. This was well placed and prepared to the highest standards, making extensive

188

use of reinforced concrete emplacements, known as pill-boxes, tunnels and deep belts of barbed wire. Although only intended as an additional defence, the Germans withdrew to it in February and March 1917, removing them from the Salient, created at great cost by the Somme battle, which had been the principal target of the allied plan of attack and necessitating a delay and change of plan. The allies went into the evacuated and devastated zone to find it was extensively booby trapped. For example, a time-delayed mine in a cellar in Villers Faucon wiped out the headquarters officers of the 6th Glosters, including former English teacher at George Watson's, Ninth and Edinburgh OTC commander, Major Robert Gerrard.

In the 51st Division's sector the enemy were holding firm, unable to develop defence in depth and unwilling to give up the strongly held Vimy Ridge. The Ninth moved up on 22 March, ready to attack at 24 hours' notice but the attack was delayed; it was probably as well as the weather had been so bad little training had been undertaken. Instead the division carried out some very large raids involving about 150 men in order to cause lasting damage to the enemy defences opposing them. In these raids they identified that they were facing the 2nd Bavarian Reserve Infantry Regiment, 1st Bavarian Reserve Division – and that they were formidable opponents.

The Ninth were on the immediate right of the Canadians when the latter made a 'reconnaissance in force' against Vimy Ridge on the night of 28 February/1 March. A deployment of gas forewarned the Germans who bombarded the Canadian trenches and a number of gas cylinders were breached, then the wind direction changed before a second release. A rare truce was held on 2 March to retrieve the wounded. It is reported that as a result of this disastrous raid, the Canadians and the 51st Division ordered the removal of gas cylinders from their lines.

When not in the line, training was undertaken near the billets, though the weather was not co-operative. Between July and December 1916 the division had changed area eighteen times, a situation not conducive to training. In fact, since March 1916 they had not been out of the line for more than ten days, and just before Arras they were in five different Corps and three Armies in a single month. General Harper had quite developed ideas about training and was now intent on building upon the success of Beaumont Hamel. He believed in individual initiative, 'it is the fittest mind which survives as much as, if not more than, the fittest body'. The enemy wire was to be cut with No.106 instantaneous fuzes, which entered widescale use in 1917. These fuzes unreeled brass tape in flight to arm the shell and the tapes fluttered down on the British front line as they waited to go.

The layout of the German trenches was taped-out on the ground and the attack practised. The British 18-pounder barrage was simulated by pipers and hostile machine guns by drummers. The assault of trenches was also practised, using reserve trenches near Villers Châtel. Great emphasis was placed on keeping well extended on the approach and shooting down the garrison before entering the enemy trench. The creeping barrage was now quite sophisticated, though as ever there were scant means of communication between the infantry and artillery. White Very lights were to be sent up to lengthen the range by 100 yards and green ones as an SOS, but only after the barrage had completed its timetabled advance. Nevertheless, the loss of men to your own barrage was considered a necessary risk, made more inevitable as artillery barrels wore out.

Bewsher brings it down to this:

> 'While the barrage was on the trench, the Bavarians would be on the dug-out step, and the Highlanders would be waiting from seventy to a hundred yards short of the trench. As the barrage lifted the race began. Would the Bavarian reach his fire-step and open fire on the Highlanders, or would the Highlanders reach the parapet and shoot the Bavarian down before he could man his trenches?'[51]

From the German perspective Jünger describes the race where men had to 'cover the small amount of ground, from the entrance of the shelter to the sentry posts. But these few steps needed to be taken in the instant of a great crescendo of fire before an attack, the precise timing of which is a matter of gut instinct and feeling.'[58] At the sudden *fortissimo piano* the fight ceased to be between artillery positioned miles to the rear and bombing and hand-to-hand combat commenced.

Grenade training, with such dangerous devices and methods, incurred a toll of its own, including the Ninth's John Sexton, wounded in 1915, and Andrew Ramsay accidentally killed at grenade school in 1916. In 1915 being selected as a 'bomber' was not popular. Tactics consisted of 'bayonet men' moving forward whilst bombs were thrown over their heads. The grenades were crude, such as the Battye, or even improvised with guncotton and jam tins and a 5-7 second length of fuse often lit from a cigarette.

The lessons Jock Brown learnt were:

1. Always leave the detonators behind – a bomb without a detonator is quite harmless.
2. Never take the safety pin out before you throw the bomb. This ensures that it will not burst if you strike the trench. The Germans will probably throw it back, but it is unlikely it will fall in your part of the trench.
3. Always have a fuse a foot long [so that it burnt for 30 seconds].

By 1916 the more reliable Mills bomb was in mass production and could be found in every infantryman's equipment, particularly on a raid. C Company suffered a loss the night before the attack when a man, possibly Thomas McDowell, turned over on his wire bed in his dug-out and the pin of a Mills bomb was caught. At some point George Houston received a Distinguished Conduct Medal, cited in *The London Gazette* when 'an enemy bomb was thrown into the trench which he and ten other men were holding. He promptly picked it up, and when it slipped from his hand with the fuse still burning, he picked it up again and threw it over the parapet. Just as it left his hand it exploded, wounding him in the face. His plucky act saved the lives of several of his comrades.'

Rifles were also fitted with dischargers to fire grenades and in April 1917 rifles for rifle grenades increased from thirty-four to sixty-four per battalion. This multitude of weapons formed part of the new platoon tactics. Although the creeping barrage was vitally important against well defended locations, the platoon of four sections had the firepower and tactics to overcome un-neutralised machine guns. One section was centred about grenadiers (bomb throwers), one the Lewis gun, another rifles and scouts and finally the rifle grenadiers; the Lewis guns and rifle grenades provided the supporting firepower.

A number of the battalion left to join specialisations such as trench mortars, the Machine Gun Corps and the Royal Engineers waterways companies, tunnelling companies and the chemical weapon Special Brigade. NCOs were asked if they wanted to take up commissions for the Tank Corps (so named in July) and Regimental Sergeant Major Peter McLachlan gave them an honest appraisal that *Subs*[23] had a life expectancy of six weeks. Nevertheless, a number of men put their names down, but may not have survived the coming months at Arras.

Away from the line there was also an opportunity for sports. The Inter-Platoon Football Tournament was concluded two days before the battalion took up positions for the Battle of Arras. Harold Silver had to adapt his goal keeping skills – he had played for the Hyde Seals water polo club. Bill Hay had great confidence, having the Broad brothers in his platoon. Finalists were No's 10 and 12 Platoons from C Company and resulted in a narrow win for No.12 Platoon. Indeed football is reported to have been compulsory in the winter of 1917 with every platoon issued with a ball. B Company won the Inter-Company Relay Race, each team consisting of one officer, one CSM, one CQSM, one sergeant, one corporal and one private, each to run 220 yards.

Thélus – Vimy Ridge

'The object of the offensive is to capture the VIMY RIDGE'

Operation Order No.70, 5 April 1917

ON the left of the Division, Corps and Army (51st Division, XVII Corps, Third Army), 154 Brigade was to attack alongside the Canadians (First Army) to their left, with 152 Brigade to their right (Map XV). The brigade attack was to be led by the 4th Seaforths, on the left against the Lille Road, and by the Ninth to their right. Their objective was the so-called Black Line, capturing the enemy's front-line system and consolidating, with other battalions to push on to the Blue and Brown lines beyond. This was the 'Leap Frog' system that Bewsher attributes to Harper, that the general staff had described as 'an extremely difficult operation'[43] in February 1916 but had issued as tactical doctrine SS144 in February 1917.

The divisional artillery were given six lanes, one per Field Artillery Brigade (the 51st Division being reinforced by four Army Field Artillery Brigades), each assigned one battery of six 18-pounders to perform wire cutting and create a creeping barrage up to the Black Line, one up to Blue and one up to Brown. They would provide two to three times the weight of barrage compared to the first day of the Somme.

Roclincourt.

The 4.5″ howitzers would form a searching barrage ahead of the creeping barrage and the 60-pounder heavies would take on strongpoints ahead of the objectives. There were to be four days of bombardment from V day and continuous bombardment throughout Y day, the day before Zero, and Stokes mortars were to give a final, intense bombardment of the front lines. In addition, 200 gas drums were to be fired as well as 1,600 4″ Stokes mortar gas shells.

The battalion disposition was initially to place C Company in the front line in Bonnal Trench, D Company in the support line in Collecteur Trench and A and B companies in dug-outs at Écurie. The day before the off 'Bunty' Walkden and his Lewis gun team had their dug-out blown in. They made a hole big enough for a man to get through and reported all present and correct. The details of the plan were that in preparation for the attack, A and D companies would move into no man's land between saps 20-22 ahead of the line, with B Company in the line and C Company in reserve. These positions were the old French trenches that the brigade had withdrawn from in 1916. Ahead of them were three enemy lines designated Red, Yellow and Black. They were to be east of Bonnal Trench by 2am on Z and their codeword that all was ready was 'Green', the CO's name. A Company on the left and D Company on the right were to attack at zero plus two minutes on a two-platoon front in two waves, the first wave against the Red Line and the second wave 100 yards behind to take the Yellow Line.

The barrage was to lift from the Red Line at zero plus four minutes and the Yellow Line at Zero plus seven minutes. B Company would then form the third wave against the Black Line – here a trench called Poser Weg – with an intermediate barrage lift at Zero plus ten minutes and a lift from their objective at Zero plus thirty-four minutes.

It was to maintain a protective barrage until Zero plus two hours six minutes. The battalion were to capture the Black Line at 7.10am, giving them just over an hour from the time the barrage lifted. C Company would remain in reserve. Each company would mop up and gain touch on both flanks, before the Argylls came through. The first contact aeroplane was due over at Zero plus one hour, and the forward infantry were to light red flares in the bottom of the trenches to indicate their position.

On 2 April, amidst heavy snowfall, Zero was fixed for 8 April. The bombardment therefore began on 4 April but the attack slipped on 5 April to make Z hour 5.30am on 9 April 1917, Easter Monday. As the Ninth came up, they passed over tank tracks that they took as a good sign. On 8 April the enemy's counter bombardment presented very hazardous conditions, and so through the night gas shells were fired by the division's counter-battery guns, successfully suppressing the enemy's retaliatory fire. There had been some snow and the ground was very soft. The men were warned to take great care in assembly not to give themselves away with rattling equipment or moonlight shining on bayonets. Lieutenant Bob Lindsay, Intelligence Officer, synchronised watches. The companies moved out from Bonnal at 10pm, where four were killed, and were in position by 4am. The Ninth had 22 officers and 698 Other Ranks going into action, leaving behind 14 officers and 217 ORs by order of GHQ.

Bill Hay of No.4 Platoon and Johnny Willocks, whom Hay called 'Bollocks', of No.2 had an habitual falling out at assembly and A Company Sergeant Major Jack Renwick had to step in: 'For god's sake pack it in. You'll be fighting the Germans in a few minutes.'[79] The rum ration was issued and they fixed bayonets at 4.30am. 'We're all in this together, boys,'[79] assured Hay. The barrage began, on cue at 5.30am.

Shortly after Zero, Second Lieutenant Bill Ferguson of No.2 Platoon, wounded at the Somme and nine months in France, was killed in his ninth action, shot dead climbing out of his assembly position, leaving his platoon to Sergeant Johnny Willocks. Sergeant David Gardner was surprised to see a British salvo falling behind them.

Bill Hay was in the second wave at Vimy:

'We soon caught the boys up who were jumping from shell hole to shell hole... Soon we got to the German front-line trench. It was smashed to bits but there were several dug-out entrances. We dealt with these first. I pulled the pin from a Mills bomb and chucked it down the steps – 'Come out, you fuckers!' There was a crash followed by shouts and screams... Up the steps came four Jerries with their hands up.'[79]

We had captured the first line and then we made to the second line and I got caught on the barbed wire between the first and the second line [Red and Yellow]. I had mitts on my hands, and my kilt and my mitts caught on the barbed wire. I found myself eventually buried and stunned, and blinded because I got muck, filth all over me. I don't know what hit me or what dropped there.'[56]

Hay thought his platoon commander, Jimmy Adams, was killed at the outset. He had promised Adams' mother he would look after the young subaltern, who came out in

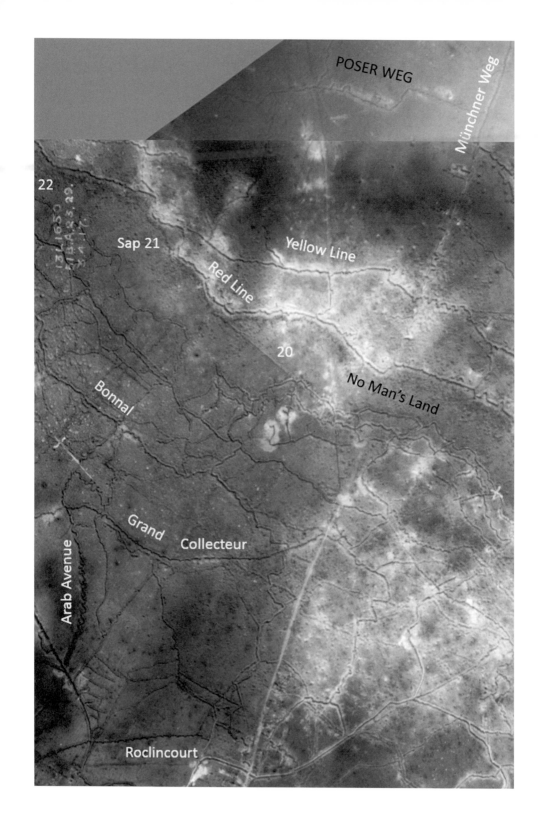

POSER WEG

Münchner Weg

22

Sap 21

Yellow Line

Red Line

20

No Man's Land

Bonnal

Grand

Collecteur

Arab Avenue

Roclincourt

January aged 19. It seems Adams led his platoon to the second line before he was killed. A third A Company subaltern, Second Lieutenant David McEwen was seriously wounded leading his platoon, and died at No.42 Casualty Clearing Station the following day.

Jimmy Adams.

In the second line the company came under fire from a sniper and Company Sergeant Major Jack Renwick and Corporal George Fernie stalked and killed him. The *London Gazette* reported that Jack Renwick 'displayed great courage and initiative in commanding the company. He captured and consolidated his objectives and sent in valuable reports.' With two signallers, he entered an enemy dug-out and captured twelve Germans, including three officers. He then made the place the company headquarters. John Laidlaw Renwick, wounded at the Somme, with the rare distinction of both a Military Cross and a Military Medal, was killed later in the month, aged 22.

William Moncur's officer was wounded, so he led the platoon to their objective; he 'turned the conflict in our favour by killing four Germans and capturing eight others.'[33] Corporal Thomas Palmer led his bombing section to knock out a machine gun hampering the advance.

The objective was attained by 7.30am after a 'stiff fight,'[33] with Major Rowbotham and Captain William Lindsay (D Company) despatching parties against a number of pockets of resistance. It was carried with 'a combination of individual dash and sharp-witted leadership.'[33]

Jackie Renwick.

With posts pushed out as far as the barrage had allowed and the line consolidated, the Ninth now provided carrying parties through heavy snowfall, from Bonnal Trench up to the Black Line, and on to the Blue Line when it fell at 12.27pm. Runners came in via sap 21 with delayed information on the progress of battle. It was reported that the brigade had succeeded in reaching the Brown line at Pont du Jour by 6.30pm and were in touch with the Canadians. However, they were in fact still short of the Brown Line. There was uncut wire on the reverse slope, observable only from the air, and it is understandable that cresting the shoulder of the ridge they might follow the fall of the slope and veer to the right, creating a gap with the Canadians.

Attempts were made through the following day to take the far objective and to bomb up Tommy and Ouse Trenches, but were held up by machine-gun fire and instead a line of posts was dug across the crest of the ridge to link up with the Canadians. The artillery were called up and the brigade prepared to renew the attack behind a creeping barrage.

At 9am on 11 April all companies of the Ninth were ordered to attack this part of the Brown Line in two waves, with two tanks moving up on the right, and were in position in Tommy Trench for Zero hour at 2pm. The artillery had been prepared for

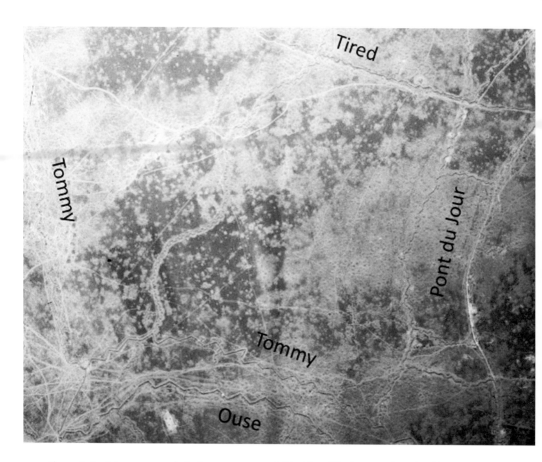

Tired

Tommy

Pont du Jour

Tommy

Ouse

the original barrage and their targets carefully identified; now they had been moved-up in poor weather to new positions. There was to be a four-hour bombardment for wire cutting, but after the heavies fired short, Zero was postponed until 4 then 5pm. The expectation was that a hard fight lay ahead.

As soon as the bombardment ceased, patrols went out to see if the wire had been cut prior to the assault and, crawling up to the enemy trench at 5.30pm, found it empty. A second trench was empty too but enemy dead lay between the two who had clearly tried to withdraw in the bombardment in order to be away before the attack. Both trenches were occupied by half the battalion and contact made to left and right with units of the brigade, while patrols made contact with the enemy on the railway. They were relieved in a blizzard at 3.30am on 12 April 1917, retiring to 'Y' Huts near Laresset for three days. The division 'shared the honour of that day with the Canadians, taking as many prisoners and gaining a great part of the ridge'.[80]

There was now clear observation over the Douai plain. Although there had been no surprise, the Germans thought the bombardment would last another week, their reserves had been too far back and too few, for they were preparing to punish Nivelle to the south.

Though Vimy was deemed a relative success, there were inevitably heavy losses. Casualties on the 9 April 1917 were 2 officers killed and 9 wounded, one being Major

J. Rowbotham, 69 ORs killed, 138 wounded and 27 missing. Thomas and Jessie Campbell, of the family firm of butchers, lost two sons in No.4 Platoon Lewis gun section on the same day: George 'Doey' and John 'Niffy' Campbell – who created the company's secret haggis recipe in 1911.

James Dobbin, a 37-year-old grocer, was conscripted in March 1916 and put his preferred unit as the Army Service Corps. Instead he was sent to the Royal Scots. He had just come through a sulphur treatment for scabies when he was sent to France and transferred to the Ninth in February 1917. He was killed at Vimy and buried in Roclincourt Valley Cemetery with a number of other Ninths. His widow and daughter received 18s 9d a week as a pension. Donald Darroch from Jura left a widow and ten children.

At 11am on 9 April the RAMC received a wire urgently requesting stretcher-bearers for an estimated 80 casualties from the Ninth. Thirty-six bearers were sent as well as orders 'to hold 50 Huns in readiness'.[36] Prisoners, once passed by Intelligence, were often used as stretcher-bearers.

We left Bill Hay in the front-line system:

'I was frightened of the noise of rats squealing and scuttling around, I hate rats anyway. Sometimes they'd start eating a man before he was dead...I had nightmares afterwards, particularly over that incident.[56]

I kept trying to get out of this shell hole and the sides were sloped and there was a snowstorm. I had a hell of a job to get out, I couldn't get out of the damned place and in any case I didn't know where I was, I couldn't see and I kept losing consciousness. I think that if the stretcher bearers saw a man unconscious in a shell hole, they wouldn't bother with him, they were picking up the wounded. So I lay there the whole of that day from early morning, and then the night and the whole of the next day before they found that I was alive and the next thing I found myself in hospital.'[56]

Jimmy Quinn in No.14 Platoon, D Company had got no further than the lull before the storm and was in his starting trench on 9 April when wounded:

'An odd shell or two came over from Jerry – some beyond us – some short – then a dud – short again. Next minute the world sort of came to an end. With a roaring scream and a great flash a shell burst right in the back of the trench... the next thing I can remember is Walkden standing up calling 'Damn me, Jimmy, I'm hit'. The other lad [Elrick] was lying across me, kicking his feet and legs about... I guessed I'd 'got it' at last.'

Quinn staggered off to the aid post with a rifle as a stick, without realising his knee was broken and that he would never be the same again. He was seen by 'Big Lawson Cairns' and he saw too that 'Bunty' Walkden, who had only dug himself out from underground the day before, was there 'all nice and comfy and bandaged'. Clyde

Elrick, born in Cincinnati, had been beyond hope. He has been recorded as missing ever since, so must have disappeared into the mud.[23]

Quinn was bounced down the road in a motor ambulance and when they stopped 'called the orderly and told him his driver was – a whole lot of things! Just with that the driver came forward and in a soft voice said: "I'm sorry I gave you such a rough passage – the road was shelled last night and it's full of holes".' She was a girl.'[23]

He was then moved by train until, at the tented 22nd General Hospital at Camiers, near Étaples, he was operated on more than once but by the end of the month they had amputated his leg. Quinn resisted going to Britain, writing later, in 1934, 'I felt I would not get better and I wanted to die in France beside the troops, but I couldn't tell anybody that.'[23] He returned to Britain overnight on the 18/19 May 1917, and recovered at the Lord Derby War Hospital at Warrington.

Going forward in the attack with B Company, Frederico Lopez, a Manchester cotton salesman, was hit in the right arm by a bullet that broke his arm in six places and then entered his chest. He was dressed and sent to hospital where his arm was amputated at the shoulder, and the bullet extracted a fortnight later.

In late 1916 the battalion journal, *The Leather Sporran*, published the latest pension rates. A missing limb was worth between 16s a week and 10s 6d depending upon how much was lost, and a right arm was valued slightly more than a left.

Just as supplies came up to the line from the Channel ports by train, then lorry, horse and by foot, so casualties travelled the other way. They were first carried to the Regimental Aid Posts (RAPs) in the trenches by stretcher-bearers; in this action left to right were Abri Mouton, a specially enlarged dug-out, Sabliers a dug-out in a sandpit, and third a newly made dug-out in Fish Avenue. A further RAP was located in a cellar in Roclincourt. The wounded were then carried to a Collecting Post (CP). A Walking Wounded Collecting Station (WWCS) was signposted for those who could make their own way. From the collecting posts, horse-drawn wagons and cars, if possible, took them to the Advanced Dressing Station (ADS) and then to the Main Dressing Station (MDS). A Motor Ambulance Convoy (MAC), usually of Ford 'Tin Lizzies', then transported them to the Casualty Clearing Station (CCS), and from there ambulance trains and hospital ships took them to base hospitals on the coast or in the UK.

Joseph Boston.

Even at this stage of their journey casualties were far from free from the dangers of war. Joseph Henry Boston was aboard the ambulance ship HMT *Donegal*, returning from Le Havre to Southampton, when it was torpedoed by *UC-21* on 17 April 1917. He survived but was killed in action in France on 31 March 1918.

Another ambulance transport ship, lost on the same route, was the HMT *Warilda*, carrying Private John Smith. At 1.30am on 3 August 1918, a U-boat was spotted fine on the starboard bow at 100 yards, and the helm thrown hard over. The captain was on the bridge in time to see the track of a torpedo, which struck between the engine room and No.4 hold. The crew in the engine room were killed but the engines continued to run. Over 100 patients, mostly cot cases, and the attendant nursing staff were killed when the hold almost instantly flooded. Smith was among the missing.

George Hutton survived a grave injury in this his first action, when he was hit in the back by a shrapnel bullet that went through his right upper chest, a day of which he never spoke. He did not pass through the war undecorated however, as mess treasurer at Glencorse, his mess mates awarded him the OBE, 'Order of the Boiled Egg'.

Casualties were not always due to enemy action. Arthur Anderson was one of many *hors de combat* from trench fever, an infectious disease carried by lice. The MO was also down with trench fever so a new doctor put him on tablets. After lying on a stretcher for 24 hours with only tea and tablets, he was moved by motor ambulance to a field hospital and put in clean clothes, then the ambulance train took him to hospital in Rouen:

'I awakened in the morning to find myself in a large tent, and a blissful feeling of being between clean sheets. In a day or so the temperature subsides, and although feeling decidedly shaky, am on my legs again by the end of the week. There are eight lads in our tent and we find the V.A.D.s both charming and attentive. The one who attends to me, oddly enough, comes from Edinburgh and we find quite a lot to talk about in her spare moments.'[28]

Bennet Clark was in the UK convalescing. He had been wounded at April 1915 and had remarked then, in hospital near L'Abeele: 'I don't know what it is unless it is being away from the Bn as well as from home, but I feel quite homesick here!'[16] He was gassed in July 1916, and his brother Allan (RAMC) saw him briefly at Abbeville and was pleased to hear he had arrived at hospital in Britain: 'Ah'm! So Miss BG and the night nurse are charming are they? You naughty, naughty boy: the next I shall be hearing is – well Ah'm, enough said….You must send me a photo! of her!! soon!!!'[16] Now in the spring of 1917 he was a convalescent at the Seven Stars Hotel in Totnes. He had to wear a blue band so that hotel staff knew not to serve him drinks, but the doctor 'prescribed' him a glass of stout at lunch and dinner and he was allowed to go anywhere until 11pm when the hotel closed up for the night. He soon acquired a suntan and found it a relief that in such an out of the way place no Assistant Provost Marshal ever stopped him to ask why he was not in uniform. However, his ambition had not left him, in 1918 he felt he had missed out on a medal because he left his company in the hands of another officer to go on a course, and this man had the audacity to win an MC.

David Edwards left this in Dolly Pickering's autograph book at the UVF Hospital: 'Oh Dolly dear but thou are queer, and full of furiosity, Your album too, is just like you, a glorious curiosity.'

Rœux

THE adjutant described Vimy Ridge as 'an easy job' but they were about to move 'to a spot worse than High Wood of last July'.[16] In order to maintain pressure, in support of the French offensive of 16 April, further advances were demanded. The Ninth left their rest on 15 April to positions near Fampoux, a village east of Arras that had been captured the week before. A and B companies were sent down the front line, Crump Trench, the *chemin creux* or sunken road next to the River Scarpe, late on 19 April with orders to attack the German positions at the west end of Rœux Wood and the trench in front of Mount Pleasant Wood (Map XVI).

On the following morning at 8.30am, following a two-hour bombardment, the two companies attempted to rush the enemy positions but found the wire was uncut and were halted by prompt and accurate machine-gun fire. The enemy were in stout possession of a trench (Ceylon Trench) that crossed to the river and a new plan was made for the following day.

At 3pm on 21 April, after a one-hour bombardment, A Company tried again. Fighting their way 200 yards up Ceylon Trench they established a post at a copse, at the junction with Colne communication trench. They also succeeded in getting down the sunken road from Ceylon Trench to Rœux Wood where they would have been advised to stop. Instead the company entered the wood where, as Ewing writes, 'it was sadly cut up by the Boche riflemen and machine-gunners and was ultimately forced back to its starting point'[33] in the sunken road.

There is some evidence that the trench the British called Cusp was extant by 20 April, and made for an unpleasant discovery by the battalion.

C and D companies also encountered a heavy barrage whilst attempting to relieve A and B companies. The net result was a post 150 yards in front of the sunken road, and a German prisoner taken from the machine-gun company of 2nd Battalion, 31st Regiment, for the loss of 10 killed and 41 wounded and missing.

Among those killed was 45-year-old Captain Taylor. Alexander Taylor, Sheriff-Substitute of Forfar, but known to the men as Daddy Taylor, originally joined the battalion in 1900 before a stint in South America. He had been shot through the thigh at Second Ypres and been invalided out, but rejoined the battalion in March 1916. Also killed was John Milne, a gardener at Bonnycraig, who knew that he was suffering from consumption when he enlisted but had been undeterred. On 22 April some 4.2″ and 5.9″ shelling was received. John Allan, the Heart of Midlothian football player was wounded and went missing, his death presumed.

Daddy Taylor.

The final objective of 154 Brigade, including the Ninth, was the infamous Chemical Works and, to the south, the village of Rœux itself with a number of copses in front of it. This was to be the third attack on the fortified village of Rœux, against newly dug trenches whose positions were not well known. In addition, there were three enemy divisions opposite with good reserves.

Having assembled on the sunken road south of the railway, with the River Scarpe behind them, the general attack began at 4.45am on the misty morning of 23 April. The attack consisted of the 7th Argylls on the right (their first wave in Ceylon and Colne Trenches), with two companies of the Ninth attached and assembled to rear. The 4th Gordons were on the left, similarly with two companies of the Ninth attached. The Gordons and Argylls had the objective of the Black Line and Blue Line, and the Ninth of consolidating the Blue Line. For this picks and shovels had to be carried in order to dig a new trench, with exceptions made for Lewis gunners, men carrying buckets of bombs, runners and signallers. Strongpoints were to be constructed by D Company on the right and B Company on the left. The barrage was to lift from the Black Line at Zero plus 19 minutes, Blue at Zero plus 100 minutes, and the Ninth were to advance from Crump Trench at Zero plus 30 minutes in one wave.

On the right, the 7th Argylls went over followed half an hour later at 5.15am by C and D companies of the Ninth. The barrage was not heavy enough to subdue the enemy and they soon caught up with the Argylls hung up 150 yards from the start by machine-gun fire from Mount Pleasant Wood and the extreme flanks.

C Company, on the right, were immediately drawn into the battle. They forced themselves into Rœux Wood amidst heavy fire and smashed trees. Bewsher describes it as 'perhaps the most savage infantry battle that the division took part in… It is certain that at one time they were well in Rœux Wood and towards Rœux village, as the bodies of Highlanders were found in those places when the Division subsequently occupied Rœux.'[51] Ewing adds, 'Bullets sped among the men from apparently every quarter, and the appalling din created by the explosion of shells and the crash of falling trees added indescribably to the awful turbulence of the scene.'[33] Rœux Wood had many snipers and four or five machine guns unaffected by the barrage. A sunken road in Rœux Wood was particularly well defended.

Lieutenant Crawford Jamieson (probably C Company), a fruit merchant, was killed leading his men in a charge. Company Sergeant Major James Dunkley was also killed. Lewis gunner George Fernie took out a German machine gun and was also able to fire on parties across the river. However, the attack south of the river had failed and fallen back and so the company's right flank also had to be withdrawn. The Argylls managed to advance through Rœux Wood, though this was not properly cleared, and on to the village. At 10.30am a strong counter-attack forced them out of the village and they held the tramline until evening.

Albert Forsyth, an 18-year-old piper 'who was a highly skilled bomber, volunteered to bomb the Germans out of a position in which they were covered by machine guns. He crawled up and succeeded in his object, but was killed.'

D Company were facing Mount Pleasant Wood. Private Alexander MacPherson describes going over the top from the sunken road:

'Dawn was breaking. The officers scrambled up the bank and with a shout inaudible in the tumult and a wave of the arm led us over the top. In a long straggling line we rushed forward over the shell-torn ground plunging into shell-holes, conscious of the need for haste and feeling as though our feet were weighted with lead and as if we were crawling along instead of running (which of course we were). All round whistled the machine-gun bullets lashing the ground as if in a spray but no one heeded them. The German barbed wire, battered and torn by shellfire, was soon passed through, though it always is as well to pick one's steps and choose an easy path in getting through that fatal barrier. Many soldiers caught on its barbs had been delayed long enough to let the Machine Guns riddle him with bullets or the sniper mark him as his prey.

We leapt into the first trench (now empty) scrambled up the other slope and ran on. Here we halted for a few minutes and took cover in the numerous shell holes while we had time to look round. In front the ground seemed to rise to a crest crowned with a clump of trees, and then dipped once more. All was shrouded in mist, but the dim light of dawn showed numerous figures running back and forward. Were these Germans or Argylls? Most decided the former and opened fire and we did so with the [Lewis] Gun.

Lamont, Orr and I were together in the same hole with two men of 15 Platoon. The Sergeant Major [probably Goodfellow] on our right signalled to us to come forward with a wave of his arm and I got out of the shell hole and on my hands and knees began to crawl to the next one dragging the Gun. Before I reached it I received a terrific blow on the left side which took my breath away and I realised I was hit. I plunged into the hole and lay down on my back keeping well undercover. Every breath caused me pain and on looking for the wound I found a hole as big as my hand in my greatcoat on my left side below the breast.'[61]

MacPherson was hospitalised and survived the war. D Company found the continuation of Ceylon Trench was full of Germans, Mount Pleasant Wood strongly defended, and found a new trench, later called Cusp Trench, along the Black Line, had been made from joined up shell holes that ran from behind Mount Pleasant Wood out to Rœux Wood.

Tank 716 abandoned.

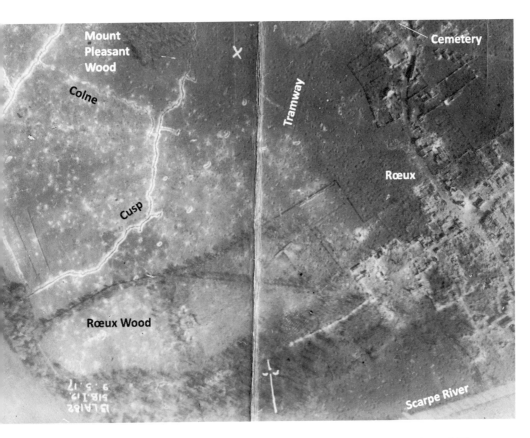

These defences held up the attack for at least one-and-a-half hours. About 6.30am the enemy began to trickle away and the arrival of a tank, about 8am, hurried them on. About thirty Germans surrendered, the others retired to Rœux. This allowed the Argylls and D Company to gain the Black Line with a bayonet charge, enter the wood and advance on the village.

The tank, C7 (No.716), a male Mk I commanded by Second Lieutenant Victor Smith, started at the railway arch, went via Mount Pleasant and the cemetery and put 200 rounds of 6-pounder into the village, firing on houses containing snipers and machine guns. Sadly, the driver of the tank had such limited visibility that on at least one occasion he crossed a shell hole containing wounded with tragic consequences. It retired having expended its ammunition and became stuck in the Scarpe marsh.

James Gair was shot in the left wrist and taken prisoner. Company Sergeant Major William Goodfellow, a 31-year-old health insurance officer, was killed. Second Lieutenant William Campbell, an actuary who had started the war as a private in the Ninth, was at the forefront. He picked up a Lewis gun and, though wounded, inspired his company by advancing on Rœux firing on the enemy. He remained in command of his platoon for the rest of the day, for which he was awarded an MC. Following the counter-attack, by 2.30pm the Ninth and 7th Argylls were in a line of shell holes parallel to the tramway.

Meanwhile A and B companies were supporting the 4th Gordons and were under

CSM David Walker leads Joseph Hanna, Robert Jamieson and Charles Arnot of B Company out of Crump Trench.

heavy fire from the Chemical Works and railway embankment. They went forward by section rushes. Captain George Strachan, commanding A Company on the right, was severely wounded. Some of B Company made it past the north of the Chemical Works but were not seen again. The remainder, with A Company, dug-in on a line facing the road between the Chemical Works and the cemetery. Here they were victim to a great many snipers as well as shelling. Company Sergeant Major Jack Renwick was last seen about 11am going to the assistance of B Company at the Chemical Works.

Captain Patrick Alexander Blair, chartered accountant and treasurer of the Scottish Geographical Society, was 'a brave and steady leader, he was much loved by the boys... for his fatherly manner'.[79] In the absence of information from runners, Pat Blair, acting Brigade Major, was sent forward on reconnaissance and found the Black Line held. On a further recce in the afternoon he was killed by a sniper at the Chemical Works.

Pat Blair.

The Black Line was consolidated by 2.30pm. Some posts near the Chemical Works were lost in a counter-attack at 8pm. That night they fell back from a line of shell holes to the west and parallel to the tramway, to the Black Line; they were relieved and after nightfall moved back to the sunken road. On the right on 24 April, patrols established that the Germans were holding the cemetery and the east of Rœux Wood, with snipers behind the 26th Northumberland Fusiliers in the narrow strip of the wood. It would take a sixth attack, on 12 May, to secure Rœux.

The casualties were as follows: 5 officers killed, 2 wounded; 54 Other Ranks killed, 115 wounded, 55 missing. The death count for the day climbed to 91 all ranks, with

The Chemical Works before and after the battle of Arras.

three company sergeant majors dead. Bennet Clark, in Totnes, wrote, 'When one thinks that 12 [officers] have gone from the Bn during these weeks it makes one wonder at being here.'[16] Casualties for the whole battle came to 500.

George Strachan later became Writer to the Signet and remained a first class shot, but at times had to finish competitions by shooting from his left shoulder due to his injuries. Two other noted shots fell at Arras, Douglas Allan, from Robert Younger breweries and John Bain, from the Southern Light Opera. Kenneth McAlpine was last seen retiring from the firing line wounded and going to the dressing station under heavy shell fire, his death presumed. Cecil Valentine died of wounds; he was one of three brothers in the battalion and their cousin was a nurse in Serbia. Homer Fraser was one of five sons killed in the war, and his mother was presented to Prince Henry, but it transpires that one of the sons was in fact in Australia suffering mental incapacity.

Finally, at 12.50am on 25 April, the Ninth marched back to Arras and moved by train to the rear. Once more new drafts of men were received and officers were attached from other battalions. The Ninth spent three weeks behind the lines, with distractions to be found in Arras, and the unwanted distraction of an ammo dump blowing up at Wanquetin. There were performances of the division's troupe, the *Balmorals*, and the division's massed pipe bands played. On 7 May Harper viewed the 4th Seaforths in training, but as they nearly killed several civilians who had not been cleared 'naturally the G.O.C. was somewhat annoyed'.[81] Two days later he inspected the Ninth at training and 'was quite satisfied with the way the work was carried out'[1] by the Ninth.

The Hielan' Division

When war was declared the chief o' the Huns
Thocht he'd march across France wi' his men and his guns.
But there's ane thing tae mind when y're mackin' provision
He didna tak coont o' the Hielan' Division
Men frae the Tweed up to auld John O' Groats
Brocht up on porridge an' haggis an' oats.
Oor Willie, wee man, twas a mournful omission;
He didna tak coont o' the Hielan' Division.

The Balmorals photographed after Arras.

The artist Peploe wrote to Cadell: 'I'm glad to hear you're enjoying the luxurious life of the trenches so much,' and Cadell wrote home: 'Everything is filthy with mud, and if cleanliness is next to Godliness our chances of heaven are few.'[59] At one time he was living in a lightless barn and wrote to his sister: 'I write this in a loft. Lots of rats and other things which should appeal to you as a lover of animals.'[59]

Cadell's 'Seated Soldier, Reading'

The Company Commander (as he appears to himself)

The Company Commander is worried night and day
He has his men to exercise, he has his men to pay
He has to guard their stomachs from nasty things to eat
He has to give them C.B. and see they wash their feet
The Sergeant goes to Blighty to train the soldiers there
The Loot becomes an Adjutant, the Col. a Brigadier
The influential Major to teach a school is gone
The Company Commander is left to carry on
He loses his lieutenants and all his N.C.O.'s
He can't get iron rations, he cannot get clean clothes
There in the muddy trenches he sits a nervous wreck
And if the Fritzes come across, he gets it in the neck
And when at last the push is on and all the orders read
He jumps the blooming parapet, and stops a bit of lead
They shove him in a shell hole in the nearest handy spot
And leave him to the only rest the blighter ever got.[10]

All too soon the brigade was back in the line continuously for the second half of May, slightly ahead of the Blue Line objective of the month before and subjected to continuous bombardment that involved digging-out and re-occupying trenches. On 16 May the division had to counter a German attack at Rœux and the Chemical Works; 154 Brigade were in position on the railway line by 11am, but the situation was stabilised. On 24 May Colonel William Green reconnoitred the trenches with Company Sergeant Major William Low and his orderly, Albert Lawrence, when, he tells us, 'a shell dropped in the trench just behind me and killed the other two outright'.

John Wilson wrote home on 23 May saying, 'Still in the trenches, but having an easy time', but was killed two days later. Heavy shelling on 27 May knocked in Sheriff Post (Map XVI) and C Company HQ in Ceylon Trench was blown in. About 10am John Thomas Johnston, a month in France, was killed 'in the Company Headquarters when the shell landed on the top and hit him in many places on the chest'. About 10.30 that night, a small party was sent out to 'scupper a German post'[1] but attracted machine-gun fire from another post and had to abandon the attempt. Johnny Willocks, who had become acting Company Sergeant Major on the death of Jack Renwick, became the fifth CSM killed at Arras.

Third Ypres – Passchendaele

'I venture to place it among the three best fighting Divisions I have met in France'

Lieutenant General Ivor Maxse

SINCE becoming commander-in-chief in December 1915, Haig had been convinced of the merits of an attack in Flanders, to break out from the Ypres Salient. Here the Germans had been stopped in a First Battle in 1914 and stopped again in the Second Battle of Ypres in 1915. He had been unable to carry out a third battle in 1916, instead committed to a joint attack with the French at the Somme; and in early 1917 at Arras as second string to Nivelle's offensive. In June 1917 he succeeded in pushing forward the southern shoulder of the Salient at Messines. Now he intended to roll up the enemy line to the north, along the Pilckem Ridge towards Passchendaele, in the Third Battle of Ypres. In this he was supported by the Admiralty, desperate to clear the Channel ports of U-boats, but the prospect horrified the Prime Minister, Lloyd George.

At the beginning of June the division moved north to the Pas-de-Calais and began a period of training with six weeks preparation for their next major action, interspersed with duty in the trenches. Once again, the exact dimensions of the enemy's defences were laid out with tracing-tapes, the British front line marked with blue flags, and the German with red flags. The 'barrage' consisted of fifty men holding up blue and white signalling flags, with drums in place of machine guns. An example of the training included 'the barrage will be lost and the rest of the advance will have to be by platoons or sections covering each other's advance and making full use of natural cover.'[1] Harper further developed his tactics with platoons learning to hold opposition frontally whilst working sections round to outflank it, which would prove apposite for taking on the pill-boxes of Passchendaele. A large-scale model of the terrain was constructed, about the size of four tennis courts, to familiarise all of the men with their objectives. The redoubtable Highlanders were to be thoroughly prepared for the coming battle.

The Division's Horse Show and Sports Day included an interesting mix of 'sports'. Lieutenant Moffat of the Ninth won the Officers' Jumping, and the battalion won the

Rifle Grenade Competition, in which each company was represented by a man firing four rounds at a target 75 yards distant. There were no casualties in June, though there were two deaths in hospital, but through July there was an increase in casualties as they approached the battle.

The Third Battle of Ypres, known as Passchendaele, began on 31 July 1917. Once more in the Salient, the division 'at the summit of its great reputation',[20] was to leave the Yser Canal, pass between Pilckem Ridge and St Julien and advance to the Steenbeek stream (Map IX). The division attacked with 152 Brigade on the right and 153 Brigade on the left with the Ninth's 154 Brigade in reserve. The Ninth were placed on immediate readiness to support 152 Brigade, as such they were required to train on the same objectives. The brigade objective was to establish a chain of posts across the Steenbeek, which was up to 10ft wide with 5ft banks, cover the crossings and the Military Road, place a company post at Mon du Rasta and send reconnaissance parties forward (Map XVIII).

By 10 July the Ninth were back in the line north of Ypres, with reserves at the canal bank and were subject to heavy shelling, including gas. When not in the line, the Ninth and 4th Seaforths continued training in the St Acaire training area, west of Poperinghe. On 30 July they moved into position on the west side of the canal near Essex Farm.

Two second lieutenants watched with binoculars the progress of the 6th Gordons from the canal bank. They were both old Watsonians who had mobilised in the ranks and had subsequently been commissioned in 1916. Jock Gellatly (24) had been twice wounded.

William Campbell.

William Campbell (22) had been thrice wounded and awarded the MC for gallantry at Rœux in April, where he had picked up a Lewis gun and inflicted many casualties. As they watched, some high velocity shells hit the canal bank and a shell killed Campbell outright and took Gellatly's arm. He was removed by ambulance, but it was hit by a shell and destroyed.

The division achieved its objectives. The next morning the Ninth relieved the 6th Gordons and 6th Seaforths in heavy rain, the start in fact of a month's rain. Such was the chaos and confusion that John Barclay was awarded a Military Medal for gallantry, carrying out his duties in traffic control under shell fire. Lieutenant Jim Annan, who had postponed his medical studies and was commissioned in March 1917, led his men over the canal on No.4 bridge:

John Gellatly.

'We only got a few stray 5.9 shells on the way across. We didn't have a single casualty until we got to Minty's Farm… Of course the Germans had every one of their own positions marked… So, just as we were coming up to Minty's Farm, the shells started falling all around. We got a slashing there all right.'[46]

209

Blockhouse at Minty Farm.

Nevertheless, Minty Farm (now a Commonwealth War Graves Commission cemetery) became battalion headquarters. On the night of 2 August the Ninth pushed four posts onto the east side of the River Steenbeek, and two more on the next day, these posts holding three to eight men. The rain raised the Steenbeek and made the surroundings extremely difficult to operate in, particularly for the runners. The unstoppable Second Lieutenant James R. Black, though wounded on the first day, made two reconnaissances near the Steenbeek under heavy fire and identified the position of the enemy.

In an effort to prevent men and horses drowning in the mud, duckboards were laid through the shattered landscape, an enduring image of the notorious battlefield. Originals in the Ninth should have recognised the area from their first assault during Second Ypres in 1915, but Ewing describes the now transformed Salient:

'The sites of the numerous groves, that had once draped with soft greenery the country-side of Flanders, were marked by a naked tangle of unsightly splintered timber. Day and night the region was buffeted by shells till the roads and buildings disappeared and the ordinary map no longer performed the office of a guide.'[33]

Up at the Steenbeek, taking turns to take shelter from rain and shellfire, Annan remembered:

'Then there was a lull in the shelling, and through the machine-gun slit on the back wall of the pillbox we heard this terrible kind of gurgling noise. It was the wounded, lying there sinking, and this liquid mud burying them alive, running over their faces into their mouth and nose. We had to keep heaving the duckboards up and trying to put some other stuff underneath, just so that the fellows wouldn't sink so much. We

210

The Ninth on 'Duckboard Parade'.

couldn't understand why, in the name of God, anyone had ordered an attack like that over terrain like that. It was impossible.'[46]

Through nightly bombardments James Thomson, formerly Transport Sergeant 1021 but now transport officer, managed to get at least iron rations up the muddy tracks with 'unfailing regularity'.[33]

A patrol captured a German and the battalion were relieved to brigade reserve, after four days on iron rations. The terrain had become so unrecognisable in just the three days they had been in the line that Annan had great difficulty in organising their relief. His runners kept getting lost trying to cross the featureless morass back to Minty Farm. Charles Carrington watched men of the division returning 'muddied up to the bare thighs, and with kilts hanging in laps and folds of clay like sculptor's work'.[20]

They were in trenches at the canal bank on 4 August; the following day a shell wiped out a section in the trench, among whom William Simpson died later. They retired to 'Dirty Bucket Camp' having amassed casualties of 15 killed, 114 wounded and 4 missing.

From the Carberry Pit at Musselburgh, Thomas Brown, who had lost the sight of his right eye in the Quintinshill rail disaster, had been wounded in action in April, but was wounded again, this time fatally.

A recent arrival to the battalion, Private William Dea, was one of the D Company Lewis gunners across the Steenbeek. Dea, from Juniper Green, was a machineman at a paper mill on the Water of Leith. He had attested in December 1915, had been placed on the Army Reserve and was mobilised in March 1917. He was 40 years old and married with three children under 4. His diary, abridged and edited, reads:

'Left Glencorse June 5th 1917. Waverley Station was a great relief, no women folk to see my going away. We went on to St Pancras and got our train for the coast at Folkestone. We got on the transport and then across the Channel with 3 others, convoyed by 5 torpedo boats. It was a lovely morning, the sea was like a pond. Boulogne a dirty seaport town, no comparison with the clean natty streets of Folkestone. Next morning we were off to the base at Étaples, what a tramp, a perfect nightmare. Those leeches who held on to the draft all the way from Boulogne to Étaples selling oranges at 2d each to men who had left their all to save their scurvy lot from Huns, the only thing that opens their miserable hearts is money nowadays. No one here that I have met have a good word for them. We met Mills at Penicuik mimicking the instructors, which he was good at. He is the only one I have had a good laugh at since coming here to this life. It was so queer coming here and meeting so many local lads from home, I did not know these lads I met in France.

Étaples, what a name from many. A horrid nightmare, which after a fortnight I was glad to see the last of for some time. What stories went at Étaples, men dying under the strain, one suicide, it was depressing, then those hospital cases. This is a life which I can't say I like, it has its drawbacks and the great thing is the scarcity of bread, in fact rations are very short at Étaples. Glencorse was bad but here it's hellish. What the line will be like I don't know. We have been going from bad to worse all the time, surely as regards grub this is the limit. The instructors here or at Glencorse are all alike, clinging on to their jobs with the desperation of despair. They groaned under their load. So did the souls with me who were forced into this cursed war. The whole world is at it now, at least the world that matters nowadays, those with men and money to put into the desperate gamble. I have written few folks, what has one to say to anyone but those who are my all. At present homesickness makes me too sulky to write much to anyone. Friday we were on draft and told to join up with Dandy Ninth. Gracious what a drop a kilt, I laughed, however I did not take it so bad either. Sat. we were off to join our new batt at front.

We have recourse to an estaminet or pub which we have given the name of the 'Spotted Frog'. The French beer is wet but that's about all that can be said about it, it's like the people, just wet. What a cheery lot was there, everyone had a smile and a shout for his neighbour. The remark went round what a difference from Étaples, where a smile was one of pity and resignation to one's fate. After all a kilt is not so very bad, I have been here now 6 days and don't feel it so draughty.

Sunday was Church Parade as usual and tobacco rations. Reveille at 5.30, out on parade at 6, physical jerks till 7, this is called adjutant's parade. Breakfast at 7.45, parade again at 9 till 12.30. Monday I was picked out for Lewis Gun and paraded with the class at 9am. We had the naming of parts of gun explained and the working of the gun, every hour we had a smoke then finished at 12.30 for the day. The sergeant is very painstaking man and is teaching a lot of duffers, it's very interesting I never saw a machine gun before let alone handle one.

Andrew [his brother] doesn't hold out much promise of a transfer so I will go on and take my chances, which as far as I hear and see are mighty slim. If things do get that way I will face it no dodging my fate, get your back up and shoot out your neck and on you go. I would liked to have given the boy at the very least a sporting chance for a start in life, however if it does not come off we can only hope that Jeannie will be spared in life, health and strength to help him on the strait road to lead a clean, healthy and manly life. I was always vexed about Jean but perhaps this time she will pull round and be a rare lassie, another Jeannie [His daughter Jean died of influenza aged 2]. Then the baby, she will never perhaps know her daddy, the bairns when they grow up will perhaps never remember such a soul. Jeannie, that wife. I have loved one of the best produced. If I go, it will go hard with her but I have no fear for her, she is a pearl and I never had all the time we were together anything but sweet thoughts for that sweet little girl who met me that July night at the Exhibition. Married five years, three children and as much in love as those happy courting days. Well we will have to look up and hope it may come again.

My transfer does not seem to make much headway, however I do hope it comes soon. I am sick of this infantry work. Parade at 7 for buckshee attack, a practice for our work up the line. A hard day, the usual tramping of wheat, barley, corn, marigold and French beans and usual broad beans. What a waste, if it goes on this way on all fronts no wonder the war costs so much. I don't know how long the line was but we had about 1½ mls to walk and it took an aeroplane to keep us all right. Word is going that we leave this place on Monday, I hope our next billet is as good as this is for mates up the line. Donaldson's shirt was a moving mass, fancy being lousy. A bottle of stout tonight, 2 francs for 3 bottles, a dear drink. We passed on Friday some German prisoners sawing wood, there were some fine looking men among them.

Monday [9 July 1917] morning opened cold and rain. We got our packs ready and tramped thro St Momelin to St Omer where we entrained for the trenches. We had a halt for the night outside Poperinghe, our arrival was heralded by a munitions dump on fire, the rattle and boom of the guns and bursting shells was not exactly a lullaby for tired men, however we managed to sleep somehow. Reveille went at six I was busy getting my boots on when a shell burst outside a hut 20 yds off, killed 2 and injured 3, not a bad start for the Ninth. We are fairly in it now, the guns are never silent, continually going. We go into trenches tonight.

Well I got safely over my first tour in the trenches and didn't feel worried but the carrying party at night was rather trying carrying those heavy cylinders over shell torn tracks in the dark. Carrying rifle and equipment was a devil, we got over it with a sigh and was glad to get back to our dug-out and our drumming up in safety, how those shells came over on Thursday night. Gas and those horrid helmets. What a relief to write here in the comfort of a tent and look back on it all. Hope I am lucky all the time.

We are on the buckshee attacks yet practising for a grand show over the bags, it's on everyone's mind and all are very anxious to have it all stopped. Our days here have been very quiet, 20 minute physical jerks then done for the day which is spent lice hunting and sleeping in bivouac, a polite way of saying dossing outside, one day was a thunderstorm which nearly washed us all out. The bivouacs are situated in a hop grove, the sheets stretched across sticks and pegged down, the worst of the place is the thunder of those guns which thro the night especially never cease, the rammie has never ceased today.

Everyone is quite hopeful of our time when the rush starts, I am often afraid they are too sure but time will tell.'[82]

William Dea had been just over a month with the battalion when he was killed by a sniper on 3 August 1917 on the far side of the Steenbeek. His diary, the spine possibly torn by the bullet which killed him, was returned home and carried within it was a ticket for the 1908 Scottish Exhibition, where he had met his Jeannie. His son Willie's earliest memory remained being held up to the window to see his father march off to war.

Poelcappelle – Stroombeek

'Dante would have found the country unspeakably worse than his inferno' [32]

THE next assault in September would put the Ninth in the thick of it once more. Having been the reserve in July, 154 Brigade were now given the objective of the Langemarck-Gheluvelt line with only one brigade used on the division's front (Map XVII and XVIII). This was intended to provide a 'jumping-off' point for an attack on Poelcappelle in October but had defeated repeated attempts to advance the British line in previous weeks. The mud was as bad as it had been in Courcelette, there was aerial bombing, the enemy made large-scale use of mustard gas, which had made its unwelcome introduction the month before and in addition, the enemy defences were bolstered by a vast number of concrete fortifications, for the water table prevented deep dug-outs. Facing the brigade was the 36th German Division; they were Prussian, 'an excellent combat division',[83] with Grenadier Regiment Nr.5 directly opposite the left of the brigade, who impressed with their stiff resistance after a heavy barrage. Two German deserters from the 5th Grenadiers crossed on 11 September.

The Ninth were to be on the right and 4th Seaforths on the left of the Lekkerboterbeek stream. In front of them was the first German trench of the Wilhelm Line, Pheasant Trench called the Black Line. About 40 yards in front of it were a number of newly constructed machine-gun emplacements. Beyond it followed a slight depression down to their objective, the Stroombeek, a small water course marked as the 'dotted Blue Line'. The terrain then rose to a slight ridge at Quebec Farm where the next wave would take the Blue Line.

In the moonlight of 1/2 September a German reconnaissance aircraft came over Murat Camp at about 600 feet and immediately attracted the attention of the machine-gunners of the Ninth, 4th Gordons and 154 MG Company. The aircraft turned, the engine stopped and it crashed on the west bank of the Yser Canal; it was doubtless claimed by all three units.

The British shelled the enemy line heavily on 10 September, though some shorts fell in their own lines. The Reverend James Cappell was wounded on 15 September and died in 1918. The brigade had been largely in camp in the weeks leading up to the attack and spent five days practising the capture of strongpoints under a barrage in a taped-out area. A practice attack at 5.30am on 18 September was completed by 7.10am.

Thorough preparations were made. For communication a wireless station was to be set up, and 'power buzzers' were to be used, a type of ground induction communication. Each company had responsibility for establishing telephone lines as well as having four runners, nine pigeons and a message-carrying rocket with a 1,000 yard range. The SOS message was by firing Very light flares. Bülow Farm had a power buzzer, and also a messenger dog. Volunteering to be a runner was ill advised as they ran great risks, especially when, as Tom Boyd discovered, you would get no rest from an 'over-zealous'[23] platoon commander. There was a buried cable to Ferdinand Farm, so this telephone link was maintained, however the three circuits that ran between Ferdinand Farm and Bülow Farm were cut in the bombardment; the intention had been to run two wires forward to New Houses when captured by the Ninth. Pigeons were to be released at Flora Cott and New Houses as they were taken. Three men of the battalion were trained at signalling to balloons using helio, electric Lucas Lamp and binoculars.

The artillery would precede the attack with 24 hours of intense bombardment. The barrage of 18-pounders would start 150 yards in front of the forming-up position, so as to fall on Pheasant Trench on the left, but in no man's land on the right. It would lift at Zero plus three minutes in 50 yard lifts every two minutes, then after 200 yards at 50 yards every three minutes to the dotted Blue Line. Supporting the Ninth were 18-pounders firing shrapnel at four rounds a minute and consisting of eleven six-gun batteries. This amounted to almost 100,000 shrapnel bullets a minute for a sustained period.

There would then be a protective barrage 200 yards beyond the dotted Blue Line at two rounds a minute, including some smoke shell, quickening eight minutes before starting again as a warning to the next wave of infantry, and taking them onto the Blue Line. As well as the main creeping barrage there was a combing barrage, to dwell on strongpoints and work up communication trenches; a neutralising barrage, of heavy guns searching further ahead and a standing barrage intended to break up counter-attack forces.

Twelve tanks of 12 Company D Battalion were assigned to assist in the capture of strongpoints. On the right No.9 Section, of four tanks (namely D42 Daphne, D43 Delysia, D44 Dracula and D54 Diadem), were to leave St Julien at Zero minus 45 minutes and drive up the Poelcappelle road. From the British front line one pair would tackle New Houses, whilst the other pair turned right at the junction to take on Flora Cott. If the infantry required help from the tank they were to wave their steel helmets on top of their rifles. However, they were not to wait for the tanks. Of the four tanks, almost immovable in the mud, D54 Diadem was hit near the start line, D42 Daphne received two direct hits such that D43 Delysia was unable to pass, and D44 Dracula made it some way up the Poelcappelle road before the engine gave out. No.7 Squadron RFC provided the 'contact' flights so that the men could indicate their position with red flares.

The 51st Division had employed a machine-gun barrage at Beaumont Hamel, with machine guns firing at long range over the heads of friendly troops, but 'so obsessed now was the higher command by the Machine Gun Barrage, that the Machine Gun Companies of every available division were crowded into line to support the offensive'.[84] The 1915 edition of the Machine Gunners Handbook prohibited overhead fire at ranges exceeding 1,500 yards; but by 1917 the advice had changed to ensuring fire was at least 20 yards over the heads of the infantry, with sandbags or battens to prevent the muzzles being depressed. Bewsher blithely tells us:

> 'The men were accordingly specially warned that the enormous volume of bullets passing over their heads would sound as if they were only a few inches above the crowns of their steel helmets, whereas in reality there would be a margin of safety of many feet.'[51]

With four Machine Gun Companies, the division had a total of sixty-four Vickers machine guns, and half were employed in the indirect machine-gun barrage. These guns were placed on wooden T-bases to prevent the tripods sinking into the mud and their elevation set at dusk the night before with inclinometers, for the targets were too distant to be observed. Captain Douglas Wimberley's 232nd MGC had twelve guns as R Battery, arranged near Haanixbeek Farm:

> 'I was very nervous of my men getting annihilated, as a number of guns were slap in the open... I fired one gun over the back of the farm itself, one at each side, and one just in front – four guns in a radius of seven yards. Others were poked higgledy-piggledy wherever there was a little concrete untouched to give protection, the remainder took their chances among the shell holes.'[85]

Liven's Projectors were to fire 250 gas drums, and therefore the infantry were to wear their respirators from Zero minus 5 minutes to Z plus 15 minutes.

The infantry had a relatively narrow no man's land to cross – on the left it was a mere 150 yards. However, the Lekkerboterbeek made for soft ground and the Ninth on the right faced a marsh at Viailhas Maisone [Vieilles Maisons]. The battalion headquarters was established at Bülow Farm, but it was not advisable to visit in daylight as 'the ground is lavishly sprinkled with shrapnel'.[1] Harper's 'little fellers' were issued their instructions: entrenching tools will be carried, but greatcoats will not, they were to have 170 rounds of Small Arms Ammunition per man, one Mills bomb and two days' rations (one 'preserved' that included jam and milk for Z day, the other 'iron' for Z+1).

After a fortnight's dry weather, the rain began again late on 19 September as the men approached their assembly positions along lines of duckboards. The shell holes on either side, often touching each other, invariably formed pools of stagnant water and also, inevitably, unmarked graves. The soft ground did, however, serve to bury shells, minimising the effects of splinters. Captain Willie Urquhart had served as platoon commander in 1915 and returned to the battalion in June 1917 with the rank of captain, commanding A Company. He received a gun shot wound to the right arm on the march up but remained at duty. The battalion were in position by 3am on 20 September with a strength going in of 15 officers and 535 ORs. They assembled in shell holes, in line with the front-line posts, to attack on a two-company front.

The 4th Seaforths were on their left, to be followed by the 4th Gordons. The Ninth were to be followed by the 7th Argylls through to the Blue Line on a three-company front, leaving a counter-attack company 200 yards in front of the dotted Blue Line. For the Ninth the objective of the dotted Blue Line was the Stroombeek. They were also responsible to 'make good' the ground up to the protective barrage where there was to be a pause. Special parties were to deal with every known concrete blockhouse. They were to put at least two sections into New House and Flora Cott as strongpoints. The brigade made clear: 'It is to be impressed on all ranks that a counter-attack is inevitable… if only the men will use their rifles, there is nothing to be feared from it.'[1]

Zero hour was at 5.40am 20 September. Douglas Wimberley watched the opening of the attack from Ferdinand Farm:

'At dawn our barrage started – it was the most stupendous bombardment I have ever seen… It was still dark – nothing could be seen but a sheet of flame a thousand yards in front where the shells were dropping, yellow in places from our projectors, which were falling thickly. One could not hear a man shouting a foot away from one… we could not even hear the German shells bursting fifty yards away for the thunderous roar of our artillery.'[85]

As the intricately organised barrage rolled forward, green SOS lights fired by the Germans were seen to rise up all along the line and the British went 'over the bags' at 5.40am. This was musket ball range, the distance of the traditional Highland charge. Both attacking companies were engaged with rifle and machine-gun fire from the start, but got well up to the barrage before the German counter-barrage began about six minutes after Zero. A Company on the right under Willie Urquhart with 'fine dash'[33] rushed the pill-boxes and displayed 'the greatest skill and gallantry',[51] using fire and movement techniques, moving between shell holes in twos and threes. A correspondent reported:

'The blockhouses were dealt with by small parties of Highlanders, who had been in training to meet them, and went like wolves about them, firing their machine-guns and rifles through the loopholes, if the garrisons would not come out.'[80]

Pheasant Trench and the associated strongpoints were consolidated by 6.45am. Robert Lawrie made it to their objective when a small piece of shell struck him in the forehead and killed him.

B Company on the left, contending with the swampy ground of the Lekkerboterbeek, came under 'ravaging'[33] machine-gun fire and 'some of the Royal Scots wavered and came back to our original line but were quickly rallied and re-organised'.[1] Company commander Lieutenant Frank 'Lofty' Scott, who had served in Gallipoli and moreover was a winner of the officer's hundred yard dash, reorganised the three platoons of the company and led them forward again, assisted by battalion intelligence officer Second Lieutenant James R. Black and artillery liaison officer Second Lieutenant Fairlie.

'This shows the hideous country from Pheasant Trench and the line of approach of the 4th Seaforths when they captured the pill-boxes.'[86]

Part of the company was already in the right of Pheasant Trench and from here Corporal Alexander Horne with two men of his bombing section made their way along the trench and destroyed the machine gun most responsible for holding up the rest of the company and 'accounted' for about twenty of the enemy. The company secured the trench 'with splendid gallantry and held their ground only by most grim endurance',[80] permitting the attack to continue. Officers who had been through several major actions remarked that they had never seen so many enemy dead, with almost a hundred in 100 yards of Pheasant Trench. Of 280 all ranks of the 5th Grenadiers' front battalion, only about twenty, mostly wounded, survived.

C Company (following A) and D (following B) now passed through onto the further objective of the Stroombeek, 'a Slough of Despond',[20] despite resistance at Flora Cott and enfilading fire from Hübner Farm, outside the divisional boundary to the right. Private James Flynn, of C Company, was the first man to reach Flora Cott, *The London Gazette* tells us, 'held by ten of the enemy. He showed great courage and initiative in bombing the occupants and killing seven of them. He finally succeeded in capturing the position', his section accounting for fifteen opponents.

Two Lewis guns and two rifle sections of C Company were employed to fix the concrete fortress of Hübner Farm, allowing 2/8th London Regiment (Post Office Rifles) from 58th Division to capture it. Rather surprisingly, as it was outside their boundary, the thirteen men who took the position included members of the Ninth. Either the Highlanders were purposely detached, or they mistook it for Flora Cott. Over seventy unwounded men surrendered. D Company suffered approaching Pheasant Trench but the battalion was established on the the Stroombeek / dotted Blue Line by 8.10am. They now defended the line from the Poelcappelle-St Julien Road on the left to Flora Cott on the right with sections up to the protective barrage. The 7th Argylls had leap frogged through in good time to catch up their barrage and on another 500 yards to the Blue Line. From here the village of Poelcappelle came under observation.

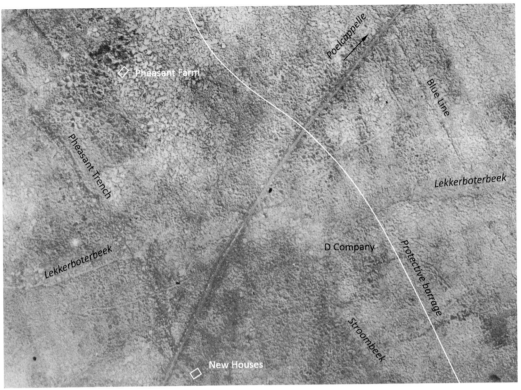

'That terrible mud battle of Poelcappelle'[32] The terrain photographed in January 1918, true backdrop to the map.

So fierce was the fighting that 12,000 rounds of rifle ammunition had to be sent up. 'The Germans as usual wandered about looking for someone to surrender to – all the Jocks being too busy to bother about them.'[85] Over a hundred unwounded, and thirty wounded men were taken prisoner.

At 3pm a large German concentration was reported by aeroplane, quickly followed by a counter-attack, but it was fought off. The wounded, streaming back warned, 'Clear out, the Boche will be here in a minute'[85] but Wimberley advised dividing such reports of the enemy by four. An intercepted wireless message at 4pm gave orders to 452nd Regiment, 234th Division to make a further counter-attack from Poelcappelle. A heavy German bombardment of the Stroombeek valley now began and the expected counter-attack developed about 6pm with intense fire on the left sector. The 4th Gordons, supported by some 8th Argylls, expended their ammunition and fell back, losing Rose House, Malta House and Delta House. The enemy came down the 'V' formed by the Poelcappelle road and Lekkerboterbeek and cut deeply into the British gains. This exposed them to significant casualties from the attentions of the 7th Argylls' north-facing defensive flank near the cemetery, and the Ninth's D Company which could enfilade the advancing enemy from the junction of the Stroombeek and Lekkerboterbeek. D Company also sent a Lewis gun forward to assist the Argylls. The enemy were stopped to the Ninth's left-front, upon the dotted Blue Line. 'In all this fighting, as far as I can find, the Highland Territorials of the 51st Division upon the left had the bloodiest fighting.'[80]

After 8.15pm the battlefield fell quiet, but a difficult night followed with a now unconsolidated line and the Ninth, supposedly in the rear, holding a flank by posts. After another day of shelling, and much sniping, the enemy counter-attacked at 6.30pm in the evening, again without avail. That night the Ninth were relieved and withdrew from the battle with their objectives achieved, one of their finest victories of the war. Harper 'estimated that more of the enemy were killed than in any previous battle'; the strategy had anticipated automatic counter-attacks and planned barrages accordingly.

William Clark.

Nevertheless, the Ninth lost 34 killed, 165 wounded and 27 missing, the deaths for the day rising to 60. They captured 100 prisoners, 8 machine guns and a trench mortar.

William Hamilton Clark of B Company, from George Heriot's and the office of the Grand Lodge of Scotland, was killed. Joel Bamford had worked as a bleach works machine man at Hayfield, Derbyshire. He was wounded and missing on 20 September, his death being accepted for official purposes in October 1918. All that could be returned to his parents were his razor and handkerchief.

Charles Isles was killed leading his platoon after his officer had become a casualty. Lieutenant Charles McLean, already twice wounded, was killed carrying forward a Lewis gun to support the battalion on the left and was buried where he fell. Twenty-two Military Medals and a Bar to an MM were awarded for 20/21 September.

Joel Bamford.

To the south the Ninth's old positions in Glencorse Wood and Nonne Bosschen were captured by the Anzacs. In the view of Hindenburg, the battles of Third Ypres put those of the Somme completely in the shade.

Lieutenant General Ivor Maxse, commanding XVIII Corps, went as far as to say of the 51st:

'I venture to place it among the three best fighting Divisions I have met in France during the past three years. Its record in this Corps comprised: ... On 20th Sept., 1917, an assault on a Sector of the LANGEMARCK-GHELUVELT line which had resisted capture for more than a month, an incursion into hostile territory... repeatedly attacked by five Prussian battalions, all of whom were defeated with sanguinary losses.'

The failure of B Company to take Pheasant Trench in the first rush was observed by Captain Andrew Bain of the 7th Argylls, as they prepared to follow on:

'The attack duly took place, the 9th Royal Scots went over and here the [British] machine guns opened up but they were falling short and they were falling into the backs of the 9th Royal Scots and practically wiped out the whole of that company and they came back and said they couldn't have gone because they were being shot from behind... Douglas Wimberley [said] 'the tripods, whenever they opened fire, they sank in the mud and depressed the muzzles and that was why they were shooting [short]'; but then they ought to have seen that.'[87]

Bain's Argylls, without machine guns, got 'right on' and, he added, 'We never wanted overhead machine gun fire again.'[87] Bain's version of events is not repeated elsewhere but it is quite possible that, at the time, attention would not be drawn to such mistakes. At Zero the guns opened up at a rate of 3,750 rounds per hour until they lifted at 6am, and in the first three hours 232nd MGC fired 102,000 rounds.

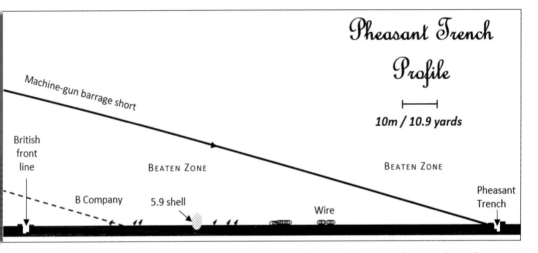

It should be appreciated that the beaten zone of a machine gun forms a long, but relatively narrow ellipse, describing an area containing nine-tenths of the fall of shot. It was usual to employ machine guns obliquely from the flanks so as to enfilade enemy lines; but these indirect barrages fired over the heads of the advancing troops. The barrage from around Haanixbeek Farm was delivered over a mile (2,000 yards or 1.8 km), the flight of each bullet would take over six seconds, reach a maximum altitude of around 60 yards and create a beaten zone some 130 yards long by 17 yards wide (119x15m). In order to shorten the range to say, Pheasant Trench, the muzzles need only depress a couple of degrees. However, the beaten zone at this range would now be 240 yards in length (219m), occupying most of no man's land, through which B Company advanced. In contrast, fire from the German lines would cross the narrowest part of no man's land in a fifth of a second, experience a drop of a few inches, remain supersonic and be capable of passing through a course of bricks.

The division and the battalion may have done well, indeed as the line was taken forward from where they had left it, they might have thought only they could do it;

but they had lost ground too and the Passchendaele offensive is rightly remembered as one of unceasing misery.

The division now moved south to the Heninel-Wancourt sector, entering the trenches at the beginning of October for a month, south of the Cojeul River. They faced French territory that had been deliberately obliterated by the Germans when they removed themselves to the Hindenburg Line earlier in the year. This scene of devastation, eradicating villages and woods, self-proclaimed as the German 'Empire of Death'[51], served to further deepen the resolve of the British. The trenches were cut out of chalk and in reasonable condition though the men were mostly in 'cubby holes'[1] cut in the side of the trench.

Here there was a great deal of patrolling activity by both sides. For example, about 3.30am on 12 October, grenades were thrown at the Ninth's posts and they immediately replied with rifles and Lewis guns. The 4th Seaforths, on the left, were expecting a patrol to return and so did not open fire until, shortly thereafter, bombs landed in their post and wounded seven. One German jumped into the trench throwing bombs until a Seaforth bayonetted him in the face and took him prisoner, but not before Alexander Lawrence of the Ninth was killed in his shelter. As ten bombs landed in one of the Ninth's posts, the NCO led his men out of the sap-head and they drove off about thirty Germans. Alexander Turner won the MM, but Norman Sutherland was killed and his body could not be found, and Louis Riley, from Bradford, became a prisoner and ended up at Soltau. Four enemy dead were found, including an officer, of II Battalion 162nd Regiment. A few days later the brigade began filling in their saps as a revised plan of defence.

With the first American units preparing to fight alongside the allies, the American 78th Division were attached in August 1917 and Shannon Samuel Dennison MD, a doctor who had studied at the University of Maryland, transferred to British service with the 51st Division and the Ninth. Major General Edwards and staff of the American Army visited the battalion and inspected them at bayonet and physical training.

Cambrai

'The whole essence of the operation being 'surprise' there will be no preliminary bombardment.'[1]

154 Brigade War Diary

TACTICALLY Cambrai, 20 November – 7 December 1917, where tanks were first used *en masse*, was a victory for the British; strategically it left little changed on the Western Front. It was something of an experimental operation, one which Haig considered would be of 'local success'.[51] There was to be no respite for the 51st Division, which had already lost over 10,000 men in 1917 and had been in almost continuous fighting for a large part of the year. They were placed in the centre of the attack. The target was once more to be the infamous Hindenburg Line. The division's objective was a line from the high ground at Bourlon Wood through Cantaing to Nine

Wood with 154 Brigade in reserve at Metz. This was a quiet sector with unbroken ground.

In order to maintain surprise, the usual preliminary bombardment was dispensed with. Instead the artillery were calibrated on ranges behind the lines and were to deliver an intense barrage with predicted fire – shooting from the map. Counter-battery targets were identified with flash and sound ranging. Aerial photography permitted detailed and up to date maps. It was the development of artillery support that opened the way to the end of the war, and the great achievement at Cambrai was the return of surprise. The artillery would cut the wire with instantaneously fuzed high explosive shells, obscure the advance with smoke shell, provide a creeping barrage and neutralise the rear areas.

Infantry tactics had also undergone an evolution, and Harper had been at the forefront of thinning his ranks to reduce casualties and training platoons to take the initiative. Notably he had placed only one brigade on the division's front in the attack at Poelcappelle. The infantry would advance close to the barrage, working across the terrain in small sections. The tank, where present, was recognised by the C-in-C as a useful adjunct, excellent at crushing wire and able to bring firepower to the point of assault, enfilading the trench lines. For this, seventy-two tanks of D and E Battalion were deployed on the division's 1,400 yard front. Harper kept his infantry 100 yards from the tanks, following within signalling distance, so that when given the 'All Clear, Come On'[1] (a red and yellow flag) they could advance up the lane of crushed wire, open out and capture each objective. Aeroplanes would also be employed in a dangerous ground attack rôle.

In preparation for the coming battle, reconnaissance of the lines was made by parties in trousers rather than kilts to avoid raising enemy suspicions. A tank demonstration showed that the wire destruction was most effective and 'great camaraderie was established',[1] with the Ninth training with tank crews at Izel-lès-Hameau through the days from 28 October, and enjoying 'colossal binges'[88] overnight. There was also a lot of sport, culminating in the anniversary of Beaumont Hamel which had been declared a holiday, a day of 'festivity and sports', blessed with good weather and with extra rations, special dinners, concerts and with the *Balmorals* using an old RFC hanger as their theatre.

Just before the attack the battalion moved to camouflaged accommodation at Metz, with the assault brigades going on to the starting lines near Trescault. On the first day, 20 November, the division was held up at the ridge at Flesquières (Map XIX) by uncut wire but by 2pm the enemy retired and they carried it the following morning and continued to Cantaing.

On 21 November 154 Brigade moved up from reserve. The 4th Gordons passed through 152 Brigade on the right at 10.30am, and the 7th Argylls through 153 on the left, with the 4th Seaforths following. The Ninth were placed in brigade reserve.

At noon ten tanks arrived and helped the Gordons carry Cantaing, though fighting continued until 3pm, drawing the Gordons to the right. The Gordons were then supported by three squadrons of the Queen's Bays (2nd Dragoon Guards) and the 9th

Cantaing.

Cavalry Brigade MG Squadron. On the left the Argylls were held up until 3.30pm but they proceeded to Fontaine with the aid of tanks and the 4th Seaforths, the latter taking over the defence of the village at 8pm.

The Gordons did not think they could hold out against a counter-attack and so that night the Ninth were ordered to relieve them in Cantaing but not go through their position. They duly moved into posts with all four companies around a squadron of the Queen's Bays that Colonel Green asked to remain – they had had 37 men wounded and 4 horses killed. It proved a quiet night and at dawn on the 22 November the left and right companies swung forward to improve their field of fire. Their right, C Company, now lay on Nine Wood in touch with the Bedford Regiment. B Company under Captain Aymer Maxwell on the left moved up to man the sunken road and obtain touch with the Seaforths. The open ground between the Ninth and eastern Fontaine could only be linked by patrols.

Arthur Gould Lee, an RFC pilot with No.46 Squadron, had been strafing near Fontaine, targetting *Feldgrau* men moving south from the road into La Folie Wood when, at an altitude of about 30ft, his Sopwith Camel B2457 was brought down by a shell burst. The machine came to a halt in the middle of no man's land under machine-gun fire from La Folie Wood 200 yards away, and he made a desperate race in his flying kit in the opposite direction to a sunken road. Walking down the road, now 300-400 yards from the enemy, a soldier called him into a trench:

'Here I found myself with the 9th Royal Scots, of the 51st Division. The Company Commander, Captain Maxwell, had seen me come down, and was surprised I wasn't pipped by the Boche opposite. His men had laid quick bets on whether I'd get away

224

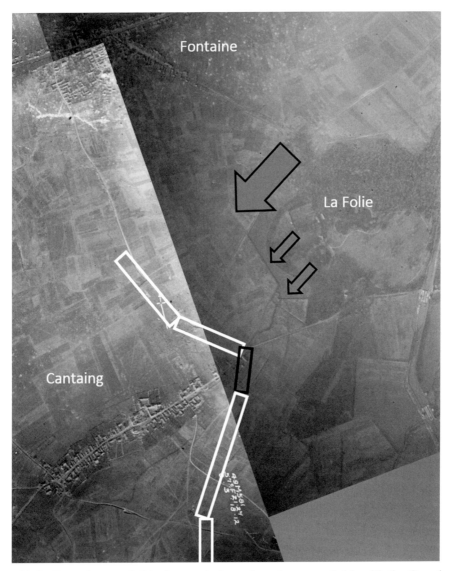

Fontaine

La Folie

Cantaing

with it. From the trench I had a good view of my immense field, with the Camel perched there looking pathetically abandoned… From here, too, I could see how the ridge on which Bourlon Wood lies dominates the whole area.

Within seconds of entering the company dug-out, Maxwell produced a bottle of whisky, and gave me a good nip. I needed it! I told him all I could about the German reinforcements coming up from Cambrai, and of my modest efforts to deter them.'[89]

By turns Lee and Maxwell were surprised at each other's perceptions. Maxwell thought Lee had deliberately landed to bring him information, and Lee told him that far from returning to his machine, he intended walking out. A runner took Lee back over the 50 yards of open ground to Cantaing, which was being shelled, the 'Scottie' fresh after the run whereas Lee, in his heavy attire, was done in.

Mid-morning a German prisoner from II Battalion, 232nd Regiment was found hiding in a cellar in Cantaing. Trench mortars were brought into the line to assist against La Folie Wood. It was at Fontaine Notre Dame on 22 November that the Germans directed their focus against the unfortunate Seaforths who were in an untenable position between German forces in Bourlon Wood to the west and in La Folie Wood on the east. At 10am a heavy shelling by 4.2″ and 5.9″ guns began of Fontaine and Cantaing, and soon SOS flares could be seen from the former. Douglas Wimberley of 232nd MGC bore witness:

'We could see Boche running out of Bourlon Wood and from La Folie on the east… As soon as we got to Cantaing we went down to Colonel Green, 9th Royal Scots, in his dug-out and told him the news. He instantly rang up the artillery, and messages were sent all round for the 9th Royal Scots and 1st Cavalry Brigade troops in Cantaing to stand to. We later got the bad news that Fontaine was lost and that a lot of the Seaforths were taken prisoner, killed or wounded.'

By noon Seaforths were coming back from Fontaine to B Company until about 120 Seaforths were drawn up on the left and reorganised by Corporal George Leighton in charge of the extreme left post. By 3.50pm the village was entirely in enemy hands, who were observed advancing between Fontaine and La Folie Wood. As the Germans reached the rise of a road, B Company opened heavy Lewis gun and rifle fire and forced them back. The enemy made no fewer than five further, unsuccessful attempts to cross the road before digging in. Bewsher, in a wartime turn of phrase, describes the Ninth as having 'had some splendid shooting during the afternoon'.[51] In the centre, A Company, with the squadron of the Queen's Bays, kept movement in La Folie Wood under fire. By evening it was quiet, patrols were sent out and the line was shifted to the left.

The following day, 23 November and the fourth day of the battle, the division made an unsuccessful attack on Fontaine using 152 Brigade who passed to the left of the Ninth, with tanks entering the village.

David Peattie took part in this attack. Private Peattie 4497, a 19-year-old dentist, was one of a score of Ninths who volunteered for the Heavy Branch Machine Gun Corps in October 1916 and were sent to a secret training area near St Pol. Here he was introduced to the Mark I tank before being assigned as a Lewis gunner in B Battalion of the Tank Corps. At Fontaine he was one of the right gunners in a female (machine gun) Mark IV tank named *Bogey II* (B35, No.4589) that had already been in action on 20 November. They now passed through to the left of his old unit at Cantaing.

Entering Fontaine from the south-west, and unsupported by 6th Gordons who were unable to cross the fire-swept approaches, the tanks met heavy resistance – barricades across the street, armour-piercing ammunition and light guns, including a truck mounted anti-aircraft gun. Bogey II worked its way well into the village, but with the driver concussed by a grenade on the roof and both of the right gunners disabled, the tank withdrew. Peattie 'stuck to his post until the end' but died in the tank. Buried at

Conqueror II (C47 No. 4651) burnt out near the church in Fontaine.

Marcoing, his grave was lost and he is commemorated on the Cambrai Memorial. Another Ninth, James Simpson, was a tank gunner in C Battalion in this attack; wounded, he died a week later.

The Ninth were in reserve for this attack, having been lent to 152 Brigade. As such CW4 (No.4514), a wire-pulling tank from C Battalion, rallied with the Ninth ready for a further attack, but thankfully this was not ordered. The battalion kept up their fire on parties of the enemy at the edge of La Folie Wood, and those crossing to Fontaine; they were themselves subject to German artillery bombardment. Maintaining a telephone connection with brigade, and providing wires from Cantaing to all the companies, was largely the achievement of Sergeant Allan Mitchell. When the telephone went down on 23 November, signalling with brigade was by lamp but this too was destroyed by shell fire, wounding two signallers. On one occasion Mitchell had to resort to a pigeon to get his message through.

On the left, Sergeant James Jamieson in B Company put stragglers of the 152 Brigade into order; he ended the war as Company Sergeant Major with DCM, MM and Bar.

On the night of 23/24 November the Ninth were relieved by the 2nd Grenadier Guards and retired to Metz. Casualties were 4 killed and 16 wounded. Company Sergeant Major Jack Brebner, 'the best of the lot'[23] of D Company, had joined in August 1914 and turned down a commission in the field after the Somme. Here he was among the wounded but insisted on staying with his company and 'near died of blood poisoning'.[23]

The division had taken the line 5 miles forward. However, in the view of Brigadier General Henry Pelham Burn, known as 'PB':

'These operations have again proved conclusively, in my opinion, that after the first day's battle further advance is impracticable until an entirely new operation has been planned and prepared, a proceeding that takes weeks rather than days. I have seen this proved again and again – Beaumont Hamel, Vimy Ridge, Arras, 3rd Battle of Ypres and Cambrai all go to prove my point.'[1]

He concludes that advancing within the effective range of field guns gave a good opportunity for success every time, but that 'breakthrough' was unlikely due to the weakening of an attack and the strengthening defence with shortened lines of communication. On the first day of Cambrai the German 54th Division was being relieved by the 20th Landwehr Division, the 107th Division was put in on the second day, on the third day the 119th and 214th Division were encountered and later the Lehr Regiment of the 3rd Guards Division, which had been resting at Ghent when the battle began, came into the line.

In contrast the lengthening British lines meant the Ninth managed to get sixty-four boxes of small arms ammunition, one per section, brought up by pack animals during their time in the line; but the Seaforths had expended all of theirs in the bitter fighting in Fontaine. The counter-attacks on the third day could not be adequately met by the artillery, which had struggled to get guns and howitzers forward despite the better ground; nor could the divisional ammunition column meet their demands for munitions. Restricted to two rounds a minute, they still needed to unload three wagons of ammunition a minute. British firepower was, however, supplemented with thousands of 7.7cm rounds fired from captured guns.

A week later the division was called away from their St Andrew's Day dinners. German forces had forced their way across the incomplete Canal du Nord near Lock No.5 at Mœuvres (Map XX) as part of a major counter offensive. A second battle then began upon the hills of Cambrai. On 1 December the battalion was moved up to the old British front line replacing the 2nd London Regiment of 56th Division and once again in sight of the brooding slope of Bourlon Wood. The next day they took over the front line with exposed flanks and extended east on the night of 3 December when B Company took over from the 2nd HLI. The relief was delayed due to a German bombing attack in progress along the communication trenches, which was briskly dealt with.

Both sides employed bombing blocks, these were hastily constructed barricades in a trench giving the defending riflemen sufficient line of sight to keep grenade throwers at bay. At 7.20am on 4 December the enemy attempted to bomb down a sap (Cimbern Weg) on the Ninth's left and this was repulsed by the platoon of Sergeant T. Smith of A Company. In the afternoon a second unsuccessful attempt was made, this time rushing a communication trench (Deutsch or Sand Lane) held by B Company, involving bombs and rifle grenades and leaving several of the enemy dead after almost an hour's fight.

Ernst Jünger was in these trenches, until wounded, although he was not sure exactly where himself. He describes bombing his way along the trenches on 2 December, where the German stick grenades had a slight advantage in range:

'The British resisted manfully. Every traverse had to be fought for. The black balls of Mills bombs crossed in the air with our own long-handled grenades. Behind every traverse we captured, we found corpses or bodies still twitching. We killed each other, sight unseen. We too suffered losses… The exchange of hand-grenades reminded me of fencing with foils; you needed to jump and stretch, almost as in a ballet. It's the deadliest of duels, as it invariably ends with one or other of the participants being blown to smithereens. Or both.'[58]

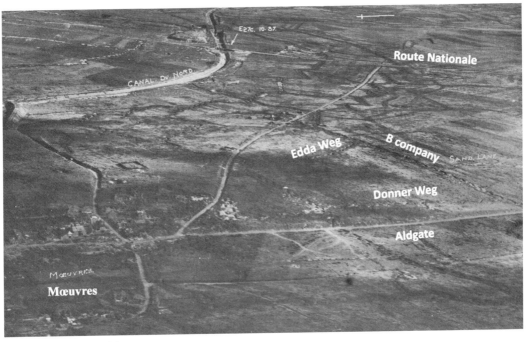

B Company at Mœuvres.

Despite the Ninth's resolute defence, the situation elsewhere was deteriorating necessitating their withdrawal and at 5.30pm on 4 December orders were received to evacuate the position and return, with some relief, to the old British line. One platoon from each company was left as a rearguard until early the following morning. Five were killed, and 18 wounded. William Middlemiss died the following day, he had been shot in the head and never regained consciousness. The battalion moved back to Fremicourt, near Bapaume. The Germans regained much of the territory they had lost in November, undoing the positional achievements of Cambrai.

The contrasts between the actions of 1915 and the present part of this history are stark. At Second Ypres the Ninth advanced in waves with fixed bayonets. At

Poelcappelle and Cambrai the various specialists prepared with full scale practices, large models of the objectives, aerial photographs studied by all men and sketch maps widely issued. They advanced with fire and movement supported by light machine guns and rifle grenades; dribbling forward in twos and threes between shell holes; fixing machine-gun posts and working around the flanks without recourse to artillery; closing on pill-boxes; co-operating with tanks and aircraft. They consolidated with trench mortars and machine guns. All the protagonists would adopt the late 1917 lessons of Riga, Caporetto and Cambrai in 1918.

Frémicourt and Furchtbarkeit

'The War Office has, I hear, just come into possession of a document of extraordinary interest... prepared by the German Headquarters Staff... It is a list of British Divisions in their order of "Furchtbarkeit", which may be translated "much to be fearedness"... In this historic list pride of place is given to the... Fifty-first Division.'

The Pall Mall Gazette, 6 February 1918

AS a result of the Highlanders' tenacious successes in 1917, it may well have been that the 51st Division was considered the most formidable division on the Western Front – certainly in their own opinion. Jim Elliot tells us that even when they joined the 51st Division in early 1916, they were known as '1st Division of Storm Troops'.[2] Right from the outset Clarence Gibb recognised this as a mixed blessing, pleased that their new acquaintances in the regulars 'consider us one of the best of the battns. out here' but adding 'the worst of this is that more is expected of the battalion'.[37] The division received the highest praise from Major General Maxse in September 1917, General Foch called them 'supermen' and it was a division that Haig allowed himself to express affection for, a division that because of results had earned for itself the dubious honour of almost constant employment in the line and in the attack.

Somehow a territorial division, in just a few months after Beaumont Hamel, had managed to take on the mantle of the regular army Highland Brigade, famous in many campaigns and in the Crimea as the 'thin red line'. The 51st (Highland) Division had become a household name of the same stature as the Guards (and they had to be 5ft 10in). They had made solid attacks at Arras and in front of Poelcappelle; their star was firmly in the ascendancy. That it might be fixed there in written records for a century says something about how reputations are made.

A German document, discovered by Dr Alex Fasse, assessed a number of British divisions and in January 1918 identified the *Besonders gute Angriffsdivision*[57] (especially good assault division) as: Guards, 7th, 9th, 29th, 33rd, 51st, 56th, 63rd Division, Canadians, Australians and New Zealanders. In February, *The Pall Mall Gazette* claimed to have seen just such a document, with 51st Division given top billing. This claim was then widely repeated in *The Evening Standard, The Times, The Illustrated London News, The Spectator,* even in the US, then subsequently in a great many memoirs and books (including this one), the list generally running: 1st – 51st Division, 2nd – 29th Division, 3rd – Guards Division.

Charles Carrington probably had it right when he said:

'One of the favourite legends of the war was the German Black List, of which one was always hearing new versions... Some divisions had so great a reputation as to appear in everyone's list and the typical order as I often heard it given was: the Guards, the 51st Highland Division, the New Zealanders, and then the division in which you happened to be serving.'[20]

Wilfrid Bion of the Tank Corps saw it thus: 'the 51st Division, Highland Territorials, had won a reputation second only to the Guards. In their own opinion, and many could be found to share it – even amongst the enemy – they ranked even higher. For steadiness and reliability the Guards could not be matched. But the virtue that was their strength also led to the defect of rigidity in some situations where the flexibility of the 51st would have been more valuable.'[88] The true value of any of this is hard to assess, but the propaganda value was clearly closely tied up with the 51st Division's *esprit de corps* and, as Napoleon believed, 'morale is to the physical as three is to one'.

Major General Douglas 'Tartan Tam' Wimberley, commanding the 51st Division in the Second World War believed, 'Tell a man his father fought well, his grandfather fought well – and when it comes to the bit he won't let you down.'[67]

Bobby Johnston 'attached the greatest importance' to pride of regiment, for morale. Johnston served with a Territorial unit, from drummer boy to platoon sergeant in the Ninth, as a regular sergeant in Salonika with 1st Royal Scots, and in Kitchener's New Army with a commission in the 16th Royal Scots. In his opinion:

Johnston, with his father.

'In order of fighting capacity and ability to soldier in any conditions I place the Regulars far ahead of the other two. Its basic training had been so thorough, the fitness and maturity of the soldiers was instantly noticeable... On the other hand, life was easier and more agreeable in the rather different atmosphere of a Territorial Battalion... Their manners and habits were more civilised. They were just as keen as the Regulars... The fighting spirit of the

231

Territorials too was high. But their officers were in the military sense quite untrained...
The T.A. officer – usually much brighter intellectually and better qualified
academically – was an amateur who was learning the hard way in 1915. As I joined
a Kitchener Army Battalion after it had been bled white on the Somme and at Arras
I felt at once that its standards were low... Its serious weakness was in N.C.O.s ('I
found only one NCO who knew his job')... They were without the regimental pride
which marks the professional soldier and in battle were therefore less efficient or
reliable.'[19]

Officers might come out to France as captains without 'recent active experience'.[19]
However men commissioned from the ranks in 1st Royal Scots were 'not really part
of the Officers' Mess' so Johnston applied for a Territorial unit. The TF and NA
officers were more able to question their CO's orders, something envied by regular
subalterns.

Johnston also believed the officer-soldier relationship to be strong in the TF and
NA officers, strengthened by the experience of battle, that they were, 'All men of
intelligence, bright young men.'[19] Ferguson certainly felt that 'in Scotland the
formation of units as Highlanders has drawn out a superior and intelligent class of
recruit,'[7] building on the Scottish education system. It was subsequently recognised
that the Territorials' 'greater intelligence enabled them to overcome training
deficiencies,'[48] testament to their self-discipline. Ferguson had taken these recruits and
instilled a powerful sense of 'esprit de corps, in the full confidence that if a good
regimental character and tradition were formed ... that those who would roll in in the
event of a real emergency would soon assimilate the spirit and habits of their older
comrades....'[7]

So it proved, not in all regiments, but in the 51st Division 'battalions would suffer
terrible casualties in officers and men; commanding officers would be killed, or
invalided, whole messes would disappear; yet the units remained the units, imbued
with the old spirit, absorbing countless reinforcements and still a great fighting unit'.[32]
Hindenburg describes the 'historic fame'[60] of a unit as a kind of indestructible cement
that holds them together, very soon permeates new members and thereby allows the
corps to be repeatedly reconstituted. Even in the Second World War:

'It would be the merest sentimentality to gloss over the fact that, towards the end of
the war, any Scottish unit might contain an actual majority of Englishmen in the
ranks. Incredibly strong and subtle, however, is the power of tradition. To be a "Jock"
soon became the pride of any good lad from south of the Border.'[70]

Here, now in the Highland Division, was a Highland-Lowlander, or indeed Lowland-
Highlander battalion. As with any self-respecting Scottish battalion, the Ninth had their
own William Wallaces, Robert Bruces and Rob Roy MacGregors. Arthur Anderson
did not feel particularly Highland when he was able to find a vacant place in a tent in
Étaples in 1916 and found the occupant Seaforths speaking Gaelic.

Yet whilst *esprit* can strengthen a regiments, it does not always promote co-operation, and may even result in feuds. Rivalry, found between sections, platoons and upward, may be robust and sanguine, or disruptive and unhealthy. We have already seen that Argylls could fight between battalions, and there was at least one punch up with the Guards on relief, after Fontaine. Less seriously the 51st's *Balmorals* were in fierce competition with the *Bow Bells* troupe of the 56th Division, and the *Balmorals* even 'kidnapped' Connel of the HLI from the 32nd Division, a female impersonator who became famous as 'Gertie'.

A unit should certainly aspire to being reliable by being efficient and disciplined, to gain the advantages of deterrence and win the psychological battle; but gaining a reputation for fierce indomitability must be paid for in blood. The *Besonders gute Angriffsdivision* all experienced heavy losses and were frequently put into battle. Only the Australians succeeded in making it clear that they had had enough in September 1918.

From 3 December into spring 1918, the division made major improvements to the trench system, following standardised instructions issued by General Harper. The division also found the energy to construct bath houses and a picture palace amongst the billets. The *Balmorals* performed a comic opera called *Turnip Tops* that was so successful a special theatre was built. Unfortunately, it was captured by the Germans on the day it was to open.

On 23 December an air raid, lasting an hour-and-a-half, on their camp at Frémicourt caused seven casualties. The division prepared 20,000 Christmas and New Year cards, one per man – issued through the canteen at tuppence each. Christmas Day was one of sleet and snow, but a holiday was enjoyed nevertheless and the men attended the divisional cinema. The bad weather delayed the Boxing Day brigade shooting competition for two days, when the Ninth's No.2 Section of 5 Platoon were the winners and No.3 Section the runners-up.

By New Year's Day they were back in the line near Demicourt in a hard frost. The men were instructed to pull their hose tops well up over their knees and were issued with long puttees.

Chapter 7

Defeat and Victory
1918

A narrowing window of opportunity presented itself to the German High Command for the spring of 1918. The Germans had already beaten Serbia, Romania and Russia. Now a million men had been liberated from the Eastern Front, but the United States had yet to field her significant army which would grow from just less than a million men in May 1918 to over a million men by the Armistice. The blockade was weakening Germany and breakthrough tactics seemed a real possibility. The initiative was in German hands and their intention was to divide the French and British, force the latter out and win the war.

Across the entire BEF, brigades were reorganised to contain three, rather than four battalions as a consequence of the losses of 1917 and the shortage of drafts from home. The Ninth, 5th Gordon Highlanders and 8th Argyll and Sutherland Highlanders – one battalion from each of the brigades of the 51st Division – were withdrawn, formed into the Highland Brigade and transferred to 61st (2nd South Midland) Division as 183 Brigade in February 1918. According to John Stirling these were 'three of its best battalions',[11] to Bewsher it was 'a great blow both to the Division and to the battalions'.[5] They had played an important part in the history of the 51st Division through its greatest period.

The massed bands of 154 Brigade played them off and between 6 and 9 February the 'highly indignant Scots'[90] marched south, crossing the Somme at Voyennes, and joined the Midlanders of the 61st Division. Their strength was 38 officers and 828 ORs. Three of the four battalions of 183 Brigade were disbanded, to be replaced with Scots, and across the British Army 175 battalions were lost. It could have been worse as the Infantry Record Office at Hamilton had heard that the Ninth were being disbanded. Instead they received a draft of 124 ORs.

Table 10. Infantry Brigades of the 61st Division

⊠	61st (2nd South Midland) Division *Major General Colin Mackenzie*	
182 Brigade *Brigadier General WK Evans*	**183 Brigade** *Brigadier General AH Spooner*	**184 Brigade** *Brigadier General Hon R White; AW Pagan*
2/6 Warwicks 2/7 Warwicks 2/8 Worcesters	1/9 Royal Scots 1/5 Gordons 1/8 Argylls	2/5 Gloucesters 2/4 Oxs and Bucks 2/4 Royal Berks
1/5 Duke of Cornwall's Light Infantry (DCLI) (Pioneers)		

In contrast to the 51st, the 61st Division was a second-line Territorial division, mainly of 'home service' men, that had fought with such disastrous consequences at Fromelles in 1916 that they had earned themselves the unfortunate nickname of the 'sixty-worst'. The Germans seemed to agree, listing them as 'poor'[63] in August 1916. The Highland Brigade was intended to stiffen the division as the British extended their line further south to replace French units across the Somme and Oise rivers. Thus the Ninth joined their new division in the former French lines north of St Quentin between the valleys of the Omignon and the Germaine rivers. Fifth Army formed the British right, within which the Ninth were part of XVIII Corps, 61st Division, 183 Brigade (Map XXII).

Following the German strategy of *defence in depth*, but finding French preparations of any kind sorely lacking, much work was undertaken on fieldworks around the Holnon plateau, the ground still devastated by the German withdrawal. The defence in depth principle was implemented as three areas of defence, each held by one of the battalions of the brigade in rotation. This entailed less time out of danger than in the four-battalion system that had previously existed. In the Front or Forward Zone, a line of outposts was held by two companies, who would fall back if attacked. This was backed by strongpoints to form a *line of resistance* 1,500-2,000 yards behind the outpost line to break-up and delay the enemy until reserves could be brought up. One company held a strongpoint, in the case of 183 Brigade this was Fresnoy Redoubt, which also accommodated a dedicated counter-attack company. In fact the orders stated: 'Each Commander, from Battalion Commander to Platoon Commander, will have a counter-attack unit.'[1] For example in early March the Ninth had B Company on the left front, C on the right front, D in Fresnoy with A Company as the counter-attack company and 'Echelon B' (transport etc) went to billets at Villevêcque.

The second area was the Battle Zone, with a battalion billeted at Marteville Huts and ready to man their stations in the event of attack. This was a line of mutually supporting posts with the same arrangement of companies. It was here an enemy attack was to be stopped.

The Reserve Battalion in the Rear Zone was billeted at Beauvois and would man the rear defences at Holnon Wood as required. Because of the angle of the River Omignon, this zone defended the rear of the whole division and came under direct orders of the division. Three company redoubts were planned with a counter-attack company at battalion HQ in a shallow quarry. On the command *Man Battle Stations*, the reserve battalion of the right brigade, 182 Brigade, would move up from Germaine to Attilly Huts and the centre reserve battalion from 184 Brigade would come from Ugny to join 183 reserve at Marteville Huts. The principal reserve was supplied by 183 Brigade with the other battalions available for counter-attack under their orders. An Army line was also to be constructed as a final back stop position.

However, across the Fifth Army sector the battle zone was incomplete and there was precious little in the rear zone. Many trenches were merely removed turf and the redoubts existed but in name. Each battalion in the Forward Zone was required to put a mining platoon to work.

Communications remained heavily reliant on telephone lines and the work of the battalions included burying cables from the redoubts to a depth of 8ft. They were supplemented by six pigeons, sent daily to Fresnoy (Nicholson says that trench stores included sporting guns to bring down pigeons). Provision was made for foggy weather in the form of intermediate repeating stations and, in dense fog, with a chain of four runner posts. Gas warnings were by Strombos Horns and gas rattles.

The brigade's artillery provided four six-gun 18-pounder batteries, less one gun located at Fresnoy for anti-tank purposes, and one 4.5″ howitzer battery. The heavy artillery came under divisional orders. There were eight SOS posts in the outpost line, each with a rifle fitted with a rifle grenade that would burst into a parachute flare of three red stars. This would instruct the artillery, whose guns were left laid on pre-arranged SOS lines, to open fire for 15 minutes.

Rab Murdoch's section, 1918.

On 2 March the Ninth moved into the Forward Zone, and at 9.30pm a raid on one of their posts was attempted by the enemy behind a barrage, but thankfully no one was missing. On 10 March they moved to Marteville Huts, and on 19 March to Beauvois. Therefore, by chance, when the roulette wheel stopped, the Ninth were in Reserve, the 8th Argylls were in the Battle Zone and the 5th Gordons were in the Forward Zone.

Kaiserschlacht – Spring Offensive

BY the spring of 1918 the Germans had amassed an army of four million on the

Western Front. For the Operation Michael offensive they outnumbered their opponents by almost three to one and had huge local superiority in artillery and aircraft. Most of the British effort had been exerted in protecting the Channel ports, heavily defending the northern end of the line in Flanders. However, Ludendorff had long selected St Quentin as the point for his breakthrough. On the German left Hutier's Eighteenth Army was to intercede between the British and the French, in the centre von der Marwitz's Second Army, north of the Omignon, was to form a pincer with von Bulow's Seventeenth Army on the right. Correspondingly, directly facing the 61st Division's 6,000 yard frontage were three German divisions with generous reserves, and the Corps' three divisions faced fourteen German divisions. All was quiet on the Western Front until 21 March.

A raid overnight on 20/21 March by the 2/6th Warwicks took fifteen prisoners and discovered two further divisions on their front. This disquieted the division to the point that they had flooded their front with gas. Meanwhile Bill Hay and his platoon in C Company were getting drunk. Either Hay knew with certainty something the rest of Fifth Army did not, or, perhaps most likely, 20 March was their first opportunity to imbibe since leaving the battle zone:

'We knew that the Germans were going to make their big attack, so everybody drew their last Franc that was owing to them up to the day, saying we might as well have it, get drunk if you like, before the attack. We were in billets, playing cards all night, drank right on to the early morning. The early morning was very misty, very foggy, and one or two shells landed in the village, so the order came to fall in and we all had to jump out from where we were, half-drunk as a matter of fact, some were sozzled. We all lined up, called the roll and put our gear on, stand to and start the march from there up into the line. Going up to the line we were in what they call Artillery Formation. We first of all marched as companies, then we broke into platoons, then into sections as we got nearer the line, because there was shell fire.'[56]

Operation Michael – St Quentin to Amiens

'The German Crown Prince's Army Group will first gain the line of the Somme south of the Omignon stream.'[60]

Orders of His Imperial Majesty the Kaiser, 10 March 1918

IN the morning mists of 21 March 1918 a German gunner pulled a lanyard to fire the first shell of Operation Michael; 3.2 million followed on this first day. Even Paris was shelled by a colossal gun from an unprecedented range of 68 miles. The expected storm had broken, driving against the southern extent of the British zone, over the Somme battlefields, and with unexpected success.

A heavy bombardment had commenced at 4.30am and twenty minutes later the division issued the order to *Man Battle Stations*. The Ninth left their billets at Beauvois under the order *Bustle* at 5.30am, were clear within an hour, and were amongst the artillery in the embryonic rear defences at Holnon Wood by 8.50am. The Official

History describes how, in fog and gas that afforded a visibility of only 10-12 yards, men had to 'hold on to each other like blind men as they stumbled forward in the darkness'.[43] There they were shelled periodically throughout the day, particularly with gas, causing casualties in A, B and especially C companies.

In the Forward Zone, *Strosstruppen* from the German 113th Division, largely unseen, infiltrated through the outpost line about 9.30am. Parties worked on the flanks with flame-throwers, light and heavy machine guns and trench mortars until the 5th Gordons in Fresnoy Redoubt came under pressure by 11.20am. An hour later they were surrounded and soon after that communications were cut. In fact all of the forward redoubts had been surrounded by about noon, and the Ninth were ordered to pay special attention to the right flank of 184 Brigade when Enghien Redoubt was surrounded. Around the same time the 8th Argylls in the Battle Zone had lost trenches and John Crawford Buchan won his VC defending a series of posts over two days. The fog prevented the SOS flares from being seen. From the eight beleaguered battalions in XVIII Corps' Forward Zone, only about fifty men got away and these few men came in through the night. However, three battalions had held up three divisions all day and the battle quietened down by 10pm.

Though more were killed on 1 July 1916 on the first day of the Somme, the highest number of casualties for the BEF on any day of the war were incurred on 21 March. Among the missing was Frank Moffat, at one time with the Ninth and now trench mortar officer; his wellbeing was notified by a postcard from Colonel McTaggart, 5th Gordons, from captivity.

The following morning was again thick with fog and ten German divisions attacked the three in XVIII Corps, most heavily in the north, where the 61st Division still held the Battle Zone, and on their left where 183 Brigade held a defensive flank against incursions along the Omignon valley. At 8.15am the 24th Division on the left were attacked along both sides of the Omignon; about 10am they began retiring and at 12.10pm the Ninth, though warned to relieve the 8th Argylls in the Battle Zone, instead were ordered to move back to the reserve line near Villevêque and 'retained a firm hold'[43] of the left flank. C Company, fighting the rearguard action, was reduced to two officers and about thirty men.

Bill Hay.

The indomitable Sergeant Bill Hay ended his fighting war at this point:

'The Germans had gone way by on the flanks and we were stuck there… There were these Germans all sitting around drinking their coffee and eating their sausages, and their rifles were all stacked together, when the mist swirled and moved and I saw this right in front of me. It was such a sitting target and I still had three magazines left on the Lewis gun. We were told to stay put and hold the Germans up until the troops could get back and reform a new line of defence. So I let them have the whole three magazines and then I'd got no ammunition so I could do nothing else then… If you're sitting behind a machine gun you've got no fear because you've got a gun, you don't realise that you're a target, an obvious target. There's a certain sense of feeling you're okay, because you've got the gun you see. You're not scared, you're so intent on doing what you want to do…

So then the machine guns opened up on us, the German machine guns, I finished my ammunition and I told the blokes to make a run for it… and I just sat in the trench, waiting. I thought well, after all these years of filth and mud at least I got my revenge on my mates that had died and what I'd been through and I can't recollect that I was scared, I can recollect that I thought "well this is the end now". I didn't know if I'd be killed or taken prisoner or what would happen. A German officer came along the trench with his revolver… Well, there's no point in saying, you know two fingers, you have to put your hands up. So I was captured... There was only about three of four of us left alive when the Germans captured me.'[56]

Among the casualties of C Company were Alex Kelly. Severely wounded by a bullet through the body on 21 March, he was left in a shell hole and probably picked up later by the Germans; his death was recorded as 22 March. Also from No.12 Platoon was John Brown who was wounded in the face and taken prisoner. Arthur Wainwright, an insurance man from Leeds, received a bullet in the right arm and was captured at Marteville; Norman M. Macdonald was picked up the next day and died of pneumonia in June.

At 1pm the 24th Division blew the bridge at Vermand having passed to the north. Arthur Conan Doyle's history explains:

'The 9th Royal Scots extended their line to the westward, and facing north presented an unbroken front to the constant hordes of Germans who were moving down the northern slopes of the Omignon valley in the direction of Caulaincourt. It was not until late in the afternoon of March 22 that the Sixty-first Division retired, still fighting, to a prepared position north of Vaux.'[91]

The Ninth at Villevêcque, set to 'watch and counter' the westward movement of the enemy, were singled out for praise by Ivor Maxse, commanding XVIII Corps, in safeguarding the left flank of the Corps. However, in late afternoon outflanking to the north and, to a lesser extent, south of the division compelled them to withdraw to the 'Army line', which was completed by 5.40pm. Shortly after the Ninth received their orders, the rest of the division were instructed to occupy the Army line, recently dug but only to a depth of 18in.

This reserve position was occupied by the Ninth on the left, up against the river, with the 8th Argylls on the brigade right and the remnants of the 5th Gordons in the centre including Echelon Bs. At 8.30pm there was shelling with gas and, following a 50-minute bombardment, the enemy attacked the Army line in force but were fended off. However, with Vaux-en-Vermandois to the south taken about 7.45pm, 184 Brigade on the right broken, Beauvois gassed, the ammunition dump on fire and the line to division cut, the position became difficult. Brigade HQ moved to the Ninth's HQ in

Pleasant Woods and from here they managed to make contact with division, receiving Corps' orders to retire overnight to the Somme. This decision, by Maxse, later came under criticism as being premature. Doubtless Maxse had in mind the retreat of August 1914 when, as a brigade commander, he had lost a battalion through 'prolonged delay'. Movement was almost impossible near Beauvois due to the weight of artillery fire, but as 183 Brigade began to retire at nearly midnight via Matigny to the Somme, Beauvois had already been taken by the enemy.

Believing the British fatally weakened, Ludendorff's plans for 23 March fanned out his armies. The Seventeenth Army (General Otto von Below) on the right had made little progress but were reinforced to continue north-west and drive the British into the sea. Second Army (General Georg von der Marwitz) in the centre, unable to swing northward in support of the Seventeenth, were now to advance without halt westward on both sides of the Somme, though it was not until 26 March that they were given Amiens as an objective. Rather than the limited objectives of securing the Somme and Crozat Canal, Eighteenth Army (General Oskar von Hutier) on the left had enjoyed far greater success and were now to relentlessly gain ground to the south-west between the British and French armies. Hutier's success in the south had therefore prompted Ludendorff to widen the attack, and this inevitably spread his resources and reduced pressure on the allies. In retrospect Hindenburg realised, 'We ought to have shouted into the ear of every single man: "Press on to Amiens. Put in your last ounce."'[60]

In contrast to the static lines and familiar place names of 1915-17, the actions of the German Spring Offensive read like a gazetteer of locations (Map XXI). Although it is the daily bread of soldering to march with heavy packs to mispronounced places, they probably had a limited grasp of where they were or where they were going.

The Ninth crossed the Somme at Voyennes at 5.30am on 23 March, barely before the bridge was blown by anxious Royal Engineers who left some heavy guns behind on the right bank (Map XXIII). The division was to hold the bridgeheads at Breuil and Buverchy but instead, 'sadly depleted',[43] went into reserve around Nesle, arriving about 9am. GHQ's Operation Order No.784 at 5pm on 23 March began: 'Fifth Army will hold the line of the Somme river at all costs.'[43]

The Germans systematically attacked the crossings of the river and canal and had established bridgeheads at Pithon and Ham to the south. As such the Ninth were dispersed to Languevoisin with a company at Breuil, near the Canal du Nord, until returned to Nesle in the evening when 184 Brigade took over the south-east flank. At Nesle they were placed under orders of the 20th Division and put into billets at one hour's notice, with pickets to the north-east. They passed a quiet night, had a chance for a wash and started their day with a breakfast of eggs and champagne.

Unconfirmed reports on the morning of 24 March from 8th Division, that the enemy had crossed at Béthencourt, resulted in divisional orders for the brigade, plus a battery of Canadian Motor Machine Guns, to assemble at Mesnil-Saint-Nicaise and counter-attack. They were approximately 600 strong. The swing bridge at Béthencourt had not been completely destroyed the day before, allowing infantry to cross in single file, and

Nesle.

opposite Fontaine-les-Pargny the enemy had spent time felling trees across the canal and constructing rafts. Orders were issued at 11.10am 'to locate the enemy and drive him over the canal'[1] as follows: the 8th Argylls, with about sixty survivors from the 5th Gordons, on the right were given the objective of Hill 80, just west of Béthencourt; the Ninth on the left were to advance up the Pargny road to Rieux Copse, immediately north of Fontaine-les-Pargny, but with their left flank in the air. Zero hour would be noon starting with a twenty-minute bombardment; the 18-pounders were to shell the hill and the heavy artillery the wood, and also Villecourt across the river.

Initially both attacks went well and they were believed to have driven the enemy back across the Somme, 'and by half-past two in the afternoon the position had once more been re-established',[91] but the German XXV Reserve Corps came on in large numbers and forced the brigade back under heavy machine-gun fire to the Morchain-Rouy road, endangering their left flank. Doctor Alexander McMurtrie who had, rightly or wrongly, a reputation for leaving cases to his orderlies, here 'took innumerable risks to succour the wounded'.[33] Stretcher-bearer John Watson went missing. One Ninth wrote:

'During our retirement, near Nesle, I was in a shell-hole with another private, when the Sergeant told us to retire further. The private and I made a rush, while the Sergeant took shelter for a minute in the shell-hole which we were leaving. Just at that moment

Pargny, Canal de la Somme.

he was hit in the head by a sniper, and I believe that he was killed, but we had to leave him.'[92]

Three sergeants were killed that day: Alexander Black, David Gowans and Peter Grant, previously the pioneer sergeant, whose brother was killed on the same day. Battalion runner James Shiell was killed by a shell splinter.

The battalion had held up German Grenadier Regiment No.12 for about four hours, however this was the worst day of the retreat for the Ninth, with 59 dead. Captain Stanley Mountford, who had worked for Norwich Union in Argentina and won an MC at Gallipoli, was killed and is one of eight buried at Pargny British Cemetery. Harry Donkin, bookseller, shot in the back and buttock, managed to get away but died in May. A large number of the wounded were taken prisoner, such as Corporal Albert Andrew of B Company, who had been shot through the mouth and right shoulder.

During the night of 24/25 March, the defences were to be thrown into confusion. At 3pm all of the 20th Division, whose right had been secure behind the Canal du Nord, were retiring, so orders were received to pull back to the north of Mesnil-Saint-Nicaise and link with the 8th Division on their left. As the latter found this impossible, at 6.50pm the orders changed again and 183 Brigade were instructed to throw a line out from Mesnil-Saint-Nicaise to Potte, about 1½ miles as the crow flies. The 8th Argylls were to be on the right and the Ninth on the extreme left of the division and Corps, with one company in Potte to keep touch with 25 Brigade, 8th Division, XIX Corps. Before they were in position, Mesnil-Saint-Nicaise was captured by the enemy and the line was set back to the west. Although communications were extremely difficult between units, limited as they were to runners and staff on horses, the sole breakdown in brigade communications occurred this night – the Ninth were cut-off from about 10pm on 24 March until late the following morning. They were attempting to find their own 8th Argylls to the right and a company of the 22nd Durham Light Infantry (Pioneers) of 8th Division on their left near Potte, but the DLI had only managed to get as far as Dreslincourt.

In the middle of the night Colonel William Green finally managed to find Brigadier General Clifford Coffin VC of 25 Brigade who told him dismissively he had withdrawn to Dreslincourt in anticipation of a major counter-attack. This was to be by the 8th Division and the 24th Division in conjunction with the French 22nd Division, who were between Rouy and Mesnil-Saint-Nicaise, to pass between Potte and Mesnil-Saint-Nicaise after 8am (later 11am) in order to regain Béthencourt. No one had told the Ninth, who were leading a lonely existence in the cold night air.

With his companies stretched to breaking point, Green had no choice but to divert the company intended for Potte to Dreslincourt to gain touch, but at 4.50am 8th Division units were ordered to be north of the wire of the old trench line by 5.30am to clear out of the way of the counter-attack. Brigadier General Spooner of 183 Brigade thought their neighbours had needlessly exposed their flank which they 'threw into the air'.[1] The gap through Potte to 8th Division, according to the Official History, was at least two miles.

The counter-attack failed to materialise, not least because the enemy attacked at 6.15am on 25 March, and unsurprisingly found the front thinly held. They were already in Potte by 8am and an estimated 5,000 entered Dreslincourt about 9am, whilst at the same time an attack south of Mesnil-le-Petit cut off some of the 8th Argylls. Therefore the overstretched brigade 'made a long and gallant fight',[43] retreating to the railway and holding up the enemy for three hours, until all ammunition was expended. Under intense pressure, the Ninth withdrew in groups in the direction of Fonches. Several men were killed as they were driven back across the railway line and some retired through Étalon. Reformed around 2pm, they were temporarily with 72 Brigade, 24th Division, XIX Corps withdrawing to Hattencourt. During the night of 25 March, having finally lost contact with the enemy, they were sent on to the 61st Division at Le Quesnel.

On the afternoon of 25 March, the French 22nd Division lost Nesle and withdrew to the south-west, further widening the gap. At 6pm, with both flanks open, the two British divisions in the open, 20th and 30th, conformed and withdrew. XVIII Corps, including the five brigades constituting the 20th and the 61st Divisions, conformed with the French and fell back to the south at midnight and in bad weather. The British, including XIX Corps, retired on a divergent line to the north and this created a 3-mile gap on the Santerre plain on what was effectively the dividing line between French and British armies, and through which Ludendorff was attempting to drive a wedge.

On the morning of 24 March Philippe Pétain, the French Commander-in-Chief replacing Nivelle, had visited Haig and told him his priority was the defence of Paris, which risked severing the allies. Haig would also have had concerns about the Channel ports. Now, on 26 March, a conference was called by the French President. Pétain told them that the British Fifth Army was broken and made an unfavourable comparison to the routed Italians at Caporetto, and that he could not help. After a bitter argument, General Ferdinand Foch, who had been sent to Italy after the heavy losses of the Somme, was made supreme co-ordinating allied commander.

The remnants of XVIII Corps, without artillery, assembled outside Roye before daybreak on 26 March, day six of the offensive. The 20th and 61st Divisions marched at 7am toward Le Quesnel, arrived about midday and went into support and reserve as the rest of the Corps began occupying old French trenches from 1916 that ran up to the River Somme at Frise. Although the gap was largely filled, the enemy were well advanced, indeed a German regiment passed behind the XVIII column soon after they had left Roye.

Returned to the 61st Division, the Ninth were sent to Beaucourt. Losses meant that on arrival a single, composite battalion had to be formed from the remnants of the brigade. Under Colonel Green, this consisted of two companies of the Ninth, one of the 8th Argylls and one of the 5th Gordons and was about 550 strong. They dug-in a series of outposts across the Amiens-Roye road east of Mézières-en-Santerre and occupied them by 5pm.

Heavy fighting continued on 27 March and the Ninth were twice advanced forward to dig-in again, once in the vicinity of Hangest. At 5.30pm Fifth Army ordered the 61st Division, with the composite battalion, north. The battalion was replaced about midnight of 27/28 March by a French unit, and they themselves were 'conveyed by omnibus'[33] in the small hours of 28 March and assembled at the railway line north of Marcelcave. Headquarters reported at 1.30am, but some of the troops, including the Ninth, were still arriving at 5am (Map XXIV).

A new crisis was developing. The evening before, two Prussian regiments had crossed the Somme from the north and the 3rd Grenadier Regiment had entered Lamotte-en-Santerre and Warfusée Abancourt on the Roman road, placing them behind the left flank of XIX Corps and 10 miles from Amiens. To Gustav Goes 'This was the way to fight, just like we were led in the East! Bristling like a hedgehog, the companies occupied the villages.'[93]

The area was known to the Ninth as their first experience of the Somme in 1915; the composite battalion, less artillery, was now placed two miles behind XIX Corps' faltering line. On this the eighth day, having arrived around 5am, they were under orders again at 7.50am to take up a position along the railway ready to attack northward if the enemy advanced west from Lamotte. The division then ordered them to attack Lamotte directly with Zero hour at 11.30am, changed to noon then changed again to *forthwith*. Corps had told them that there were very few of the enemy in Lamotte and that the attack must take place with little artillery support.

The now very weak and tired 183 and 184 Brigades, at 11.50am on 28 March, set off across 2,500 yards of featureless terrain – though our own wire presented an obstacle – north against Lamotte. A Company were ordered to occupy the village but at 300 yards from their objective they were pinned down by machine-gun fire. Gustav Goes was in the village:

'Lieutenant d. R. Röhnisch lowered his binoculars. His 11th Company was already set up to provide a splendid reception. Lamotte suddenly appeared deserted but snipers and machine guns were lurking behind hedges and bushes. The British marched into the village, unaware – Koenigsberg Fusiliers surrounded them immediately and disarmed them affably... Oberleutnant Schwarck worked equally well at the eastern entrance to Lamotte... Lieutenant d. Res. Zimmermann stirred up a machine-gun nest at the western exit; Offizierstellvertreter [equivalent of Warrant Officer] Sommerey ("Iron" as he was called), rushed the nest with a Stoßtrupp and smoked it out of the farmhouse.'[93]

The British attack stalled 200 yards from the enemy, though on the right one company pushed up to the outskirts of the village. On the left the attack was held up by machine-gun fire from Warfusée Abancourt and attempts to work a company round the north-west side of Warfusée failed. John Heggie, a golf club maker, was killed while leading a patrol reconnoitring Warfusée. Though orders were received not to press the attack around 3.40pm, the composite battalion steadfastly remained until ordered to retire at 5.30pm; withdrawal was complete by 8pm. Corporal William Telfer's Lewis gun protected their retirement.

The Official History notes that with armies on the left and right retiring, the position could not have been held even if it had been retaken. They had, however succeeded in delaying the German advance on this crucial part of the line until a defence could be organised.

Behind them the village of Marcelcave was heavily shelled and attacked but had already been abandoned by XIX Corps' improvised forces. Retiring to the railway cutting north of Marcelcave, the composite battalion were enfiladed along the railway line and threatened from behind. Therefore the brigade repaired half a mile to the west of Marcelcave and dug in as part of a new line of defence between the Roman road to the north and the edge of a wood on the La Luce stream to the south. Eighteen men were killed on 28 March, including 28-year-old Company Sergeant Major William Gibb 350006, who had joined in 1912. Marcelcave was taken by the enemy by dawn on 29 March.

At the new line of defence they were shelled for two days, though not attacked by infantry, and observed Demuin and Aubercourt changing hands more than once to their immediate south. An Australian counter-attack, intended to restore the line between Marcelcave and Aubercourt, was planned for 30 March and this prompted two sets of orders for the composite battalion. Firstly, rifle fire from Morgemont Wood to the south (renamed Lancer Wood, east of Bois de Hangard) told them parties of the enemy had

Marcelcave.

Cave Copse

Looking east along the railway with Marcelcave to the south.

entered it on the afternoon of 30 March, threatening the counter-attack, and one company was sent to work through the wood from the north-east corner to the far side. 'The enemy made the most of every gun he had and shelled Lancer Wood... very heavily with 5.9s – 4.2s – and 77s, also captured 18 pounders.'[1] Though taking heavy casualties they held the ground until the counter-attack came through about 4.30pm.

Secondly, to prevent high ground south-west of Marcelcave being occupied before the Australian counter-attack, Captain Harry Wakelin's C Company was ordered to attack and hold this ridge, which they achieved under heavy machine-gun fire from the south-east. Wakelin, seeing the enemy coming on, succeeded in changing front in ten minutes and delivering an attack to the right, which stopped them.

By about 5pm the Australians had passed through Lancer Wood and 'got to the Boche with the bayonet' against the 91st Oldenburg Regiment. The composite battalion reassembled in their former support position west of Marcelcave.

The Ninth were finally relieved overnight 30/31 March to Gentelles, but had to relocate outside the village during daylight and lie in artillery formation due to shelling. That evening, day eleven of the ordeal, they occupied all the available cellars. They held the line again on 1 and 2 April, but after fourteen days the composite battalion was dissolved on 3 April and the Ninth made billets at Vergies.

Estimated casualties for the Ninth were 17 officers and 550 other ranks, killed, wounded or missing. Fatalities for the eleven days of the retreat settled at 115 with a large number commemorated on the Pozières Memorial. A huge draft of 528 arrived on 6 April 1918, which would have included many boys aged 18½, and for the month totalled 19 officers and 652 other ranks.

It is conventional to speak of the turning tide, but there was nothing inevitable about bringing this offensive to an end, death marked every mile. The Germans had rushed headlong and heedless of their losses, unravelling as they lost touch with their lines. The Ninth had stood near the epicentre at the start of the onslaught and fought it all the way back to its final halt, about 40 miles as the crow flies, practically to the gates of Amiens, a city that had fallen to the Spanish in 1597 and the Prussians in 1870. The Official History sums up the achievements of units such as theirs:

'Truly the survivors of the Fifth Army, who were still holding a 19-mile front, deserved well of their country. Far from being swept away and destroyed by the onslaught of three or four times their numbers, the XVIII and XIX Corps… had, with little reinforcement, not only brought the Germans to a standstill, but after ten days' heavy fighting were still in the line.'[43]

The BEF's total tally of fifty-eight infantry divisions had fifteen exhausted divisions in or near the line, including the 61st Division, and but a single fresh division.

Robert Grubb typically worked in no man's land as a sniper and had won the MM in December 1917. During the withdrawal he was out on the flank, like an ancient skirmisher, when he saw an enemy machine gun being set up in his direction and wisely decided to retire. However, before he made it back he was badly wounded. The battalion were under orders to leave but his mates said, 'We can't leave Bobby out there' so went out and fetched him in. His right leg had to be amputated above the knee and he returned to civilian life with an artificial leg at the age of 21. When offered a white feather on an Edinburgh tram, all he could do was silently get up and leave as best he could.

On being taken prisoner Bill Hay felt a great sense of relief to be taken beyond the range of bullets and shells. He and another prisoner, and two German escorts, carried a badly wounded German officer to the dressing station on a barn door and then they went to the rear, the escort as relieved as them to be away from the fighting. Whilst sharing rations at the side of the road a German column came up:

'One came over and tried to lift my kilt, to see what you wear under your kilt, and I gave him a kick in the shins and he hopped around holding his leg, so the others, instead of being set on by them, they sort of ridiculed him because he was obviously one of these cheeky devils.' [56]

Prisoners on all sides were kept in barbed-wire cages, open to the elements, and Hay contracted pneumonia before he was sent to the camp at Stendal. He survived the war having been all but blinded in the left eye, gassed, hit in the leg by shrapnel bullets and taken prisoner.

A great many of the wounded fell into enemy hands including Lance Corporal Walter Neill. Neill had joined up in November 1915 as a 21-year-old iron storeman, and first served in France in July 1916. He suffered a gunshot wound to the right elbow which shattered the bone on 23 March at Nesle and was captured shortly afterwards. The large numbers of wounded German and Allied troops made conditions worse than for previous prisoners (abridged):

'I was kept at the dressing station for about five days, but did not receive any treatment. Then I was taken to a large field hospital. We were not taken in an ambulance train, but open trucks. Nobody looked after us at all. I never saw a doctor or orderly and received no treatment of any kind. I got no food except such as I could get for myself. Some of the prisoners got soup, but I was too weak to stand waiting about for it.'

A fortnight after his injury he arrived at a hospital at Brie and was operated on the same day by a German doctor who was an exchanged prisoner. In August Neill heard that he might be exchanged and on 9 September he, and twenty-three other wounded prisoners, went on a three-day train journey to Aachen, near the Dutch border. Thirteen were passed by a board of German doctors and the rest were sent back to camp. Neill went on to Rotterdam and was repatriated on 23 September 1918.

Meanwhile Captain Norman Macdonald, who after three-and-a-half months on the front had been interned as a prisoner of war for three-and-a-half years – half his career – was also repatriated. Macdonald had been a prisoner at Gütersloh since his capture in June 1915. Well known for sports, here he played football and hockey in winter and lawn tennis in summer. He discussed languages, music and literature with French and Russian officers, a number of the latter bearing Scottish names, producing a thoroughly civilised, though perhaps not entirely accurate image of life as a prisoner of war. However, he was moved to the infamous camp at Holzminden, nicknamed *Hellminden*, a *strafe* or punishment camp for troublesome officers, that opened in September 1917, and where, a tunnel was started immediately from which a mass escape took place in June 1918.

In April 1918, Macdonald was 'repatriated' to the neutral Netherlands as part of measures that had been agreed to alleviate their conditions. In a series of halting agreements, invalid civilians and combatants from both sides were repatriated through, or interned in the Netherlands, by a Hague Agreement brokered in July 1917 which also covered officers who had been held prisoner for more than eighteen months. On at least one occasion a British and a German officer found themselves sitting at the same table in Rotterdam. Another man in Holland was William Stow – one of the Ordnance Survey men who had enlisted at the outbreak of war. Wounded in the right shoulder and back at High Wood, the Red Cross listing him as a Korporal of C Kompanie 99th Royal Scots. He arrived in June 1918 and made it back to Britain in November.

The only other officer taken prisoner was Second Lieutenant Denis Wallace, 4th Royal Scots attached, who had been shot in the upper thigh on 24 March 1918. Sadly, he died less than a month later at a military hospital at Guise, north-east of St Quentin, and was buried by the Germans at the military cemetery of La Desolation nearby. Surprisingly, the first news that a missing officer was in fact a prisoner of war often came when he cashed a cheque in Germany and it passed through their agents Messrs. Cox & Co. at Charing Cross.

Among those anxiously awaiting news was Miss Jane Rice of Leith. She had been routinely receiving Field Service postcards from her brother Colin through early 1918, bearing the simple printed statement 'I am quite well'. Then, in mid-May she received a letter from Lieutenant Alex Cameron that Colin had been wounded on the 24 March in the counter-attack at Mesnil. As the Ninth had heard no news of him, Cameron thought he had probably become a prisoner of war. With what must have been dwindling hope she wrote to the War Office a month later for news. They did not reply until September, and then to inform her that Colin was officially missing. The Army Council concluded he was dead in September 1919. He had been one of the 59 killed that day in stemming the German advance.

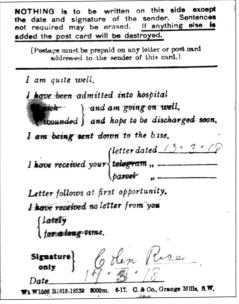

Rice's last Field Service Postcard.

Jane persevered for information with the British Red Cross and they wrote sympathetically in March 1920, with the closing of the Enquiry Department for Wounded and Missing: 'His name was on our lists for months, and we asked all the men of his unit whom we were able to see, both in English hospitals and at the bases abroad, but none of them threw any light on his casualty. We have also questioned released prisoners but have learnt nothing.' Finally, in May 1920 Colin's father Peter received a War Gratuity of £11, of which Jane was entitled to half, and the balance of Colin's pay and allowances of £2 10s 2d. In passing we might add that Douglas Haig's War Gratuity was £100,000.

The Red Cross were swamped with requests to find the missing in prisoner of war camps but all too often, as in Rice's case in July 1918, replied *Négatif envoyé*. David Gowans' parents received news from the German government that he had died of wounds. The family of Myles Lavin were more fortunate. He had been in C Company's rearguard action on the opening day and recorded as killed, when this was corrected to 'Man Alive + Prisoner of War at Stendal.

At the end of the month *The Scotsman* recorded a number of decorations for the Ninth: one bar to the Distinguished Service Order (DSO), fifteen Military Crosses (MC), one bar to the MC, nine Distinguished Conduct Medals (DCM), eighty Military Medals (MM), several foreign decorations and a number of Mentions in Despatches (MID).

Operation Georgette – Lys

'Every position must be held to the last man: there must be no retirement. With our backs to the wall and believing in the justice of our cause each one of us must fight on to the end.'

Haig's Special Order of the Day, 11 April

BEGINNING on 9 April, after a two-day bombardment, Ludendorff made a second push called Operation Georgette, known to the British as the Battle of the Lys and the Portuguese as Batalha de La Lys. This second attack was mounted in Flanders, astride the River Lys, with the aim of taking the Flanders hills and reaching the Channel ports. The Germans had a total of 199 divisions on the Western Front (many of them fresh), reaching 205 by 14 April as more arrived from the east. This permitted a large proportion to oppose 59 British divisions (of which all but six had already been engaged) and the French 133rd Division despatched north to assist. The attack was conducted with twenty-six fresh divisions, adding nine more as the battle developed, initially against the Portuguese. By 11 April the Germans had advanced, at the maximum point, 9 miles in the vicinity of the Lys.

Impromptu arrangements made by XI Corps positioned the 51st, 50th and 61st Divisions on a 6-mile front astride the Lys, with 5th Division in reserve. The 61st Division were to form a support line with the front line to the east held by the 51st (Highland) Division.

The Ninth, containing many untrained drafts, was rushed up by train late on 10 April from the Somme area to Steenbecque. They should all have got away that night, but the logistical pressures meant that the final company was on a fourth train that left at 6.30am on 11 April on a twelve-hour journey. By evening they had marched to a position south-west of Merville, where the River Lys had been 'canalised' and was more significant than the old Lys, also called the *vieille*, or even *ancienne* Lys, that wandered to its south (Map XXV). They took up a south-east-facing flank at the crossing of the River Clarence at Calonne about 10pm. Already in position to their left by 4pm were the first units of 183 Brigade to arrive – the 5th Gordons and 5th Duke of Cornwall's Light Infantry (DCLI) (Pioneers) with the 8th Argylls coming up behind the next morning; 182 Brigade was on the right, with 2/7 Warwicks against the bridge, and 184 Brigade to the rear.

> 'The... district was remarkable for its well-stocked farms, and with the general flight of the civilians large numbers of unmilked cows, geese, goats, hens, and all manner of farmyard creatures commenced to stray across the fields and down the roads.'[94]

That night the brigade was instructed to take over the section up to the canal from the 7th Durham Light Infantry (Pioneers) of the 50th Division and accordingly the 5th Gordons extended north to the canal and the Ninth extended their line to the east. Meanwhile the enemy were working their way around Merville and by the morning of 12 April there was sniping on the left flank.

At 5am on 12 April the 51st Division were penetrated by the German 16th Division at Pacaut and withdrew behind the River Clarence. The Germans boldly pushed outward. North of the Pacaut gap the 5th DCLI and 5th Gordons, enfiladed from the south and with flanking fire from the north fell back at 7.50am. Although successive stands were made along the railway, as the morning wore on the greater part of the two battalions were forced to withdraw across the Lys Canal, south of Le Sart, under heavy machine-gun fire with most of the 5th Gordons north of canal around 10am.

The 7th Black Watch of the 51st Division, were in front of Calonne and Lieutenant Colonel John Millar, commanding, wrote of 12 April (edited):

'The day broke beautifully clear and the enemy had 4 balloons up by 5.30am. The DCLI moved along the road and back through our lines [7am]. The officer who brought up the rear of this party reported that our right flank was enfiladed. Two of the posts heard him and bolted. The remainder left their posts. The enemy were observed "dribbling" into an assembly position and pushing forward a Machine Gun among haystacks. The rot having started the entire left flank broke and ran. Infection spread to the centre which also broke. This overcame the right flank and the rout was complete.'[1]

Only two NCOs had been in France before and their posts were the only ones to hold, the rest were pouring through the Ninth's position where CSM David Walker was rallying his men (he had been the only surviving company sergeant major at Rœux). Around 8am an enemy field gun was brought up and scored five direct hits on the 7th Gordon Highlanders HQ at L'Ecang Farm. By 9am the HQ had been overrun and soon after the last of the stragglers had also retired across the Clarence.

The Ninth then came under intense machine-gun fire from L'Ecang Farm on the right flank. Unbeknownst to the Ninth, the German 16th Division had placed great importance on the capture of Calonne 'cost what it may'[43], and II/68th, III/68th and the left wing of 28th Regiment via Bouzateux Farm at 6.30am, attacked with effective artillery fire. The forward posts of the Ninth were forced in but they made a stand through the morning. The 28th Regiment account reports:

'During the approach, the regiment had turned to the left and now encountered Calonne, which was being stormed. In this place was an English crew with numerous MGs, skilfully deployed from roof hatches and from the high church tower making the approach very difficult. Nevertheless, the attack went on, as on the practice sites. An approximately 6-800 m wide, free and level terrain in front of the village was overcome by leaps and bounds. The shock battery, driving up again to the front line, made a hit in the church tower and we managed to breathe. The MWs [Minenwerfers] put the outskirts under fire. Extensive use was made of our MGs. So the companies came up quite fast. A dashing Englishman, who at the last moment wanted to blow up a bridge in front of the village, fell by an infantry shot. From the east and southeast our people entered the village. Here it came to persistent close combat, in which, among other things, the 12/28 particularly distinguished themselves. Three MGs and 40 men became their prey.'[95]

Another German account reads: 'After lively house-to-house fighting a passage over the Clarence was achieved at 10.30 a.m. The bridge was found undamaged and about 11 a.m. [10am British time] the western edge of Calonne was occupied.'[43] There was particularly fierce fighting across the schoolyard. A British officer, escaping through the window, exchanged simultaneous pistol shots with a German officer, hitting the latter in the shoulder. By 10.30am the enemy had broken through Calonne in considerable numbers and most of the battalion were in slits just north of the old Lys or on the railway.

Le Pont de la Clarence, 1918.

The 2/4th Oxfordshire and Buckinghamshire Light Infantry saw the scene from near Baquerolles Farm: 'All day very severe fighting was in progress a mile to our left. Merville and Calonne were almost blotted out by smoke, and the air was thronged with aeroplanes.'[94] At this point, there were no friendly forces to the Ninth's left, right, front or rear and they were forced to swing round to face east across the railway and behind a loop of the old Lys. In this position they succeeded in making contact with the 5th Gordons north of the canal, but the enemy were infiltrating between their right and 182 Brigade. At 12.10pm they were under fire from north of the canal and were reported as being pressed back at 1.40pm and 3pm, by which time they were following orders from 2pm to withdraw to a new general line.

With assistance from the 8th Argylls and conforming to a new front line with 182 Brigade, the reversals of the day were halted. The Ninth were relieved at 8pm and made into a composite battalion. In the view of the Official History, the 61st Division had saved the 51st from destruction. On the following day, 13 April, the Germans opposite XI Corps: 16th Division, 8th Bavarian Reserve and the 8th (Prussian) Division, made fierce attacks but were unable to make further gains against British artillery fire.

The composite units manned trenches near St Venant. On 14 April four attacks were made against 183 Brigade (8th Argylls) on the southern bank of the Lys with little effect but at great loss to themselves, and on 15 April companies of the Ninth, in composite units, were in the line again. Here the line stabilised; from 16 April their front became quiet and they remained in the area until the end of May.

Company Sergeant Major Jack Brebner, back having been wounded at Cambrai, was bandaging one of his men when he was killed on 12 April. Quinn mourned his

Looking east – the Ninth withdrew toward the camera through the afternoon, and north of the railway, the German advance stopped near the road and marked crossing at Q2a1.1.

loss: 'I wish I'd known him longer and better, for Jake was a real man.'[23] James Johnston was awarded a posthumous Military Medal; his brother-in-law Isaac McMeachan, also in the battalion, had been killed less than three weeks before on 24 March.

Ewing accurately describes the German successes in March and April as Pyrrhic. Nevertheless, estimated casualties for the Ninth for April were 16 killed, 142 wounded, 144 missing and 2 died of wounds. The high rate of 'the infinitely worse "missing"'[35] was due to the retiring actions that had been fought, leaving many men behind. PoWs included James Mackie from Crail, repatriated in November, and John Sharp whose parents had no news for two months, but who was growing vegetables at Soltau. Fatalities climbed to 71 for the month, including the death of Major George Cowan.

Issac McMeachan (left) and James Johnston (right), 1918.

In both battles the Ninth had been right at the spearhead of the attacks, halting the enemy at their furthest point of penetration.

Another major reorganisation was now required due to the heavy losses. Lieutenant Colonel Green, who had gained two bars to his Distinguished Service Order whilst in command, left to become the new GOC of 153 Brigade on 14 April 1918. The following day 'sterling'[33] Lieutenant Colonel John 'Jock' Muir, Black Watch, assumed command. The Ninth were transferred to the 15th (Scottish) Division on 1 June 1918, replacing the 4th/5th Black Watch in 46 Brigade.

James Meek's watch-chain has the bullet attached that lodged in his thigh on 12 April 1918.

Table 11. Infantry Brigades of the 15th Division (July 1918)

15th (Scottish) Division		
GOC Major General Hamilton L Reed VC		
44 Brigade *Brigadier General NA Thomson*	**45 Brigade** *Brigadier General NA Orr-Ewing*	**46 Brigade** *Brigadier General VM Fortune*
4/5 Black Watch 8/Seaforths 5/Gordons	13/Royal Scots 6/Camerons 8/Argylls	9/Royal Scots 7/8 KOSB 10/Scottish Rifles
9th Gordons (Pioneers)		

It will be seen that 183 Brigade was divided amongst the brigades of the 15th Division – 44 Brigade was referred to as the Highland Brigade, 45 as a mixed brigade, and, tellingly for the dual identity of the Ninth, 46 as the Lowland Brigade. On 15 June the strength of the division was 10,035. On 24 June, Brigadier General A.F. Lumsden commanding 46 Brigade was killed by shell-fire. The 10th Scottish Rifles were commanded by Lieutenant Colonel Douglas Foulis, formerly Private 2196 of the Ninth, from September 1918.

The 15th Division, originally a Kitchener K2 division, had gained fame for action at Loos, where Piper Laidlaw of the 7th KOSB won his VC for playing upon the parapet. It was commanded by Hamilton Reed, another holder of the Victoria Cross, earned at Colenso in the Boer War.

The Ninth joined near Athies, east of Arras. It could be argued that Ferguson's Highland quorum had now diminished whilst the battalion passed from Highland Division, to Highland Brigade to Lowland Brigade in the space of a couple of months and risked being Highlanders in nought but name. At the end of June they were further weakened by rampant Pyrexia, of Unknown Origin (PUO). However, there was an opportunity to regain their strength. When in billets the battalion HQ was located at 46 Rue de Trois Visages in the heart of Arras, with officers billeted nearby and other ranks in the cellars of the Hotel de Ville and Petit Place, connected to the vast tunnel network beneath the city. The Ninth were given three days access to the baths at Anzin which had a capacity of 120 men per hour, their clothing to be steamed while they waited. The cinema was signed over to the battalion on two nights (officers 1 Franc, ORs 20c), the football ground on two days, and the band, through seniority, were the first to play for the forming of the Brigade Guard.

Operation Friedensturm – Soissons

'On July 30 and 31, the German rate of retreat slackened and the resistance stiffened. ... but on August 1 further Allied forces arrived on the scene and the Germans abandoned any hope they might have had of attempting a general stand'

Bertram Benedict, *A History of the Great War*

HINDENBURG and Ludendorff wished to tie up the French and allied reserves and then succeed in their original aim of forcing the British out of Flanders. As such the next three German operations were in the south, threatening Paris, but with ever reducing progress. They began on 27 May 1918 but by 15 July extended to *La Deuxième Bataille de la Marne* and here in Soissonnais, crucially, on 18 July the French went over to the offensive. Maréchal Foch requested four British divisions to move south and Haig duly despatched the 15th, 34th, 51st and 62nd Divisions, forming XXII Corps under Lieutenant General Sir Alexander Godley. On 17 July, whilst *en route,* the destinations were changed, and the 15th and 34th Divisions passed from the French Third Army to come under the direct orders of the French GAR (Reserve Army Group), specifically Tenth Army under General Mangin whose French and American forces were making successful attacks south of Soissons. The Ninth found themselves in Champagne. To BC they had been 'lent to the French and Yanks'.[16]

On 21 July a night march brought the 15th Division up to Coeuvres, though a full moon shining onto the dusty columns exposed them to the attentions of enemy bomber aircraft. By 3am, near Chazelles, the Ninth replaced Regiment Banford, 1st Brigade, 1st Division 'The Big Red One', US Army in the left sector of the French XX Corps, the *Corps de Fer.* The French 87th Division were to the right and the French 69th Division to the left. Here were horizon-blue poilus, olive drab doughboys, khaki tommies, and, in this case, hunting stewart jocks. The information provided by the incumbent French and American troops was so scant that a patrol of the 8th Argylls stumbled upon a German post. Thereby warned that a relief was in progress, heavy shelling of the division ensued.

William Rennoldson remembers their first day: 'When the Americans came in I was sent out on a mopping up party, about six of us and a lance corporal and I didn't

US 1st Division artillery 20 July 1918 near Ploisy.

know what to do because they were all lying in heaps. So we just dug some holes and put them in.'[96]

The division had taken on a two-brigade front. On the right 46 Brigade had as their objective the village of Rozières, with the Ninth as brigade reserve; 45 Brigade were on their left with orders to take La Sucrerie, and 44 Brigade were in reserve. The US Army recorded that it was the first time French, British and American artillery had worked together. The division stated that there had been insufficient time to relieve the American artillery, so they would cover the attack – insufficiently as it turned out. Nor had there been time to reconnoitre the ground ahead.

The attack began at 5am on 23 July 1918 with 46 Brigade making a few hundred yards against heavy machine-gun fire, but by 8.15am thoughts of further advance had to be abandoned. Neither French division had been able to advance, leaving the 15th Division's flanks in the air and requiring additional companies to secure them. At 6pm a counter-attack from Chivry Farm was repulsed without disrupting the division's

Schneider Tanks, June 1918.

Troupes écossaises, Hartennes 31 July 1918.

consolidation which continued overnight when the Ninth took over their entire brigade front with the 13th Royal Scots doing the same to their left. Casualties were cleared through American and French ambulances, so that many wounded were reported missing.

It should be noted that to the south the French 412th Infantry Regiment, 58th Colonial Division were unsuccessfully engaged against Taux at this time. Supported by Schneider tanks from Groupement I, they were forced back by a counter-attack and the *412ᵉ Régiment d'Infanterie* was reduced by losses of 900 *hommes hors de combat.* That night they were replaced by the French 12th Division who secured Villemontoire on 25 July.

During 24 and 25 July the enemy attempted to remove the Scots with very heavy shelling, the Ninth had 15 killed, and on the night of 25/26 July 46 Brigade switched with 44 Brigade in reserve. On 26 July the divisional boundary was extended to the south, and from along this line on 28 July 44 Brigade attacked 'the village, park and chateau of Buzancy, a position formidably organized by the enemy for defence',[97] for reasons of surprise, at lunchtime. The Ninth stood-to for much of the day.

The village was briefly held, but the 8th Seaforths on the right were dangerously exposed by the failure of the French division to the south to advance, and during the afternoon they fired an SOS signal flare and began a fighting withdrawal. The division was forced back to the starting line after a day of losses. In many of these co-operations the contemporaries are rather brusque about their allies, the French. On this occasion however, the history of the 15th Division makes it clear that the terrain was very difficult, and that the strain of campaign had taken the *poilus* almost to breaking-point.

That night, without notice, the Ninth relieved the French 1/67th Regiment, though there were gaps in the line that needed patrolling and an inundation of gas shells meant that respirators had to be worn for most of the night. The 15th Division and French 87th Division had swapped places, their respective artillery batteries still in their original positions. This artillery was to provide the barrage for an attack, without preliminary bombardment. At dawn on 29 July the new line was held, from right to left, by the Ninth, 7/8th KOSB, 9th Gordons (Pioneers) (later replaced by 6th Cameron Highlanders) and 13th Royal Scots. Opposite the Ninth was a 1,000 yard long ridge surmounted on the right by three hillocks, *Les Trois Mamelons*, strongpoints in the enemy defences (Map XXVI). Littered across the field were destroyed Renault and Schneider tanks from the attack on 23 July. This position was completely overlooked by the enemy, who had been reinforced by XVII Corps, and the terrain offered no opportunity for cover.

The attack, planned for 30 July but postponed to 1 August, was for the 15th Division to envelope the Bois d'Hartennes from the north, in conjunction with the French 12th Division working around from the south. The Ninth were to make the main thrust; it was a formidably difficult job.

Zero hour awaited a signal to be dropped by aeroplane, this being conditional on the success of a French attack to the south. On the right 46 Brigade had objectives to be taken in two bounds: the first, Green Line, by the Ninth who were to advance up the slope, take the two northern wooded *Mamelons* and go forward as far as the Soissons road; and then the second by the 10th Scottish Rifles to the Red Line. Then 44 Brigade would pass through onto Taux and meet up with the French. To the left 45 Brigade were to straighten out the line and construct a long defensive flank on their left.

German infantry watch British artillery cut their wire, Soissons 1918.

The Ninth's right-hand position put them into contact with the French 12th Division and a platoon of B Company was assigned as liaison with the French 54th Regiment. The bombardment was to start three minutes before Zero, 150 yards ahead of the front line and then lift as a rolling barrage at the rate of 100 yards in three minutes. When 250 yards beyond the Red Line it was to wait for one-and-a-half-hours for 44 Brigade to move up.

Lieutenant James Thomson, having done good work at Third Ypres, now kept supplies of ammunition, water and hot food moving through the enemy's barrage on 29 July, losing two men and six horses. The battalion continued to be shelled on 30 and 31 July, with 'blue cross' gas which hung about a long time in the mist. On the night of 30/31 July, with more gas shelling, they filled in mustard gas shell holes, including one near the battalion HQ near Raperie (a sugar beet mill).

Before dawn on 1 August the supporting companies of 10th Scottish Rifles were guided into place by the Ninth and lay hidden in standing corn. Douglas Bannatyne's D Company and the liaison platoon assembled behind a hedge with the other companies dug-in behind or in a quarry called the 'Sandpit'. The aeroplane signal was received at 8.25am, repeated by the artillery with smoke shells, and a clear half-hour set Zero for 9am.

The barrage opened and 'it was thin and placed several hundred yards in front of jumping off positions. The start was ragged.'[1] The enemy machine gunners were 'not troubled by our barrage'[1] and as soon as the barrage opened the enemy opened up a heavy crossfire, this particularly enfiladed the start line from the right and D Company was caught climbing out, but also included machine guns hidden in the derelict tanks in front – tanks which were supposed to have been destroyed by artillery on the previous afternoon.

The advance up the ridge across very open ground toward well-defended, wooded hills proved an impossibility. C Company attempted to follow at 9.07am. The two companies were severely damaged in just 100-250 yards having advanced 'with the greatest gallantry'.[71] With Captain Richard Murray the only unhurt officer, and the barrage having moved on, they took what cover they could find while under direct machine-gun fire from high ground 200 yards away.

B Company, now on the start line, sent one platoon over to help C Company and were badly cut-up. They reported that none of the men who had gone over could move due to enfilade machine-gun fire from right and left. Acting Sergeant Alexander Lockie went forward under machine-gun fire to restore order, and this involved killing two of the enemy who attempted to penetrate their disorganised line.

William Rennoldson from Sunderland had already served with the 3rd Durham Light Infantry, 9th Royal Scots and the Labour Corps when he was returned to the Ninth in April 1918. He recalls the chaos of the attack (abridged):

'As soon as I got over, the little Lance Corporal got wounded straight away. Then I went straight on, following the rest. The bullets were flying all over but we still went on. Each time I got up and down and went on, I couldn't see anybody. I had gone quite a way then and then I turned round and couldn't see anybody and I came on my way back, crawling back all the way. I was crawling back from about half past 9 and I was crawling back all the way through the field and every time I made a move they were firing at us. I couldn't see anybody. I was going like that for about three or four hours. On my way back a machine gun bullet came through here [his chest].'[96]

He was not as alone as he felt, a number of men had great difficulty getting back, as the slightest movement brought on heavy machine-gun fire and attracted snipers. Captain Murray rallied the survivors back at the jumping off line, assisted by Kenneth Baird. Sergeant John Fraser 'showed great gallantry and resource' when all the company officers and company sergeant major had become casualties, he assumed command of his company and reorganised them under heavy machine-gun fire.

Behind the front, the Quarry, also under direct observation, was a 'death-trap'.[33] At 12.55pm Colonel Jock Muir informed brigade that unless the French, who had advanced about 50 yards and then immediately returned to their start line, could move forward and deal with the machine guns on the right flank, they would be unlikely to make further progress. It was confirmed that no one had made it to the woods before a new barrage was planned. The French, they argued, had to take the *Mamelon* on the right (south-west), where the enemy could be distinctly seen, before the Ninth and 10th Scottish Rifles made their assault as the enemy machine guns were directly to their right and rear.

The Quarry near Raperie, 6 pm on 1 August 1918, also showing three derelict Schneiders and a Renault.

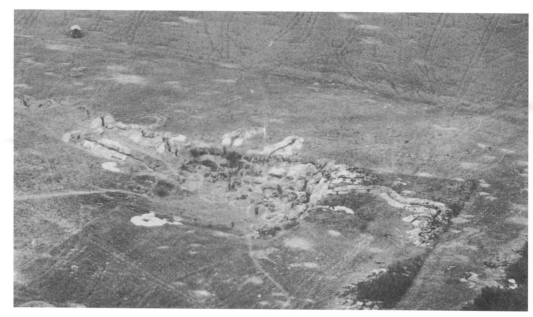

Detail: 9th Royal Scots HQ in the Quarry. Note derelict Schneider top left and tank tracks.

A new plan was formulated to take the *Mamelons*, limiting troops to within the Green Line. Stokes mortars were to target the tanks to allow their capture. A bombardment of the objectives would begin at 3pm, the barrage would start at 3.27pm and lift at Zero 3.30pm, advancing 100 yards in three minutes. The Ninth were to attack the central *Mamelon*, 10th Scottish Rifles passing through them to the east to take the next. Meanwhile at 2.20pm the enemy took a small hillock on the right rear, driving out the French garrison, and established a machine-gun post. The French to the south had briefly held Tigny but had been forced out around 2.45pm.

The bombardment was 'rather scattered'.[1] The Ninth's second wave, A Company under Findlay Ross, had already suffered heavily at assembly. They went over at 3.30pm and although the barrage was better on this occasion, in a repetition of the morning, as soon as the barrage started the enemy machine guns opened up once more 'like sheets of driving rain'[33] and they experienced predictably high casualties getting out of their trenches. Within ten minutes they were held up after 50-100 yards, and at 4.50pm, when the attack was abandoned, A Company could not 'be found' owing to heavy loss. By 5.20pm they were notified that the French 12th Division attack had also failed, though it was clear to those on the spot that on this occasion the neighbouring French did not manage to leave their lines at all.

Any attempt by casualties to move was met with heavy machine-gun fire, but by 8.15pm some men had got back and the front was now quiet. The 10th Scottish Rifles were about 50 yards forward of the original front line and reported that they had seen nothing of the Ninth's liaison platoon. From this platoon only two men returned. The Ninth moved back to close support at night.

Rennoldson, wounded in the chest, had taken shelter in a short section of trench, but he was told to clear out because the Scottish Rifles were coming through in a second wave attack.

> 'I was following him and all of a sudden ping went and I was hit just above the ankle. The Germans fired two shots and he missed me. I hopped all the way to the dressing station and when I got in I was the last in line there and I was the first out. They carried us over the trenches, they were shelling like nobody's business.'[96]

William Rennoldson, aged 21 and 5ft 1in tall, was returned to Britain ten days later. On account of his wounds and dependent mother, he received a weekly pension of 8s 3d. The wife and child of Private John C. Houston received 20s 5d a week from February 1919.

The Regimental Aid Post (RAP), with one NCO and eight men, was at Raperie where most of the casualties gathered. However, it was subject to rifle and machine-gun fire, so although motor ambulances came in from all parts of the front, arrangements had to be made to get the wounded away by stretcher bearers. A number of cars braved the gunfire and made it there in daylight at 6pm and were very busy through the night.

Bandsman Wilfred Baggaley, a professional clarinet player, who had previously been wounded several times as a stretcher bearer, was killed by machine-gun fire. Private Richard Owenson, Scottish Rifles, was decorated for his selfless bravery in attending to the wounded of his own battalion and those of the Ninth who lay in sight of the enemy, as were Privates Mark Clougherty and Alexander Campbell of the Ninth.

The Ninth's losses of 108 killed, 300 wounded and 13 missing, a total of about 80 per cent of the battalion's strength, made this the worst day of the war for the battalion.

Wilfred Baggaley.

Alexander Haig volunteered to act as runner when all except one of the regular runners had become casualties and made many journeys under very heavy machine-gun fire; 'he made the delivery of his messages his first consideration, and entirely disregarded his personal safety', reads his medal citation. Private William Dobbin, a miner, who had served with a number of Royal Scots battalions and had been wounded at Loos and the Somme, transferred to the Ninth in September 1916 and won the Military Medal and *Croix de Guerre* with Palm. He had received a gun shot wound to the right arm at the end of Operation Michael when the battalion was shelled in Gentelles. Here, with '*parfait mépris du danger*' (perfect contempt for danger) he won a Bar to his MM having carried messages from brigade HQ several times across ground swept by machine guns with '*beaucoup de sang-froid*'. Similarly Lieutenant Andrew Hughson, liaison officer, possessed '*merveilleux sang-froid*' (wonderful composure, or literally 'cold-blood').

George Hart had served in Gallipoli (his brother had been killed in the Quintinshill rail disaster of 1915) and won an MM with the Ninth at Arras for holding his position against a large enemy force with his Lewis gun. His parents were informed that he had been killed in action, but to their great relief two weeks later received a postcard from him stating he was a prisoner of war in Germany. James Little, married the year before, had also had a long war having been gassed, had dysentery twice and a bad case of trench fever. James Little and 'nearly all his platoon were killed'.

However, as the battalion was being relieved after nightfall by 4th/5th Black Watch, a remarkable thing was happening: the Germans flooded their dug-outs with gas and withdrew along the whole front. The following morning the French 12th Division pushed east, past Hartennes and the Germans retired before them, the French 87th Division to the north advanced and 15th Division patrols passed through the *Mamelons* and Taux to Amberif without interference. The French Tenth Army was ordered to advance at 11.30am and 46 Brigade were commanded to stand by. By nightfall on 2 August the division had advanced a further 3 miles and crossed the River Crise north of Charcrise.

George Hart.

'And so, on August 2, the enemy gave way; that day the Allies crossed the [Crise] valley along its entire length, and advanced across the eastern side of the plateau as far as the Vesle. On the same day they entered Soissons—at last. The ancient capital of the French kings, the city which formerly disputed the claim of Paris to be called the metropolis, is now no more than a mass of ruins... Here ended the second battle of the Marne. The Allies have regained possession of the whole plateau which extends from the Marne to the Vesle and the Aisne.'[98]

The deaths represented a full company: 5 officers, including the two company commanders Douglas Bannatyne and Findlay Ross; Company Sergeant Major William Moncur, a hero of Arras; 3 sergeants and lance sergeants; 13 corporals and lance corporals; 86 privates.

The body of 40-year-old Lieutenant Douglas Bannatyne, D Company, was found further forward than any other man in the attack. Bannatyne was a classics scholar, lawyer, District Commissioner of the Boy Scouts and organiser of Episcopalian missions to the east end of Glasgow. He had been in France since April 1918 and 'his pluck and endless gameness in spite of his years was greatly admired in the Battalion'. The Bishop of Aberdeen and Orkney regarded him as a 'saint'.

The Divisional Burial Officer created a cemetery at Raperie quarry on 9 August and buried 103 men, almost all of them fatalities of the Ninth from 1 August. After the Armistice these men were reburied by the Commonwealth War Graves Commission 400 yards to the west in Raperie British Cemetery which consolidated a number of smaller cemeteries.

General Mangin wrote of the 15th and 34th British divisions:

'During the whole day of the 1ˢᵗ of August, side by side with your French comrades, you stormed the ridge dominating the whole country between the Aisne and the Ourcq, which the defenders had received orders to hold at all costs. Having failed in his attempts to retake the ridge with his last reserves, the enemy had to beat a retreat pursued and harassed for 12 kilometres...To-day's success has been made possible by the conduct of all concerned, and particularly by the sacrifices of the Scottish... The victory of August 1 puts the finishing touch to that of July 18, and is ending in a rout.'[1]

Writing in 1921 he added that the 15ᵗʰ and 34ᵗʰ Divisions 'contributed largely to the Allies' victory'[71] in the decisive battles of July 1918. Similarly, General Fayolle, GAR, wrote to Haig that the 15ᵗʰ and 34ᵗʰ Divisions 'by their dash, their courage, and their devotion have excited the admiration of the French troops'. Colonel Blair told a crowd in Edinburgh that General Mangin had said he was proud of the 'brave mountaineers of Edinburgh' the Dandy Ninth, who had done a large share of the work memorialised as 'Here for Ever the Roses of France are Entwined with the Thistles of Scotland.'[6]

Ici fleurira Toujours le glorieux chardon d'Écosse Parmi les roses de France. Memorial erected by French 17th Division to 15th (Scottish) Division above Buzancy.

Cimetière Anglais La Raperie, rank and file of the Dandy Ninth.

The Official History recognises that their part in the first victorious Allied offensive has been largely overlooked in Britain. Indeed, although there may be agreement that the turning point came sometime between 15 July, the last German strike, and 8 August, when Fourth Army made its remarkable advance, 1 August could contend as the German apogee before the fall. 'The actual extent of ground gained in the fight of August 1st was small, but its consequences were far-reaching.'[97]

The Germans had attempted to tie-up the French in Soissons by threatening the capital so that Operation Hagen, a final Flanders assault could be made to secure the Channel ports and even shell Britain. However, the reserves intended for the resumption of battle in the north had been consumed in the south and the withdrawal from the Marne Salient in the first days of August 'meant the end of our hopes of dealing our long-planned decisive blow at the English Army,'[60] wrote Hindenburg in 1919. The Official History records the German view that 'much worse was the loss of confidence in final victory'.[43] The Ninth saw things similarly: 'The German defence was broken, and a few hours after the attacks on 1st August the enemy were in full retreat towards and over the River Aisne. This was the beginning of the German retreat which ended in the Armistice.'[99]

The Ninth were back on operations on 2 August and pushed forward to dig-in on high ground north of Taux, south of Buzancy. In the early hours of 3 August the 15th Division were relieved along the Raperie road, after eight days of fighting, by the French 17th Division. The expected motor lorries and buses did not arrive, and an 18 mile march carried the division to the environs of Vivières and on into the night.

The Hundred Days

'Please inform 9th Royal Scots how much the success of the Battalion is appreciated. Number of prisoners testify to resistance offered by the enemy to capture of this most important tactical feature which was the key of the position on this front. Well done 9th Royal Scots.'[1]

Brigadier General Officer Commanding 46 Brigade

THE final hundred days until the Armistice, evoking Waterloo, began with the Ninth recovering from their battle losses at Maizières, west of Arras. Here there were baths, recreational games and parades, including the presentation of French decorations to the men. However, after some time patrolling to make contact with the retreating enemy, having been so badly mauled in the retreat, the battalion was sent some miles north to 'one of the dullest spots on the front'[33] in the Mazingarbe district, near Loos, much to their disgust, says Ewing.

Joining in August were 13 officers and 292 ORs; and absorbed from the disbanded 16th Royal Scots were 8 officers and 26 ORs. They included Annan Ness, a footballer from Hearts, who was Regimental Sergeant Major in the 16th Royal Scots and, on the day they were disbanded, took a commission in the Ninth. At the end of the month command of the battalion passed to Lieutenant Colonel Arthur Stephenson from 16th Royal Scots. Stephenson was a man of 'splendid leadership'[19] who had served as a trooper in the Boer War, won an MC at Loos and 'knew his officers and men, and saw them always, visiting his front and support lines often twice a day and always if there was a patrol in no man's land'.[19]

The Ninth took over the line in front of La Philosophe, where they had to make frequent contact to check the enemy were present; they were found to be 'very alert'[1] and large enemy patrols could be encountered. In one such action of 4 September Captain 'BC' Bennet Clark and A Company raided the enemy lines. They assembled in no man's land before dawn and at daybreak advanced with a barrage to an empty front line; no prisoners were taken but six of the raiders were missing. Three had fallen foul of the British barrage. Robert L. Lawson was missing having been taken prisoner. They went out the following night with a similar result, proving the Germans were still in force in his second line.

They were briefly at Vermelles living in damp tunnels, then into captured trenches around the Quarries at St Elie near Hulluch, where communication trenches still ran into German held territory making for tense sentry duty. Alexander Stewart had been wounded at Gallipoli, wounded in Palestine and went missing at Hulluch. With relief they were withdrawn on 28 September for a rest. That month they had 358 drafts, 50 wounded and 11 missing.

Whilst out of the line, in early October the enemy began emptying his ammunition dumps via his guns, and to retire. The division followed up briskly and found the Germans determined to hold on at Vendin-le-Vieil, a bridgehead on the Haute Deûle Canal (Map XXVII). A German deserter incorrectly told them that his comrades had crossed to the east side of the Deûle Canal and destroyed the bridges. Although the enemy were strongly posted on the east bank of the canal, any patrols approaching the west bank experienced heavy machine-gun fire.

Back into the right of the line on 11 October, 46 Brigade had to deal with booby-trapped dug-outs, buildings and roads. They were under orders to capture Vendin-le-Vieil the following day, a heavily fortified village and this responsibility passed to the Ninth. Annay to the right was to be captured first and so the Ninth spent an anxious day awaiting the result. As soon as Annay fell that afternoon, they were ordered to go in.

The Operation Order reads:

> 'It is not definitely known how the enemy holds the area to be attacked, but it is thought that it is held by small outposts in the village of Vendin le Vieil. There is a certain number of old gun pits in the village which probably will have dug-outs connected with them or in the vicinity… In an operation of this nature each section or group must necessarily act largely on its own initiative and the main point to keep in view is that a forward movement must be maintained…Hot tea will if possible be provided under Coy. arrangements before men move off to jumping off positions.'[1]

As well as a barrage across the village and canal, the bombardment began with a ruse of harmless gas and the ringing of German 'gas gongs', and ended with a smokescreen on the far bank of the canal.

William S. Leslie, when as a sergeant, had searched no man's land for Macdonald and Ross in 1915. Now a second lieutenant, he led A Company on the right against the industrial site, a maze of railway sidings, coke ovens and buildings. C Company on the left were opposite the fortified mining village.

Coke Ovens.

13   VENDIN LE-VIEIL — Les fours à cokes

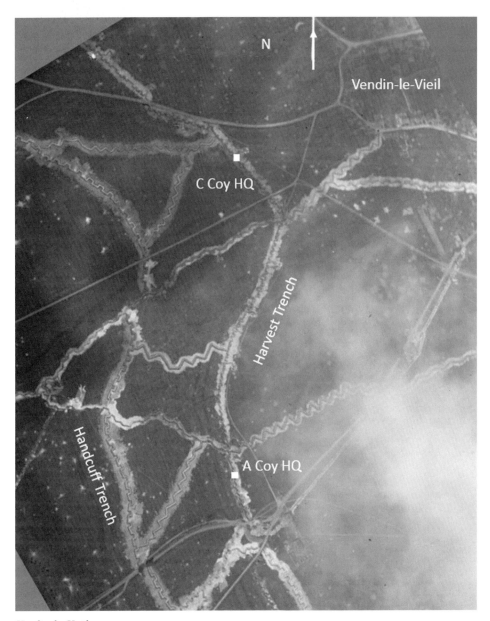

Vendin-le-Vieil.

The Ninth rushed across the open ground, swept by machine-gun fire, entered Vendin and 'desperate hand-to-hand fighting took place'[71] in a series of isolated incidents, using phosphorus bombs to deal with numerous concrete emplacements. Private Gilbert Briggs, providing covering fire with his Lewis gun, allowed Sergeant William Allan to capture an emplacement and take fourteen prisoners.

When Second Lieutenant Andrew Forsyth was killed, Lance Corporal John Hynds led the platoon against a pill box and killed the NCO and gunner at close quarters, allowing the advance to proceed. He had been awarded the MM at Soissons and received the DCM for this action.

Similarly, the platoon of Private Samuel Salberg, one of a number of Jewish soldiers with distinguished records, was held up in marshy ground by a machine gun and, with the officer wounded, he led a renewed attack personally killing the gunner.

The retreating enemy were considerably harassed and posts established along the side of the canal, thereby capturing the key tactical feature for the division. Thirty-five prisoners were taken. The success allowed the line to be brought forward on both flanks and the next two days were spent consolidating the new position. The prospect of crossing the canal under fire, however, could not inspire confidence.

Samuel Salberg.

The enemy now started to fall back apace and the Ninth crossed the canal on 15 October by hastily constructed bridges, but not before Second Lieutenant James Haig and Sergeant Thomas Macdonald had outflanked a machine gun. On the following day they held the brigade's outpost line on the division's right with patrols exploring Epinoy Wood, where 41-year-old grocer Walter Beaton was killed. Andrew Simpson was maintaining contact as a mounted orderly and had two horses wounded under him.

The next day 45 Brigade took up the pursuit, with the 8th Argylls passing through the Ninth and the latter following in reserve. The Germans offered little resistance until ensconced behind the River Scheldt, here canalised, around Hollain which the division reached on 21 October. The position was a difficult one and whilst waiting for the flanking divisions, it became yet more difficult as the Germans flooded the ground east of Hollain. Corps informed the division not to move, and so they established posts in the marshy ground. The villages of Hollain and Jollain Merlin were heavily shelled with 2-3,000 gas shells in the small hours of 29 October and the Ninth were relieved for road repairing.

Bob Lindsay described being gassed as like men drowning all around him. Frank Bell, a gamekeeper, was badly gassed and was sent to No.15 Casualty Clearing Station where he died on 3 November. October casualties amounted to 7 killed, 77 wounded and 3 missing. About this time Bennet Clark was told by a member of the Brigade Staff that the Ninth was considered by far the best battalion in the brigade.

With the neighbouring 16th Division in place on 7 November, Corps instructed the 15th Division to cross the Scheldt the following day. There was further 'Blue Cross' gas shelling of the villages that night, the last artillery fire the division suffered, and at noon they crossed by barrel bridge and occupied the east side with heavy artillery support. The Ninth were at Deroderie when the enemy was reported to be retiring, and the battalion was given short notice to move forward. Advanced patrols met with no opposition on 9 November and they followed the enemy cautiously through Antoing the next day which 'had a canal that would have been a deadly place to have attacked',[16] to Pipaix. The enemy, 2nd Guards Regiment, were similarly disinclined to take risks. It was now known that the enemy sought an armistice and few Germans were met on the next two days as the division continued to advance.

Bennet Clark wrote to his mother on 10 November of 'a new experience for me just marching along and hardly hearing a gun fire… We still wait however for the news of Peace or No Peace and as you may imagine this is the main topic of conversation.'[16]

The division had just begun to cross the Dendre Canal, when news reached them at 10.30am on 11 November 1918 that hostilities would cease at 11 o'clock. The Division Signal Company had in fact intercepted Foch's wireless message to Higher Command at 6am, giving them advance warning of the Armistice.

BC was able to able to follow up with another letter:

'We got the news that the Armistice was signed while on the march yesterday. We had halted in a large village when a Cyclist Orderly passed and gave us the news as official from the Corps. Some of our planes flew over us at the same time very low and from the waving of hands etc we gathered what had happened. It is difficult to realise that hostilities have ceased, and in all probability for good. When we got in to our new billets, the C.O. had all the officers round to HQ and we drank "to the day" in the national beverage…

It is wonderful how the villages we pass through are all decorated with flags and triumphal arches. I just escaped yesterday being presented with a huge bunch of flowers on the march. However my horse was wearing a bunch. This village welcomed us with their brass band… I can tell you I was glad to be with the Bn yesterday. The Second in Command [Major William Lindsay] and myself were the only two who came out with the Bn as officers and were with it "on the day". It is something to remember.'[16]

The wave of emotion can scarcely be imagined. Even as volunteers they had hardly been offered a Heraclean choice: a life of ease or one of hardship and glory. However the Ninth, alongside many other units of all services and sides, completed their trials of Heracles, but with scant glory. They had laboured in snow and swamp, dug trenches, held cloths over their mouths against poison gas, suffered Stymphalian bombardments and stood at the very gates of Hades. Now they could ascend back to the streets and fields of civilisation. Yet, even if we do not accept the narrow precept of courage in entering the war for the protection of Belgium, we can nevertheless admire the spirit of men fighting their way out from under sentence of death, to peace once more.

The War Diary for the long-awaited 11 November dispassionately reports:

'The Battn was ordered to proceed to ERVAUX by march route but on arrival there was ordered to push forward. A halt for 2 hours was made in a field on SOUTHERN outskirts of BLICQUY where it was officially announced that an Armistice had been signed and had come into operation. The Battn then moved to ORMEIGNIES arriving at 1600 hours.'[1]

Casualties for the month were nil.

Armistice

'Varied and picturesque experiences have been the lot of the 9ᵗʰ Royal Scots in the fair land of France and the flat lands of Flanders. They have held posts in the cold and the wet, amidst scenes of inconceivable desolation. On dream-like summer evenings they were in trenches that ran through an orchard where the cherries were red or ripening, where birds were singing, and lines of solemn owls could be seen sitting on the branches in the moonlight. Luxuriant grass in front of the trenches had to be cut at night by patrol parties armed with scythes and hooks. A touch of the weird is associated with one of these excursions – when a German with a scythe was heard and seen sharpening his blade with a hone, like a sinister figure of death on No Man's Land, unaware or heedless of the danger that lurked around him.'[6]

THE day after the Armistice was signed the march on the Rhine was in prospect as the 15ᵗʰ Division were transferred to III Corps, but to their disappointment it was cancelled on 21 November (the day the German fleet entered the Firth of Forth and surrendered) and the Corps was sent to the Brussels area. One consolation was billeting at Chateau Attre where the wines, buried in the garden since 1914, had just been recovered. In the middle of December the battalion moved to Braine l'Alleud, on the edge of the battlefield of Waterloo.

On 7 December a party, including the band, but without steel helmets or respirators, marched 12 miles to line the road at Willapuis and welcome King George V on his visit. Consisting of 9 officers and 135 men, drawn from all of the companies, they were about twenty men deep on each side. The king walked down the crown of the road and GOC General Reed had to force his way through the jubilant crowds on either side. The division were confident they had shown His Majesty greater enthusiasm than at any other part of his tour.

The winding down of the battalion began soon after the Armistice, though there was still a war on until peace was signed. 'Educational and recreational training' were now the order of the day, under the direction of ex-Ninth John Wishart. English and arithmetic classes started on 23 November and by February 1919 the daily pattern had settled down to working parties for the Royal Engineers, drill and route-marching in the morning and classes in the afternoon in English, French, arithmetic, Latin, 'practical gardening' and shorthand.

Important for the home economy, the miners promptly began demobilisation on 11 December, and 221 ORs were demobilised in January 1919. They were without John Jeffrey who had been mobilised in 1914, worked in the mines for a year at Penicuik, was remobilised in April 1917 and died of influenza in 1918. Men were still rejoining the battalion from hospital, but influenza was now sweeping the world and Bennet Clark wrote to his father, 'It is an awful job here dealing with cases of men who get telegrams of dangerous illness and deaths at home.'[16]

Sport, of course, also featured and the Ninth won the Brigade Challenge Cup. There was a Benson Cup for Association Football and the 46 Brigade Athletic Cup. At the

The Colour Party in Edinburgh.

cross-country race they managed second place. The divisional boxing matches were won by Privates William Davidson (light weight) and John Driscoll (middle weight) who went on to the Army competition at Lille where Davidson was defeated and Driscoll lost after extra rounds on points and 'a sensational bout'. Finally, there was a victory, Private Robert Munro won the 100 yards sprint. Bennet Clark concluded, 'The Bn I think came out top in the Sports as it generally does.'[16] The War Diary makes its excuses: 'Owing to the Demobilization of many of the best exponents of sport the high standard hitherto maintained by the battalion could not be reached.'[1]

At noon on 17 December the Ninth's colours were returned to the battalion. The colours, given at Windsor in 1909, had been in the safekeeping of the Territorial Force Association and now the Lord Provost handed them over to an escort from France led by Lieutenants Thomas Lawson and James Haig. Lawson was one of the four young subalterns who joined the battalion in the first draft during Second Ypres. With them were three originals: Company Sergeant Major Robert Thomson, Sergeant William Crichton and Sergeant Tommy Lamb. Lamb had served right through with Maxims and Lewis guns. He carried George Hogg off the field at Second Ypres, was given a shock when a cartridge went off in a brazier near the Somme and used to sing with Harry Hills.

273

The Pipes and Drums December 1918.

Also present were James Clark's widow and Colonel Blair, who said of their departure in 1915 that he 'did not know that any of them realised what we were up against when we marched into the Caledonian Station on that wintry night. Since, it had become well known in Edinburgh that they had fought at Ypres and the Somme; but it was not as well known the sacrifice they had made at Soissons. He sent the colours out with good wishes and love, to join those of the French who were dipping theirs in the waters of the Rhine.'[26]

As December came upon them there must have been palpable disappointment that the end of the war would not be over by Christmas. It was not until the following June that the cadre were repatriated. Officers left behind joined 11th Royal Scots in Germany, and some of the men were posted and transferred.

Apart from Thomas Wilfrid Bennet Clark and William Carruthers Smith Lindsay, with the battalion on Armistice Day, what was the fate of the other twenty-eight original officers who crossed to France in February 1915?

Colonel Blair remained in command at Abancourt until December 1917 and Major Taylor Cameron became Judge Advocate at Scottish Command. Of the ten captains, four were dead and David Bell and Dr John Bowie had both been badly wounded in the legs. The Adjutant, Robert Dudgeon, commanded three different battalions before being appointed to command 51 Brigade. Dick Moncrieff was at the War Office, Frederick Lucas rose to DADMS in the RAMC, and George Green went from being an RFC balloon officer to equipment officer with the famous 56 Squadron.

This leaves fifteen lieutenants: William Liddle died from pneumonia on 27 September 1918 at a Casualty Clearing Station. Three served on the staff, and one was probably at the War Office. Cyril Falconer Stewart became Assitant Provost Marshal for Dunfermline. Willie Urquhart went from an RFC Cadet School Instructor to administration. Norman Macdonald was a prisoner of war, now in the Netherlands. Patrick J. Blair became Commanding Officer of 13th Black Watch. David Ross Haddon, wounded three times, ended the war as a major in the RAMC. Aymer Maxwell went back to medicine, and post-war went to Rangoon with 1st Royal Scots where he joined Edgar Robb. William Richard was sent to Craiglockhart War Hospital, the psychiatric hospital famous for treating Wilfred Owen and Siegfried Sassoon, and near where the Ninth used to carry out tactical exercises. Andrew Gordon, who had been instrumental in the raising of the Ninth, served as quartermaster until May 1918. It seems his son may have been killed in an accident in Edinburgh, involving a pistol, whilst waiting to serve abroad with the Red Cross. Gordon, a golfer and yachtsman, died in 1921.

At the Armistice, Frank 'Lofty' Scott and John Morrison Dalziel were still at war, serving in North Russia. Scott would go on to serve in Ireland with the Auxiliaries 1920-1922, and in the British Gendarmerie of the Palestine Police. Dalziel, an apprentice dentist, had joined the Ninth as a private and when we last met him he had been wounded outside the Abbaye in Ypres in 1915, the first of

John Dalziel.

three woundings. Commissioned into 3rd Royal Scots, attached 2/10th Royal Scots, he learnt of the Armistice on 12 November whilst under artillery fire.

In North Russia the Royal Scots were mostly men recovered from wounds and listed as medical category B. They were part of an allied River Column numbering about 500, including Canadians, Poles and Americans, at Tulgas near the confluence of the Dvina and Vaga rivers. The necessity of removing the allied gunboats before the river froze at Archangel, 200 miles to the north, gave the Bolsheviks a brief window of opportunity before they had to remove their gunboats to the south. Supported by artillery fire from the gunboats, and on orders from Lenin, on 11 November 1918 2,500 of Trotsky's Petrograd Red Guards surrounded Tulgas and attacked from the woods. The Canadian field artillery had to about turn and fire at point blank range.

The American Silver Parrish wrote: 'We licked the Bolo good and hard but... the Royal Scots lost 36 men and many wounded... The Bolo lost about 475 men.'[100] Ewing, in the manner of a serving officer, described the fighting after 11 November as 'bickering'.[33] On the other side of the river the Bolsheviks rushed the forward post on 14 November and, according to his commanding officer, wounded and then murdered Second Lieutenant John Dalziel. He is buried at Bereznik.

Blockhouse at Tulgas.

Bolo Prisoners — Bereznik

Bolo Prisoners.

Jim Elliot was also still at war. Commissioned into the 7th Gordons in June 1916, he was wounded the following month at Mametz and deemed fit only for home service by his medical board and so he transferred to the King's African Rifles near Nairobi as an instructor. Whilst *en route*, the German force under Paul von Lettow-Vorbeck had pushed south into Portuguese East Africa. Contrary to his medical classification,

German 10.5cm gun from SMS Königsberg, Deutsch-Ostafrika.

Elliot got himself posted into 2nd/3rd KAR and in January 1918 shipped south with a battalion of *askaris* to defend coastal stations. He eventually found himself at the mouth of the Rio dos Bons Sinais in July aboard the rusty SS *Luna* with half the battalion. The first half of the battalion were keeping Lettow 10 miles outside the town of Quelimane but received a 'drumming'. Elliot and a drunken Scots skipper came up river, bumping over sand bars, and put the Portuguese town into a state of defence. Lettow now turned to the north-west and Elliot's company followed. Herbert Edgar, Robert Shaw and Sergeant Robert B.S. Tait were also in the King's African Rifles.

Elliot's war ended on 14 November when British despatch riders from Nyasaland, carrying news of the Armistice, reached the Germans first at Kasama, in present day Zambia, and they in turn came over under a white flag of truce. Lettow surrendered at Abercorn, now Mbala, and the Germans were ferried over Lake Tanganyika and taken onward by train. Hostilities may have ended but Elliot was 600 miles from the coast and it was not until Christmas Eve, when a force reduced to half by malaria and influenza, reached Lindi by foot. For Hogmanay, Elliot was among the Scots at Dar-es-Salaam who were guests of Lettow, himself, it might be said, a guest at His Majesty's pleasure. At midnight they sang '*God Save the King, Deutschland Über Alles* and, finally, the international anthem of *Auld Lang Syne*, a song the Germans knew as well as we did.'[2]

Although commissioned into the Gordon Highlanders and having had distinguished service in the KAR, Elliot considered that 'The 'Dandy Ninth' was the best Battalion a man could wish to be in and I still think it. I am still a Dandy at heart.'[2]

Many of the Ninth, particularly as so many received commissions, went far and wide in the course of the war. There were Ninths in the Balkans at Salonika / Macedonia, Mesopotamia, Italy and in Egypt and Palestine. Dentist Reginald Page served aboard HMS *Neptune*. Dr Neil Macleod was a Surgeon Probationer with the destroyer screen at Jutland and was hoisted aboard HMS *Petard* to try and save the lives of her many wounded. He was shot dead in 1946. It appears Alexander Anderson deserted from the Ninth, and became a seaplane mechanic with HMS *Hyacinth* and *Manica* off the East African coast. Ian Molyneaux was in Jerusalem, but killed in France in July 1918.

Malcolm Macfarlane.

As part of the famous action by the 52nd Division in Palestine, John West got his men across the flooded River Auja on box-like boats pulled by ropes. The transport officer said, 'I bet you a fiver you get the MC' but instead he received the Romanian Order of Michael the Brave.

George Cochrane was an officer in the 1st Gurkha Rifles when they took Baghdad and is commemorated on the Basra Memorial. Herbert Gammie, recommended for a commission at Boreham House, 'fell in the heroic fight against overwhelming odds at the evacuation of Baku'.

There is a puzzle in the service of Gordon Dickson, who had lived in China and so became an officer in the Chinese Labour Corps, before serving in the ranks of the Ninth, and being wounded at Soissons.

Arthur Campbell, a pharmacist, with the Ninth since 1906 and who had been instrumental in establishing the 2/9th and 3/9th Royal Scots, served as Embarkation Staff Officer and Detention Superintendent in Sierra Leone from 1917-19. Charles R. Brown instructed an American division in the USA and similarly George Borthwick taught bayonet fighting in North Carolina. Malcolm Macfarlane of the recruiting mission was described as 'the first British soldier to be buried in the United States in over one hundred years' after his death from pneumonia.

William Millar had already had a Whippet tank knocked out in August 1918 when he was given another and was killed the same day near Achiet-le-Grand. Israel Stoller, transferred from the Ninth to the MGC in October 1916, was sent to Egypt and became an armoured car gunner at Akaba. Alastair Shannon was commissioned in the Highland Light Infantry, captured at Kut-al-Amara and, as a Turkish prisoner of war, survived the 'Death March' across the Syrian desert. Prior to repatriation in December 1918 he wrote 'A Song in the Night', probably at Afion Karahissar [excerpt]:

Comrades that I loved fell at my side, silently
embracing the Unknown; without a sigh, without a
moan, they dropped like stones at my feet.
I passed on, my Beloved, trampling their poor bodies into the
reeking clay, crushing with my boots the faces I had
known so well...

The ranks clash together.
The bellows of rage blacken the face of the sun.
The bayonets sink deep, deep.
O God of Heaven, every thrust made is a thrust
into one's own heart.
There is something broken there.
It will never be healed —
Your ear close. Beloved!
Closer! Let it be whispered to you only:
I have slain my friends[101]

A number of men finished their service in the RAF, formed on 1 April 1918 from the Royal Flying Corps and Royal Naval Air Service. Among the approximately twenty-five records of Ninths turned aircrew (pilots and observers) we have Victor Bush, born in Bangkok, at that time in Siam, to Admiral John Bush and Meh Plien. He was attached to the RFC in 1916 and taught at No.1 School of Air Fighting at Ayr. On 8 February 1918 one of the planes of his Sopwith Camel B5565 buckled in the air, the uncontrollable machine crashed at Kincaidston Farm and he was instantly killed.

Victor Bush.

William Moyes was shot down in an FE2d in April 1917 by Max Müller, south of Ploegsteert, when they turned back to assist another machine. John Neill flew two-seat DH4s with 55 Squadron, part of the Independent Air Force. Returning from bombing the sidings at Melle, near Ghent, in September 1917, they were attacked by ten enemy aircraft of Jasta 18. They had fallen behind with a poor engine, were engaged by two aircraft and shot down by Rudolf Berthold. Seen going down in a steep spiral with smoke coming from the fuselage, they succeeded in landing and setting fire to their machine. Made a prisoner of war, Neill was repatriated in August 1918 through Holland.

In September 1918, from the same squadron, the writer W.E. Johns was shot down in F5712 followed by ex-Ninth George Dunlop in F5714, all becoming prisoners. Archibald Stewart Clark survived three crashes as an observer in Armstrong Whitworth FKs in Salonika, and a flat spin into the sea off Aboukir. James Young was a private at the time of Arras and an observer in the RNAS in July on long distant raids in the Mediterranean, and the Caucasus. He was mentioned in despatches for Coastal Command in the Second World War.

Alex Mitchell flew an SE5a in Palestine and was four times wounded in an air campaign that T.E. Lawrence described as having 'converted the Turkish retreat into rout'.[102] Arthur Lechler, born in Madras, was flying the new Bristol Fighter in April 1917 when he was shot down and taken prisoner, in the same fight as William Leefe Robinson VC. The victor had been Richthofen who proudly placed tail A3340 of the Bristol on his 'trophy wall'.

Rob Roy MacGregor had lied about his age to join the Ninth. Having been gassed at Arras he joined the RFC but went missing from a bombing raid on billets near Roulers in an FE2 and became a PoW. After the war he worked in the 'movies' at Lasky Studio, later part of Paramount, and in a goldmine in Alaska before becoming an accountant.

John Gordon Smith Grant was the highest scoring pilot of the Ninth. He had inherited the Glenlivet distillery from his father. With the Ninth from 1913, in France he commanded 5 Platoon until seconded to the RFC in November 1916. As a Sopwith Camel pilot in 1917 he shot down two enemy aircraft. Wounded after trying to destroy a detonator, he was posted to Italy and shot down three Aviatiks in the space of three days. Back in France in 1918, he increased his score to six in May. He was wounded in combat six days later and was being operated on in No.3 Canadian Stationary Hospital that evening when it was bombed by enemy aircraft and he was killed.

John Smith Grant.

Wull Grossart, late of the machine-gun section, had been hospitalised at Courcelette and, finding himself with the reserve battalion at Catterick, became an RFC cadet there in November 1917 and learnt to fly in three months. His prior experience consisted only of riding a push bike. Grossart's friends in the Ninth had given him the helpful advice, 'You will only fall out once.'[5] However his excellent instructor, Captain Valentine 'old devil' Baker (co-founder of Martin-Baker), 'did not like to kill any more of his pupils than he could help'.[5] Grossart soloed on 5 January 1918 in a DH6 'feeling as brave as in the barrage in "Death Valley" ("Happy Valley" near Mametz Wood, Somme)'[5] but landed 'twenty feet up' and pancaked onto the ground with his instructor doubled up with laughter. He first flew a DH4 on 9 March and two weeks later, as the Germans advanced, he was sent hurriedly to France and the next day was passed out as a fully qualified service pilot on DH4s. Grossart joined No.205 Squadron operating over Villers Bretonneux. The citation for his Distinguished Flying Cross in September reads:

'During the last two and a half months this officer has carried out twenty-seven successful bombing raids and twenty-five special photographic reconnaissances, his services on the latter duty being exceptionally valuable. This officer possesses a fine spirit of determination; neither strong opposition nor adverse weather conditions deters him from achieving his object.'

This work supported the big push in August. Although ostensibly a bomber pilot, he and his observers accumulated five aerial victories. He reflected:

'How different to the life we knew together. There was no quiet walk in the evening for us after Beaumont Hamel, no contact with Nature undisturbed by war. It was dig, dig, dig to the encouraging screech of the enemy shells. There was no peaceful sleep in comfortable beds for us then, only the lean in the corner of a snow-covered trench among chalky mud, frozen, miserable, and waiting for the relief we knew to be some days away... Perhaps the best fun I had during this time was spending a few minutes after emptying my guns and getting rid of the bombs, in prowling about at low altitudes over the old spots where you and I drummed up, cussed, or laughed according to the circumstances of the moment... Over Curlu, Fargny Mill and Vaux with the mile of marsh where the comedy of outposts was perpetrated, where we lived mostly on rum and had a perpetual "sair heid" in consequence, where Rutherford was captured at the Crows Nest; over Suzanne of evil memory.'[5]

'Auld Reekie,' the motor ambulance, Rab Murdoch sitting in the doorway.

The experience of war meant that the survivors, even the uninjured survivors, cannot have been expected to have remained inviolate. Bill Hay had nightmares about the rats. Years later James Quinn woke from anaesthetic in hospital remembering his friend carrying Small Arms Ammunition outside the trench in Sanctuary Wood, and frightened the medical team by screaming 'Jim, Jim, come back, you …….. They'll get you!'[23]

'Wee Rab' Murdoch was a 5ft 3in Lewis gunner, twice wounded. As a shipping clerk at Kilsyth in 1933, he came home one Sunday night to see the lights on at his house. His wife stayed outside with their son and pram, and he went inside and found burglars. He took an automatic pistol from a drawer and when unemployed miner Daniel Brady tried to rush him, or perhaps get past him from the scullery, Murdoch shot him in the throat. Murdoch was bailed for culpable homicide, the jury found no charge to answer and he 'didn't lose a lot of sleep over it'.[103]

Thomas Hart settled as a bread van driver in Sligo. In March 1940 he left his coat, hat and money belt under a bridge and drowned himself in the deep-water dock. After his body had been recovered, some five days later, the coroner recorded his death as 'suicide by drowning while the balance of his mind was unsettled owing to a head wound received in the Great War'.

About a quarter of men returning had some form of disability, the most that many of them could expect was an unskilled wage, as a full pension was 25s a week. Wattie Scott had been invalided out of the army with a poisoned leg. In the back of his diary can be found his long division to show that the £50 for his first year equated to 19s 3d a week. However he served again with the Labour Corps. Lawrence Mitchell had heart disease when he was signed off with no incapacity; the Royal Hospital at Chelsea felt obliged to write 'it would seem highly improbable for the man to be completely cured in three months'.

Questions were asked of Robert Virtue's pension in Parliament, for his family were destitute. John Clapperton had his right arm amputated in March 1918. 'If I have suffered & given much for the old flag, so have thousands more. But if only we win at the finish & secured victory for Christianity then we will not have suffered in vain.'[75]

William John Watt lost his right hand and left arm at Arras in 1917 and remained in hospital until October 1919. He ran a newsagent's shop at the Scottish Veterans Garden City Scheme at Longniddry 'but could measure out quarters of sweeties from jars with practised ease'. The veteran in the adjoining shop cut his own throat with a razor. Not only did Watt cope, but he expanded his horizons with art classes and around 1930, with a brush strapped to his forearm by elastic bands and an old gramophone as a turntable, he began decorating pottery. He sold his prodigious output, under the name 'Stump', from his newsagent's shop.

The last word belongs to the ever-enthusiastic Jimmy Quinn, 'stoutest heart in the old gun team,'[5] who enlisted on the day of mobilisation and was the last of the original machine-gun section in the battalion when a shell broke his leg on the slopes of Vimy Ridge in April 1917. He had a difficult time settling into civilian life:

'Four of us went to a Dance – all 9th men. Three on leave and myself... one of whom brought another girl to me. By that time I had slid into a corner. When the girl came over I stood up and one of them fair screeched at me standing on one leg (one forgets

William 'Stump' Watt at work in his studio.

odd sights like this in hospital). She cried out '*Oh! Oh! You've lost a – you can't – I didn't know*' and fair turned and ran away crying! All of us were a bit upset and I felt like drowning myself and cleared out miserable from the heart outwards!'[23]

However, Quinn battled on, was fitted with an artificial limb at Edenhall, in three weeks had learnt to walk with it, was given a civilian suit and his discharge. Confounding any simplistic view of the Great War, he finishes his memoir:

'Well – I liked – no I won't say all – but most of it and have not one regret whatever happens in the future and has happened since '14 to me. I can aye say '*I was a man ance and took my place amongst men.*'[23]

Postscript
1919 to date

Peace 1919-1923

'They have lost heavily in killed and wounded; and possibly more than any other regiment they furnished officers for the rapidly expanding British Army.'[6]

IN the new year, on 25 January 1919, the battalion moved to 'peace and plenty'[32] Brussels and were greeted riotously despite the heavy snow. The Ninth had first been billeted at Tubize on 17 December 1918, and they were permanently there for their last few months from March 1919. Strikes at home resulted in the frustrating cancellation of leave on 22 March.

Training diminished as men were demobilised and fatigues were still an ongoing requirement, and in April training stopped with the provision of escorts for prisoners of war. Three Prisoner of War Companies, Numbers 287, 332 and 323 were formed consisting of 80 men for the first two, and a remainder of 52 men for the third. By May the battalion was reduced to cadre strength under Major William Lindsay. At least one man tarried, a baker married a Belgian girl and set up a patisserie.

'Bunty' Cadell had resisted a commission until 1918, when he joined the Argylls. From home Peploe complained of a lack of new material, writing:

'I notice you are using your beautiful sketch book for meaner uses than you intended, but I can quite understand. There can't be much to inspire one in a dug-out... This habit of yours of living in dug-outs must inevitably result in a new development in your painting. I can see you will absolutely give up the use of flake white. After all why shouldn't one? Is it not quite unnecessary for a colourist? And at the present price it would also be an economy... Do you ever see "Colour" in the trenches?'[59]

Cadell was wounded in July but returned to joint-command of 278 POW Company in early November 1918. His duties occurred on alternate days, starting with a 6am parade '(i.e. seeing that all the prisoners are there and that none have escaped)'[59] and then sending them out under escort to work on the roads or on salvage. Five-hundred *Huns* goose-stepping past, with '*Achtung! Die Augen links*' (eyes left), was 'Terrifying!!'[59] He then had the day to himself until another parade was held at 5pm, and finally at 11pm he had to walk around the outside of the compound with his sergeant.

'When do you think you will get home?' asked Peploe, surmising 'I'm afraid Art is not one of the "*pivotal*" trades in a modern State, but rather considered as some foreign substance, like dirt, on the rim of the wheel liable at any moment to be dropped off.' In the event, Cadell served until 1919 and on returning home almost immediately

'Their colours wreathed with laurel,' Waverley Station 18 June 1919.

returned to painting in Iona, commencing the greatest period of his career creating indelible images of Edinburgh's New Town and adding lustre to the Highlands.

The final entry in the War Diary was at Tubize, Belgium for May 1919 and ends:

'Sport: On 28th May the Battalion engaged in a cricket match with the XVth Div. M.T. Coy R.A.S.C., and an enjoyable game resulted in a win for the Battalion by 43 runs. The weather for the month was very dry and warm.'[1]

The Ninth returned to Edinburgh in small parties as they demobilised. Seven months after the Armistice came into force and nine days before the peace was signed at Versailles, the colour party of the Ninth returned to Edinburgh shortly after 4pm on 18 June 1919. Led by Lieutenant Andrew Hughson, it consisted of seven officers and NCOs. Two of them, David Anderson and Frederick Reid had been with the battalion when they went out in February 1915. To their surprise, awaiting them on the platform were the Lord Provost and the band of the 2nd Royal Scots, along with a large crowd made up principally of demobilised men of the Ninth. Mrs Clark laureated the gilt tops of the flag-staffs to the National Anthem, and they proceeded along Princes Street following the band to Wemyss Place, their old headquarters and at that time those of the Territorial Force Association. The two lieutenants carried the colours, guarded by four of the NCOs with bayonets fixed, and the seventh man led the donkey mascot, replete with red rosettes.

The 2/10th Royal Scots returned from active service in Northern Russia at the same time, including David Deas who had been wounded at Merville, and the battalions were fêted alike. On the following day the members of the battalion were entertained by the Provost and City at their old drill hall on Forrest Road.

The original members of the battalion, those who had crossed to France in 1915, formed the 'Inventor Club', named for the ship that had carried them across the Channel. The first annual dinner, on the anniversary of their departure, was held by some 200 members of the Ninth at the Royal Scots Club on 23 February 1920. At this time the RSC was located in the YMCA huts in St Andrew Square, until the present premises opened in 1922.

There was much myth making and mirth. Comrades laughed as Sergeant Cook Bob Tait recounted trying to climb into his cooker when a *Zepp* dropped bombs on *Vlam*[23]; B Company were questioned anew about 'the dog that no one killed'[10] and it was recalled how Duncan Geekie had asked Bill Innes 'how his blisters and rheumatics were now!'[23] as they caught their breath in a bullet-swept shell hole advancing on High Wood.

Alexander Blair was present, the commanding officer from 1912 to 1916, he was in many ways still at the heart of the battalion. Blair became honorary treasurer of the British Legion of Scotland at which he worked tirelessly as 'a labour of love' until his death in 1936 aged 71. Sir Ian Hamilton, whose reputation had perhaps rather unfairly foundered on the beaches of Gallipoli, was Scottish President of the Legion, and also presided over the reunion. Toasts were proposed to the Colonel-in-Chief, Princess Mary, and 'Our Fallen Comrades', asking all present to 'devote a few moments to the remembrance of those who had not returned with them from their great reconnaissance into the regions of immortality. He shared the ideas of the Japanese generals who, when they empty a cup of saki to dead warriors, address them directly and as if they heard every word that was said.'[6]

In memory of Norman Howard Small, depicted as St Stephen, and his brother William Small (Royal Horse Guards), stained glass windows were presented to Mayfield Parish Church, now known as Craigmillar Park Church, by their parents.

As practical memorials, Edinburgh gave her support via the British League of Help to a number of French villages in need of agricultural machines and seed. One of these was Avricourt, connected to the Ninth from the fighting near Nesle in 1918.

The lasting memorial to the regiment has been the Royal Scots Club in Edinburgh, a stroll beside the gardens along Heriot Row from Ferguson's drill hall on Wemyss Place, where the life of the Dandy Ninth began.

During 1919 all seven of the Territorial battalions of the Royal Scots were disbanded, save the 2/10th Royal Scots who were disbanded in February 1920. Days later, on 18 February 1920, recruitment for the new Territorials commenced. Service would normally be for four years, with £5 (later £3) efficiency bonus payable and with full pay on camp, level with the Regulars and 'treble the pre-war rate'[26] so that he 'will not only get a healthy holiday free of any expense to himself, but will be able to accumulate a substantial contribution to the expenses of the annual holiday of other members of his family'.[26]

An Anniversary Dinner.

The last Church Parade.

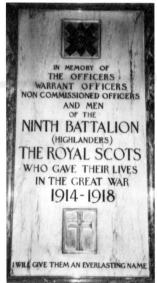

Memorial in St Giles'
Cathedral, Edinburgh. Blair
had proposed 'Living or
dead, comrades all.'

Investiture at Buckingham Palace, July 1919, Bob Lindsay and
Mrs Frederick Paulin.

It was also recognised that any expansion in time of war would be through the Territorials and all officers and men were required to sign the Imperial Service Obligation. On the first night the Ninth had nine men sign. At the beginning of March 1921 the 'newly resuscitated'[6] Ninth were recruiting with a concert held at East Claremont Street under the command of Lieutenant Colonel Patrick James Blair, formerly 'Young Blair', and the recruiting sergeants were kept busy to a late hour.

Defence Force 1921
OWNERSHIP of Britain's coal mines, state controlled through the war, returned to private hands on 31 March 1921: wages were cut and strike action followed. A State of Emergency was declared. This was exactly a year since the Z class reserve had been disbanded and an attempt was made to activate the Territorial battalions. However, the attestation forms explicitly excluded their use in 'civil commotion'. New forms were

printed overnight under the name of the Defence Force and from 9 April men of military experience 'capable of bearing arms' were asked to sign up for a maximum of 90 days. They were expected to wear their uniform and carry their arms, those who provided their own clothing were given a £5 grant.

The recruitment was rapid and popular. The Territorial drill halls were opened for recruitment, with preference given to serving Territorials, with the intention of their being re-embodied as the 'DF'. Edinburgh's battalions recruited briskly with all of the officers being obtained by 12 April from their parent units. As had been the case in the Boer War, the volunteers were treated as temporary regulars, with the 9th Royal Scots (Defence Force) being commanded by Temporary Lieutenant Colonel Patrick Blair, joined by such familiar names as William Lindsay and Norman Macdonald. Almost all of the men were unemployed ex-servicemen for whom pay as regular soldiers was welcomed. At one church parade in England a DF volunteer was heard to say, 'O! Lord, please make the Bolshies good again – but not just yet.'[6]

The Scotsman was clear: 'The best preventive of the spread of this revolutionary and destructive spirit is the immediate filling up of the ranks of the defence force,'[6] though they had to make clear that there was no question of being sent abroad or to Ireland, nor to work in the mines.

The Defence Force, 75,000 strong, was created in order to protect the country's infrastructure, such as the railways and ports. 9th Royal Scots (DF) were deployed in the Addiewell district and also at Cardenden, Fife. An immediate necessity was to restart the mine pumps. Many collieries in Lothian had their pumps stopped around 7 April 1921 for a week, and though arrests were made for riotous behaviour, the situation was restored relatively quickly when compared with Fife. Here there were police baton charges and some Justices of the Peace resigned before being required to read the Riot Act giving the army recourse to lethal force.

9th RS Defence Force.

The threat of general strike collapsed on 15 April and the government provided a temporary subsidy. Yet the precautions were costing the government a million pounds a week. Having ceased recruitment on 19 April, it was not until mid-July 1921 that most of the miners were back at work, the force was disbanded and the Territorials were then free to re-enlist in their units on an assumption of continuous service.

Amalgamation 1922

THE infantry of the new Territorial Army, so named in October 1921, was costed and set out as fourteen divisions of twelve battalions each, to make a peace time establishment of 4,704 officers and 114,240 other ranks. Of the 40 surplus battalions, 19 were converted to technical arms or suspended, leaving an excess of 21.

At the anniversary dinner in 1920 *weel kent* Lieutenant Colonel Alexander Blair spoke of 'annihilation', saying the War Office 'had launched an attack of poison gas against the battalion, and they did not know whether they were dead or alive. Meantime they were in the Casualty Clearing Station – (laughter) – and he would appeal to their Colonel [Hamilton] for first aid. (Renewed laughter).'[6] The Ninth were seen as at risk as 'the junior battalion'[26] and indeed that seems to have been the War Office's original plan, but 'the proposals met with considerable opposition in Edinburgh'[26] and by early March 1920 it was believed the country would retain the services of three out of seven battalions: 4th/5th, 6th and 9th Royal Scots.

In the event the 6th and 8th Royal Scots joined the artillery, and 10th Royal Scots joined the engineers early in 1921. This left four battalions in the Edinburgh and Midlothian Association (4th, 5th, 7th and 9th Royal Scots) with a total strength of 937, against a peace establishment of 2,720, and of which the 7th had a strength of only 126. The focus now fell on the 7th Royal Scots through the summer. The 7th (Leith) Battalion had origins dating to 1859, had suffered severe losses at the Quintinshill rail disaster near Gretna in May 1915 and had fought with distinction in Gallipoli, Palestine and Flanders during the war. Lord Rosebery and William Wedgwood Benn, the Liberal MP for Leith, defended the battalion and Lord Salvesen said in July 1921:

'The Seventh was the only battalion connected with Greater Edinburgh which wore the distinctive uniform of the Royal Scots – a uniform that appealed to him far more than the black [rifle] uniform characteristic of the Edinburgh Battalion, or even the kilted uniform that had attracted so many to the Ninth.'[6]

The men, answering a postcard poll, stated six to one that they would prefer to quit rather than transfer.

Of the four battalions, it was decided that two of them must go and amalgamation was sought rather than disbandment. It was officially announced in October 1921 that the Army Council had approved amalgamations to create the 4th/5th and 7th/9th battalions of the Royal Scots, to be completed by 1 January 1922. The War Office had intimated that the half-battalions could keep their separate drill halls and distinctive uniforms, but it later transpired the 7th would have to pay for their own hall and the uniform pledge also fell by the way in 1922; although the 7th, apparently 'all asked to be allowed to wear the kilt'.[98] In November 1921, the 7th deposited their colours in South Leith Parish Church and their CO Archibald Maclaine Mitchell addressed the battalion:

'They had had to bow to the inevitable in being forced into an amalgamation which practically meant the disbandment of the battalion… To amalgamate a Highland and a Lowland battalion was one of those things that could only be suggested by one who knew and cared nothing for Scotland… London did not recognise anything Scottish without a kilt, but nevertheless their regiment was famous before there was a War Office.'

Nineteen officers resigned and applications for discharge were received from 543 men. Of those officers transferred to form 4th/5th Royal Scots and 7th/9th Royal Scots, *The London Gazette* only lists two from the 7th Battalion: Honorary Colonel the Earl of Rosebery and Lieutenant Hugh McCrostie.

Through either choice or necessity Iver Salvesen, of the great Leith shipping and whaling firm, joined the Ninth in 1921, served in the 9th DF and later in the 7th/9th. Iver was the youngest of seven and had two older brothers who had served with the 7th Battalion. Christian died in the tragic Quintinshill train disaster in 1915, from which his body could not be identified; Eric went missing at the Scarpe in 1917.

In the event, it was not until 1923 that the amalgamation was completed with the transfer of officers; of which Captain Norman Pringle-Pattison may have been the only one not to object, having served in both battalions during the Great War, firstly with the 7th in Gallipoli, and with the Ninth from May 1917. Among the officers was Arthur Chapman. He and his brother Samuel both joined the Ninth as privates on the outbreak of war, both were commissioned into 7th Camerons, but Samuel was killed in 1916.

Consequently, the new 4th/5th (Queen's Edinburgh) continued to reside at Forrest Hill, the drill hall of the old QRVB; and the 7th/9th (Highlanders) adopted the dress, drill hall and distinction 'Highlanders' (1924) of the Ninth and the nickname '*Dandy Ninth*' also endured. So too, the annual church parade which continued to mark the departure of the Ninth for France but with wreaths laid at the memorials of both battalions in St Giles' Cathedral. Finally, their commanding officer was also a Ninth in the form of Patrick Blair, followed in due course by other Ninths until a new generation of men took over and led the battalion in the Second World War.

Between the wars the *Dandy Ninth* continued their traditions, winning many shooting competitions, such as the Velongdis Cup at Bisley. However, there was change, 'Territorial Battalions were very much more democratic after the war'[19] and economic difficulties meant Territorial camps were cancelled in 1933, despite the fact that this was the Tercentenary of the Royal Scots. They lined the street for the coronation of George VI in 1936. The 4th/5th (Queen's Edinburgh) became an anti-aircraft unit in 1938, but in the summer of 1939 the 8th Royal Scots (Lothians and Peeblesshire) were reformed. In this next war Ninths could again be found in many parts of the world.

In the Home Guard, Patrick James Blair commanded Lothian in the Second World War, Norman Macdonald had a command in Glasgow, Alastair Murray in Edinburgh, Colin Penney the anti-aircraft guns at Craigentinny. Oswald Walker, chemistry lecturer, was with the Special Operations Executive. Drummer John Wilson from Hearts had twice been wounded in action. In the Home Guard he contracted pneumonia at Inchcolm and died in February 1940. John Falconer was Chief Air Raid Warden in Edinburgh until he became Lord Provost in 1944, later playing his part in instigating the Edinburgh International Festival in 1947. Bobby Johnston commanded the 8th Gordons, which became an Anti-Tank Regiment in Burma.

Here ends the history of the 9th (Highlanders) Royal Scots, but the thread of the Ninth is present still in the strands of the British Army and can be traced to men serving the colours today.

> *'There's nane o' my ain to care,*
> *There's nane to mind me noo,*
> *There's nane o' my ain to comb my hair,*
> *There's nane to sponge my mou'.*
> *There's nane o' my ain to care,*
> *Strange han's sall straighten me,*
> *Strangers sall fauld about my limbs*
> *The claes o' my deid body.'*

Lance Corporal William Ogilvie

The Second World War

'No man ought to join the Territorial Army who is not prepared to go to the rescue of France and Belgium if wrongfully attacked by Germany in the sort of circumstances that prevailed in 1914, or to defend the Empire, if it is vitally assailed, and go within a very few months, or even weeks, of the outbreak of war.'[26]

Winston Churchill, 1920

THE 7th/9th Royal Scots *Dandy Ninth* were embodied under the command of Lieutenant Colonel Iver Salvesen, who might be considered the last of the Ninth, on 3 September 1939 at the start of the Second World War. They formed part of 155 Brigade of the 52nd (Lowland) Division. The compressed 7th/9th Royal Scots became two again with a second-line battalion in March 1939 and they marched in Edinburgh that summer with their duplicate battalion in civilian 'mufti', still awaiting uniforms.

Table 12. Infantry Brigades of the 52nd Division (Territorials) on 3 September 1939

52nd (Lowland) Division *Major General James Drew*		
155 (East Scottish) Brigade *Brigadier T Grainger-Stewart*	**156 (West Scottish) Brigade** *Brigadier FG Chalmer*	**157 (HLI) Brigade** *Brigadier NR Campbell*
7th/9th Royal Scots	4th/5th RSF	1st Glasgow Highlanders, HLI
4th KOSB	6th Cameronians	5th HLI
5th KOSB	7th Cameronians	6th HLI
Royal Armoured Corps, Royal Signals, Royal Artillery & Royal Engineers		

Former Dandy Ninths included Brigadier Thomas Grainger-Stewart, and Colonel David Carnegie, commanding Glasgow Highlanders. KOSB King's Own Scottish Borderers, HLI Highland Light Infantry, RSF Royal Scots Fusiliers

On the same day that Neville Chamberlain resigned as Prime Minister in favour of Winston Churchill, the quiet unease of the 'Phoney War' ended. The German blitzkrieg rolled across the Low Countries and France and in just ten days from 10 May 1940, Panzer Group von Kleist had fought its way from the Ardennes to the Channel at Abbeville, on the River Somme. This cut-off the bulk of the British Expeditionary Force to the north, who consequently were forced to evacuate from Dunkirk between 27 May and 4 June. Sadly the 51st (Highland) Division were captured, though the Ninth's old brigade, 154 Brigade escaped and became the nucleus of the new 51st (Highland) Division.

Scotland's other Territorial division, the 52nd, was hastily sent to France on 8 June, a few days *after* the evacuation at Dunkirk. The 7th/9th Royal Scots disembarked on 13 June 200 miles to the south-west at Cherbourg as part of the so-called Second BEF. The advanced brigade, 157 Brigade, had already been attached to the French Tenth Army at the front now near Rouen and plans were made for the other brigades to follow. However, the Tenth Army and the Army of Paris were withdrawing on divergent courses, a widening gap the division could not close. A plan to hold Brittany was also briefly entertained but realising that no stand could be taken in France, the division was ordered to evacuate back through Cherbourg on 14 June. However on the following day, with other units embarking for home, Churchill vacillated as to the effect of the withdrawal on French morale, and the division was halted. The evacuation shipping was lying idle at Cherbourg. Twenty-four hours later the order to depart was reinstated, with Pétain requesting an armistice, the gap in the French defences exceeding 50 miles in width and 157 Brigade engaged in fighting.

John McGurk, a 7th/9th piper:

'We got into these trucks and of course they were packed to the gunnies, and Christ if you wanted a pee it wouldnae stop, they wanted to get to Cherbourg and you had to pee out the side of the bloody trucks. And you passing the bridges and people were flinging flowers... Until eventually we got into Cherbourg and they put the trucks on fire.'[104]

With the 5th KOSB defending the city, the division began embarkation on 16 June, as part of Operation Ariel in which RMS *Lancastria* was sunk off the coast of St Nazaire with untold loss of life

The *Dandy Ninth* recovered only one of their Bren carriers, and all their PU vehicles went off the quay. The last boat left Cherbourg at 4pm on 18 June with the Germans 3 miles from the harbour. The division had been in France less than a week; the allies were not to return for four years.

The division was then made part of Coastal Defences, uniquely trained in mountain and snow warfare in 1942, with Norway in their sights, and in an air transport role in July 1944. Seven operations were planned, the last was to land to the north of Arnhem but nine hours before heading to their airfields the unfolding disaster on the bridges cancelled the final operations. They were consigned to be infantry 'known to us by the somewhat contemptuous title of "flat".'[70]

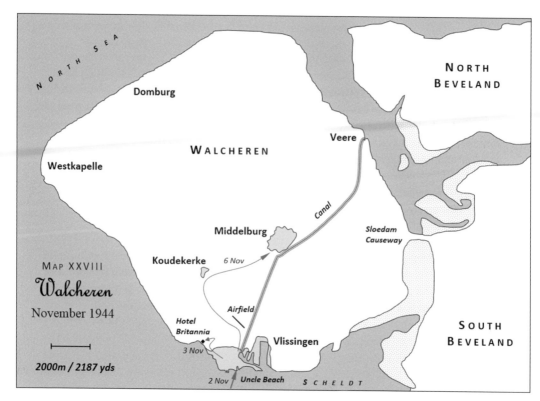

MAP XXVIII

Walcheren

November 1944

2000m / 2187 yds

Eventually the division joined the British Liberation Army in Holland in October 1944 at a critical time. It was vital to open the port of Antwerp, already in British hands, in order to supply the Allied advance. The island of Walcheren throughout history has dominated the River Scheldt, in fact the Royal Scots had landed at Domburg and fought the French on Walcheren in 1809, the British Army losing 4,000 men to disease. In 1944 the estuary was heavily mined and the island was a stronghold of Hitler's Atlantic Wall held mainly by the German 70th Division with some of the 64th Division, who had experience in Russia. To hamper the defenders the RAF bombed the dykes, flooding the interior so that the island was effectively 'sunk'.

The Canadian Army had been given the daunting task of storming the 1,200 yard causeway from the east of the island, a forlorn hope that took several days to accomplish. An amphibious operation was now planned, like the hellburners of Antwerp breaking the siege.

On 1 November 1944 the Commandos went in at Westkapelle and Vlissingen, anglicised as Flushing. The 4th KOSB of 155 Brigade crossed the Scheldt from Breskens and landed on 'Uncle Beach'. Their landing craft were shelled and they were immediately engaged in street fighting facing a maze of pillboxes and a multitude of mines ashore. The next day they held the docks and town centre whilst the rest of the brigade passed through, the 5th KOSB to go east and 7th/9th RS to go west.

The 7th/9th had landed at Uncle Beach early on 2 November, had cleared streets and snipers, and assisted in the evacuation of civilians. That night they were given the objective of a German strongpoint at the Hotel Britannia with an estimated garrison of fifty. In the dark they made their way out of town on roads flooded waist deep with seawater and a 5-knot current, holding their weapons and incongruous 'Mountain' shoulder badges clear of the seawater, to assemble 300 yards behind the hotel. The water here was in places at least shoulder deep, but routes were found to commence the attack at 4.15am. Unexpectedly the strongpoint was held in strength and comprehensively protected by trenches and pillboxes, by machine guns and a four-barrelled 20mm cannon on the roof.

There was desperate fighting inside, the building was now on fire, and Lieutenant Beveridge scaled the outside to reach the roof. About 10am an underground bunker was entered and it was discovered that the hotel was in fact German headquarters for Vlissingen. Private Robert Love:

'I led the Bren-gun team towards a pillbox, there didn't seem to be any life or movement and as we stood at the entrance a German came towards us from one of the various rooms. I challenged him and he immediately turned and ran back from where he came and I gave a burst of Bren gun fire which dealt with him and within minutes twenty-five of the enemy came out of various rooms and surrendered.'[105]

Artillery firing across the Scheldt land a shell close to the Hotel Britannia.

The Hotel Britannia, before and after the Highlanders visit.

The hotel was subdued by noon, General Reinhardt and 600 men were captured. The following day British minesweepers entered the Scheldt.

With Vlissingen secure, there remained the difficulty of taking the regional capital Middelburg, an island within an inundated island. On 6 November A Company of the 7th/9th under Major Hugh Johnston left Vlissingen aboard amphibious Landing Vehicle Tracked 'Buffaloes' of A Squadron, 11 Royal Tank Regiment, following a circuitous route through the flooded land to the west.

> 'There was a pill box away across when we were going up, and the company commander asked us to go across to investigate... it was all mined, but unfortunately for us we'd already gone across the barbed wire and were blown up, and we lost quite a few. I was in the back of this and my bloody pipes were broken... a lot of the boys were killed and thrown into the water by the blast... and I don't know that they found them until they drained the place.'[104]

The lead company in eight Buffaloes found German resistance, so strong up to this point, had broken. Major Johnston:

> 'It was a curious sensation floating up deserted streets, looking into the top-storey rooms of houses. We crossed a bridge with the water shelving rapidly, and turned a sharp corner on to dry land, to behold the two leading Buffaloes surrounded by an excited throng of Dutch civilians.'[106]

'The LVT party drove cautiously'[1] into Middelburg and an inebriated General Wilhelm Daser was found in his headquarters but he insisted that he would only capitulate to a senior officer. 'In view of the heavy preponderance of field grey in the square,' thought Hugh Johnston, 'the time seemed ripe for some accelerated promotion, and so I forthwith became a colonel.'[106] A more colourful account is that 'hastily borrowing a subaltern's pips to add to the crown on his shoulder, he assumed the 'local and temporary' rank of colonel'[70] and took the surrender. General Daser, the capital and its surviving garrison exceeding 2,000 had surrendered to a company of Royal Scots numbering 200.

With the Scheldt navigable, Antwerp was restored to service though still bombed heavily. Iver Salvesen, whose shipping skills had kept him occupied fuelling the convoys on the Gold Coast, West Africa, was brought in to help open the docks. Liberty ships entered the harbour at the end of the month and on 1 December alone, 10,000 tons were put ashore.

The German offensive from the Ardennes (Battle of the Bulge) was intended to retake Antwerp, and this saw the division on the right of the British line adjoining the Americans in December, but the offensive collapsed in the last hours of the year.

In January 1945 the division advanced east with the battalions leap-frogging through. Kloster Lilbosch fell to the Royal Scots who took sixteen prisoners. Their

LVT Buffaloes heading through Markt into Lange Delft, Middelburg 6 November 1944.

Robert Love at
Bremen.

next objective, *en route* for the Roer, was Heinsberg. The 7th/9th undertook a night march of 13 miles to cut the town off over night on 23/24 January and saw off a Tiger tank with their 6-pounder anti-tank gun. In the morning the 4th KOSB cleared the town. The 7th/9th Bren gunner Robert Love:

> 'We fought our way into the centre of the town, the Germans seemed to appear from nowhere, and most of them had white camouflaged suits on and were difficult to see, every house had to be cleared of the enemy, snipers were everywhere, we would throw in a grenade then rush into the house and shoot anything that was moving. We were getting dangerously low on ammunition, plus it was getting dark so it was decided by the Battalion H.Q. to hold our positions that we had captured, if possible

until more ammunition was brought up to us. I found myself with 4 Section, in a reasonably undamaged house, we made ourselves as comfortable as possible, but there was to be no rest for us, sleep was impossible as the Germans occupied the house next door "not very nice neighbours to have". They were reasonably quiet though and except for a few rifle shots, we had more or less a peaceful night.

I set up my Bren-gun at a window overlooking the street, it was a bitterly cold night, at dawn the Germans counter attacked... Anyway, we were under heavy shelling at the time and were expecting another counter-attack so we had to stay at our positions when all of a sudden there was an almighty explosion just above us. We had received a direct hit and the upstairs came tumbling down on top of us, my number two and I were buried. I thought Christ I've had it, I couldn't move and then I realised that my head was on something soft and there was a queer taste in my mouth, I came to the conclusion that the soft thing must be my mate... I heard movement nearby and voices, good old Scottish voices, not German. I remember thinking, Christ I hope they don't think we are dead and leave us... My mate was dead and I had been lucky as all I had were a few cuts and bruises.'[105]

They crossed the Rhine on 25 March and fought with 7th Armoured Division to Soltau, of which the Commanding Officer, Lieutenant Colonel John Dawson wrote: 'We moved off the next morning, with a large assortment of Armour, to capture a town on the main axis which the Armour had had to by-pass. We eventually got in and captured it amid flames just as darkness was falling. A fairly hectic night for all concerned trying to open the road, put out flames and rout out Germans.'[106]

The Desert Rats were bent on reaching Hamburg, but the battalion reverted to the 52nd (Lowland) Division at Achim. By the end of April 1945 they had gained possession of the centre of Bremen on the River Weser. The city possessed both a Focke-Wulf aircraft factory and was in the process of completing, with forced labour, a supposedly bomb-proof U-boat factory. An uneasy ceasefire lasted until Victory in Europe was secured on 8 May 1945.

Far from the finery of Edinburgh's Esplanade, Charles Mackay's heavily laden Highlander, shown in the Preface, was going into war in March 1915; and so Pat Crosby's left Heinsberg toward the end of war, nigh thirty years later.

"WHEN YOU'SE GUYS LEAVE THE TOWN YOU CERTAINLY TAKE IT WITH YOU."

Leaving Heinsberg.

299

Postwar 1945 to date

WAR was followed by a year of occupation at Detmold, Germany as part of the British Army of the Rhine (BAOR). With a heavy duty of care for refugees, they took to shooting deer in the forest to provide food; though they were able to end 1945 with a Christmas Day England v Scotland 'International' football match. Disbanded on 26 June 1946, they were reconstituted on 1 May 1947 at East Claremont Street, the same pattern that had followed the First World War. Territorial life then returned. 'I joined the 7th/9th in the TA in 1953 after I had finished my two years national service with the regular 1st Battalion,' remembers Robin Bell, 'We quite enjoyed being kilted Highlanders, though we were laughed at a little as "Princes Street Highlanders."'

The Territorials were now subject to the seemingly cyclic requirements of expansion and reduction. The perennial problems were recognised by Niall Macpherson, MP for Dumfries, as early as 1948:

'If we are to get an efficient volunteer service we must create prestige units… if we formed a *corps d'élite* of volunteers it would produce a tremendous recruiting power at once. To a certain extent it has been done in the Special Air Service Regiments, and other units with special prestige can do it, for example, the "Dandy Ninth".'[107]

On 1 March 1961 the 7th/9th and 8th Royal Scots amalgamated to form 8th/9th Royal Scots which still did not meet regulation strength, and the kilt was dropped. On 1 April 1967 the TA was replaced with the Territorial and Army Volunteer Reserve (TAVR), and a consequent reduction in manpower finally ended the territorial battalion, 8th/9th Royal Scots reduced to A (Royal Scots) Company, The 52nd Lowland Volunteers, still in the same drill hall.

In 1971 expansion created 1st and 2nd Battalions of the 52nd Lowland Volunteers. The TA name was re-adopted in 1982 with reorganisation but the force was reduced again in 1992. The Royal Scots themselves narrowly avoided amalgamation in 1993. The 52nd Lowland Regiment was formed in July 1999, the only TA infantry battalion in Lowland Scotland, and the only Royal Scots element was A (The Royal Scots) Company, East Claremont Street. The Royal Scots had the patronage of two Princess Royals as Colonel-in-Chief: HRH Princess Mary (1918-65) and HRH Princess Anne (1983-2006).

In 2006 it was a case of farewell even to the Royal Scots name, so famed in martial story, in the creation of The Royal Regiment of Scotland, a former appellation of the Royal Scots. The regulars of The Royal Scots became part of 1st Battalion, alongside two territorial battalions: 52nd Lowland 6th Battalion and 51st Highland 7th Battalion, either of which, as we have seen, would have been acceptable homes for the Ninth with their dual identity as Lowlanders and Highlanders. The Ninth's lineage therefore continues to this day as part of Army Reserve A (Royal Scots Borderers) Company, 6th Battalion, The Royal Regiment of Scotland (6 SCOTS) with headquarters at Colonel Clark's drill hall on East Claremont Street and with HRH The Princess Royal as Royal Colonel.

Appendix A

South African War Roll

Service Companies, Royal Scots
Broun, J.C.C., Lt, 3rd Service Company
Simpson, Pte, 1st Service Coy
Ormiston, G.H., Pte, 2nd Service Coy
Chalmers, J.S., Pte, 3rd Service Coy
Geddes, J.H., Pte, 3rd Service Coy
Kidd, G.F., Pte, 3rd Service Coy

City Imperial Volunteers (CIV)
Campbell, A., Sgt

Scottish Horse, Imperial Yeomanry
Stewart, J., Sgt
Ruxton, A.J., Cpl
Macduff, G., L/Cpl
Lee, J.F.F., Pte
Milbourne, P., Pte
Chapman, A.J., Pte
Calder, H.G., Pte
Rutherford, W., Drummer
Renton, R.W., Pte
Fraser, J., Pte

Fincastle's Horse, Imperial Yeomanry
Murray, D.W., Sgt
Kerr, W.W., Farrier-Sgt
Macdonald, J., Pte

Other Yeomanry Regiments
Holmes, A., Cpl
Anderson, G.W., Pte
Gray, R.A., Pte
Kirk, J., Pte
Milne, F.W., Pte
Traill, J.C., Pte
Macdonald, E.R., Pte
Watson, G.K., Pte †
Hunter, W., Pte
Potter, G., Pte
Drummond, C.C., Pte
MacLeod, W., jun., Pte
Ponton, T.V., Pte
Wood, W.B., Pte
McKay, W., Pte
Lockie, T.B., Pte
Sutherland, A., Pte

South African Constabulary
Bowden, A.H., Pte
Scott, T., Pte
Treasurer, R.C., Pte
Ferguson, J.L., Pte
Lyon, J., Pte
Macdonald, W., Pte
MacLeod, R., Pte
Martin, H., Pte

† Deceased

Ferguson

301

Appendix B

Commanding Officers

9th Royal Scots, subsequently 1/9th Royal Scots

James Ferguson of Kinmundy (1857–1917)
24 July 1900 – 3 December 1904
Lieutenant Colonel and Honorary Colonel

His father was a Director of the Great North of Scotland Railway Company and laird of Kinmundy, Aberdeenshire. Educated Birkenhead, Craigmount and Edinburgh University.

He married Georgina Agnew in 1885 and had two sons, James in 1886, killed at High Wood, and John in 1887, died February 1904.

Advocate 1870, called to the Bar in 1879, was King's Counsel (KC) in 1902 and variously Sheriff of Argyll; Inverness, Moray and Nairn and Forfarshire.

In 1874 he was commissioned sub lieutenant in the 17th Aberdeenshire Rifle Volunteer Corps (Old Deer), becoming honorary major in 1889 of 3rd Volunteer Battalion (The Buchan) Gordon Highlanders. He was the first commanding officer, 9th Battalion Royal Scots, resigned his commission in 1904, his father having died on 11 September of that year.

At the outbreak of war Ferguson took command of the new second-line battalion 2/9th, and later formed the third-line battalion. He retired in March 1917 and died at Edinburgh the following month.

Ferguson was the author of various books, including *Two Scottish Soldiers* on his ancestors General James Ferguson 'a soldier of 1688 and Blenheim' and Lieutenant Colonel Patrick Ferguson 'a soldier of the American Revolution' and inventor of the breechloading rifle. Of the latter he writes, 'He saw no difficulties in combining the character of a soldier with that of a citizen'.

His widow Georgina survived him by more than 30 years. On her death, without an heir, eighteenth-century Kinmundy

Signature of Commanding Officer.

Kinmundy House, the home of James Ferguson.

House fell into ruin in the 1950s and is now part of farm buildings.

He was 'The epitome of the enthusiastic and successful Territorial Colonel of the old school'.[10]

Major James Charles Wardrop was in temporary command 3-16 December 1904.

James Clark (1859–1915)
December 1904 – 1912

Clark's father was a thread manufacturer. From a family of thread manufacturers and the son of a ship owner, James was educated at Pau Lycée, Paisley Grammar School and Glasgow University. He married his second cousin Norah Clark in 1889.

Served in 5th Volunteer Battalion (Deeside Highland) Gordon Highlanders 1876-77; Mounted Infantry QRVB 1886-90; 9th Royal Scots 1900-1912.

Advocate 1883, KC 1908, Chairman of the Edinburgh School Board, Member of Edinburgh Town Council and Chairman of the City of Edinburgh Territorial Association. The School Board named a school in his honour on St Leonard's Lane.

He took command of 9th (Dumbartonshire) Argyll and Sutherland Highlanders in September 1914. On 10 May 1915 the battalion moved up to support 2nd Cameron Highlanders just as the Germans advanced on the 27th Division astride the Menin Road near Hooge. Clark was killed shortly afterwards, aged 56. According to accounts of the time a party of Germans in Cameron kilts approached and when they were recognised Clark was forced to lead a charge in which he was killed by a shell.

Alexander Stevenson Blair (1865–1936)
1912 – April 1916, then on Staff as Commandant of Abancourt Area
to November 1917.

His father had been a judge in Jamaica, and Sheriff-Substitute of
Invernesshire, Moray and Nairn.

Educated Loretto School; Brazenose College, Oxford BA 1886;
Writer to the Signet, 1889. Appointed captain of D Company, 9th
Royal Scots, December 1900.

At Oxford he played in the First XV and XI. Blair was a fast
three-quarter back (a centre or wing) in the innovative Oxford
University team of the 1880s but his potential to play for Scotland
was wrecked by a knee injury.

President of the Scottish Rugby Union, treasurer of the British
Legion of Scotland.

He married Elinor Dixon and they lost a son in the war, Second
Lieutenant Patrick Edward Adam Blair, 1st Black Watch (William
Green's battalion) wounded at Gheluvelt and missing since 29
October 1914.

Oxford University XV 1884, AS Blair top-left.

Percy Thuillier Westmorland (1863–1929)
April 1916 – May 1916, left to command 151 Brigade

Royal Warwickshire Regiment (Reserve of Officers)
Second Lieutenant in the Bedfordshire Regiment 1882. He
served in Gambia 1894, on the Ashanti Expedition 1895-96,
Boer War, Gambia 1902, North-West Frontier India. Retired
1912. Served 1914-18 War, commanded 5th Lincolnshire
Regiment November 1915 - April 1916, 9th Royal Scots April
– May 1916, GOC 151 Brigade.

William Green (1882–1947)
May 1916 – April 1918, left to command 153 Brigade

Son of Sir William Green (1836-1897), who served at the
Crimea, 'Indian Mutiny', Tel-el-Kebir, Sudan, Nile and
commanded 1st Black Watch (Royal Highlanders).

1st Black Watch, served in Boer War and in the Great War
from August 1914. Wounded in the Battle of the Aisne 15
September 1914, and at Aubers Ridge 9 May 1915. Former
captain and adjutant of the Ninth 1908-1912, rejoined battalion
as major on April 1916, in command May 1916 - April 1918,
promoted Brigadier General 153 Brigade, 51st Division.

Bewsher describes him as 'a most capable battalion
commander… one of the best infantry leaders that had served
with'[51] [the division]; Ewing described him as a 'tried and
esteemed leader.'[33]

Major General 1935, Governor of Portsmouth, Commander
South-Western Area 1938. Golf Army Champion. Married
Lesley Hannaford.

Major William Thorburn in temporary command April 1918,
appointed to command 8th Royal Scots

John Balderston Muir (1874–1955)
April 1918 – August 1918, on proceeding to UK

4th Black Watch (Royal Highlanders), twice wounded. Took command of 2/1st Oxfordshire and Buckinghamshire Light Infantry August 1916 where he was known as 'Jock' Muir, 'had the experience of a dozen years' service with Territorials, in peace and war, firmness, tact, and last but not least, a keen sense of humour, in giving expression to which he was a past-master'.[108] Described by Ewing as 'sterling'.[33]

In business with Thos Muir, Son, & Patton Ltd, coal merchants, carting contractors and builders' merchants.

Major Robert Gifford Moir, 8th Argylls temporarily assumed command May 1918 with Muir on month's leave

Arthur Stephenson (1881–1950)
August 1918 – March 1919, on proceeding to UK

Known in 16th Royal Scots as 'Steve'.

Stephenson was born at Stoke Damerel, near Devonport. He moved to South Africa in 1900 and worked for the post office. In the Boer War he served with the Imperial Light Horse. He became an Inspector in the Native Labour Bureau in Rhodesia and served in the Southern Rhodesian Volunteers. Stephenson sailed to the UK in May 1915 and went to France with the 9th King's Own Yorkshire Light Infantry in September. Wounded by shrapnel on 1 July 1916 on the assault south of Round Wood, he had a run in with Haig. Assumed command 16th Royal Scots August 1916 'where he showed us splendid leadership. He knew his officers and men and saw them always.'[19] On 16 May 1918, following heavy losses, the 34th Division was disbanded. Commanded 9th Royal Scots from August 1918. In 1919 he returned to Africa and became Commandant Northern Rhodesian Police in 1925. In the Second World War he was Lieutenant Colonel East African Forces, 1939-42.

In the absence of Major William Lindsay, Captain John Burns assumed temporary command.

306

William Carruthers Smith Lindsay (1891–1969)
March 1919 in command Cadre, returned UK June 1919

Coal exporter, his father had also been a colliery manager. Educated Daniel Stewart's College and Edinburgh University. Cadet Edinburgh University OTC, Second Lieutenant 9th Royal Scots 1910, served through First World War, Major, wounded September 1916. Military Cross 1917 for company command and assuming command of battalion until relieved. Unmarried.

2/9th Battalion:
1. Captain Arthur Campbell Aitken, briefly commanded in September 1914
2. James Ferguson, September 1914 to February 1915
3. Thomas George Clark, February to May 1915
4. Charles Thomas Gordon, May 1915 to June 1916
5. Arthur Frederick Egerton, June 1916 to July 1918
Disbanded in Ireland, July 1918.

3/9th Battalion:
1. James Ferguson, June 1915 to March 1917
2. Claude Prendergast Doig, March 1917 to April 1917, became Commanding Officer 4th (Reserve) Royal Scots.
Amalgamated with 4th (Reserve) Battalion July 1917, disbanded March 1919.

5th Scottish Provisional Battalion:
William Lachlan Forbes was in command of 5th Scottish Provisional Battalion at Dundee

7th/9th Royal Scots:
Patrick James Blair was promoted Lieutenant Colonel of 9th Royal Scots in February 1920 and served through into the 7th/9th Royal Scots. In 1927 command of the battalion was in the hands of Thomas Wilfrid Bennet Clark, in turn handed on to Norman Macdonald in 1931. Thomas Grainger-Stewart took over in 1932 until he became a brigadier in 1938. Iver Salvesen was in command at the start of the Second World War. All five of these officers had served with the Ninth. Through the war the Commanding Officers to VE day were I.R.S. Salvesen, F.L. Johnston, J.T. Campbell, E.C. Colville (Gordons), M.E. Melvill (wounded at Walcheren October 1944), J.G. Dawson.

Honorary Colonel:
Sir Ian Hamilton was the honorary colonel for over 30 years. Brigadier General Robert Maxwell Dudgeon, former adjutant, held the post in 1932, Patrick James Blair in 1945 and Brigadier Thomas Grainger-Stewart 1955-60.

Ian Hamilton.

Nomenclature

12 July 1900	The Highland Battalion, Queen's Rifle Volunteer Brigade, The Royal Scots (Lothian Regiment)
11 July 1901	9th Volunteer Battalion (Highlanders), The Royal Scots (Lothian Regiment). Part of Regimental District, No. 1, order of precedence No. 80
1 April 1908	9th (Highlanders) Battalion, The Royal Scots (Lothian Regiment) (Territorial Force)
12 September 1914	9th (Service) Battalion (Highlanders), The Royal Scots, on formation of Reserve Battalion.
8 February 1915	1/9th (Highlanders) Battalion, The Royal Scots (Lothian Regiment)
7 February 1920	9th (Highlanders) Battalion, The Royal Scots (The Royal Regiment)

Second-Line

12 September 1914	9th (Reserve) Battalion (Highlanders), The Royal Scots
2 October 1914	9th (Home Service) Battalion (Highlanders), The Royal Scots
2 December 1914	9th (Reserve) Battalion (Highlanders), The Royal Scots, the original name restored

With the creation of a third-line these two became First Reserve Battalion and Second Reserve Battalion.

8 February 1915 – 1/9th, 2/9th and 3/9th designations introduced

Appendix D

Strength and Numbers

James Ferguson was the first officer appointed on 24 July 1900. Volunteer Force service records are rare, the earliest number presently noted is that of Alf Ruxton, No.323, who joined on 18 August 1900. George Peddie, a 30-year-old warehouseman in Leith when he attested as No.486 in March 1901, served with 2/9th and 5th Scottish Provisional Battalion until discharged at Dundee in 1916.

Watson graduating from the University of Edinburgh.

John Watson was a 17-year-old schoolboy at Boroughmuir when he joined the Volunteer Force (on his attestation papers his employer is recorded as the Edinburgh school board), he was one of the last to do so in March 1908 as No.1602. At the end of the month the VF ceased to be, and in early April he re-enlisted in the Territorial Force as No.199. After almost seven years of service, but only four months after mobilisation, Watson was found medically unfit with heart murmurs and was discharged. He died on 19 February 1915 at the age of 24, a few days before his battalion departed for France.

When members of the Volunteer Force joined the Territorial Force in April 1908, there were naturally a lot of numbers issued in the space of a few days, but the battalion only achieved half-strength. This rise was repeated in the intense recruitment of March 1909, as described in the main text and shown in the graph.

The graph shows the attestation dates of the battalion in the Territorial Force from 1908 to the end of 1916. Initially the serial numbers closely follow the battalion strength. Thereafter men joined and left at a fairly steady rate, about 150 a year, until war was declared and there were suddenly queues at the recruiting stations. The earliest wartime serial number recorded thus far is No.1818, Andrew Hinde who had served at Tientsin, China with the Camerons. The rate of recruitment slowed in 1915, until late in the year we can see a large number of men attesting under the Derby Scheme. These men were placed on the Army Reserve and mobilised (and given their regimental numbers) in the following months. Conscription began in March 1916 with the Military Service Act. The character of the battalion would have been quite changed as the war progressed. Direct enlistment in the TF ceased in December 1915 with drafts now being brought in from across the country, and in the haphazard circumstances of 1918 from a great many other units.

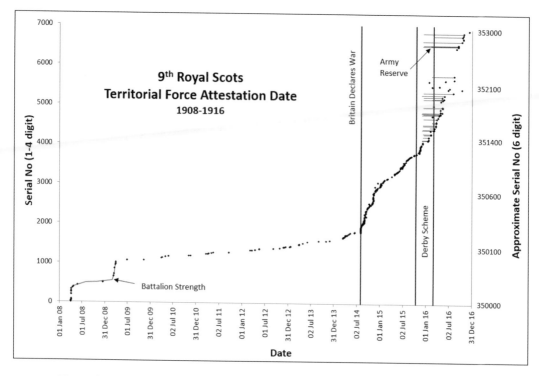

From the beginning of 1917 the original battalion TF numbers (1-4 digits) were renumbered as regimental 6-digit numbers, for the 9th battalion this was a block 350001-375000.

Five-digit numbers are not original 9th Royal Scots; but over a tenth of the battalion's dead were 5-digit men drafted in without renumbering. Post-war the Territorial Army employed 7-digit numbering.

David McGovern may have had the full set: Volunteer Force 1411, Territorial Force 67 then 350008 in 1917, Territorial Army 3044227 in 7th/9th Royal Scots. Archibald Fleming and Edward Fleeting were also old soldiers who carried on with the TA. Nichol Wilson, a gardener, was a member of the TA and was listed for the Defence Force as Army No. 9RS/108, serving eighty-four days.

A total number of those who served is not easy to estimate. According to the battalion pamphlet '200 Officers and 6000 Other Ranks'[98] served with the battalion in theatre. Bill Hay estimated 3-4,000. The Medal Rolls for the British War Medal and Victory Medal, which will underestimate the total, add up to 4,198 men.

A number of drafts were sent to the 1/9th on the Western Front. One of the biggest was draft number 7 with over 300 men, this preventing any chance of the 2/9th being sent out. As the 1/9th had been able to draw in around 100 men from other battalions before the draft arrived, it seems around 100 of the draft were redeployed. The biggest draft was in 1918. The Ninth had been much reduced in strength fighting all the way back from in front of St Quentin to Amiens in the German offensive in March. The War Diary tells us they had a huge draft of 528 on 6 April 1918. A substantial number of these men were from the HLI, Training Reserve Battalion No. 2 District.

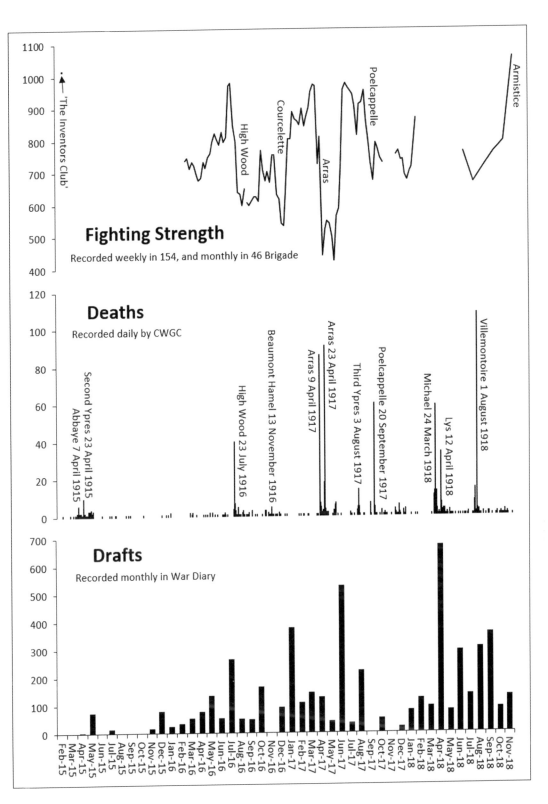

Fighting Strength

Recorded weekly in 154, and monthly in 46 Brigade

Deaths

Recorded daily by CWGC

Drafts

Recorded monthly in War Diary

'The Inventors Club'

High Wood

Courcelette

Arras

Poelcappelle

Armistice

Abbaye 7 April 1915

Second Ypres 23 April 1915

High Wood 23 July 1916

Beaumont Hamel 13 November 1916

Arras 9 April 1917

Arras 23 April 1917

Third Ypres 3 August 1917

Poelcappelle 20 September 1917

Michael 24 March 1918

Lys 12 April 1918

Villemontoire 1 August 1918

The original battalion strength in France in February 1915 was 1,017, adding all of the drafts, which would include the great number of men returned after wounds etc, making the total 6,299 all ranks.

From the timeline it is easy to identify the major actions fought by the Ninth, most clearly from deaths, but also in the loss of fighting strength and the consequent drafts. Note also that fighting strength diminished rapidly in the winter at Courcelette. The average fighting strength of the battalion in the 51st Division was 30 officers and 719 men. The greatest loss on a single day was 108, suffered on 1 August 1918 at Villemontoire, near Soissons. If we apply a moving average, we find the heaviest loss of life over 3-day, 5-day and 7-day periods are all at Arras in April 1917. However the war became more lethal year on year.

The average deaths per day are as follows:

Table 13. Average deaths per day

From February 1915	1916	1917	1918 to November	Total for war service
0.26	0.39	1.21	1.24	0.78 average deaths per day

There are 18 deaths outside of this period.

The Commonwealth War Graves Commission records 1,072 deaths for the Ninth for 1914-21. This dataset, including 30 men identified as 'attached', 'formerly' and 'posted' as well as the 2/9th and 3/9th, forms the basis of the following section. The number is greater than the all ranks establishment of the battalion on arrival in France in 1915, in fact it is 105 per cent.

The CWGC account opens on 1 September 1914 with George Ledingham in the billets at St Ann's Maltings; three members of the Ninth died in the UK prior to deployment. The last death recorded by the CWGC was George Stobie from Portobello on 12 July 1921, a 26-year-old market gardener who had served in four battalions of the Royal Scots. He was one of fifteen Ninths who died between the Armistice and the closing of the records on 31 August 1921. Many others would have had ongoing health issues and shortened lives as a result of the First World War.

These men are buried or commemorated in 185 cemeteries with 802 in France, 217 in Belgium, 46 in the UK and 5 in Germany, all these last being PoWs who died in captivity, or immediately afterwards; though many others taken prisoner died in France. Two men attributed to the Ninth died elsewhere: David Callander in Egypt, but he was almost certainly 7th Royal Scots; and James Mudie in Greece, he would appear to have been in the Royal Scots Fusiliers. Commemorated on ten memorials are 372 men (35 per cent) who have no known grave. Of these only the Hollybrook memorial, at Southampton, is outside of France and Belgium, and this for John Smith who died when the *Warilda* was torpedoed. The highest number in a single cemetery lie at Raperie Cemetery at Villemontoire, near Soissons. Almost all of them were from the Ninth, 95 died on 1 August 1918 and 97 are commemorated there.

Of the 1,072, 49 were officers, approximately the same average ratio of officers to other ranks for the British Army generally. This Roll of Honour therefore makes a battalion by itself, consisting of all ranks between the 797 privates and two majors (Jimmy Ferguson and George Cowan) and a drummer and a piper (Thomas Gibson and William Forsyth respectively); just as the losses on 1 August 1918 make a company.

Though the 1/9th commanding officers survived the war, former CO James Clark was killed and James Ferguson died shortly after relinquishing his command of 3/9th on Home Service. Among the dead are one Distinguished Conduct Medal, four Military Crosses, eighteen Military Medals, one MC and MM and one Mention in Despatches.

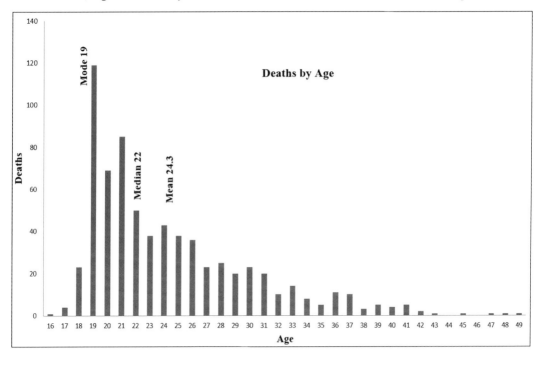

The average age of those who died was 24, but as can be seen, the toll fell heaviest on 19 year olds, the youngest age at which men were supposed to serve overseas until 1918. Twenty-eight men died under the age of 19, though eleven of these were 18 year olds in 1918. David Steedman set sail for France on his eighteenth birthday. One lad was just 16 years old, James Brown Morgan. The oldest was 49 (actually 50), Alexander Fowler from Fife. Both youngest and oldest lied about their age, Fowler claimed to be 33 when he attested in 1915 and served with 3/9th in the borders. He was hospitalised twice with rheumatism and died of pneumonia shortly after release from hospital.

313

Farm servant James Black enlisted in June 1915 and was on the Western Front in October. It was not until August 1916 that he was returned under age to the UK, still only about 17. Some men were discharged as under 17 more promptly: Angus Litster was in five months, Alexander Grieve six weeks and Walter Thomson two weeks. These youths had stated they were 19.

James Low was discharged after three days because Dr John Cumming noted that 'on further observation has been found to be... unfit to become an efficient soldier on account of melancholia'. William Bracelin landed at Cape Helles with 1st KOSB, but disciplined for fraudulent enlistment, he then joined the Ninth.

Families that stand out for their loss include these pairs of brothers: G.E. and W.B. Brown (9 and 18 April 1917 respectively), J.A. and H. McGilp, A.H. and G.L. Ramsay, D. and D.J.E. Thompson and G. and D. Webster.

Speculatively, if one in six (17 per cent) lost their lives this can be compared against the figures for the British Regular and Territorial Forces in France as a whole at: 12.06 per cent killed and died, 37.56 per cent wounded, 6.37 per cent missing and prisoners; totalling 55.99 per cent. However, the infantry strength in France (1 March 1918) was 36.38

William Tully on his wedding day, January 1918, with four wound stripes.

per cent of the total strength and these might be expected to have borne the heaviest toll. In all theatres 19.96 per cent of the infantry were killed or died.

Others were luckier, Walter Blyth was wounded six times, won the *Croix de Guerre (Etoile)* at Soissons and served from November 1915 until demobilised in 1919. Three times the number of fatalities can be expected to have been wounded, missing or prisoners, totalling over half of those serving. The 154 Brigade figures for the Ninth (March 1916 – July 1917) show 223 killed, 761 wounded, 118 missing. This means that for every man killed 3.41 were wounded and 0.53 missing. This is more fatal than 1:5.2 in the BEF generally. Of those admitted to hospital in the BEF 3.32 per cent died, 54.04 per cent returned to duty, 41.32 per cent were evacuated overseas and 1.32 per cent remained in medical charge on 21 December 1918. John Thomson and Peter Cobban were both admitted for shell shock; Alex Ritchie for 'gun-deafness'.

Purely for illustration, if we assume that the nationality of those killed is the same as their relatives' location, then we have: Scots 551 (77 per cent), English 143, Irish 5, Welsh 1, American 2, Tobagonian 1, Anglo-Scots 8, Anglo-Irish 1, Canadian-Scot 2, Australian-Scot 1, American-Scot 1.

During 1915, for every 'English' death in the Ninth, 7.3 'Scots' died; whereas in 1918 it was one Englishman for every 2.6 Scotsmen. This reflects the way that conscription and drafts weakened the links between the traditional regimental recruiting area in an era of total war.

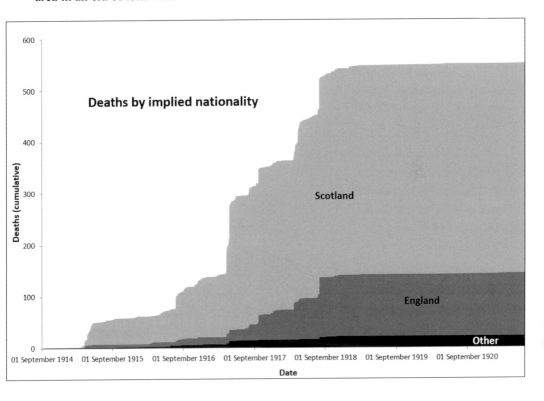

Notes

Acknowledgements

'Of the seventeen battalions of which the Royal Scots… consisted… about one half have gone out of existence without leaving any representative. These defunct battalions have a glorious record which ought to be given to the public as part of the achievements of the regiment as a whole.'
E.T. Salvesen, *The Spectator*, 27 August 1920

My foremost thanks go to those who have provided me with diaries and letters from battalion members, principally Margaret Donaldson for the diary of her uncle, James Lawson Cairns, Malcolm Fergusson for the diary of William Dea, Graham Gibb for his grandfather's letters and Alistair Murdoch for the letters of his great uncle Arthur Lawson, pictured on the cover.

The text is clearly enriched by the images, for whom I thank, among others, John Duncan and his excellent Newbattleatwar website, Erik Geissler in Grenoble, John Johnston in New Zealand, Matthew Lucas, George Souness, Tony Allen, Aurel Sercu in Ypres, Janet Gyford at Witham and Tanker from forum.pages14-18 in France. Reasonable efforts have been made to contact copyright holders, but please contact me regarding omissions.

George McCosh.

I have also enjoyed enlightening correspondence with Richard Brooks, Ian Verrinder, Ron Abbott, Heather Jack, Jon Nicholls, Gordon Barclay, Tim Gale, Alasdair Hutton, Derek Robertson and conversations with George Grubb and Robin and Alastair Salvesen.

I am indebted to the professionals, Colour Sergeant Bell and Lance Corporal Kelly at East Claremont Street, as well as Tom Gordon and the late Colonel Bob Paterson at Edinburgh Castle, and Roddy Riddell and Charles Grant of the Ross Bequest Trust. I am grateful to the Imperial War Museum, University of Leeds, University of Aberdeen, National Library of Scotland, National Library of Wales, Museums of Scotland and Edinburgh Castle Museum Library.

Perhaps the greatest resource is that provided daily on Chris Baker's online Great War Forum, highly recommended for information and assistance. I am particularly grateful to Gordon92 on uniforms, Robert Dunlop for translating Fraktur, AOK4,

Pierssc, David Murdoch, Robbie56, Barkalotloudly, Steven Broomfield, and to many others who have contributed their time and expertise in assistance. Gratitude is of course due to the patience of Irene Moore, Nigel Cave and all at Pen & Sword. *Lapsus calami* are mine.

Finally, my sincere appreciation goes to my family for their encouragement, the vast quantity of transcription my mother has undertaken for the index of personnel, my father's photographs and the support of my wife Karen. This book is dedicated to Eva and Alex, and their cousins, great-great-grandchildren of a *Dandy Ninth*.

Notes on the Text

PREFACE

Costs: At the Infantry Base Depot at Étaples a ruinous rate of exchange ran at 140c to the shilling, but this was in many ways an abnormal place and here a ten-shilling gold half-sovereign could be 'swopped' for fifteen shillings. Inflated costs were encountered as the war proceeded, and always nearing the front line. 'Cherry' Thin and his platoon enjoyed eggs, fried potatoes and five rounds of drinks for a shilling each in 1915. The following year Arthur Anderson could buy a good bière for tuppence or twenty centimes at an estaminet off Rue Gambetta in Arras. However in 1917 William Dea complains at two francs for three bottles of stout at Wulverdinghe. Whisky was sometimes available for only 3/6 a bottle, though *Spey Royal* soon got the nickname *Spare Oil*.[87] Equally it could be an exorbitant 7s 6d or 9 francs a bottle.

CHAPTER ONE – Volunteers & Territorials 1900-1913

Attestation: Ten shillings was the same scale that the Edinburgh volunteers had paid in 1860, though the Artisan Companies could not afford a rifle at £4 each so they drilled with shared Brown Bess muskets until the War Office sent them rifles from the Crimean War. Meanwhile the Advocates Company drilled at Parliament House with their wigs on in case they were called into court. There was also a Teetotallers Company.

A Metamorphosis: with some guesswork.

CHAPTER TWO – Defence of the Realm 1914

Spies: Before the war Armgaard Graves had been a celebrated German spy, convicted in Edinburgh in 1912 for having obtained naval secrets in Edinburgh and Glasgow. The publication of his memoir in 1914 helped fuel spymania. Germany's pre-war spy ring in Britain, twenty-two agents, were imprisoned at the outbreak of war, except for one who escaped to Germany. This network had been uncovered when the Kaiser was visiting for the funeral of Edward VII in 1910 and a captain in his entourage was followed one evening to a barber's in Islington. Recent research suggests this was an MI5 myth to help push through the Aliens Restriction Act. As well as Lody, a half-dozen other new spies, many graduates of the Espionage School in Antwerp, had their movements co-ordinated so that they passed through Edinburgh in succession: Ludovico Hurwitz-y-Zender (sometime between 12 April and 24 May 1915); Robert Rosenthal (possibly November 1914 and May 1915); Willem Johannes Roos (18-27 May 1915); Louise Emily Wertheim (28-30 May 1915); Augusto Alfredo Roggen (5-8 June 1915) and Irving Guy Ries (Carl Hensel 21-26 July 1915). All were arrested and executed except Lizzie Wertheim, a 'rather flashy-looking person of the boarding-house type', according to Basil Thomson of CID. She died in Broodmoor in 1920. Unidentified spies may have included Pauline Slager, Fred Herrman, Jules Silber and a man named de Bie.

CHAPTER THREE – France & Flanders – 1915

St Jean: The regimental historian Major John Ewing is alone in placing C and D Companies either side of DCLI in the initial assault. Similarly, there is no clear disposition for the reunited battalion. The war diary has Colonel Blair back at Wieltje at 5pm, advancing in support, and puts A, B and C at the northerly extent by 7.30pm. Ewing suggests A Company are supporting D on the left of 2nd DCLI, with B Company extending the line right. Some reports of A Company overnight put them to the left of DCLI and west facing, and of B Company relieving them at an advanced trench on the following day.

Mouse Trap Farm was rechristened many times: simply marked as chateau, then chateau du nord, or to the Germans as Wieltje Chateau and the British officially as 'farm in C.22.b', it was unofficially called Shell Trap Farm or confusingly Canadian Farm. The ominous-sounding Shell Trap was changed by V Corps orders to Mouse Trap Farm.[43]

Gordon and Asquith 12 December 1914. Asquith first: 'An excited Belgian officer, with a few other men, ran up to me and, pointing to a high mound, said would I not like to see the German guns, as one could only die once. As Major Gordon had left me to go to a further cemetery, I was glad enough to accompany them. Frightfully excited and almost deafened by the Crack! Crack!! Crack!!! Boom!! Boom!!! I tore up to the top of the hill with the officer holding my elbow... I began to think Major Gordon must be killed... when he returned his face was bathed in perspiration.' Gordon: 'I then hid the car behind a ruined building, leaving Mrs Asquith to write up her diary... I expected to find my charge in a nervous state, but instead she was calmly writing in the car quite unappreciative of the severity of the enemy fire.'[22]

Abbaye: The nuns, present in Ypres from 1665, relocated via Britain to Kylemore Abbey in 1920. The Abbaye had briefly suffered occupation in the revolutionary wars beginning 1793, and 80-year-old Dame Josephine, who did not survive the flight to England, remembered sisters who had lived through that time. Ypres was briefly occupied by the Germans in 1914 and the washerwoman of the Abbaye had troops billeted upon her, resulting in stories of nun's undergarments being used by German troops to dry their faces.

Gas masks: Within days of Second Ypres, cotton wads were issued as protection,

318

followed within a month by cotton mouth pads (the Black Veil Respirator that did not need to be dipped in solution). These were replaced by the British Smoke Hood (Hypo helmet with a mica window) from June, in turn replaced by the Tube Helmet (with two mica eyepieces and with P, PH and PHG variants against various gases). Finally, in 1916, the Large and then Small Box Respirators were introduced, the latter design continuing largely unchanged into the Second World War.

CHAPTER FOUR – Highland Division 1916

High Wood: 'Wanton waste' was the charge made against Major General Charles Barter, commanding 47th Division which attacked the wood in September; he was relieved of command.

Beaumont Hamel: The picture is rather obscure. The Official History says: 'A Coy of the 1/9th Royal Scots (also 154th Brigade) was set to bomb forward along Leave Avenue, but this isolated effort could not make much progress.'[43] The Argylls report that Cowan's D Company arrived at 11am 14 November, and it may have been they were late for a 6am zero. 152 Brigade claim that one company was lost and could not be found, whilst the Ninth are crossed out of 154 Brigade war diary for this action. It is not clear on which day the 'brilliant charge'[33] took place.

Alec Wright: Bill Hay's account suggests Alexander Wright 1257, without being definitive.

Highlanders: Something of the tensions present are contained in the tale that 6th Cameronians (Scottish Rifles) protested at being brigaded with Highland units in the 51st Division, having their traditions in Covenanting opposition to the Jacobites. The 6th battalion were moved from the division before the Ninth joined. Childers had tried and failed to link the Cameronians with Highlanders in his amalgamations and even in the twentieth century the 1st battalion called themselves the Cameronians and the 2nd battalion, with origins in Perthshire, the Scottish Rifles. They may well have been satisfied to know that Crown Prince Rupprecht of Bavaria, commanding the army group opposite the BEF, was in the Jacobite line of succession.

CHAPTER SIX – Offensive Spirit 1917

Vimy: The brigade Observation Post signalled that the Black Line was taken at 6.46am, but not confirmed by the battalion until 9.5am. The battalion have the capture at 7.30am. The 7th Argylls were to pass through *en route* to the Blue line. Because the Ninth were delayed in their objective, the Argylls assisted in the capture of the Black Line but lost the barrage and had to battle through machine-gun fire. The Seaforths on the right were also 'late'.

Poelcappelle: The 18-pounders expended 67,000 rounds in the 24 hours between noon on 19 and noon on 20 September, whilst the six 4.5″ howitzer batteries fired 14,000 rounds. On the morning of the assault the twelve 6″ howitzer batteries fired 5,561 rounds and the three batteries of 9.2″ howitzers fired 685 rounds. There were also 60-pounders and other artillery involved, and the sixteen trench mortars fired

2,700 rounds. In a bizarre legal proceeding, Vickers of Great Britain paid Krupps of Germany £40,000 in 1926 in licence fees for fuzes manufactured during the war, though only a few percent of what was owed. The fee was based on the calculation that the British had fired 4,160,000 shells and (implausibly) killed a German with every other one.

Cambrai: The delay at Flesquières has been the cause of much discussion. It is generally agreed that the tanks could not keep up with the barrage, the wire was uncut, the German artillery was very effective, that the tanks failed to crest the ridge abreast and that the infantry were not close enough and not present in the village. To Liddell Hart, an exponent of the tank, it was Harper's tactics that were at fault. In contrast Bewsher praised Harper's tactics throughout the period he commanded the division and stressed that the 'leap frog' method was superior to German tactics at the time and quickly adopted by other divisions. The close training, he says, and 'the co-operation between the tanks and the infantry were admirable'.[51] However he admits that the infantry were held up by wire at the crest and were unable to support the first action in the village. Harper wrote unequivocally that tanks could not operate independently. From a German perspective Guderian, the influential Panzer commander of the blitzkrieg, commends the officer in the village, Major Krebs, who countermanded orders for futile counter-attacks and instead made a steadfast defence of the village until nightfall before retiring. Some of these arguments, *reductio ad absurdum*, seem to be between the infantry following at 100 yards in file 'worms,' as promoted by the Tank Corps; versus following at 100 yards in extended ranks, as ordered by Harper; approaches debated in infantry tactics at the time.

Lee: Captain Arthur Stanley Gould Lee of 46 Squadron, was downed on 22, 26 and 30 November. Previously in the month, both Maxwell and Lee had witnessed the fatal crash of a Bristol Fighter at the 51st Division games, held to celebrate the anniversary of Beaumont Hamel. The escape from a Camel in no man's land, and falling in with the Royal Scots appears as a story in the first Biggles book by W.E. Johns, meeting 'Major Mackay of the Royal Scots, the fust of foot, the right of the line and pride of the British Army'.

Robert Graves on reputation: 'It seemed to be agreed that about a third of the troops forming the British Expeditionary Force were dependable on all occasions: those always called upon for important tasks... The mess agreed dispassionately that the most dependable troops were the midland county regiments, industrial Yorkshire and Lancashire troops, and Londoners. The Ulstermen, Lowland Scot, and Northern English ranked pretty high. The Catholic Irish and Highland Scots took unnecessary risks in trenches and had unnecessary casualties; and in battle, though they usually reached their objective, too often lost it in the counter-attack; without officers they became useless.'

CHAPTER SEVEN – Defeat & Victory 1918

Voyennes: *En route* to Calais in October 1415, Henry V had worked his way up the Somme to Nesle and crossed at Voyennes, where the French had attempted to delay him by digging holes in the causeway. He was in a precarious situation, hemmed in between the river and marshes where the canal now runs and coming into contact with bodies of French horse. A week later he defeated his enemies at Agincourt.

Le Quesnoy: One hundred men, under Captain Eddie Combe (2nd Royal Scots), held Le Quesnoy until nightfall on 26 March. He reported 'Held on to W. end of village till 6-40pm. by which time enemy was closing in on both flanks, and remainder of garrison (9 Men) were withdrawn as enemy attacked and overran our positions.'[1] Haig described it as 'a very gallant feat of arms'. Ewing, in his regimental history, inserts this significant sacrifice chronologically between two paragraphs on the Ninth and this has given rise to readers, historians and even serving members of the battalion being misled that the Ninth fought this action with only eleven survivors. Instead they were at the similarly named Le Quesnel, and not far apart geographically at only 4-5 miles.

Albert: The Official History of Australia in the War of 1914-1918 describes 'remnants of half-a-dozen Scottish battalions' holding the railway line, including 'Scotties' of the 'weary' Ninth on 27 March. However the location of this was near Albert, and it seems unlikely that even scattered remnants would be this far north.

Calonne: 1st Royal Scots were at Calonne on the retreat to Dunkirk in May 1940. There was fierce fighting at Paradis, a short distance to the south, also the scene of a war crime.

Soissons: 'Regiment Banford' may refer to Brigadier General Frank Bamford.

North Russia: The polar explorer Frank Worsley, who had famously navigated an open boat to South Georgia in 1916, and as the captain of a Q Ship had rammed and sunk *UC-33* in the Irish Sea in 1917, was briefly a fellow officer of Dalziel's as Lieutenant Commander 'Tally-ho' Worsley, in the company of the Royal Scots. He had then commanded the gunboat HMS *Cricket* and had been withdrawn in October 1918.

More tales from the RAF: Another 55 Squadron man was William Legge 'believed shot down in flames' in June 1918. Thomas Sturrock was seen going down near Harlebeke in a Morane in October 1916 and died of wounds as a prisoner. George Doughty was killed in his FE2b in November 1916. Thomas Millar was brought down in a Sopwith two-seater in May 1917 and was repatriated in January 1919. Robert Young was badly hit by anti-aircraft fire whilst spotting for the artillery in a BE2c in 1917. Harry Melville had already been wounded once in a DH9 in June 1918, the following month he raided Saarbrucken and went missing. George Raine was killed in a mid-air collision. Charles Robson was brought down in a Bristol Fighter and taken prisoner. William Steel had two crashes, after one of which civilians stole a number of parts from his DH4. John Balfour's Camel was strafing at Cernoy in June 1918 when his petrol tank was holed and he was forced to land. James Kidd landed in a shell hole after two propeller blades were shot off his Bristol Fighter during firing practice. Two weeks later he was seen diving steeply over the Foret de Mormal, and his death presumed.

POSTSCRIPT – 1919 to date

Approximate awards for the battalion: CMG 2, DSO and Bars 3, MC and Bars 25, DCM 20, MM and Bars 138, MSM 4, French *Medaille Militaire* 3, *Legion d'Honneur* 2, *Croix de Guerre* 8. Total 205.

Second BEF: 157 Brigade was attached to the French Tenth Army on the night of 12/13 June. There was an 8-mile gap on its right. On 14 June the Prime Minister enquired whether the rest of the 52nd Division could support the front line. General Alan Brooke replied that there was now a 30-mile gap between the Tenth Army and the Army of Paris. The division was ordered to evacuate, halted the next day, to be again commanded to evacuate on 16 June. Meanwhile following further French withdrawals in the face of German armoured columns, 157 Brigade was forced to disengage, was embussed by midnight on 16 June and transported 200 miles to Cherbourg, covered by 5th KOSB.

Further Reading

A selected bibliography for further reading would include the divisional histories, foremost Bewsher's of the 51st Division (archive.org) and for the last months of the war, Stewart and Buchan's of 15th Division. Ferguson is the main source for 1900-1909. A grand wee book for February-May 1915 is Young's *B Company* (neillgilhooley.com); for 1915 see also *Private Beatson's War*. Lyn Macdonald's books have quotes from Ninths. *Cheerful Sacrifice* is excellent for Arras, particularly as Jon Nicholls knew Bill Hay well. A worthwhile audio interview is that of Bobby Johnston (IWM.org). Finally, the Official History (Military Operations) is very readable, though naturally lengthy. The Second World War is dealt with only as a short postscript here, so please see the superb *Walcheren 1944* by Richard Brooks, and *Mountain and Flood* by George Blake.

Abbreviations

AWM Australian War Memorial, CC Crown Copyright, EED *Edinburgh Evening Despatch*, EEN *Edinburgh Evening News*, GWF Great War Forum, HC Huie Collection, IWM Imperial War Museum, LaC *La Contemporaine (L'Argonnaute, Fonds des Albums Valois)*, McM courtesy of the Lloyd Reeds Map Collection at McMaster University, NBW Newbattle at War website, NLS National Library of Scotland, NMS National Museums of Scotland, NRS National Records of Scotland, PC Postcard, TNA The National Archives (Kew), WO War Office.

Bibliography

For biographical information see Index of the 9th Royal Scots at neillgilhooley.com

The 61st Division had the reputation of being a poorly performing formation. How did it acquire this reputation and was it a justified description?, 984318, MA Dissertation, University of Birmingham

The 9th Battalion (Highlanders) The Royal Scots (The Royal Regiment), Edinburgh, 1925 (12 page pamphlet)

Aitken, Dudley W., *Guerrilla Warfare*, October 1900 - May 1902: *Boer attacks on the Pretoria-Delagoa Bay Railway Line*, Military History Journal, Vol. 11 No. 6, December 2000, *Die Suid-Afrikaanse Krygshistoriese Vereniging* (The South African Military History Society) (quoting Gustav S. Preller, *Kaptein Hindon*, 1916); also *The British Defence of the Pretoria - Delagoa Bay Railway*, Military History Journal, Vol. 11 No. 3/4, October 1999

Alexander, Jack, *McCrae's Battalion*, 2003

Anderson, Arthur, IWM Documents 3608

Andrews, Clarence Edward (editor), *From the Front*, 1918, with Lyon, WSS, Lines Written in a Fire-Trench, noting 'Written in a fire-trench above "Glencorse Wood", Westhoeck, April 11, 1915'; Easter at Ypres: 1915, noting 'Written in a dug-out called "Mon Privilège" in Glencorse Wood by Westhoek near Ypres, 9-10 April, Easter Week, 1915' (Easter was 4 April 1915)

Asquith, Margot, *The Autobiography of Margot Asquith*, 1922

Bain, Andrew Ramsey, audio IWM catalogue no 375, 1974. Note this is the only source found for the 'friendly fire' incident. Although Bain specifically mentions Wimberley, it is possible that 152 MGC, as P Battery, were the more likely to fire short.

Becke, A.F., *Order of Battle of Divisions*, 1935-1945

Beckett, Ian Frederick William and Simpson, Keith (editors), *A Nation in Arms*, 1985; specifically Chapter 5 The Territorial Force by Ian Beckett, includes quote on intelligence from Report of the Committee on the Lessons of the Great War, by the Kirke Committee, 1932

Beckett, Ian F.W., *Riflemen Form*, 2007

Bell, J.R.S., *Ian, A Memoir*, 2016

Benedict, Bertram, *A History of the Great War*, 1919

Bennet Clark, T.W. Letters written by sons to mother (Willie, 1st Royal Scots; Wilfrid, 9th Royal Scots and Allan, RAMC), 1994.106, National War Museum

Scotland Library, Edinburgh Castle. Diary excerpts courtesy of Robbie56 at GWF, also GWF and rsdiarybennetclark.webs.com

Bennett, Will, *Absent-Minded Beggars, Volunteers in the Boer War*, 1999

Bewsher, F.W., *History of the 51st (Highland) Division 1914-1918, 1921*

Bird, Derek, *The Spirit of the Troops is Excellent*, 2008

Blake, George, *Mountain and Flood*, 1950

Brooke, Alan, Operations of the British Expeditionary Force, France from 12th June, 1940 to 19th June, 1940, 22 June 1940

Brooks, Richard, *Walcheren 1944, Storming Hitler's Island Fortress*, 2011

Brown, John, *Letters, Essays and Verses*, 1921

Building News and Engineering Journal, Volume 102, January to June 1912

Bureauofmilitaryhistory.ie witness statements relating to Limerick

Cadell, F.C.B., Letters, NLS Acc.11224

Campbell, Colin, *Engine of Destruction*, 2013. Quotes HStAS M33/2 †B 536, *Abteilung Fremde Heere Nr. 4610* (Dr Alex Fasse per Jack Sheldon, and Judith Bolsinger, Haupstaatarchiv, Stuttgart)

Cannon, Roderick, *The Highland Bagpipe and Its Music*, 2002

Carrington, Charles, *Soldier from the Wars Returning*, 1965

Cecil, Hugh and Liddle, Peter H. (editors), *Facing Armageddon*, 2003; particularly Spiers, Edward, The Scottish Soldier at War, Chapter 24

Chambers, Robert, *History of the Rebellion in Scotland in 1745-46*, 1827

Clapperton, John Warnock, GD1/1228, NRS

Clausewitz, Carl von, *Vom Kriege*, 1832; translated as *On War* by Colonel James John Graham, 1873

Cochrane, Peter, *Scottish Military Dress*, 1987

Cole, Reginald Price, manuscript reference code BP/51, National Library of Wales

Conan Doyle, Arthur, *A History of the Great War, The British Campaign in France and Flanders, Volume V – January to July 1918, 1919*

Cox & Co, List of British Officers taken prisoner in the various Theatres of War between August 1914 and November 1918, 1919

Creswicke, Louis, *South Africa and the Transvaal War*, 1901

Crozier, F.P., *A Brass Hat in No-Man's Land*, 1930 (Crozier writes 'Shankhill')

Crutchley, C.E. (editor), *Machine Gunner 1914-1918*, 1973, for Third Ypres quoting *History and Memoir of the 33rd Battalion Machine Gun Corps*

Darroch, G.R.S., *Deeds of a Great Railway*, 1920

de Wet, Christiaan Rudolf, *Three Years' War*, 1902

Dea, William, Diary, courtesy of Malcolm Fergusson

Diary of Services of The First Battalion The Royal Scots, During the Boer War. South Africa, 1899-1902, 1904

Dixon, John, *Magnificent but not War*, 2003

Dove, Richard (editor), *"Totally Un-English"?: Britain's Internment of "enemy*

Aliens" in Two World Wars, 2005 specifically, Manz, Stefan, 'Civilian Internment in Scotland during the First World War'

Down, Norman Cecil, *Temporary Heroes*, 1917

Duffy, Christopher, *Through German Eyes*, 2006

Dunbar, John Telfer, *History of Highland Dress*, 1964

Edmonds, J.E. et al., *Military Operations, France and Belgium, 1927-1948* (Official History)

Elliot, J. (or Elliott), IWM Documents 5912

Ellsworth-Jones, Will, *We Will Not Fight*, 2007

Ewing, John, *The Royal Scots, 1914-1919*, 1925

Farrell, Fred, with an introduction by Neil Munro, *The 51st Division War Sketches*, 1920

Ferguson of Kinmundy papers, University of Aberdeen, MS 3816

Ferguson, James, *Record of the 9th (Volunteer) battalion (Highlanders), the Royal Scots*, 1909

Fidler, John P, IWM audio catalogue number 24879

Foley, Archie and Monroe, Margaret, *Portobello and the Great War*, 2013

Foley, Michael, *Prisoners of the British*, 2015

French, Craig, *Friends Are Good On the Day of Battle*, 2016; The 51st (Highland) Division during the First World War, PhD Thesis, University of Glasgow, 2006

French, John, Eighth Despatch, 15 June 1915

Gale, Tim, *French Tanks of the Great War*, 2016

Gibb, Clarence William, letters to his fiancée Annie, courtesy of his grandson, Graham Gibb

Gibbs, Philip, *From Bapaume to Passchendaele*, 1918

Gibson, Craig, *Behind the Front: British Soldiers and French Civilians*, 2014 Reference: Mersch, *avocet, to bourgmestre*, Ypres, 8 April 1915, Doos 17, *Militaire Opvorderingen, Schade berokkend door de troepen* (Military requisition, damage caused by the troops), 542.7, SAI

Goes, Gustav, *Der Tag X*, 1933, translated by Robert Dunlop

Gordon, A.A., *Culled from a Diary (1867-1939)*, 1941

Graves, Armgaard Karl, *The Secrets of the German War Office*, 1914

Graves, Robert, *Goodbye to All That*, 1929

Grayson, Richard, *Belfast Boys*, 2009

Grierson, James Moncrieff, *Records of the Scottish Volunteer Force, 1859-1908*, 1909

Griffith, Paddy, *Battle Tactics of the Western Front*, 1994

Grossart, W, IWM Documents 5929

Guderian, Heinz, *Achtung-Panzer*, 1937; translated by Christopher Duffy, 1992

Haig, Douglas, Despatches

Hammond, Bryn, *Cambrai 1917: The Myth of the First Great Tank Battle*, 2009.

Quotes 'colossal binges' Horace Birks, Tank Corps; 'a reputation second only to the Guards' Wilfrid Bion, Tank Corps

Hay, William, audio, IWM Catalogue 16455, 1984 (see also Macdonald, L and Nicholls, J)

Hennessey, Thomas, Spooks: *The Unofficial History of MI5*, 2010

Hesketh-Prichard, H., *Sniping in France*, 1920

Hindenburg, Paul Ludwig Hans Anton von Beneckendorff und von, *The Great War*, 1919, edited by Charles Messenger, 2006

Histories of the Two Hundred and Fifty-One Divisions of the German Army which Participated in the War (1914-1918), 1920

Hogg, Ian V., *The Guns 1914-18*, 1971

Holmer, BC, IWM Documents 17250

Hooper, Colette, *Railways of the Great War with Michael Portillo*, 2014, referring to the work of Geoff Clarke

Horsfall, Jack, Cave, Nigel and Gorczynski, Philippe, *Bourlon Wood*, 2002

Humphries, Mark and Rosenthal, Lyndsay, *Sir Richard Turner and the Second Battle of Ypres*, Canadian Military History Volume 24 Issue 1, 2015

Hussey, A.H. and Inman, D.S., *The Fifth Division in the Great War*, 1921

Johns, W.E., *The Camels are Coming,* 1932, subsequently *Biggles, Pioneer Air Fighter*

Johnston, Robert William Fairfield, IWM Documents 4474 and IWM audio catalogue number 13586, 1975

Johnston, Rory, *A Major Hoodwink*, 2012

Journal of an Edinburgh Mountaineer, probably the diary of RHF Moncrieff, excerpts courtesy of Barkalotloudly at GWF

Jünger, Ernst, *Storm of Steel (In Stahlgewittern)*, 1920, translation by Michael Hofmann based on 1978 version, 2003

Keegan, John, *The First World War*, 1998

Kipling, Rudyard, *A Song of French Roads*, 1923; *Bridge-Guard in the Karoo*, 1901

Lawrence, T.E, *Seven Pillars of Wisdom*, 1926

Leask, J.C. and McCance, H.M,. *Regimental Records of the Royal Scots*, 1915

Leather Sporran, The Magazine of Battalions of The Royal Scots. Vol. 1, No. 1 1 September 1916, The Journal of the 2/9th Royal Scots, 3d; Vol. 1, No. 2 1 November 1916, The Journal of the Highlanders, The Royal Scots, 4d; Vol. 1, No. 4 June 1917, The Magazine of Battalions of The Royal Scots, 4d

Lee, Arthur Stanley Gould, *No Parachute*, 1968 and *Open Cockpit*, 1969

Lees, Andrew Gray, WO 161/99/123 No. 983, 1917

Lewis-Stempel, John, *The War Behind the Wire*, 2014

Lidell Hart, B.H., *A History of the First World War,* 1930

Litz, Brett T. and Schlenger, William E., *PTSD in Service Members and New Veterans of the Iraq and Afghanistan Wars*, 2009

Love, Robert Gray quoted by Joe Lawler Brown ww2talk.com

Lyon, W.S.S,. see Andrews, C.E.

M & GN Circle Bulletin, issue 649, April 2015

Macdonald, Catriona MM, *Scotland and the Great War*, 2014, see Chapter 5 by Ian S. Wood.

Macdonald, J.H.A., *Fifty Years Of It*, 1909

Macdonald, Lyn, *They Called It Passchendaele*, 1978; *Somme,* 1983; 1914-1918 *Voices and Images of the Great War,* 1988; 1915: *The Death of Innocence*, 1997; *To the Last Man,* 1998

Mackenzie, T.A., Ewart, J.S. and Findlay, C., *Historical Records of the 79th Queen's Own Cameron Highlanders,* 1887

Maclean, Fitzroy, *Highlanders*, 1995

MacPherson, A.F., diary presented to the 51st Division 51hd.co.uk

MacQueen, John and Winifred (selectors), *A Choice of Scottish Verse 1470-1570*, 1972; quoting the Bannatyne MS of 1568

Manz, Stefan, *Migranten und Internierte: Deutsche in Glasgow, 1864-1918*, 2003 (see also Dove)

Marshall, F. (editor), *Football, The Rugby Union Game*, 1892

Martin, David, *Duelling with Long Toms*, 1988

Martin, David, *Londoners on the Western Front: The 58th (2/1st London) Division in the Great War*, 2014

Matthews, E.C., *With the Cornwall Territorials on the Western Front*, 1921

Maurice, John Frederick, *History of the War in South Africa, 1899-1902*, 1906-1910

Maxwell, Herbert (editor), *The Lowland Scots Regiments*, chapter on The Royal Scots by MM Haldane, 1918

McGurk, John, audio IWM Catalogue No 25278

McVeigh, Patrick, *Look After the Bairns*, 1999

Memorials of Rugbeians Who Fell In The Great War, 1921

Mitchell, T.J., and Smith, G.M., *Official Medical History of the War, Medical Service*s, 1931

Moore, Irene, *Armourer* Militaria Magazine, issue 2, 1994

Moore, William, *A Wood Called Bourlon*, 1988

Moore-Bick, Christopher, *Playing the Game: The British Junior Infantry Officer on the Western Front 1914-18*, 2011

Mullay, Alexander J, *Blighty's Railways*, 2014

Munro, Kevin, *Scotland's First World War*, 2014

Münstermann, Paul and Begau, Robert, Geschichte des Infanterie-Regiments von Goeben (2. Rheinisches) Nr. 28 im Weltkriege 1914–1918, 1932, courtesy GWF AOK4

Murland, Jerry, *Retreat and Rearguard Somme 1918*, 2014

Murray, William, Liddle/ww1/gs/1848 Special Collections, University of Leeds

Newark, Tim, *Highlander*, 2010, on Wimberley quotes Borthwick, J, *The 51st Highland Division in Africa & Sicily*, 1945

Nicholls, Jonathan, *Cheerful Sacrifice*, 1990

Nicholson, Walter Norris, *Behind the Lines*, 1939

Norman, Terry, *The Hell they Called High Wood*, 1984

Pakenham, Thomas, *The Boer War*, 1979

Panayi, Panikos, *Prisoners of Britain*, 2012

Parrish, Silver, Diary, Bentley Historical Library, University of Michigan

Paterson, Robert Haston, *Pontius Pilate's Bodyguard: a History of the First or the Royal Regiment of Foot*, The Royal Scots History Committee, 2000. Quote from Major RHB Johnston (edited), published The Thistle, July 1946; letter from JG Dawson, 30 April 1945

Pratt, E.A., *British Railways and the Great War*, Vol.2, 1921

Quinn, James, IWM Documents 5992

Rennoldson, William, Liddle/ww1/tr/06/37 Special Collections, University of Leeds

Reynolds, Francis J., *World's War Events*, 1919

Rice collection, courtesy family via capitalcollections.org.uk, records relating to Colin Rice

Rinaldi, Richard A, *Order of Battle of the British Army 1914*, 2008

Robins, Simon, *British Generalship on the Western Front*, 2005

Rorie, David, *A Medico's Luck in the War*, 1929

Rose, G.K., *The Story of the 2/4th Oxfordshire and Buckinghamshire Light Infantry*, 1920

Ross, Robert B. (7th Gordon Highlanders), *The Fifty-First in France*, illustrated by Jessie K Ross, 1918

Ross, William, TNA WO 161/99/22

Royle, Trevor, *The Royal Scots*, 2006 and *The Flowers of the Forest*, 2006

Russell, William Howard, Russell's *Despatches from the Crimea 1854-1856*

Saunders, Anthony, *Trench Warfare 1850-1950*, 2010

Sclater, John Robert Paterson and Maclean, Norman, *God and the Soldier*, 1918

Scott, Alex, Fife Force, *A Phantom Army, Sydney Morning Herald*, 19 March 1932

Scott, Walter, Diary, TNA catalogue NRAS4284 NRA 44886

Sellers, Leonard, *Shot in the Tower*, 1997

Seton, Bruce, *The Pipes of War*, 1920

Sewell, EHD, *The Rugby Roll of Honour*, 1919

Shannon, John Alastair or Alastair, *Morning Knowledge: the Story of the New Inquisition*, 1920, courtesy Yvonne Wilkie; see also Young, William P.

Sheffield, Gary and Todman, Dan (editors), *Command and Control on the Western Front*, 2004

Simkins, Peter, *Kitchener's Army: The Raising of the New Armies 1914-1916*

Skeil, A.P., The River Column in North Russia, in *The Long Road to Victory* edited by John Buchan, 1920

Somner, Graeme, *George Gibson & Co*, World Ship Society

Springer, Shaun, Humphreys, Stuart (editors), *Private Beatson's War*, 2009

Statistics of the Military Effort of the British Empire during The Great War 1914-1920, HMSO, 1922

Stevenson, David, *With Our Backs to the Wall*, 2011

Stewart, J., and Buchan, John, *The Fifteenth (Scottish) Division, 1914-1919*, 1926

Stirling, John, *Our Regiments in South Africa, 1899-1902*: Their Record, based on Dispatches, 1903 (Captain, 7th Volunteer Battalion, Royal Scots)

Stirling, John, *The Territorial Divisions 1914-1918*, 1922

Swann, J.C. *Citizen Soldiers of Bucks*, 1930

Tait, Derek, *Edinburgh in the Great War*, 2016

Thackeray, Francis, *A History of the Right Honourable William Pitt*, 1827

Thin, Russell Gibson, NMS M.2009.44.1, M.2009.44.2

Thomson, Basil, *Queer People*, 1922, republished as *Odd People*, 2015

Trevor-Roper, Hugh, *The Invention of Tradition: The Highland Tradition of Scotland*, in Hobsbawm, Eric and Ranger, Terence (editors), *The Invention of Tradition*, 1983

United States Army in the World War, 1917-1919, Military Operations of the American Expeditionary Forces

Verrinder, Ian, *Tank Action in the Great War*, 2009

Viljoen, Ben, *My Reminiscences of the Anglo-Boer War*, 1902

War Diaries: principally 9th Royal Scots a) February-December 1915, WO 95/2264/2, b) January 1916 – January 1918, WO 95/2887/5, c) February 1918 – May 1919, WO 95/1954/1; 154 Brigade, 51st Division War Diaries WO 95/2883/2 through to 95/2885/1; but also the War Diaries of other units as required

Weaver, Lawrence, *The Story of the Royal Scots*, 1915

Weekes, Alan, *A Bloody Picnic: Tommy's Humour 1914-18*, 2010

Wells, H.G., *The Outline of History*, 1921

West, Nigel, *Historical Dictionary of World War I Intelligence*, 2013

Westlake, Ray, *Military Metal Shoulder Titles*, 1977

Wilson, Herbert Wrigley, *With the Flag to Pretoria*, 1902; *After Pretoria: The Guerrilla War*, 1902

Wimberley, Douglas, *Scottish Soldier*, NLS Acc.6119

Wyrell, Everard, *The History of the Duke of Cornwall's Light Infantry 1914-1919*

Young, John, IWM audio Catalogue no 11315, 1990

Young, WP, *Soldier to the Church*, 1919; and published anonymously 9th Royal Scots (T.F.), *B Company on Active Service from a Private's Diary*, February-May 1915, 1916, with appendix by 'Another Private' John/Alastair Shannon; see also Shannon

Images

Images have at times been cropped, annotated or edited to suit

PREFACE 0-01 No. 1827 Charles Alexander Mackay, Leather Sporran 0-02 Map I

CHAPTER 1 1-01 Edward Read in Wilson, HW 1-02 Alec Ball in Wilson, HW 1-03 *The Scotsman* 1-04 Ferguson 1-05 Ferguson 1-06 EEN 1-07 Diary of Services 1-08 Diary of Services 1-09 Map II 1-10 Diary of Services 1-11 Wilson, HW 1-12 Wilson, HW 1-13 Wilson, HW 1-14 Stephen Luscombe and Charles Griffin's Britishempire.co.uk 1-15 Diary of Services 1-16 Ferguson 1-17 Map III 1-18 Montage 1: 1903 Maxim, Ferguson; 1903, PC; entrain, Ferguson; B Company under Captain Clark 1904, PC; 1904, PC; drummer, Ferguson; 1908, HC; Bde, Gordon92 GWF; 1910, HC; 1909, GWF; 1911 Irvine, HC 1-19 Montage 2: 1911, HC; A Company under Captain Alexander Taylor 1911, Dorothy Dargie nee Wright courtesy Ian Dargie; 1911, HC; 1912, HC: 1912, HC; 1913, HC; 1913, HC; 1912 Gordon Barclay; 1913, PC 1-20 PC 1-21 Ferguson 1-22 Ferguson 1-23 PC 1-24 *Black & White Magazine* 23 September 1905, by Charles M Sheldon 1-25 *Illustrated London News* 17 October 1908 1-26 *The Sphere* 4 July 1908 1-27 Map IV 1-28 Britishempire.co.uk 1-29 PC 1-30 HC 1-31 Thardy1 on flickr 1-32 Thardy1 on flickr 1-33 EEN 1-34 Courtesy Matthew Lucas GWF 1-35 HC 1-36 Gordon Barclay 1-37 Montage 3: PCs from 1914

CHAPTER 2 2-01 HC 2-02 HC 2-04 PC *'Englische Royal Scots (Hochländer) auf Vorposten in den Dünen'* 2-05 Douglas Harries, courtesy Open Bolt GWF 2-06 *The Sketch* 18 November 1914 2-07 PC 2-08 Armoured train, *The Railway Magazine*, 1919, via NRM blog by Simon Batchelor, 2015 2-09 RS Lindsay 2-10 Map V, CC 1946, 1950, SW modern 2-11 BC Clayton c.1920 2-12 Map VI 2-13 HC 2-14 Gunn, The Book of Remembrance for Tweeddale, 1925 2-15 HC 2-16 Tatler 19 May 1915

CHAPTER 3 3-01 Cadell, FCB 3-02 RS Museum 3-04 Ruvigny Roll of Honour 3-05 RS Lindsay 3-06 NBW 3-07 NBW 3-08 HC 3-09 Tatler 3-10 Ewing 3-11 HC 3-12 Daily Record 3-13 NBW/EED 3-14 Courtesy of John Johnston 3-15 Leather Sporran 3-16 Bone (courtesy Scott Green), John Craigie, Our First Resting Place in Ypres, 26 March 1915 3-17 Map VII, CC 1917, gates PCs, Abbaye from Aurel Sercu 3-18 Aurel Sercu 3-20 NBW/EED 3-21 EED 3-22 EED 3-23EED 3-24 NBW/EED 3-25 NBW/EED 3-26 NBW/EED 3-27 NBW/EED 3-28 WWI and English Poetry 3-30 CC July 1915 3-31 1st York and Lancaster War Diary WO 95/2275/2 CC 1915 3-32 NBW 3-33 NBW/EED 3-34 Profile 3-35 NBW 3-36 NBW 3-37 NBW/EED 3-38 NBW/EED 3-39 PC 3-40 Courtesy of John Johnston 3-41 NBW/EED 3-43 NBW/EED 3-44 Ewing

3-45 NLS/74549252 X.25052 Acc.3155 3-46 Watsonian War Record 3-47 AWM EZ0172E, EZ0172D, EZ0172C c.1917 3-48 Robertson, Derek, Hawick and the War, 2014 3-49 Hammerton, John Alexander, *The War Illustrated Album de Luxe*, 1916 3-50 Geissler, William, courtesy of Erik Geissler 3-51 Cadell, FCB 3-52 Frederick Henry Townsend, *Punch*, April 1916 3-53 *Daily Record* 7 July 1915 3-54 boltonrevisited.org.uk 3-55 Geissler 3-56 Brown, J 3-57 Alistair Murdoch 3-58 Geissler 3-59 Geissler 3-60 NBW/EED 3-61 NBW/EED 3-62 CC c.1916 3-63 LaC VAL 443/065 SPA123586, Reussner, July 1916 3-64 Geissler 3-65 George Souness 3-66 PC AWM concession C04897

COLOUR C-01 to C-20 Map VIII to XXVII C-21 PC C-22 PC ('Defence not defiance' was the motto of the Volunteer Force from the poem by Martin Tupper. Tennyson also wrote poems supportive of volunteering. Similarly, the motto of Scotland and the Royal Scots is *nemo me impune*, latinised deterrent) C-23 Bone (courtesy Scott Green), John Craigie, A peep through a periscope looking towards Lille with the German Lines in the middle distance, August 1915 (Bobby Johnston tells us the water tower in Lille dominated the landscape) C-24 Bone, Muirhead, Billets in a farm in Flanders (with A Company the 9th Royal Scots in France) (detail) C-25 Anderson, Douglas N (d.1954), 1917 C-26 RS Museum C-27 Bone, John Craigie, The Clearing in Sanctuary Wood, April 1915 (detail) C-28 Cadell, FCB, Jack and Tommy, 1916 C-29 Brian Gilhooley C-30 Montage VBs Grierson, uniforms Ferguson

CHAPTER 4 4-01 Chain of command 4-02 Wauchope, A.G., A History of the Black Watch in the Great War, 1925 4-03 Geissler 4-04 Geissler 4-05 LaC VAL 438/138 SPA 117373, July 1917 4-06 CC 1916 4-07 NBW/EED 4-08 PC Doug Johnson GWF 4-09 *BIM (originally British Interned Mürren, later British Interned Magazine)* Vol. 1, No. 10, Xmas 1917 4-10 CC 1916 4-11 Landesarchiv Baden-Württemberg 456 F Nr 19 Foto 128, August 1916; plus CC 1916 4-12 AWM C310429 accession H08507, November 1916 4-13 LaC VAL 436/039, SPA 17202 D 556, November 1916 4-14 Bairnsfather, Bruce, Bullets and Billets, 1916 4-15 Courtesy John Johnston 4-16 Geissler

CHAPTER 5 5-01 NBW/EED 5-02 Watsonian War Record 5-03 *The Times History of the War* and the *Daily Record* 5-04 Poster 5-05 Andrew Wylie, courtesy Victor Judge 5-06 Watsonian War Record 5-07 Geissler 5-08 Courtesy the Pepper Gallery 5-09 Billcliffe, Roger, The Scottish Colourists, 1989 5-10 Football and the First World War 5-11 British Jewry Book of Honour 5-12 Tony Allen, franked 12 October 1916, worldwar1postcards 5-13 Bruce, William S, Scottish National Antarctic Expedition 1902-04, March 1903 5-14 Cannon, Roderick 5-15 Janet Gyford, History of Witham, from June Clarke 5-16 Shoulder title 5-17 Leather Sporran 5-18 Daily Record 7 April 1915 5-19 PC 5-20 NBW courtesy Max Espie 5-22 Courtesy jim30 at arrse.co.uk 5-21 and 5-23 Janet Gyford, History of Witham, photographs by WE Bull, from Sue Littlewood 5-24 Photograph by W.E. Bull, Maldon Road, Witham 5-25 scotsatwar (originally the Poor House of 1774, this building was besieged in the Irish Civil War in 1922, and large holes were knocked in it by a Free State 18-pounder firing across the River Shannon) 5-26 Michelle (Shelley) Hughes 5-27 twitter 5-28 Courtesy pierssc GWF

CHAPTER 6 6-01 NLS/74545882 C.1737 Acc.3155 6-02 LaC VAL 288/085, SPA 110421, June 1917 6-03 CC 3 and 5 April 1917 6-04 *The Sphere* 6-05 EED 6-06 CC June 1917 6-07 Courtesy Will Murray at Coldstream History Society 6-08 NBW/EED 6-09 sites.google landships 6-10 McMaster WW1AIR00259 9 May 1917 6-11 Farrell, F 6-12 Edinburgh University Roll of Honour 6-13 and 6-14 GWF 6-15 NLS/74548192 D.1384 Acc.3155 6-16 Cadell, courtesy FCBC flickr 6-17 and 6-18 Watsonian War Record 6-19 George Watson 1938, B.1.6, note may be mirror image, courtesy Bob Grundy, GWF 6-20 MacPherson, Alexander Fraser, *The Watsonian*, July 1918, courtesy Graham Gibb and Fiona MacFarlane at George Watson's College 6-21 Farrell, F 6-22 WW1AIR398 McMaster RFC 29 January 1918 6-23 George Heriot's Roll of Honour 6-24 Courtesy J. Thompson 6-25 Profile 6-26 Bundesarchiv Bild 104-0933 February 1918 6-27 CC 1918 6-28 Bundesarchiv, Bild 146-1971-092-06 Frankreich, bei Cambrai, Ruinen, November 1917 6-29 McMaster WW1AIR545 September 1917 6-30 Paterson, R

CHAPTER 7 7-01 David Murdoch 7-02 Nicholls, J 7-03 NLS/74548428 D.1088 Acc.3155 7-04 LaC VAL 456/157 SPA 138926, January 1918 7-05 McMaster WW1AIR00330 7-06 Courtesy Rice family, via capitalcollections 7-07 CC July 1918 7-08 Courtesy David Penman at the 130th (St John) Field Ambulance Research Group 130thstjohnfieldambulance.co.uk 7-09 McMaster WW1AIR511 9 May 1918 7-10 Donald Johnston via Peter Stubbs at Edinphoto.org 7-11 Courtesy Tom Gordon, RS Museum 7-12 American Armies and Battlefields in Europe: A History, Guide and Reference Book, 1938 7-13 AWM H04490 7-14 LaC VAL 014/8 7-15 AWM H12327 7-16 and 7-17 Spa 42 reproduced in 'Miroir ou Illustration,' courtesy Tanker on forum.pages14-18 7-18 Nottinghamshire Free Press August 1918 7-19 Armdale and District War Memorial Association 7-20 Stewart, J 7-21 PC 7-22 PC 1917 7-23 CC 7-24 British Jewry Book of Honour 7-25 NBW/EED 7-26 PC 7-27 George Heriot's Roll of Honour 7-28 American Armies and Battlefields in Europe 7-29 Courtesy Mike Grobbel 7-30 Bundesarchiv Bild 105-DOA3100, Walther Dobbertin, Rufiji delta 1915 7-31 GWF 7-32 Watsonian War Record 7-34 David Murdoch (earlier motor ambulances had been respectfully named after eminent surgeons) 7-35 William Watt junior

POSTSCRIPT 8-01 NBW 8-02 RS Museum 8-03 Gunn, The Book of Remembrance for Tweeddale, 1920 8-04 RS Lindsay 8-05 Brian Gilhooley 8-06 RS Lindsay 8-07 Map XXVIII 8-08 Blake, G 8-09 PC 8-10 Blake, G 8-11 Blake, G 8-12 Love, RG via Joe Lawler Brown on ww2talk.com 8-13 Pat Crosby via Joe Lawler Brown on ww2talk.com

The most famous photograph of the 9th Royal Scots is probably them 'marching in wet weather,' however this shows the 15th Division in 1916 so is not the Ninth, but perhaps the 9th Gordons (Pioneers).

APPENDICES 9-01 Ferguson 9-02 Ferguson 9-03 Records of Robert Scott 9-04 Ferguson, James and Fergusson, Robert Menzies, Records of the clan and name of Fergusson, Ferguson and Fergus, 1895 9-05 Ferguson 9-07 Ferguson 9-08 Ewing 9-09 *The Scotsman* 1936 9-10 War Diary 9-11 Philips, RJ, The Story of Scottish Rugby, 1925 9-13 War Diary 9-14 RSC 9-15 Ancestry 9-17 Joseph Gray, After Neuve Chapelle (10 March 1915) in which we see the back of Muir's head! 9-18 *Dundee Courier* 1936 9-19 War Diary 9-20 Alexander, Jack, McCrae's Battalion, 2003 9-21 War Diary 9-22 Ewing 9-23 War Diary 9-24 Ferguson 9-25 Edinburgh University Roll of Honour 9-26 Graph 9-27 Graph 9-28 Graph 9-29 Courtesy Irene Moore 9-30 Graph 9-31 Gilhooley 9-32 royalscots.co.uk

Please also see John Duncan's Newbattle at war website.

The Fallen

The Commonwealth War Graves Commission records 1,072 deaths for the Ninth for 1914-21, including 30 men identified as 'attached', 'formerly' and 'posted' as well as the 2/9th and 3/9th Royal Scots.

1914
Ledingham, George Douglas Bishop
Nelson, James Martin

1915
Watson, John David Moncur
Crichton, Thomas
Bennett, Frederick Ernest
Stewart, Robert
Cullen, William Geoffrey Langley
McDonald, John William Scott
Munro, Charles Melville
Frost, Gerard Garton Stacy
Mackay, George
Mackenzie, Charles A.
Mathieson, John
Newsham, Charles
Walker, Edward George
Aikin, Hugh
Scott, Robert James
Brown, Bertram
Brass, James Allan
Burgess, James Reginald Holmes
McCracken, Clement
Patrick, Francis Alexander
Cheyne, Andrew
Wharam, Allan
Black, William McLeod
Young, Charles
Dennis, William
Gray, Edward Curtis Murray
Hardie, Gordon
Kent, William
Laing, William
Lindsay, Alexander Cameron
Mackay, Neil

Reekie, John Johnston
Small, Norman Howard
Smith, Thomas
Smith, Albert Edward
Robinson, Reginald John
Smart, James
Templeton, Robert
Walker, Samuel Reid
Waddie, Thomas Wallace
Mackay, Alastair Sutton
Keenan, William Henderson
Morgan, James Brown
Millikin, William Sime
Moultray, John Ferguson
Affleck, Robert Bell
Cowan, Louis Victor
Lyon, Walter Scott Stuart
MacLennan, Roderick
Moore, David Sydney
Russell, James
Fraser, Archibald
Campbell, Duncan Mcleod
Smith, James
Thomson, Walter
Durie, Alexander
Macfarlane, Alastair Hunter
McGilp, Hugh
Meston, John F.
Mason, John James
Arnot, William
Brown, Andrew
Hutton, Ian Campbell
McDougall, Alexander J.
Jack, Frank Cotton
Grant, Donald
Smith, Ivan

Maxwell, James Hamilton
Pearson, James
Whitlie, William Jeffrey
Gibson, Robert Horsburgh
Hinde, David Edward
Swan, James Blair
Wellwood, Thomas Goodwin
Couper, James
Tod, John
Wintour, Angus George
Hyslop, Frederick Alexander
Farquharson, Alexander
Corrie, Thomas Andrew
Myles, Richard Glover
Roberts, James

1916

Fowler, Alexander
Caldwell, William
Grenville, Edward Archibald
Carter, William Samuel
Wilson, John Cairns
Hampson, Harold
Leach, George
Peddie, David Clark
Williamson, John Reuben
Templeman, Charles Gray
Hastie, James
Hume, Robert
Bird, William
Stenhouse, David
Scott, Walter Brown
Spalding, Robert Wallace
Ramsay, Andrew Hotson
French, Harold Stuart
Brown, Charles Lawrie
Kerr, George
Forster, Lionel Helden
Sharp, Michael
Bisset, John Skirving
Wood, Henry
Cartwright, Bertram
Ferguson, James

Gowans, Francis
Laverick, James
Smith, Robert Dyer
Alston, Thomas
Ballantyne, Robert
Beatson, James Nicol
Blanchard, Charles W.
Blaylock, Arthur
Byrne, Peter
Cessford, James
Coghill, William Taylor
Cormack, John
Dymock, Bryce Sinclair
Eagar, Herbert Gore
Easton, William
Elder, Alexander
Forrest, William
Fraser, Simon Sinclair
Gibson, Robert
Goodall, John
Haddow, John Campbell
Hamilton, George
Harley, John
Hutton, Stewart
Innes, James
Irving, Archibald
Jeffrey, George Peter Alexander
Johnstone, Andrew
Kelly, John Michael
Lawson, William
McKillop, John
Mitchell, Andrew
Ross, John Brown
Rutherford, Philip Flucker
Sibbald, David
Stow, Frederick James
Thompson, Dugald
Trotter, Thomas
Turnbull, John
Vallance, George C.
Wilson, George S.
Wilson, James
Wood, David

Allison, Thomas James
Wright, William
Cassidy, John
Chivas, George
Ellison, Matthew Fenney
Gerrard, Thomas
Hamilton, James Reginald
Henderson, Basil
Macrae, Thomas Colclough
Dougall, Thomas Arthur
Mclennan, Hugh Ross
Thompson, Fredrick
Clifford, Daniel
Coats, John McGregor
Gibson, Thomas
Millar, John Ovenstone
White, John
Wilson, John
Morison, Mark John Forsyth
Sumner, Thomas
Nimmo, John
Macaulay, William Birrell
Grant, William
Jamieson, William C.
Archibald, Harry
Cunningham, Adam
Darcy, John
Dudgeon, James Philip
Mather, Thomas Blackshaw
Noble, Charles
Purves, Robert Andrew Lomax
Bryce, James
Kilpatrick, John
Hood, Johnson Latto
Wright, Alexander
Lowe, John
MacDonald, Robert
Coull, Stewart McLeod
Douglas, Archibald Halliday
Young, John Irving
McFadden, Peter
Mudie, James
McDonald, Alexander

Laing, David Davidson
Gillon, Thomas
Gray, Robert Scott
Taggart, Thomas
Hayes, James
McNab, James
Neilson, James
Clugston, John
Howie, Thomas
Sloan, William W.
Blair, Robert
Muir, Alan Steele
Borthwick, George
Chisholm, David
Hay, James Alexander
Keay, James
Schofield, Harry
Brown, Alexander Webster
Rutherford, Alexander R.
Gourlay, David Watt
Robertson, William
Halliday, George Pauline
Fleming, John
Wilson, Hugh Munro
Brown, Thomas Wilson
Davie, John Swan
Gibson, John
Pow, Thomas
Neill, William Proudfoot
Mein, James Bryson

1917
Marchant, Horace
Reid, Henry
Spens, Walter Thomas Patrick
Paterson, George
MacDonald, John Row Mackenzie
Haining, William
Berman, Manuel
Knowles, Robert Wilson
Butlers, Leo John
Carson, Jonathan
Golden, James

McDowell, Thomas Orr
Adams, James Alison Wilson
Allan, Douglas
Allen, Frederick Arthur
Atkinson, Robert
Bain, James Richardson
Benn, Thomas Strickland
Boyle, James
Brown, George Elder
Brown, William
Brown, John
Cairncross, Douglas
Cameron, William
Campbell, John Mitchell
Campbell, George Storrie
Campbell, George
Child, Joe
Colley, James Ross
Conner, Alexander
Cranston, George Brodie
Crawford, Robert
Cresswell, James Henry
Darroch, Donald
Davidson, George Johnston
Dennis, Charles
Dickson, John
Dobbie, James William
Doig, James
Duffield, William George
Dundas, Robert
Easton, Henry Taylor
Elder, James
Elrick, Clyde
Ferguson, John
Ferguson, William Percival
Forsyth, David
Fryman, Herbert
Gibson, John James
Goldstein, Samuel
Gowan, Ian Dalgleish
Graves, John Lawrence Victor
Gray, John
Halley, William

Hannah, William
Hardie, Andrew
Henderson, James Laing
Ingle, Ernest
Inglis, Joseph Horsburgh
Jackson, Arthur Edward
Kay, John Telfer
Kirkpatrick, William
Leishman, John Stewart
MacGregor, John
Martin, Robert
McCulloch, Richard
McDonald, David S.
McGill, William
McKinstry, Daniel
McTague, Peter
McVey, Alexander
Messer, David
Mitchell, David
Montgomery, David
Morrow, Ralph
Nisbet, Peter
Robertson, Peter
Ronald, John H.
Ross, John
Shingler, Richard
Simpson, William
Smith, Laurence Alexander
Spence, Charles Frederick
Steel, Robert Page
Stewart, Alexander
Stuart, Peter Maxwell
Symington, David Scott
Tait, George
Taylor, Robert Watt
Tearle, Sydney Thomas
Templeton, John
Thomson, Thomas Gibson
Virtue, Robert
Walter, George Butler
Walton, John M.
Watts, Sydney
Waugh, Archibald Stenhouse

Whitehead, James
Feather, Thomas William
Kirkland, Charles Sinclair
MacEwen, David Campbell
McManus, Francis
Starkey, Harry
West, Reginald
White, Thomas
Ainslie, John
Annal, James
Brown, Robert Cunningham
Shankie, Robert Brash
Watson, George
Anderson, John Hall
Kirkhope, Walter Dickson
Mackie, George
Neilson, Thomas Scott
Smith, Herbert Shaw
McLeish, David Hardie
Sandison, Burnett
Bertram, George Dawson
Walkingshaw, Gideon
Brown, William Burnet
Burrows, Henry
Forsyth, James Elliot
Hewison, J.E.
Sinclair, Charles
Marshall, John
Pagan, John
Russell, John
Bain, John
Begbie, Alexander
Cordiner, Alexander
Fettes, John Mcdonald
Flynn, Charles
Forsyth, Alexander Phillip
Kerr, William
Lang, John
McAleney, William
Milne, John Lindsay
Muress, Thomas
Scott, Arthur
Seth, David

Simpson, William
Smith, William
Taylor, Alexander
Thomson, William Henry
Weston, Arthur Graham
Allan, John
Douglas, James
Snodgrass, Robert
Templeton, George
Watt, Harry Edward
Young, Alexander
Aitken, Thomas
Aitken, William Neil
Anderson, Peter Hendry
Archibald, Thomas
Baillie, Robert
Baillie, John Orr
Beirne, Francis
Bell, John
Birrell, John
Blair, James Thomson
Blair, Patrick Alexander
Boyes, Frank
Brisland, Edwin P.
Brown, Archibald
Buchanan, Thomas
Budge, Thomas
Burns, John
Burns, Thomas
Burns, Stewart Cameron
Cameron, William B.
Campbell, Duncan
Carmichael, Gilbert
Chamberlain, Philip
Colville, Alexander
Coop, John
Cruickshank, Colin
Dunkley, James
Edgar, James
Fleming, Samuel White
Forsyth, Albert Laurie
Fraser, Homer
Fyfe, James

Goodfellow, William
Goodlet, John Cameron
Grant, James
Grewcock, Joseph
Hatton, George
Hempseed, Robert Banks
Hill, James
Hobson, Harry
Jackson, Frank
Jamieson, Crawford
Johnston, Robert
Johnstone, John
Landsborough, Alexander
Leslie, Albert Edgar
Lillystone, Sydney Charles
Linklater, Alexander Edgar
Mathieson, Alexander
Mcalpine, Kenneth
McAughey, Herbert
McGilp, John Allison
McGimpsey, James
McGroarty, Dennis
McKinnon, Matthew Cowan
McLaren, Robert
McRitchie, John
Meighan, John McNeil
Millar, Thomas Hind
Monro, James
Morrison, William
Muir, William Edward
Muir, David
Murray, James Cooper
Pegg, Joseph
Pringle, George Cranston
Pryde, Robert
Pulford, Cecil Roland
Renwick, John Laidlaw
Richardson, William Purves
Rigby, James
Ritchie, Donald Forbes
Rodger, James
Sellar, Robert John
Shirley, Thomas

Skelding, Royle David
Smith, David Orr
Smith, Charles Hoyle
Stewart, Alexander
Strachan, Alexander
Sutherland, John MacIntyre
Taylor, William
Thomson, Charles
Turnbull, Robert
Wallace, Walter George
Waterston, William K.
Webster, George Livingstone
White, Alexander
Wilcock, Arthur
Wilson, Edward
Wright, Alexander George
Brown, John Ballantine
Brunsdon, Henry George
Gordon, Herbert
McLetchie, Charles
Walls, Alexander Rolland
Cameron, John
Hutchison, James Spiers
Johnston, Charlie
Weir, Thomas Dunbar
Anderson, David
Johnston, James M.
Philp, J.
Henderson, Robert Cowan
Kerr, David William
Mathison, Andrew
Swallow, John H.
Carmichael, Richard
Houston, John
Loftus, Duncan
Geddes, John
Keddie, Thomas Halliday
Small, William Lamont
Todd, George Dickson
Clark, Pringle
Harkness, John Robson
Turnbull, William
Lauder, George

Lawrence, Albert Robert
Low, William Gordon
Bird, James
Dunlop, Robert
Farquharson, Alexander McNaughton
Todd, Joseph
Watt, William
Wilson, John Law
Archibald, David
Brooks, John Scott
Henderson, Bertie Collett
Johnston, John Thomas
Storrar, Andrew
Willocks, John Simpson
Wood, William
Bowhill, James Sholto
Valentine, Cecil
Lazarus, Harry
Pendrigh, Thomas
Daniels, Harry
Hall, John Anthony
Campbell, William
Gellatly, John Stewart
Traill, Robert Walls
Dickinson, Thomas
Fairbairn, Peter
Gornall, Charles
Johnston, David
Matthews, William
Henderson, Thomas Brown
Bamforth, Thomas Henry
Cartledge, Samuel
Clark, George Simpson
Dea, William
Dewar, William
Ferguson, Sydney
Henderson, Andrew K.
Hewson, William Walter
Lawrence, Claude Mitchell
Macfarlane, Nicol
Reid, Allan
Steedman, Andrew Chalmers
Weaver, John

Whitehouse, Alexander
Elliott, Frank Alfred Richard
Rattray, John
Simpson, John William
Taylor, Tom
Watson, Robert
Corrall, Alexander
Simpson, William
Brown, Thomas
Smith, Horace Alfred
Michie, James
Burnside, James
Aitchison, James
Anderson, George
Baldwinson, Charles Herbert
Carrie, Stephen
Glen, Robert Newlands
Quigley, Peter Mcpherson
Wood, John William
Murray, William
Baines, Frederick
Barnes, Ernest
Garside, John
Halder, James Wilfred
Addison, Alexander
Alexander, James Kidd
Armstrong, Richard
Bailey, Thomas
Ball, John
Bamford, Joel
Banks, Alexander Mair
Cant, John
Chandler, Henry
Clark, William Hamilton
Cooke, John Henry
Cooper, William
Cormack, David
Dawson, Silas Douglas
Deans, Dudley
Diggle, Albert Percy
Edmonston, Andrew
Edwards, Albert George
Ellis, William

Ellis, John Taylor
Forrest, Alexander Redpath
Fraser, William
Gourlay, John Robertson
Hodgson, George William Fowler
Isles, Charles Ritchie
Jack, James
Johnson, Hugh
Landreth, James
Lawrie, Robert
Lawson, William
Longmuir, John
Mackie, George
Mclean, Charles John
McLuckie, George
McNeill, John
McQue, Walter
Miller, Andrew B.
Morgan, Joseph W.
Mumberson, John
Napier, Arthur
Newton, David
O'Neil, Francis
Orr, David Fairbairn
Pirie, Alexander
Pollock, Robert
Ramsay, George Lumsden
Reeve, Arthur
Rothery, John Henry
Shaw, Alfred Ernest
Simpson, Adam
Smith, Edward
Stewart, Peter Deuchars
Stewart, George
Stubbs, Herbert
Swain, James Herbert
Turner, Bernard
Webb, Arthur
Wilkinson, George
Winter, William
Wylie, John
Butchart, William
Davidson, Andrew

Patterson, James
Reichall, Michael
Sinclair, William George Syme
Ovenston, William
Marshall, George Fairholm
Cowie, George William Irving
Fowler, Hugh
Rogerson, Edward George
Fynn, Felix F.
Lawrence, Alexander Sutherland
Sutherland, Norman Edward
Champion, Raymond
Andrews, Isaac
Goldstein, Harris
Forsyth, William Harrison
Meston, John
Swanney, William
Henderson, John Williamson
Mason, Charles
McCraw, Alexander
Noble, John William
Black, Malcolm
Callander, David
Heatlie, Robert Walter
Jones, H.P.
Ross, James
Airlie, Charles
Booth, John Henry
Bust, Fred
De Rome, George Henry
Hutchison, James
Ross, John
Middlemiss, William
Spence, James
Durie, Archibald Bald
Jones, Thomas Allen
Stevenson, John
Thornton, Jack
Milroy, Robert
French, John Douglas
Hannay, Hugh
Sharp, George Norman
Welsh, John

1918

Evans, Leonard Hywel
Weaver, William
Duff, Alexander
Sibbald, James
Fitzgerald, William
Burgess, James
Collier, James Edward
Drysdale, Alexander
Graham, Frank Bernard
Learmouth, John
Leishman, William
McQuade, George
Richardson, George J.
Saveall, William
Shaw, Alexander
Stewart, Jacob
Forsyth, Alexander Roberton
Gibson, Andrew
Izzitt, George Edward
Kelly, Alexander
King, Alfred
McLean, Hugh
Meadows, Herbert James
Newby, Thomas
Robinson, James
Smith, Thomas Finlayson
Swanston, William
Todd, Robert
Watson, Andrew
Hellewell, Ernest
Alston, Andrew
Anderson, James Sharp
Black, Alexander
Blagdurn, Arthur Joyce
Bowden, Douglas
Boyle, James
Bradley, John Robert
Brodie, William
Cairns, John
Calderhead, James
Cantellow, Robert Richard
Carswell, William J.

Clark, Ernest
Couston, Alexander
Drysdale, Thomas Balmain
Geekie, Thomas Irvine
Gordon, Alfred
Gowans, David
Grant, Peter
Gunn, William Cranston
Harris, Frank
Hartopp, Tom
Hogg, Arthur
Hunt, William Ernest
Jackson, John Joseph
Jones, James
Kearney, John
King, Arthur William
Little, James Arthur
Lloyd, Arthur
Lyell, Alfred
McCabe, James
McDonald, Hugh
McLaughlan, Martin
McMeachan, Isaac
Mountford, Stanley
Murdie, Thomas
Nairn, Robert Johnston
Porter, Robert
Price, Arthur William
Quinney, Thomas
Ramsay, Thomas
Reid, Stewart
Rice, Colin
Robertson, William
Shiell, James
Skeldon, Samuel Cowan
Slater, Sydney
Snowball, Edwin
Spackman, Horace
Stevenson, Edward
Strangeways, Alexander Leishman
Swindall, Thomas W.
Taylor, Reginald J.
Turnbull, James

Verity, John Arthur
Watson, John
Watt, Thomas Goodall
Younger, David
Ashcroft, Charles
Leeder, Frederick Robert
Leitch, Ernest
Oliver, James
Walker, John
Mackay, Donald
Buchanan, Alexander
Cairns, James Alexander
Forrest, Thomas Swainson
McLeod, Alexander
Bell, John McKenzie
Cowan, Alexander
Gibb, William James
Grosset, Thomas
Heggie, John
Kerr, John
Mahaffy, Samuel
McIntyre, Archibald
Pakey, Ernest
Rowe, George William
Turnbull, Henry
Watson, Alexander
Weir, John McMichael
Henderson, William
Aitchison, Gordon MacLaren
Anderson, William Sinclair
MacDonald, Robert
Anderson, Harry
Boston, Joseph Henry
Smith, Andrew
Watt, George McR.
Halloran, John
Fairley, William Graham
Clunie, William Halkerston
Gowans, David Reid
Purves, George
Cunningham, Robert
Affleck, William
Binns, George Herbert

Boyle, James
Brebner, John
Burnside, George Colquhoun
Campbell, Robert
Clachers, James Fleming
Conacher, John
Crosby, James
Dowdalls, John
Downie, Archie
Ferguson, John
Forsyth, Thomas B.
Gethin, John
Henderson,
Hislop, Robert C.
Johnston, James
Kiltie, Robert
King, Robert
Larnach, Archibald
Leadbetter, William James S.
Liddell, George Leslie
Livingstone, John
McKernan, Andrew Petrie
McLellan, John
Muir, Harry McL.
Myles, David
Oxborough, James Ernest
Roe, James Nichol
Russell, Thomas
Semple, Robert A.
Tierney, Francis
Turnbull, George
Wallace, Robert Cowan
Dewar, William
Duffy, Thomas
Elliott, David
Miller, David
Reid, Henry George
Robertson, James Stewart
Shepherd, William Andrew
Howell, Alfred
Lennie, William
Parsons, Harry
Thompson, Daniel J. E.

Ward, Myles
McIlwraith, James
Greenwood, Alexander McMillan
Methven, David
Pattison, Edward
Wallace, Denis
Dove, Archie
Bell, John
Cameron, Duncan
Miller, George
Donaldson, Duncan
Richmond, John
Little, Johnstone
Ricks, Harry
Scott, John
White, William
Cowan, George Deas
Purves, Francis
Dansken, James Angus
Moore, Thomas
Philips, William Theodore Caldwell
Weir, John McMichael
Harrison, Harold Victor
Hillon, John
Preacher, John
Scarth, Frederick W.
Gallacher, James
Cake, James Albert Bertram
Donkin, Harry Semmons
Lythgoe, Arthur
Jones, David
Waters, James
Edwards, Thomas Harold
Small, John
MacDonald, Norman Morrison
McKee, William
McMath, Cornelius
Angus, David
Trousdale, James
Grant, James
McRoberts, William Cowan
Boon, William
Hallsworth, James McD.

Blair, James
Frew, William
Robley, George
Andrews, George Edward David
Beal, Thomas
Higgins, Robert Edwards
Johnstone, Albert William
Koch, Frank
Mayes, George Henry Cardon
McCall, James
Patterson, Andrew Allan
Barrowman, James C.
Fairbairn, William
Field, Walter
Frew, Robert
Gray, Andrew
Harrison, Henry Francis
Hunter, Thomas
Jordan, Horace
Lawrie, Thomas Helm
Linsley, George Victor
Scott, William
Shaw, John
Ward, William George
Will, Arthur C.
Willison, John Downie
Duffy, Patrick
Tindall, William
Chalmers, William Turnbull
Adams, David
Adams, Robert
Baggaley, Wilfred
Bannatyne, Douglas Alexander
Barclay, George
Barrs, Thomas William
Beecham, Herman
Black, James Muir
Bonella, Henry M.
Borrett, Albert Henry
Bradford, Alexander Whyte
Brown, Peter Russell Gibson
Brown, Joseph
Brown, Philip

Burton, George
Cantrell, William
Christie, John
Clark, George
Clarke, Hugh
Collie, William
Cowie, James A.
Crozier, George
Cruickshank, Colin
Cryan, Robert
Culley, Frank Charles
Currie, John
Davie, James
Doughty, Joseph
Dunlop, Harry Adams
Elks, William Fred
Ezzi, Emilio
Ferguson, David Macintosh
Ferrall, Crawford
Forrester, Alex Stevenson
Forster, Ernest
Gerard, Alexander
Gillespie, Archibald Thompson
Gradwell, Donald
Graham, David
Grassie, James C.
Gray, James
Haddock, Thomas
Hadkiss, William Frederick
Hamilton, John Mitchell
Harris, Thomas
Harris, John
Houston, John Copland
Hutton, Duncan R.
Jackson, James Crosby
James, Thomas John
Jeffrey, Robert
Johnson, Joseph
Johnston, Bert Edwin
Johnstone, George H.
Johnstone, Robert
Kennedy, James Daniel Stewart
Knight, Horace

Laird, Andrew
Laughton, James Craigie
Little, Frederick
Little, James
Lloyd, David Thomas
Lyall, William
MacLean, Hector
Mallon, John
McCreadie, Richard
McGhie, Peter
McIntosh, John
McMurray, James
Menzies, Alexander Cameron
Mitchell, John
Moncur, William
Mosley, Harry
Newton, John
Nicol, James
Northcote, Albert William
Pace, Charles William
Paterson, Alexander
Pickford, Harold
Porter, Walter
Rankin, Robert
Robertson, James
Roden, William Enoch
Ross, Findlay MacFadyen
Sandilands, James
Scott, Archibald Mitchell
Sinclair, Bruce
Smeath, Robert
Smelt, Hugh
Smith, Thomas
Soles, William
Spedding, John
Stevenson, Tom
Stewart, Hugh
Stewart, William G.
Strachan, James
Swindell, Thomas
Taylor, John Air
Toutkus, Victor
Turnbull, John Robert

Turner, James A.
Walker, Francis John
Wardle, Mark Clifford
Warr, George
Weatherston, Maxwell
Webb, Charles Arthur
Wilson, Richard N.
Young, James
Auld, Robert
Peattie, James
Robertson, William Maxwell
Smith, David
McCulloch, John
Ogden, Joseph Adam
Smith, John
Ellis, Edward Gordon
Black, John Burgoyne
Brockie, John
McKenna, Gilbert
Wilson, James Foster
Huie, Henry William Richard
Milne, James Laird
Ormiston, Archibald Murray
Mackenzie, Kenneth
Peden, Adam
Stewart, Alexander
McDougall, Thomas
Webster, Bruce
Smith, John
Liddle, William
Murphy, Charles Edward Findlay
Thomson, Alexander Hossack
White, William
Nelson, John

Elliott, Norman
Morrison, William
Beaton, Walter
Brown, Charles E.
Levi, Rees
Kirk, Charles Edward
Thomson, James
Weston, James
Watt, James
Henderson, James
Jeffreys, John
Connor, David
Bell, Frank
Dolphin, Ivor
Edwards, David

1919
Gibson, John A.
Robertson, Thomas
Logan, Henry
Webster, David Gifford
Henderson, James Smith
Ross, John
Crutchley, Albert
Dunnet, Donald

1920
Logan, Thomas
Steuart, James William Harvie

1921
Ferguson, William
Haslam, John Guy
Stobie, George

Index

Amiens, xvi, 109, 112, 121, 187, 240, 244, 247, 310

Ancre, 144, 150

Anderson, Arthur, 46, 99, 100, 125, 127-30, 138, 142, 155, 161, 174-75, 185, 187, 199, 232, 317 (*quotes-28*)

Annan, James, 209-11

Annandale, Arthur, 106

Armentières, xviii, 94-9, 103-105, 107-108, 119, 124, 126, 140-41

Armistice, xvi, 234, 264, 266-67, 271-77, 284-86, 312

Armoured train, 16, 41-2

Arras, xvi, 107, 121, 125-30, 158, 166, 168, 185, 187-98, 200-205, 207-208, 228, 230, 232, 255-56, 263-64, 267, 279-80, 282, 312, 317, 319, 323 (*maps XIV-XVI*)

Asquith, Margot, 62, 318

Bain, Andrew R., 220-21

Balmoral, South Africa, 13, 15, 17

Balmorals troupe, 141, 205-206, 223, 233

Bannatyne, Douglas, 260, 264, 347

Beatson, James, (*quotes-42*) 65, 68, 72, 95-6, 98, 105, 107-108, 111, 130, 156, 323, 338

Beaumont Hamel, xviii, 144-52, 189, 215, 223, 228, 230, 281, 319, 320 (*map XIII*)

Bell, David, 32, 47, 50-1, 56-7, 80, 83, 274

Bennet Clark 'BC', Thomas Wilfrid, 41-2, 50, 56, 80-1, 88, 93, 100, 124-25, 133, 163, 199, 205, 256, 267, 270-74, 307 (*quotes-16*)

Berman, Manuel, 166-67, 339

Beveridge, William, 73, 95

Black, James R., 116, 145, 210, 217

Blair, Alexander S., 5-6, 27, 29, 35, 39-40, 50, 54, 56-9, 62, 67, 72-5, 78-9, 84, 86, 90, 92, 95, 101, 106-107, 122, 124, 168-69, 174, 178, 265, 274, 286, 288, 290, 304, 318

Blair, Pat A., xv, 50, 56-8, 143, 148, 204, 341

Blair, Patrick J., 50, 56, 58, 126, 275, 288-89, 291, 307

Blaylock, Arthur, 106, 338

Bone, John C., 62, 164-65 *(& colour plates)*

Bowie, John, 56, 62, 68, 82, 99, 274

Brebner, Jack, 131, 227, 253, 346

Brentwood, 82, 179

Broun, J.C.C., 17, 301

Brown, Bertram, 67, 159, 337

Brown, John, 42, 56, 60, 66, 73, 78, 90, 94, 100, 109, 112-13, 155, 190 (*quotes-4*)

Buchanan, James, 31-2, 41

Cadell, F.C.B., 52, 102, 130, 165, 206, 207, 284 (*quotes-59 & colour plate*)

Cairns, James Lawson, 56, 62, 68, 74, 82, 86, 92, 95-6, 99, 101, 107, 197 (*quotes-39*)

Calonne, 250-53, 321 (*map XXV*)

Cambrai, 164, 168, 222-30, 253, 320 (map XIX)

Campbell, William, 203, 209, 343

Cantaing, 222-27

Chemical Works, 200, 204-205, 207

Clapperton, John, 173, 282 (*quotes-75*)

Clark, James and Norah, 5, 24, 26-7, 29-30, 37, 48, 55, 90, 171, 274, 285, 300, 303, 313

Clark, Thomas, 5, 172, 174, 307

Courcelette, 152-53, 156-57, 187, 214, 280, 312

Cowan, George D., 50-1, 56-7, 148, 254, 313, 319, 347

Crichton, Thomas, 61-2, 337

Dalziel, John, 69, 275, 321

Dea, William, 211-4, 317, 343

Dickebusch, 58, 100

Divisions

See also Royal Scots

American

  1st, 256-7

  78th, 222

Belgian

  6th, 73

British

  Australian, 131, 144, 230, 233, 245-47

  Canadian, 49, 65, 72-5, 77-8, 80-1, 105, 187, 189, 191, 195-96, 230, 240

  Guards, 18, 227, 230-31, 233

  Lahore, 101

  New Zealand, 125, 142, 230-31

  2nd, 148

  5th, 114, 119, 121, 123, 133-34, 250

  7th, 123, 131, 230

  7th (Armoured), 299

  8th, 240, 242-3

  9th, 230

  15th, 155, 255-6, 258-59, 264-66, 270, 272, 336

  16th, 270

  19th, 132, 134

  20th, 240, 242-44

  24th, 238-39, 243

  27th, xv, 54, 65, 72, 74-5, 85, 112, 303

  28th, 54, 72, 86, 93

  29th, 230-31

  30th, 243

  32nd, 121, 233

  33rd, 123, 131, 230

  34th, 256, 264-65, 306

  47th, 319

  50th, 250-1

  51st, 49, 122-23, 125-26, 141, 144, 148, 152, 170, 187-89, 191, 206, 215, 220, 222, 224, 230-35, 250-51, 253, 256, 293, 305, 312, 319-20

  52nd, 278, 292-3, 299, 322

  56th, 228, 230, 233

  58th, 218

  59th, 182

  61st, 234-35, 237-39, 243-44, 247, 250, 253

  62nd, 256

  63rd (RND), 34, 230

  65th, 179, 182, 184

French

  12th, 258-60, 262, 264

  17th, 65, 265-6

  22nd, 243

  23rd, 125

  32nd, 54

  45th, 73

  58th, 258

  69th, 256

  87th, 73, 256, 259, 264

  133rd, 250

German

  1st Bavarian Reserve, 189

  1st Guard Reserve, 126

  3rd Guards, 228

  4th Guard, 126

  8th (Prussian), 253

  8th Bavarian Reserve, 253

  12th, 147, 151

  16th, 251-3

  20th Landwehr, 228

  30th, 86

36th, 214
39th, 86
46th Reserve, 73
51st Reserve, 73
52nd Reserve, 73
54th, 228
64th, 294
70th, 294
107th, 228
113th, 238
119th, 228
214th, 228
234th, 219
Portuguese, 250

Dudgeon, Robert, 35, 39-41, 50, 56, 61, 79. 82-4, 100, 121, 168, 274, 307
Dundee, 2, 46, 164, 170, 174-75, 307, 309

Écurie, 125-26, 192
Edinburgh (*map V*)
 Bruntsfield School, 39-42, 51, 168, 173
 Craigentinny, 42, 44, 291
 East Claremont Street, xv, 27, 30, 35, 42, 160, 164, 172-73, 175, 288, 300 (*colour plate*)
 Forrest Road, 3-4, 27, 42, 167, 286, 291 (*colour plate*)
 George Watson's College, 23, 36, 175, 189
 Hunter's Bog, 7, 42
 Leith, 3, 6, 27, 35, 39, 42, 44, 46-7, 49, 57, 61, 117, 121, 166, 172, 173, 249, 290-91, 309
 Liberton Tower, 42, 44, 173 (*map VI*)
 London Street School, 172
 Meadowhead farm, 42, 44, 46
 Olympia, 42, 172
 Redford Barracks, 40, 42, 46-9
 St Ann's Maltings, 35-7, 40, 42, 172, 312

Warrender Park School, 40, 42, 173, 175
Wemyss Place, 6, 42, 285-86 (*colour plate*)
Elliot, James, xv, 84, 91, 111, 116, 120-21, 126, 157, 230, 276-78 (*quotes-2*)
Étaples, 113, 185, 198, 212, 232, 317
Étrun, 126, 128-29
Evans, Leonard H., 167, 344

Ferguson, James, xv, 3-8, 18, 22-4, 29, 49, 52, 109, 153, 162, 169, 171-72, 174-76, 178, 232, 255, 286, 302, 307, 309, 313 (*quotes-7*)
Ferguson, James junior, 23-4, 50, 52, 56-7, 89, 92, 124, 134, 138, 178, 302, 313, 338
Fermoy, 166, 182
Fernie, George, 195, 201
Fidler, John P., 160 (*quotes-72*)
Flushing, 294-97
Flynn, James, 218
Fontaine-lès-Cappy, 110-11
Frankfort Trench, 146-8
Fremicourt, 229-30, 233
French, John, 60, 90, 93
Frise, 115-17, 244

Geissler, William, 101, 117, 165
Gibb, Clarence W., 54-5, 58, 61, 100, 163, 230 (*quotes-37*)
Glencorse Barracks, 30, 66, 95, 199, 212
Glencorse Wood, 66, 68, 81, 85, 87, 101, 220
Goes, Gustav, 244-45 (*quotes-93*)
Gordon, Andrew, 2-3, 5, 50, 56, 85, 93, 102, 275, 318
Gordon, Archibald A., 4-5, 34, 62, 64, 85, 109 (*quotes-22*)
Gordon, William, of Threave, 2, 6, 10
Green, William, 27, 124, 126, 129, 144, 147, 185, 188, 192, 208, 224, 226, 243-44, 255, 304-305

Grossart, William, xvii, 65, 73, 111, 280
(*quotes-5*)
Grubb, Robert, 247

Haig, Douglas, 105, 120, 123, 148, 152,
167, 208, 222, 230, 244, 250, 256,
265, 306, 321
Hamilton, Ian S.M., xvii, 8, 11-12, 30,
286, 290, 307
Happy Valley, 132-33, 138, 280
Harper, George M., 122, 131, 143-4,
146, 151, 156, 188-9, 191, 205, 208,
216, 220, 223, 320
Haute Deûle Canal, 267
Hay, Bill, 73-4, 78, 80, 105, 115-16,
134, 137, 143, 153-54, 158, 191, 193,
197, 237-39, 247-48, 281, 310, 319
(*quotes-56, also in J. Nicholls and L.
Macdonald*)
Hepburn, John, xvi, 154
High Wood, xviii, 106, 130-39, 141,
144, 146, 200, 249, 286, 302, 319
(*map XII*)
Hill Top, 73, 75-6, 78-81
Holmer, Bernard, 51, 67, 72, 76, 82-3,
95, 99, 113, 176 (*quotes-24*)
Holnon, 235, 237
Horne, Alexander, 218
Huie, David, 22, 35, 47, 50

Imperial Yeomanry, 8-10, 18, 50, 108,
301
Intermediate Trench (High Wood), 132,
135
Ireland, 2, 10, 24, 64, 182-84, 275, 289,
307

Joffre, Joseph, 156, 187
Johnston, Robert W.F., 30-1, 36, 89-90,
92-4, 96, 101, 103, 105, 111-3, 158,
185, 231-2, 291 (*quotes-19*)
Jünger, Ernst, 125, 128, 155, 190, 229
(*quotes-58*)

Kerr, Duncan, 169
Kilmarnock, 173
Kinmundy, 4, 169, 302-303
Kitchener, 7, 9, 13, 16-7, 38, 49-50, 90,
94, 120, 128, 231-32, 255
Klingler, Fritz, 49

La Folie Wood, 224, 226-27
Labyrinth, 124-30 (*see also* Vimy Ridge)
Lamotte-en-Santerre, 110, 113, 244-45
Laubach, Herbert, 32, 170
Lawson, Arthur, 66, 88, 113-14 (*quotes-
44*)
Lee, Arthur S.G. (RFC), 224-25, 320
(*quotes-89*)
Lees, Andrew, 139-40 (*quotes-65*)
Lekkerboterbeek, 214, 216-17, 219
Limerick, 182-83
Lindsay, Robert S., 50, 56, 94, 193, 270,
288
Lindsay, William C.S., 50, 56, 195, 271,
274, 284, 289, 306-307
Lloyd George, David, 50, 208
Love, Robert G., 295, 298 (*quotes-105*)
Lowe, Thomas, 32, 175
Lucas, Frederick, 22, 29, 39, 50, 56-7,
168, 275
Lyon, Walter S.S., 72, 77, 87, 88, 337
Lys, 95, 141, 143, 250-54 (*map XXV*)

Macdonald, Norman, 50, 56, 103-104,
168, 248-49, 268, 275, 289, 291, 307
Macfarlane, Alastair, 88-9, 172, 337
Mackenzie, Kenneth, 46-7, 162, 172,
349
MacPherson, Alexander, 137, 147-48,
201-202, 211 (*quotes-61*)
Macrae, Horatio, 3, 6
Magersfontein, 1-2
Mamelons, 259, 261-62, 264
Manchester, 32, 69, 106, 139, 160-61,
166, 171, 198
Marcelcave, 244-47 (*map XXIV*)

Marœuil, 128-29
Maxwell, Aymer, 50, 56, 91-2, 103, 105, 127, 224-25, 275, 320
May, William, 167-8
McGurk, John, 293 (*quotes-104*)
McLachlan, Peter, 31, 72, 191
Merrylees, Thomas, 143
Merville, 250-51, 253, 286
Mesnil-Saint-Nicaise, 240-43
Middelburg, Netherlands, 297-98
Middelburg, South Africa, 13, 15, 17
Mœuvres, 228-29 (*map XX*)
Moncrieff, Richard, 41, 50, 56-7, 75, 102, 134-37, 275
Moore Park, 182
Morgan, James, 86, 313, 337
Morrison, James, 30-31
Mount Pleasant Wood, 200-203
Muir, John, 255, 261, 306
Munich Trench, 147-48
Murdoch, Robert, 236, 281-82

Neill, Walter, 248
Nesle, 240-41, 243, 248, 286, 320
Netherlands, 17, 249, 275, 279, 294
Nivelle, Robert, 187, 196, 208, 244

Ormiston, George, 13, 160, 301

Parrish, Silver, 275 (*quote-100*)
Passchendaele, 208-222, 319 (*maps XVII & XVIII*)
Pearson, James, 29, 36, 53, 92-3, 165, 337
Peattie, David, 226
Peebles, 171, 174-76
Pétain, Philippe, 244, 293
Pheasant Trench, 214-15, 217-18, 220-21
Poelcappelle, xvi, 65, 214-23, 230, 319 (*maps XVII & XVIII*)
Pont du Jour, 195
Poser Weg, 192

Potte, 242-43
Purves, Robert, 138-39, 339

Quinn, James, 35-6, 47, 56, 65, 74, 81, 84-5, 88, 91, 94, 96, 102-103, 111, 115-16, 118, 120, 124, 135, 137, 147, 152, 155, 158, 186, 197-98, 253, 281-83 (*quotes-23*)

Raperie, xvi, 260-66, 312
Rennoldson, William, 256, 260-63 (*quotes-96*)
Renwick, Jack, 193, 195, 204, 208, 342
Rice, Colin, 249-50, 345
Ritchie, Mary, 168
Roclincourt, 125, 129, 192, 197-98
Rœux, 200-209, 252 (*map XVI*)
Rorie, David (RAMC), 102, 138, 150 (*quotes-36*)
Ross Haddon, David A., 56, 99, 275
Ross, Findlay, 143, 262, 264, 348
Ross, William, 103-105, 140 (*quotes-53*)
Royal Scots
  Volunteer Force
    Queen's Rifle Volunteer Brigade (QRVB), 3-4, 7-8, 24, 27, 104, 109, 154, 170, 291, 303
    1st VB, 3, 27
    2nd VB, 3, 27
    3rd VB, 3, 27
    4th VB, 3, 22, 27
    5th VB, 3, 27
    6th VB, 27
    7th VB, 27
    8th VB, 27
    Highland Battalion / 9th VB, *passim*
  Regular Force
    1st Bn RF, xvi, 2, 10-17, 27, 54-5, 68, 91-2, 105, 112, 231-32, 275, 321
    2nd Bn RF, xvi, 2, 10, 27, 285, 321
  Territorial Force
    4th RS, 27, 38, 44, 57, 160, 179, 249, 290-91

5th RS, 27, 38, 44, 169, 290-91

6th RS, 27, 38, 290

7th RS, 27, 32, 38, 165, 179, 290-91, 312

8th RS, 27, 38, 122, 137, 148, 162, 165, 179, 290, 305

9th RS, *passim*

10th RS, 27, 275, 286, 290, 321

Militia / Special Reserve
   3rd RS, 2, 27, 157, 275

Territorial Army / Army Reserve, xvi, 2, 289-300, 307, 310

Volunteer Service Companies, 8-17, 301

Defence Force, 288-89, 310

Russia, 6, 153, 234, 248, 275-76, 286, 294, 321

Rutherford, Thomas, 117, 281

Salvesen, Iver, 291-92, 297, 307

Sanctuary Wood, xviii, 66-7, 85-94, 96, 99, 124, 282 (*colour plate*)

Scarpe, xvi, 128, 187, 188, 200-201, 203, 291

Scheldt, 34, 270, 294-95, 297

Sclater, John R.P., 140, 163, 168 (*quotes-66*)

Scott, Frank, 217, 275

Scott, Walter, 55, 84, 91, 95, 282 (*quotes-38*)

Selkirk, 83, 175-76, 178-79, 182, 185

Shannon, John Alastair, 94, 278 (*quotes-101, also in W.P. Young*)

Smith Grant, John Gordon, 50, 280

Soissons, xviii, 188, 256-266, 270, 274, 278, 312, 314, 321 (*map XXVI*)

Soles, William, 164, 348

Somme, xvi, 95, 106, 109-121, 126, 130-38, 142, 144-52, 158, 181, 187, 189, 191, 193, 195, 208, 220, 227, 232, 234-35, 237-38, 240-44, 250, 263, 273-74, 280, 293, 320 (*maps XI, XII & XXIII*) (*see also High Wood & Beaumont Hamel*)

South Africa and Boer, 1-2, 6-18, 22, 26, 30-2, 36, 50, 71, 90, 100, 108-109, 124, 159-160, 255, 267, 289, 301, 305-306 (*map II*)

St Jean, 73-85, 88, 318 (*map X*)

St Quentin, 109, 235, 237, 249, 310 (*map XXI*)

Stephen, Alexander, 31, 172, 175,

Stephenson, Arthur, 267, 306

Stobs, 22-6, 30-2, 35, 48, 85, 168, 178, 181

Strachan, George, 7, 50, 172, 204-205

Stroombeek, 214, 217-19

Suzanne, 114-15, 119-21, 281

Switzerland, 32, 140, 160

Tait, Robert, 32, 65, 72, 99, 116, 286

Taylor, Alexander, 50, 56-7, 94, 145, 200, 341

Terling, 181

Thélus, 126, 191-98, 319 (*map XV*)

Thin, Russell G., xv, 58, 65, 71, 77, 85, 95-7, 99, 107-108, 317 (*quotes-3*)

Tillicoultry, 179

Tralee, 182

Turnbull, John R., 183, 348

Urquhart, William M., 50, 56, 58, 178, 216-17, 275

Vaux (Somme), 115-16, 118, 157, 281

Vendin-le-Vieil, 267-70 (*map XXVII*)

Villemontoire, 258-64, 312 (*map XXVI*)

Villevêcque, 235, 239

Vimy Ridge, xvi, xviii, 125, 128, 188-98, 200, 228, 282, 319 (*map XV*)

Vlamertinghe, 68, 72, 93, 286

Vlissingen, 294-97

Voormezeele, 58, 65, 98, 113

Voyennes, 234, 240, 320

Walcheren, 294-8 (*map XXVIII*)

Watson, David, 134-37, 150

355

Watson, George, 10, 301
Watt, William J., 282-83
Wieltje, 75, 77-9, 318
Willocks, John, 193, 208, 343
Wimberley, Douglas, 216-17, 219, 221,
   226, 231 (*quotes-85*)
Witham, 171, 179-82
Wright, Alec, 143, 319, 339

Yeats, Basil, 50, 88

Young, Norman, 55-6
Young, William P., 52, 59-61, 64, 67,
   70-80, 84, 163-64 (*quotes-35*)
Ypres
   Abbaye, 62, 63-5, 68, 75, 83, 275,
      318
   Grand Place, 'the square', 66, 74
   Lille Gate, 71
   Menin Gate, 65, 74, 86, 88
   Yser, 209, 214